MANDEVILLE'S

FABLE OF THE BEES

THE

FABLE

OF THE

BEES:

O R,

Private Vices, Publick Benefits.

By

BERNARD MANDEVILLE.

With a Commentary

Critical, Historical, and Explanatory by

F. B. KAYE

The SECOND VOLUME

OXFORD:

At the Clarendon Press

MDCCCCXXIV

The Fable of the Bees

or Private Vices, Publick Benefits.

BY BERNARD MANDEVILLE

WITH A COMMENTARY

CRITICAL, HISTORICAL, AND EXPLANATORY

BY F. B. KAYE ☐ VOLUME TWO

Liberty Fund

INDIANAPOLIS

This book is published by Liberty Fund, Inc., a foundation established to encourage study of the ideal of a society of free and responsible individuals.

The cuneiform inscription that serves as our logo and as the design motif for our endpapers is the earliest-known written appearance of the word "freedom" (*amagi*), or "liberty." It is taken from a clay document written about 2300 B.C. in the Sumerian city-state of Lagash.

This Liberty Fund edition of 1988 is an exact photographic reproduction of the edition published by Oxford University Press in 1924. Permission to reprint has been granted by the Yale University Library, New Haven, CT who own the rights to the 1924 edition. Copy for reprint from Indiana University Library, Bloomington, IN.

Liberty Fund, Inc.
8335 Allison Pointe Trail, Suite 300
Indianapolis, IN 46250-1684

Library of Congress Cataloging-in-Publication Data

Mandeville, Bernard, 1670–1733.
The fable of the bees, or, Private vices, publick benefits/by Bernard Mandeville ; with a commentary, critical, historical, and explanatory/by F.B. Kaye.
Previously published: Oxford : Clarendon Press, 1924.
Includes index.
1. Ethics—Early works to 1800. 2. Virtue—Early works to 1800. 3. Charity-schools—Early works to 1800. I. Title. II. Title: Private vices, publick benefits.
BJ1520.M4 1988   88-646
170—dc 19   CIP

ISBN 0-86597-072-6 (set)
ISBN 0-86597-073-4 (v. 1)
ISBN 0-86597-074-2 (v. 2)
ISBN 0-86597-075-0 (pbk. : set)
ISBN 0-86597-076-9 (pbk. : v. 1)
ISBN 0-86597-077-7 (pbk. : v. 2)

13 12 11 10 09 08 07 06   C 7 6 5 4
13 12 11 10 09 08 07 06   P 9 8 7 6

This book is printed on paper that is acid-free and meets the requirements of the American National Standard for Permanence of Paper for Printed Library Materials, Z39.48–1992. ∞

COVER DESIGN BY BETTY BINNS GRAPHICS, NEW YORK, NY
PRINTED AND BOUND BY EDWARDS BROTHERS, INC., ANN ARBOR, MI

THE CONTENTS

VOLUME TWO

THE FABLE OF THE BEES. Part II

APPENDIXES

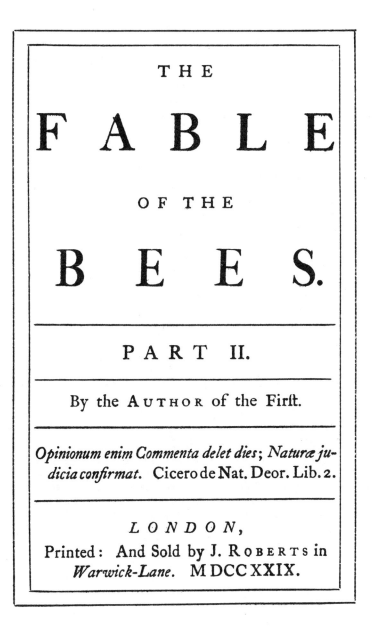

THE

FABLE

OF THE

BEES.

PART II.

By the AUTHOR of the First.

Opinionum enim Commenta delet dies; Naturæ judicia confirmat. Cicero de Nat. Deor. Lib. 2.

LONDON,
Printed: And Sold by J. ROBERTS in *Warwick-Lane*. MDCCXXIX.

[Note on the original publisher of this volume ; see title-page on recto of this leaf :]

James Roberts was the son of Robert Roberts, a printer (see MS. Register of Freemen of Stationers' Company for 7 Nov. 1692), and possibly a descendant of the James Roberts who printed several Shakespeare quartos. This ancestry is indicated by the identity of name and trade—doubly significant considering the possibilities then of family succession in these matters. The later James was admitted a freeman of the Stationers' Company 7 Nov. 1692 and clothed 1 July 1695 (MS. Court Book of Stationers' Company, 1683–97, f. 227). He became Under Warden in 1723 and 1724, Upper Warden in 1727, and was made Master of the Company in 1729, 1730, 1731, and 1732 (Court Book, 1717–33, pp. 150, 179, 271, 335, 376, 427, and 454). He died at eighty-five (Nichols, *Literary Anecdotes of the Eighteenth Century*, ed. 1812, iii. 737) and was buried 7 Nov. 1754 in the church of St. Martin, Ludgate (by the parish register).

From his career it is evident that his contemporaries thought him one of the great printers of his generation, and his books substantiate their judgement. His printing ranks with the finest of his age. Among imposing volumes which should apparently be credited to him are the original editions of Pope's *Odyssey* and Shakespeare, Garth's *Ovid* (1717), Prior's *Poems on Several Occasions* (1718), and Gay's *Fables* (1727). (That Roberts printed these books is shown by the complete identity of certain ornaments in them with those in books whose printing is ascribed to Roberts on the title-page.) As a publisher, Roberts issued first editions for Pope, Fielding, Steele, Defoe, Prior, Swift, Young, Congreve, Addison, Lord Hervey, and Dr. Johnson. In addition, he was a copious publisher of pamphlets, with a leaning towards unorthodox ones. That he printed often for Tonson (if the evidence of ornaments is to be trusted), and alternated with Tonson in the publication of the various editions of the *Fable*, indicates close business relations between the two men.

Roberts published and printed for Mandeville (according to title-page) all the separate editions of Part II of the *Fable*, the 1720 *Free Thoughts*, the *Executions at Tyburn*, and the *Letter to Dion*, and published the 1714 editions of the *Fable* and the *Mischiefs that ought justly to be apprehended from a Whig-Government* (both editions). If the evidence of the ornaments can be trusted, he also printed all the octavo editions of the first part of the *Fable* after 1723 up to and including that of 1732 (they contain ornaments identical with those in Part II of the *Fable*), the *Origin of Honour* (which shares cuts with the *Letter to Dion*), and the 1730 *Treatise of the Hypochondriack and Hysterick Diseases* (which contains the same ornaments as the octavo editions of the *Fable*).

THE

PREFACE.

*ONSIDERING the manifold Clamours, that have been rais'd from several Quarters, against the* Fable of the Bees, *even after I had publish'd the Vindication of it, many of my Readers will wonder to* [a] *see me come out with a Second Part, before I have taken any further Notice of what has been said against the First. Whatever is Publish'd, I take it for granted, is submitted to the Judgment of all the World that see it; but it is very unreasonable that Authors should not be upon the same Footing with their Criticks. The Treatment I have receiv'd, and the Liberties some | Gentlemen have taken* *with me, being well known, the Publick must be convinced before now, that, in point of Civility, I owe my Adversaries nothing: And if those, who have taken upon them to school and reprimand me, had an undoubted Right to censure what they thought fit, without asking my Leave, and to say of me what they pleas'd, I ought to have an equal Privilege to examine their Censures,*

[a] to] to to 29

A 2

4 *The* PREFACE.

and, without consulting them, to judge in my Turn, whether they are worth answering or not. The Publick must be the Umpire between us. From the Appendix that has been added to the First Part ever since the third Edition, it is manifest, that I have been far from endeavouring to stifle, either the Arguments or the Invectives that were made against me ; and, not to have left the Reader uninform'd of any thing extant of either sort, I once thought to have taken this Opportunity of presenting him with a List of the Adversaries that have appeared in Print against me ;[1] but as they are in nothing so considerable as they are in their Numbers, I was afraid it would have look'd like Ostentation, unless I would have answered them all, which I shall never attempt. The Reason therefore of my obstinate Silence has been all along, that hitherto I have not been accused of any thing, that is criminal or immoral, for which every middling Capacity could not have framed a very good Answer, from some Part or other, either of the Vindication or the Book it self.

[iii] *| However, I have wrote, and had by me near two Years, a Defence of the* Fable of the Bees,[2] *in which I have stated and endeavour'd to solve all the Objections that might reasonably be made against it, as to the Doctrine contain'd in it, and the Detriment it might be of to others : For this is the only thing about which I ever had any Concern. Being conscious, that I have*

---

[1] Cf. below, ii. 418 sqq.

[2] This seems not to have been published independently. It may, however, have formed part of *Remarks upon Two Late Presentments* (1729), if this work is, as is very possible, by Mandeville. (As to its authorship see my article 'The Writings of Bernard Mandeville ', in the *Journal of English and Germanic Philology* for 1921, xx. 457–60.) Although the *Remarks* dealt with both presentments by the Grand Jury of the *Fable*, the earlier portion of the *Remarks*, according to its own statement (pp. 12 and 16), related only to the first presentment, and, therefore, could easily have been written two years before 1728, and, indeed, seems to have been (see *Remarks*, p. 16). Perhaps, however, the defence spoken of may have been worked into the *Origin of Honour* (1732) and the *Letter to Dion* (1732).

wrote with no ill Design, I should be sorry to lye under the Imputation of it : But as to the Goodness or Badness of the Performance it self, the Thought was never worth my Care ; and therefore those Criticks, that found Fault with my bad Reasoning, and said of the Book, that it is ill wrote, that there is nothing new in it, that it is incoherent Stuff, that the Language is barbarous, the Humour low, and the Style mean and pitiful ; those Criticks, I say, are all very wellcome to say what they please : In the main, I believe they are in the right ; but if they are not, I shall never give my self the Trouble to contradict them ; for I never think an Author more foolishly employ'd, than when he is vindicating his own Abilities. As I wrote it for my Diversion, so I have had my Ends ; if those who read it have not had theirs, I am sorry for it, tho' I think my self not at all answer-able for the Disappointment. It was not wrote by Subscription, nor have I ever warranted, any where, what Use or Goodness it would be of : On the contrary, in the very Preface, I have called it an inconsiderable Trifle, and since that, I have publickly | own'd that it was [iv] *a Rhapsody.*[1] *If People will buy Books without looking into them, or knowing what they are, I can't see whom they have to blame but themselves, when they don't answer Expectation. Besides, it is no new thing for People to dislike Books after they have bought them : This will happen sometimes, even when Men of con-siderable Figure had given them the strongest Assurances, before hand, that they would be pleas'd with them.*

A considerable Part of the Defence I mention'd, has been seen by several of my Friends, who have been in Expectation of it for some time. I have stay'd neither for Types nor Paper, and yet I have several Reasons, why I do not yet publish it ; which, having touch'd no body's Money, nor made any Promise concerning it, I beg leave to keep to my self. Most of my Adversaries,

---

[1] In *Fable* i. 404.

*whenever it comes out, will think it soon enough, and no
body suffers by the Delay but my self.*

*Since I was first attack'd, it has long been a Matter
of Wonder and Perplexity to me to find out, why and
how Men should conceive, that I had wrote with an
Intent to debauch the Nation, and promote all Manner
of Vice : And it was a great while before I could derive
the Charge from any thing, but wilful Mistake and
premeditated Malice ; but since I have seen, that Men
could be serious in apprehending the Encrease of Rogues
and Robberies, from the frequent Representations of the*
[v] Beggar's Opera,[1] *I am per-|suaded, that there really
are such* Wrongheads *in the* World, *as will fancy Vices
to be encouraged, when they see them expos'd. To the
same Perverseness of Judgment it must have been owing,
that some of my Adversaries were highly incens'd with
me, for having own'd in the Vindication, that* hitherto
I had not been able to conquer my Vanity, as well
as I could have wish'd.[2] *From their Censure it is
manifest, that they must have imagin'd, that to complain
of a Frailty, was the same as to brag of it. But if these
angry Gentlemen had been less blinded with Passion, or
seen with better Eyes, they would easily have perceiv'd,
unless they were too well pleas'd with their Pride ; that
to have made the same Confession themselves, they
wanted nothing but Sincerity. Whoever boasts of his
Vanity, and at the same time shews his Arrogance, is
unpardonable. But when we hear a Man complain of*

---

[1] Sir John Fielding told Hugh
Kelly ' that ever since the first
representation of this piece [in
the same year Mandeville signed
this preface], there had been,
on every successful run, a pro-
portionate number of highwaymen brought to the office . . .'
(W. Cook, *Memoirs of Charles
Macklin*, ed. 1804, p. 64). Dr.

Johnson gave some typically sane
testimony on the other side in his
life of Gay.

[2] William Law, for instance, in
*Remarks upon a Late Book, En-
titled the Fable of the Bees* (1724),
pp. 88–9, George Bluet in his
Enquiry (1725), p. 106, and
Innes in ΑΡΕΤΗ-ΛΟΓΙΑ (1728),
p. xxiii.

an *Infirmity, and his Want of Power entirely to cure it,
whilst he suffers no Symptoms of it to appear, that we
could justly upbraid him with, we are so far from being
offended, that we are pleas'd with the Ingenuity, and
applaud his Candor : And when such an Author takes
no greater Liberties with his Readers, than what is usual
in the same manner of writing, and owns That to be the
Result of Vanity, which others tell a thousand Lies about,
his Confession is a Compliment, and the Frankness of it
ought not to be look'd upon otherwise, than as a Civility
to the Publick, a Condescen-|sion he was not obliged to* [vi]
*make. It is not in feeling the Passions, or in being
affected with the Frailties of Nature, that Vice consists ;
but in indulging and obeying the Call of them, contrary
to the Dictates of Reason. Whoever pays great Deference
to his Readers, respectfully submitting himself to their
Judgment, and tells them at the same time, that he is
entirely destitute of Pride ; whoever, I say, does this,
spoils his Compliment whilst he is making of it : For it
is no better than bragging, that it costs him nothing.
Persons of Taste, and the least Delicacy, can be but little
affected with a Man's Modesty, of whom they are sure,
that he is wholly void of Pride within : The Absence
of the one makes the Virtue of the other cease ; at least
the Merit of it is not greater than that of Chastity in
an Eunuch, or Humility in a Beggar. What Glory
would it be to the Memory of* Cato, *that he refused to
touch the Water that was brought him, if it was not
supposed that he was very thirsty when he did it ?* [1]

*The Reader will find, that in this Second Part I have
endeavoured to illustrate and explain several Things, that
were obscure and only hinted at in the First.*

*Whilst I was forming this Design, I found on the one hand,
that, as to my self, the easiest way of executing it, would
be by Dialogue ; but I knew, on the other, that to discuss*

[1] See *Fable* i. 165, where Mandeville tells the anecdote to which
this passage is an allusion.

Opinions, and manage Controversies, it is counted the most unfair Manner of Writing. When partial Men [vii] | *have a mind to demolish an Adversary, and triumph over him with little Expence, it has long been a frequent Practice to attack him with Dialogues, in which the Champion, who is to lose the Battel, appears at the very beginning of the Engagement, to be the Victim, that is to be sacrifised, and seldom makes a better Figure, than Cocks on* Shrove-Tuesday, *that receive Blows, but return none, and are visibly set up on purpose to be knock'd down.*[1] *That this is to be said against Dialogues, is certainly true ;*[2] *but it is as true, that there is no other manner of writing, by which greater Reputation has been obtain'd. Those, who have most excell'd all others in it were the two most famous Authors of all Antiquity,* Plato *and* Cicero : *The one wrote almost all his Philosophical Works in Dialogues, and the other has left us nothing else. It is evident then, that the Fault of those, who have not succeeded in Dialogues, was in the Management, and not in the manner of Writing ; and that nothing but the ill use that has been made of it, could ever have brought it into Disrepute. The Reason why* Plato *preferr'd Dialogues to any other manner of Writing, he said, was, that Things thereby might look, as if they were acted, rather than told : The same was afterwards given by* Cicero *in the same Words, rendred into his own Language.*[3] *The greatest Objection that*

---

[1] Throwing sticks at a cock tied to a stake was formerly a Shrovetide pastime.

[2] Shaftesbury had similarly stated the dangers of dialogue-writing : ' If he [the philosopher] represents his philosophy as making any figure in conversation, if he triumphs in the debate, and gives his own wisdom the advantage over that of the world, he may be liable to sound raillery...' (*Characteristics,* ed. Robertson, 1900, ii. 7). Shaftesbury had also given a defence of dialogues similar to that below in this paragraph (see *Characteristics* i. 132).

[3] No such statement is found in Plato or Cicero. Professor Paul Shorey sends me the suggestion that Mandeville was probably thinking of a somewhat similar statement made by Plato in *Theaetetus* 143 B, C, which Cicero repeated in *De Amicitia* 3.

in reality lies against it, is the Difficulty there is in writing them well. The chief of Plato's *Interlocutors was always his Master* So-|crates, *who every where* [viii] *maintains his Character with great Dignity; but it would have been impossible to have made such an extraordinary Person speak like himself on so many Emergencies, if* Plato *had not been as great a Man as* Socrates.

Cicero, *who study'd nothing more than to imitate* Plato, *introduced in his Dialogues some of the greatest Men in* Rome *his Contemporaries, that were known to be of different Opinions, and made them maintain and defend every one his own Sentiments, as strenuously and in as lively a manner, as they could possibly have done themselves; and in reading his Dialogues a Man may easily imagine himself, to be in company with several learned Men of different Tastes and Studies. But to do this a Man must have* Cicero's *Capacity.* Lucian *likewise, and several others among the Ancients, chose for their Speakers, Persons of known Characters. That this interests and engages the Reader more, than strange Names, is undeniable; but then, when the Personages fall short of those Characters, it plainly shews, that the Author undertook what he was not able to execute. To avoid this Inconveniency, most Dialogue Writers among the Moderns have made use of fictitious Names, which they either invented themselves, or borrow'd of others. These are, generally speaking, judicious Compounds, taken from the* Greek, *that serve for short Characters of the imaginary Persons they are given to, denoting either the | Party they side with, or what it is they love* [ix] *or hate. But of all these happy Compounds there is not one, that has appear'd equally charming to so many Authors of different Views and Talents, as* Philalethes; *a plain Demonstration of the great Regard Mankind generally have to Truth. There has not been a Paper-War of note, these two hundred Years, in which both Parties, at one time or other, have not made use of this victorious Champion; who, which Side soever he has fought on, has hitherto, like* Dryden's Almanzor,[1] *been Conqueror, and constantly carried all before him. But, as by this means the Event of the Battel must always be known, as soon as the Combatants are named, and before a Blow is struck ; and as all Men are not equally peaceable in their Dispositions, many Readers have complain'd, that they had not Sport enough for their Money, and that knowing so much before-hand, spoil'd all their Diversion. This Humour having prevail'd for some time, Authors are grown less sollicitous about the Names of the Personages they introduce : This careless Way seeming to me, at least, as reasonable as any other, I have follow'd ; and had no other Meaning by the Names I have given my Interlocutors, than to distinguish them; without the least Regard to the Derivation of the* ª *Words, or any thing relating to the Etymology of them : All the Care I have taken about them, that I know of, is, that the Pronunciation of them should not be harsh, nor the Sounds offensive.*

[x] | *But tho' the Names I have chosen are feign'd, and the Circumstances of the Persons fictitious, the Characters themselves are real, and as faithfully copied from Nature, as I have been able to take them. I have known Criticks find fault with Play-wrights for annexing short Characters to the Names they gave the Persons of the* Drama ; *alledging, that it is forestalling their Pleasure, and that whatever the Actors are represented to be, they want no Monitor, and are wise enough to find it out themselves. But I could never approve of this Censure ; there is a Satisfaction, I think, in knowing ones Company ; and when I am to converse with People for a considerable time, I desire to be well acquainted with them, and the sooner the better. It is for this reason, I thought it proper to give the Reader some account of the Persons, that are to entertain him. As they are supposed to be People of*

ª *the* om. 30

[1] In his *Virgin Unmask'd* (1724), p. 132, Mandeville had already referred unfavourably to the romantic hero of *The Conquest of Granada.*

Quality, *I beg leave, before I come to Particulars, to premise some things concerning the* Beau Monde *in general; which, tho' most People perhaps know them, every Body does not always attend to. Among the fashionable part of Mankind throughout Christendom, there are in all Countries Persons, who, tho' they feel a just Abhorrence to Atheism and profess'd Infidelity, yet have very little Religion, and are scarce Half-Believers when their Lives come to be look'd into, and their Sentiments examin'd. What is chiefly aim'd at in a refined Education is to procure as much Ease and Pleasure upon Earth, as | that can afford: Therefore Men are first instructed* [xi] *in all the various Arts of rendring their Behaviour agreeable to others, with the least Disturbance to themselves. Secondly, they are imbued with the Knowledge of all the elegant Comforts of Life, as well as the Lessons of human Prudence, to avoid Pain and Trouble, in order to enjoy as much of the World, and with as little Opposition, as it is possible: whilst thus Men study their own private Interest, in assisting each other to promote and encrease the Pleasures of Life in general, they find by Experience, that to compass those Ends, every thing ought to be banish'd from Conversation, that can have the least Tendency of making others uneasy; and to reproach Men with their Faults or Imperfections, Neglects or Omissions, or to put them in Mind of their Duty, are Offices that none are allow'd to take upon them, but Parents or profess'd Masters and Tutors; nor even they before Company: But to reprove and pretend to teach others, we have no Authority over, is ill Manners, even in a Clergyman out of the Pulpit; nor is he there to talk magisterially, or ever to mention things, that are melancholly or dismal, if he would pass for a polite Preacher: But whatever we may vouchsafe to hear at Church; neither the Certainty of a future State, nor the Necessity of Repentance, nor any thing else relating to the Essentials of Christianity, are ever to be talk'd of when we are out of it, among the* Beau Monde, *upon*

[xii] *any Account whatever. The | Subject is not diverting : Besides, every Body is supposed to know those things, and to take care accordingly ; nay it is unmannerly to think otherwise. The Decency in Fashion being the chief, if not the only Rule, all modish People walk by, not a few of them go to Church, and receive the Sacrament, from the same Principle, that obliges them to pay Visits to one another, and now and then to make an Entertainment. But as the greatest Care of the* Beau Monde *is to be agreeable, and appear well-bred, so most of them take particular Care, and many against their Consciences, not to seem burden'd with more Religion, than it is fashionable to have ; for fear of being thought, to be either Hypocrites or Bigots.*

Virtue however is a very fashionable Word, and some of the most luxurious are extremely fond of the amiable sound ; tho' they mean nothing by it, but a great Veneration for whatever is courtly or sublime, and an equal Aversion to every thing, that is vulgar or unbecoming. They seem to imagine, that it chiefly consists in a strict Compliance to the Rules of Politeness, and all the Laws of Honour, that have any regard to the Respect that is due to themselves. It is the Existence of this Virtue, that is often maintain'd with so much Pomp of Words, and for the Eternity of which so many Champions are ready to take up Arms : Whilst the Votaries of it deny themselves no Pleasure, they can enjoy, either fashionably or
[xiii] *in secret ; and, instead | of sacrificing the Heart to the Love of real Virtue, can only condescend to abandon the outward Deformity of Vice, for the Satisfaction they receive from appearing to be well-bred. It is counted ridiculous for Men to commit Violence upon themselves, or to maintain, that Virtue requires Self-denial ; all Court-Philosophers are agreed, that nothing can be lovely or desirable, that is mortifying or uneasy. A civil Behaviour among the Fair in Publick, and a Deportment, inoffensive both in Words and Actions, is all the Chastity, the polite World requires in Men. What*

Liberties soever a Man gives himself in private, his Reputation shall never suffer, whilst he conceals his Amours from all those, that are not unmannerly inquisitive, and takes care, that nothing criminal can ever be proved upon him. Si non castè saltem cautè, *is a Precept that sufficiently shews, what every Body expects; and tho' Incontinence is own'd to be a Sin, yet never to have been guilty of it is a Character, which most single Men under thirty would not be fond of, even amongst modest Women.*

As the World every where, in Compliment to itself, desires to be counted really virtuous, so bare-fac'd Vices, and all Trespasses committed in Sight of it, are heinous and unpardonable. To see a Man drunk in the open Street or any serious Assembly at Noon-day is shocking; because it is a Violation of the Laws of Decency, and plainly shews a Want of Respect, and Ne-|glect of [xiv] *Duty, which every Body is supposed to owe to the Publick. Men of mean Circumstances likewise may be blamed for spending more Time or Money in drinking, than they can afford; but when these and all worldly Considerations are out of the Question, Drunkenness itself, as it is a Sin, an Offence to Heaven, is seldom censured; and no Man of Fortune scruples to own, that he was at such a Time in such a Company, where* ᵃ *they drank very hard. Where nothing is committed, that is either beastly, or otherwise extravagant, Societies, that meet on purpose to drink, and be merry, reckon their manner of passing away the time as innocent, as any other, tho' most Days in the Year they spend five or six Hours of the four and twenty in that Diversion. No Man had ever the Reputation of being a good Companion, that would never drink to excess; and if a Man's Constitution be so strong, or himself so cautious, that the Dose he takes over-night, never disorders him the next Day, the worst that shall be said of him, is, that he loves his Bottle with Moderation: Tho' every Night constantly he makes drinking his Pastime, and hardly ever goes to Bed entirely sober.*

ᵃ were 29

Avarice, it is true, is generally detested; *but as Men may be as guilty of it by scraping Money together, as they can be by hoarding it up, so all the base, the sordid and unreasonable means of acquiring Wealth, ought to be equally condemn'd and exploded, with the vile, the* [xv] *pitiful | and penurious ways of saving it*; *but the World is more indulgent*; *no Man is tax'd with Avarice, that will conform with the* Beau Monde, *and live every way in Splendour, tho' he should always be raising the Rents of his Estate, and hardly suffer his Tenants to live under him*; *tho' he should enrich himself by Usury, and all the barbarous Advantages that Extortion can make of the Necessities of others*; *and tho' moreover he should be a bad Pay-master himself, and an unmerciful Creditor to the unfortunate*; *it is all one, no man is counted covetous, who entertains well, and will allow his Family what is fashionable for a Person in his Condition. How often do we see Men of very large Estates unreasonably sollicitous after greater Riches! What Greediness do some Men discover in extending the Perquisites of their Offices! What dishonourable Condescensions are made for Places of Profit! What slavish Attendance is given, and what low Submissions and unmanly Cringes are made to Favorites for Pensions, by Men that could subsist without them! Yet these things are no Reproach to Men, and they are never upbraided with them but by their Enemies, or those that envy them, and perhaps the Discontented and the Poor. On the contrary, most of the well-bred People, that live in Affluence themselves, will commend them for their Diligence and Activity*; *and say of them, that they take care of the Main Chance*; [xvi] *that they are industrious Men | for their Families, and that they know how, and are fit, to live in the World.*

But these kind Constructions are not more hurtful to the Practice of Christianity, than the high Opinion, which in an artful Education Men are taught to have of their Species, is to the Belief of its Doctrine, if a right use be not made of it. That the great Preeminence we

*have over all other Creatures, we are acquainted with,
consists in our rational Faculty, is very true ; but it is
as true, that the more we are taught to admire ourselves,
the more our Pride encreases, and the greater Stress we
lay on the Sufficiency of our Reason : For as Experience
teaches us, that the greater and the more transcendent
the Esteem is, which Men have for their own Worth, the
less capable they generally are to bear Injuries without
Resentment ; so we see in like manner, that the more
exalted the Notions are, which Men entertain of their
better part, their reasoning Faculty, the more remote and
averse they'll be from giving their Assent to any thing
that seems to insult over or contradict it : And asking
a Man to admit of any thing, he cannot comprehend, the
Proud Reasoner calls an Affront to human Understanding. But as Ease and Pleasure are the grand Aim of
the* Beau Monde, *and Civility is inseparable from their
Behaviour, whether they are Believers or not, so well-
bred People never quarrel with the Religion they are
brought up in : They'll | readily comply with every* [xvii]
*Ceremony in Divine Worship, they have been used to,
and never dispute with you, either about the* Old *or the*
New Testament, *if in your turn you'll forbear laying
great Stress upon Faith and Mysteries, and allow them
to give an allegorical or any other figurative Sense to the
History of the Creation, and whatever else they cannot
comprehend or account for by the Light of Nature.*

*I am far from believing that among the fashionable
People there are not in all Christian Countries many
Persons of stricter Virtue and greater Sincerity in
Religion, than I have here described ; but that a con-
siderable part of Mankind have a great Resemblance to
the Picture I have been drawing, I appeal to every
knowing and candid Reader.* Horatio, Cleomenes, *and*
Fulvia *are the Names I have given to my Interlocutors :
The first represents one of the modish People I have been
speaking of, but rather of the better sort of them as to
Morality ; tho' he seems to have a greater Distrust of*

the *Sincerity of Clergymen, than he has of that of any other Profession, and to be of the Opinion, which is express'd in that trite and specious as well as false and injurious saying,* Priests of all Religions are the same. *As to his Studies, he is suppos'd to be tolerably well vers'd in the Classicks, and to have read more than is usual for People of Quality, that are born to great Estates.* [xviii] *He is a Man of strict Honour, and of | Justice as well as Humanity ; rather profuse than covetous, and altogether disinterested in his Principles. He has been Abroad, seen the World, and is supposed to be possess'd of the greatest part of the Accomplishments, that usually gain a Man the Reputation of being very much of a Gentleman.*

Cleomenes *had been just such another, but was much reform'd. As he had formerly, for his Amusement only, been dipping into Anatomy, and several parts of natural Philosophy ; so, since he was come Home from his Travels, he had study'd human Nature, and the Knowledge of himself, with great Application. It is supposed, that, whilst he was thus employing most of his leisure Hours, he met with* the Fable of the Bees ; *and making a right use of what he read, compared what he felt himself, within, as well as what he had seen in the World, with the Sentiments set forth in that Book, and found the Insincerity of Men fully as universal, as it was there represented. He had no Opinion of the Pleas and Excuses, that are commonly made to cover the real Desires of the Heart ; and he ever suspected the Sincerity of Men, whom he saw to be fond of the World, and with Eagerness grasping at Wealth and Power, when they pretended that the great End of their Labours was to have Opportunities of doing good to others upon Earth, and becoming themselves more thankful to Heaven ; especially,* [xix] *if they conform'd with the* Beau | Monde, *and seem'd to take delight in a fashionable way of living : He had the same Suspicion of all Men of Sense, who, having read and consider'd the Gospel, would maintain the Possibility that Persons might pursue Worldly Glory with all their*

Strength, and at the same time be good Christians.
Cleomenes *himself believ'd the Bible to be the Word
of God, without reserve, and was entirely convinced of
the mysterious as well as historical Truths that are
contain'd in it. But as he was fully persuaded, not
only of the Veracity of the Christian Religion, but likewise of the Severity of its Precepts, so he attack'd his
Passions with Vigor, but never scrupled to own his want
of Power to subdue them, or the violent Opposition he felt
from within; often complaining, that the Obstacles he
met with from Flesh and Blood, were insurmountable.
As he understood perfectly well the difficulty of the Task
required in the Gospel, so he ever opposed those easy
Casuists, that endeavour'd to lessen and extenuate it for
their own Ends; and he loudly maintain'd, that Men's
Gratitude to Heaven was an unacceptable Offering,
whilst they continued to live in Ease and Luxury, and
were visibly sollicitous after their Share of the Pomp
and Vanity of this World. In the very Politeness of
Conversation, the Complacency, with which fashionable
People are continually soothing each other's Frailties,
and in almost every part of a Gentleman's | Behaviour,* [xx]
*he thought, there was a Disagreement between the outward
Appearances, and what is felt within, that was clashing
with Uprightness and Sincerity.* Cleomenes *was of
Opinion, that of all religious Virtues, nothing was more
scarce, or more difficult to acquire, than Christian
Humility; and that to destroy the Possibility of ever
attaining to it, nothing was so effectual as what is call'd
a Gentleman's Education; and that the more dextrous,
by this Means, Men grew in concealing the outward
Signs, and every Symptom of Pride, the more entirely
they became enslaved by it within. He carefully examin'd
into the Felicity that accrues from the Applause of others,
and the invisible Wages which Men of Sense and judicious
Fancy receiv'd for their Labours; and what it was at
the Bottom, that rendred those airy Rewards so ravishing
to Mortals. He had often observed, and watch'd narrowly*

*the Countenances and Behaviour of Men, when any thing
of theirs was admired or commended, such as the Choice
of their Furniture, the Politeness of their Entertainments,
the Elegancy of their Equipages, their Dress, their Diversions, or the fine Taste display'd in their Buildings.*

Cleomenes *seemed charitable, and was a Man of
strict Morals, yet he would often complain that he was
not possess'd of one Christian Virtue, and found fault
with his own Actions, that had all the Appearances of*
[xxi] *Goodness ; be-|cause he was conscious, he said, that they
were perform'd from a wrong Principle. The Effects of
his Education, and his Aversion to Infamy, had always
been strong enough to keep him from Turpitude ; but
this he ascribed to his Vanity, which he complain'd was
in such full Possession of his Heart, that he knew no
Gratification of any Appetite from which he was able
to exclude it. Having always been a Man of unblameable
Behaviour, the Sincerity of his Belief had made no
visible Alteration in his Conduct to outward Appearances ; but in private he never ceas'd from examining
himself. As no Man was less prone to Enthusiasm than
himself, so his Life was very uniform ; and as he never
pretended to high Flights of Devotion, so he never was
guilty of enormous Offences. He had a strong Aversion
to Rigorists of all sorts ; and when he saw Men quarrelling
about Forms of Creeds, and the Interpretation of obscure
Places, and requiring of others the strictest Compliance
to their own Opinions in disputable Matters, it rais'd
his Indignation to see the Generality of them want
Charity, and many of them scandalously remiss, in the
plainest and most necessary Duties. He took uncommon
Pains to search into human Nature, and left no Stone
unturn'd, to detect the Pride and Hypocrisy of it, and
among his intimate Friends to expose the Stratagems of
the one, and the exorbitant Power of the other. He was*
[xxii] *sure, that the Satisfaction which arose | from worldly
Enjoyments, was something distinct from Gratitude, and
foreign to Religion ; and he felt plainly, that as it pro-*

The PREFACE.

ceeded from within, so it center'd in himself : The very Relish of Life, he said, was accompanied with an Elevation of Mind, that seem'd to be inseparable from his Being. Whatever Principle was the Cause of this, he was convinced within himself, that the Sacrifice of the Heart, which the Gospel requires, consisted in the utter Extirpation of that Principle; confessing at the same time, that this Satisfaction he found in himself, this Elevation of Mind, caused his chief Pleasure; and that in all the Comforts of Life, it made the greatest Part of the Enjoyment.

Cleomenes with grief often own'd his Fears, that his Attachment to the World would never cease whilst he lived; the Reasons he gave, were the great Regard he continued to have for the Opinion of worldly Men; the Stubborness of his indocile Heart, that could not be brought to change the Objects of its Pride; and refused to be ashamed of what from his Infancy it had been taught to glory in; and lastly, the Impossibility, he found in himself, of being ever reconciled to Contempt, and enduring, with Patience, to be laugh'd at and despised for any Cause, or on any Consideration whatever. These were the Obstacles, he said, that hindered him from breaking off all Commerce with the Beau Monde, *and entirely changing his manner of Living; with-|out which he thought it Mockery to talk of re-* [xxiii] *nouncing the World, and bidding adieu to all the Pomp and Vanity of it.*

The part of Fulvia, *who is the third Person, is so inconsiderable, she just appearing only in the first Dialogue, that it would be impertinent to trouble the Reader with a Character of her. I had a Mind to say some things on Painting and* Operas, *which I thought might by introducing her be brought in more naturally, and with less Trouble, than they could have been without her. The Ladies, I hope, will find no reason, from the little she does say, to suspect that she wants either Virtue or Understanding.*

As to the Fable, or what is supposed to have occasioned the first Dialogue between Horatio *and* Cleomenes, *it is this.* Horatio, *who had found great Delight in my Lord* Shaftsbury's *polite manner of Writing, his fine Raillery, and blending Virtue with good Manners, was a great Stickler for the Social System; and wonder'd how* Cleomenes *could be an Advocate for such a Book as the* Fable of the Bees, *of which he had heard a very vile Character from several Quarters.* Cleomenes, *who loved and had a great friendship for* Horatio, *wanted to undeceive him; but the other, who hated Satyr, was prepossess'd, and having been told likewise, that martial Courage, and Honour itself, were ridicul'd in that Book, he was very much exasperated against the Author and* [xxiv] *his whole | Scheme: He had two or three times heard* Cleomenes *discourse on this Subject with others; but would never enter into the Argument himself; and finding his Friend often pressing to come to it, he began to look coolly upon him, and at last to avoid all opportunities of being alone with him: 'till* Cleomenes *drew him in, by the Stratagem which the Reader will see he made use of, as* Horatio *was one day taking his leave after a short complimentary Visit.*

I should not wonder to see Men of Candor, as well as good Sense, find fault with the Manner, in which I have chose to publish these Thoughts of mine to the World; there certainly is something in it, which I confess I don't know how to justify to my own Satisfaction. That such a Man as Cleomenes, *having met with a Book agreeable to his own Sentiments, should desire to be acquainted with the Author of it, has nothing in it, that is improbable or unseemly; but then it will be objected, that, whoever the Interlocutors are, it was I myself who wrote the Dialogues; and that it is contrary to all Decency, that a Man should proclaim concerning his own Work, all that a Friend of his, perhaps, might be allow'd to say: This is true; and the best Answer, which, I think, can be made to it, is, that such an impartial Man, and such a Lover of*

Truth, as Cleomenes *is represented to be, would be as cautious in speaking of his Friend's Merit, as he would be of his own.* It | *might be urg'd likewise, that when* [xxv] *a Man professes himself to be an Author's Friend, and exactly to entertain the same Sentiments with another, it must naturally put every Reader upon his guard, and render him as suspicious and distrustful of such a Man, as he would be of the Author himself.* But how good soever the Excuses are, that might be made for this manner of Writing, I would never have ventur'd upon it, if I had not liked it in the famous Gassendus,[1] who by the help of several Dialogues and a Friend, who is the chief Personage in them, has not only explain'd and illustrated his System, but likewise refuted his Adversaries : Him I have followed, and I hope the Reader will find, that whatever Opportunity I have had by this Means, of speaking well of my self indirectly, I had no Design to make that, or any other ill Use of it.

As it is supposed, that Cleomenes *is my Friend, and speaks my Sentiments, so it is but Justice, that every Thing which he advances should be look'd upon and consider'd as my own;* but no Man in his Senses would think, that I ought to be equally responsible for every Thing that Horatio *says, who is his Antagonist.*[2] *If*

[1] Cf. above, i. cv-cvi, 181, *n.* 1, and below, ii. 139, *n.* 1, and 166, *n.* 1. I find no such dialogues in Gassendi.

[2] This is a device by which Mandeville evades responsibility for unorthodox sentiments. Of the two speakers in the dialogues it is not always Cleomenes who is Mandeville's spokesman. Cleomenes' frequent statement of belief in the biblical account of Creation, in the midst of his demonstration of the incompatibility of this account with a scientific explanation, is an ironical pose, as is his repeated invocation of miraculous providential intervention to explain history. It is in Horatio's unorthodox disagreement with this that Mandeville himself speaks. This device is given away, by his temporary unwillingness to sustain it, in a passage (ii. 236-9) which inquires into the means by which primitive man contrived to survive the ravages of wild beasts. At first Cleomenes argues that this survival could be due only to providential interference ; but, questioned further by the

ever he offers any thing that savours of Libertinism, or is otherwise exceptionable, which Cleomenes does not reprove him for in the best and most serious Manner, or to which he gives not the most satisfactory and convincing [xxvi] | Answer that can be made, I am to blame, otherwise not. Yet from the Fate the first Volume has met with, I expect to see in a little time several things transcrib'd and cited from this, in that manner, by themselves, without the Replies that are made to them, and so shewn to the World, as my Words and my Opinion. The Opportunity of doing this will be greater in this Book than it was in the former, and should I always have fair play, and never be attack'd, but by such Adversaries, as would make their Quotations from me without Artifice, and use me with common Honesty, it would go a great Way to the refuting of me; and I should myself begin to suspect the Truth of several Things I have advanced, and which hitherto I can't help believing.

A Stroke made in this manner, —— which the Reader will sometimes meet with in the following Dialogues, is a Sign, either of Interruption, when the Person speaking is not suffer'd to go on with what he was going to say, or else of a Pause, during which something is supposed to be said or done, not relating to the Discourse.

As in this Volume I have not alter'd the Subject, on which a former, known by the Name of the Fable of the Bees, was wrote; and the same unbiass'd Method of searching after Truth and enquiring into the Nature

doubting Horatio, explains this interference away by interpreting it in terms of natural law. A similar procedure is pursued in another passage (ii. 320–1). Such belief in the universality of natural law is Mandeville's real tenet. Indeed, Horatio here (ii. 320) uses the very argument employed by Mandeville in Fable i. 117, that Providence works 'not without Means'. Wherever Cleomenes argues otherwise, then in the disingenuousness of his reasoning and the cogency of Horatio's answers (as in ii. 307–8) it is, I think, apparent that Mandeville has his tongue in his cheek and that Horatio is his real mouthpiece.

The PREFACE. 23

of Man and Society, made use of in that, is continued in this, | I thought it unnecessary to look out for another [xxvii] Title; and being myself a great Lover of Simplicity, and my Invention none of the most fruitful, the Reader, I hope, will pardon the bald, inelegant Aspect, and unusual Emptiness of the Title Page.

Here I would have made an End of my Preface, which I know very well is too long already: But the World having been very grosly imposed upon by a false Report, that some Months ago was very solemnly made, and as industriously spread in most of the News-Papers, for a considerable Time, I think, it would be an unpardonable Neglect in me, of the Publick, should I suffer them to remain in the Error they were led into, when I am actually addressing them, and there is no other Person, from whom they can so justly expect to be undeceiv'd. In the London Evening-Post of Saturday March 9, 1727-8. the following Paragraph was printed in small Italick, at the End of the Home-News.

On *Friday* Evening the first Instant, A Gentleman, well dress'd, appeared at the Bonefire before St. *James*'s-Gate,[1] who declared himself the Author of a Book, entituled, *The Fable of the Bees:* And that he was sorry for writing the same: and recollecting his former Promise,[2] pronounced these Words: *I commit my Book to the Flames*; and threw it in accordingly.[3]

[1] The bonfire on this occasion was for Queen Caroline's birthday (see below, ii. 28, *n.* 1).
[2] See *Fable* i. 412.
[3] *The Comedian, or Philosophic Enquirer. Numb. IX* for 1733, pp. 30–1, gives this account of the fraud—an apocryphal account, according to Mandeville (see below, ii. 26):
'... the Booksellers ... hired a Fellow, whom they dressed like a Gentleman, to go up to the Fire with *the Fable of the Bees* in his Hand, and to declare to the Mob that he was the Author thereof. ... This Story I had from a Bookseller in *Paternoster-row*, a Man of Worth and Honour, to whom one of the Scoundrels who hired the Fellow to personate Dr. *Mandeville* was weak enough to relate the Fact. ... I am mistaken if those very

24 *The* PREFACE.

| *The* Monday *following the same piece of News was repeated in the* Daily Journal, *and after that for a considerable time, as I have said, in most of the Papers :* [1] *But since the* Saturday *mention'd, which was the only time it was printed by itself, it appear'd always with a small Addition to it, and annex'd (with a* N.B. *before it) to the following Advertisement.*

ΑΡΕΤΗ-ΛΟΓΙΑ.

Or an Enquiry into the Original of Moral Virtue, wherein the false Notions of *Machiavel,*[2] *Hobbs, Spinosa,* and Mr. *Bayle,*[3] as they are collected and digested by the Author of *the Fable of the Bees,* are examined and confuted ; and the eternal and unalterable Law of Nature and Obligation of Moral

Persons, who hired the Fellow, did not likewise pyrate the Edition of the Answer to *the Fable.* . . .'

Apparently this anecdote about the burning of the *Fable* became current. An essay satirizing the effects of Whiston's prophecies noted, in its imaginary record of the end-of-the-world scenes inspired by a general belief in these prophecies, that, ' At St. Bride's church in Fleet-street, Mr. Woolston, (who writ against the miracles of our Saviour,) in the utmost terrors of conscience, made a public recantation. Dr. Mandeville (who had been groundlessly reported formerly to have done the same,) did it now in good earnest at St. James's gate' (*Prose Works of Jonathan Swift,* ed. Temple Scott, iv. 283).

[1] For instance, in the *London Evening Post,* 16–19 Mar. 1728 (p. 4), and in the *Whitehall Even-*

ing Post, 21–23 Mar. 1728 (p. 4).

[2] Like Mandeville, Machiavelli held that man, judged by Christian ethics, is naturally evil, and that the social order must be based on this unidealistic fact (cf. *Il Principe,* ch. 17 and 18). Machiavelli, too, believed Christianity unconducive to worldly greatness, because Christianity leads its devotees to ' stimare meno l'onore del mondo ' (*Opere,* Milan, 1804, ii. 231, in *Discorsi* II. ii), and because a prince must often ' operare contro alla fede, contro alla carità, contro alla umanità, contra alla religione' (*Il Principe,* ch. 18). For three parallels, see above, i. 39, *n.* 1, 46, *n.* 1, and 72, *n.* 1. These parallels, however, are scarcely enough to show Mandeville indebted to Machiavelli.

[3] As to Hobbes, Spinoza, and Bayle, see above, i. cix-cxi and ciii-cv.

Virtue is stated and vindicated ; to which is prefixed
a Prefatory Introduction, in a Letter to that Author.
By *Alexander Innes*, D. D. Preacher-Assistant at St.
Margaret's Westminster.[1]

[1] The two people who protested
most abusively against the immorality of Mandeville's doctrines
were, both of them, notorious.
The guilt of Hendley (cf. below,
ii. 421), who was tried for em-
bezzling charity funds, was doubt-
ful. But there is no doubt about
Innes.—The near relation of
Brigadier Lauder, who was gover-
nor of Sluys, Innes first appears
accompanying the Scottish regi-
ment garrisoned there. While at
Sluys, he met George Psalmanazar, who was then hardly more
than a boy. Psalmanazar claimed
to be a native of Formosa, concerning which he invented such
sensational anecdotes that he
managed to arouse popular interest in himself. He had, besides,
a genius for the impromptu
invention of languages. Innes,
although knowing him for a cheat,
realized that he might make
capital of Psalmanazar, and
opened communication with the
Bishop of London, expecting a
preferment from the Bishop as
the reward for converting Psalmanazar from his supposed For-
mosan heathenry and introducing
him for ethnological study into
England. He therefore baptized
Psalmanazar, coached him in
his fraud, and took him to
England.

The experiment was a success,
and Innes was made chaplain-
general to the English forces in
Portugal, whither he departed,
just in time to avoid being turned
(for a second time) out of his
lodgings because of immorality.
Meanwhile, he was made a doctor
of divinity by a Scottish university.

Some time after, in 1726, Innes
met his countryman, Professor
Archibald Campbell, in London,
and the latter entrusted him with
a manuscript to place with a
publisher. Innes did place it
with a publisher, but as his own
work, with the title of ΑΡΕΤΗ-
ΛΟΓΙΑ—adding a preface in which
he attacked Mandeville. As a
result of this book, the Bishop of
London gave him a good living
in Essex. In 1730 Campbell
reappeared on the scene, and, as
he put it, made Innes ' tremble
in his shoes '. Innes's cousin,
Stuart, physician to the queen,
interceded, however, and Campbell was persuaded to be satisfied
with an advertisement stating his
authorship, which read only that,
' for some certain reasons ', the
book had appeared as Innes's.
Even this was delayed so that
Innes could remove to his bene-
fice in Essex before it appeared.
It was time, anyhow, for him to
give up his assistant preachership
at St. Margaret's, Westminster,
for he was discovered to have
been guilty of malversation there.
The remainder of his life was
spent very privately, according
to Psalmanazar, who adds that he
hopes that Innes ' made the best

The small Addition which I said was made to that notable piece of News, after it came to be annex'd to this Advertisement, consisted of these five Words (upon reading the above Book) *which were put in after* sorry for writing the same. *This Story having been often repeated in the Papers, and never publickly contradicted, many People, it seems, were credulous enough to believe, not-* [xxix] *withstanding the Improbability of it.* | *But the least attentive would have suspected the whole, as soon as they had seen the Addition that was made to it, the second time it was publish'd; for supposing it to be intelligible, as it follows the Advertisement, it cannot be pretended, that the repenting Gentleman pronounced those very Words. He must have named the Book; and if he had said, that his Sorrow was occasion'd by reading the* ΑΡΕΤΗ-ΛΟΓΙΑ, *or the new Book of the reverend Dr.* Innes, *how came such a remarkable part of his Confession to be omitted in the first Publication, where the well-dress'd Gentleman's Words and Actions seem to be set down with so much Care and Exactness? Besides, every Body knows the great Industry, and general Intelligence of our News-Writers: If such a Farce had really been acted, and a Man had been hired to pronounce the Words mention'd, and throw a Book into the Fire, which I have often wonder'd was not done; is it credible at all, that a thing so remarkable, done so openly, and before so many Witnesses the first Day of* March, *should not be taken Notice of in any of the Papers before the Ninth, and never be repeated afterwards, or ever mention'd but as an Appendix of the Advertisement to recommend Dr.* Innes's *Book?*

However, this Story has been much talk'd of, and occasion'd a great deal of Mirth among my Acquaintance, several of whom have earnestly press'd me more than once

use of his solitude.' (See *Memoirs of ****. Commonly Known by the Name of George Psalmanazar*, ed. 1765, pp. 148 sqq. ; Psalmanazar, *Description of Formosa* (1705), pp. 288 sqq. ; the article on Archibald Campbell in the *Dictionary of National Biography*; and *The Comedian, or Philosophic Enquirer. Numb. IX*, 1733, pp. 30-1.)

The PREFACE.

to advertise the Fal-|sity of it, which I would never [xxx] *comply with for fear of being laugh'd at, as some Years ago poor Dr.* Patridge[1] *was, for seriously maintaining, that he was not dead. But all this while we were in the dark, and no Body could tell how this Report came into the World, or what it could be that had given a Handle to it, when one Evening a Friend of mine, who had borrow'd Dr.* Innes's *Book, which till then I had never seen, shew'd me in it the following Lines.*

But *à propos*, Sir, if I rightly remember the ingenious Mr. *Law*, in his Remarks upon your FABLE OF THE BEES, puts you in mind of a Promise you had made, by which you oblig'd yourself to burn that Book at any Time or Place your Adversary should appoint, if any Thing should be found in it tending to Immorality or the Corruption of Manners.[2] I have a great Respect for that Gentleman, tho' I am not personally acquainted with him, but I cannot but condemn his excessive Credulity and good Nature, in believing that a Man of your Principles could be a Slave to his Word ; for my own part, I think, I know you too well to be so easily imposed upon ; or if, after all, you should really persist in your Resolution, and commit it to the

[1] Swift's hoax, aimed at this almanac-maker, in which Swift first predicted in detail and then reported Partridge's death, had such success that poor Partridge in vain protested that he still lived. People either believed him an impostor or pretended to for the sake of the joke.

Misspelling Partridge's name, as the *Fable* did, was part of the joke (see, for instance, Swift's *Elegy on Mr. Patrige* ... *1708*). Partridge ended his *Merlinus Redivivus* (1714) with a notice about 'Pamphlets, that had my Name ... shamm'd with the want of a Letter '.

[2] Law thus concluded the section on Mandeville in his *Remarks upon a Late Book, Entituled, the Fable of the Bees* (ed. 1724, p. 98) : ' You say, if any one can shew the *least Tittle* of *Blasphemy* . . . in your Book, or *any Thing tending to Immorality* . . . *you will burn it yourself, at any Time or Place your Adversary shall appoint*. I appoint the first Time and the most publick Place. . . .'

For information as to Law's book see below, ii. 401–6. For Mandeville's promise see *Fable* i. 412.

Flames, I appoint the first of *March* before St. *James*'s Gate, for that purpose, it being the Birth-day of the [xxxi] best | and most glorious Queen upon Earth ;[1] and the burning of your Book the smallest Atonement you can make, for endeavouring to corrupt and debauch his Majesty's Subjects in their Principles. Now, Sir, if you agree to this, I hope you are not so destitute of Friends, but that you may find some charitable Neighbour or other, who will lend you a helping Hand, and throw in the Author at the same time by way of Appendix ; the doing of which will, in my Opinion, complete the Solemnity of the Day.[2] I am not your Patient, but

Your most humble Servant.

Thus ends what in the A P E T H - Λ O Γ I A *Doctor* Innes *is pleased to call a Prefatory Introduction in a Letter to the Author of* the Fable of the Bees. *It is signed* A. I. *and dated* Tot-hill-fields [3] Westminster, Jan. 20. 1727-8.

Now all our Wonder ceas'd. The judicious Reader will easily allow me, that, having read thus much,, I had an ample Dispensation from going on any further : Therefore I can say nothing of the Book ; *and as to the Reverend Author of it, who seems to think himself so well acquainted with my Principles, I have not the honour to know either him or his Morals, otherwise than from what I have quoted here.* Ex pede Herculem.

London, Octob. 20. 1728.[a]

[a] *In* 29 *a one-page list of errata followed Preface. This list is here omitted, since the corrections have been made in the text.*

[1] Queen Caroline, consort of George II, was born 1 March 1683.

[2] In his index to Part II, Mandeville humorously refers to ' *Proposal* (a) of a Reverend Divine for an human Sacrifice, to compleat the Solemnity of a Birth-Day '.

[3] This place is near St. Margaret's, Westminster, of which Innes was Preacher's Assistant.

DIALOGUE

BETWEEN

Horatio, *Cleomenes*, and *Fulvia*.

C L E O M E N E S.

Lways in haste, *Horatio?*
Hor. I must beg of you to
excuse me, I am oblig'd to go.
Cleo. Whether you have other
Engagements than you used to
have, or whether your Temper is
chang'd, I can't tell, but something has made an Alteration in
you, of which I cannot compre-
hend the Cause. There is no Man in the World whose
Friendship I value more than I do yours, or whose
Company I like better, yet I can never have it. I profess I have thought sometimes, that you have avoided
me on purpose.

| *Hor.* I am sorry, *Cleomenes*, I should have been [2]
wanting in Civility to you. I come every Week
constantly to pay my Respects to you, and if ever
I fail, I always send to enquire after your Health.

Cleo. No Man out-does *Horatio* in Civility; but I thought something more was due to our Affections and long Acquaintance, besides Compliments and Ceremony : Of late I have never been to wait upon you, but you are gone abroad, or I find you engaged; and when I have the Honour to see you here, your Stay is only momentary. Pray pardon my Rudeness for once; What is it that hinders you now from keeping me Company for an Hour or two? My Cousin talks of going out, and I shall be all alone.

Hor. I know better than to rob you of such an Opportunity for Speculation?

Cleo. Speculation! on what, pray?

Hor. That Vileness of our Species in the refin'd Way of thinking you have of late been so fond of, I call it the Scheme of Deformity, the Partizans of which study chiefly to make every thing in our Nature appear as ugly and contemptible as it is possible, and take uncommon Pains to perswade Men that they are Devils.

Cleo. If that be all, I shall soon convince you.

Hor. No Conviction to me, I beseech you : I am [3] determin'd and fully persuaded, that | there is Good in the World, as well as Evil; and that the Words, Honesty, Benevolence, and Humanity, and even Charity, are not empty Sounds only, but that there are such Things in spight of the Fable of the Bees; and I am resolved to believe, that, notwithstanding the Degeneracy of Mankind, and the Wickedness of the Age, there are Men now living, who are actually possess'd of those Virtues.

Cleo. But you don't know what I am going to say : I am----

Hor. That may be, but I will not hear one Word; all you can say is lost upon me, and if you will not give me leave to speak out, I am gone this Moment. That cursed Book has bewitch'd you, and made you deny the Existence of those very Virtues that had

gain'd you the Esteem of your Friends. You know
this is not my usual Language ; I hate to say harsh
Things : But what Regard can or ought one to have
for an Author that treats every Body *de haut en bas,*
makes a Jest of Virtue and Honour, calls *Alexander* the
Great a Madman,[1] and spares Kings and Princes no
more than any one would the most abject of the
People ? The Business of his Philosophy is just the
Reverse to that of the Herald's Office ; for as there
they are always contriving and finding out high and
illustrious Pedigrees for low and obscure People, so
your Author is ever searching after, and inventing
| mean contemptible Origins for worthy and honour- [4]
able Actions. I am your very humble Servant.

Cleo. Stay. I am of your Opinion ; what I offered
to convince you of was, how entirely I am recover'd
of the Folly which you have so justly expos'd : I have
left that Error.

Hor. Are you in earnest ?

Cleo. No Man more : There is no greater Stickler
for the Social Virtues than my self, and I much
question, whether there is any of Lord *Shaftsbury's* [2]
Admirers that will go my Lengths !

Hor. I shall be glad to see you go my Lengths first,
and as many more as you please. You cannot conceive, *Cleomenes,* how it has griev'd me, when I have
seen, how many Enemies you made yourself by that
extravagant Way of arguing. If you are but serious,
whence comes this Change?

Cleo. In the first Place I grew weary of having every
Body against me : and in the Second, there is more
Room for Invention in the other System. Poets and
Orators in the Social System have fine Opportunities
of exerting themselves.

Hor. I very much suspect the Recovery you boast
of : Are you convinced, that the other System was

---

[1] *Fable* i. 54–5.   [2] See above, i. lxxii-lxxv and 336, *n.* 1.

false, which you might have easily learn'd from seeing every body against you?

[5] | *Cleo.* False to be sure; but what you alledge is no Proof of it : for if the greatest Part of Mankind were not against that Scheme of Deformity, as you justly call it, Insincerity could not be so general, as the Scheme itself supposes it to be : But since my Eyes have been open'd I have found out that Truth and Probability are the silliest Things in the World ; they are of no manner of use, especially among the People *de bon gout.*

Hor. I thought what a Convert you was : but what new Madness has seiz'd you now?

Cleo. No Madness at all : I say and will maintain it to the World, that Truth, in the *Sublime*, is very impertinent ; and that in the Arts and Sciences, fit for Men of Taste to look into, a Master cannot commit a more unpardonable Fault, than sticking to, or being influenc'd by Truth, where it interferes with what is agreeable.

Hor. Homely Truths indeed----

Cleo. Look upon that *Dutch* Piece of the Nativity : what charming Colouring there is ! what a fine Pencil, and how just are the Out-Lines for a Piece so curiously finish'd ! But what a Fool the Fellow was to draw Hay and Straw and Cattle, and a Rack as well as a Manger : it is a Wonder he did not put the *Bambino* into the Manger.

Ful. The *Bambino*? That is the Child, I suppose ; why it should be in the Manger ; should it not?
[6] Does not the History tell us, | that the Child was laid in the Manger? I have no Skill in Painting, but I can see whether things are drawn to the Life or not ; sure nothing can be more like the Head of an Ox than that there. A Picture then pleases me best when the Art in such a Manner deceives my Eye, that without making any Allowances, I can imagine I see the Things in reality which the Painter has endeavour'd to repre-

sent. I have always thought it an admirable Piece; sure nothing in the World can be more like Nature.

Cleo. Like Nature! So much the worse: Indeed, Cousin, it is easily seen that you have no Skill in Painting. It is not Nature, but agreeable Nature, *la belle Nature*, that is to be represented; all Things that are abject, low, pitiful and mean, are carefully to be avoided, and kept out of Sight; because to Men of the true Taste they are as offensive as Things that are shocking, and really nasty.

Ful. At that rate, the Virgin *Mary*'s Condition, and our Saviour's Birth, are never to be painted.

Cleo. That's your Mistake; the Subject it self is noble: Let us go but in the next Room and I'll shew you the Difference.——Look upon that Picture, which is the same History. There's fine Architecture, there's a Colonnade; Can any thing be thought of more Magnificent? How skilfully is that | Ass removed, and [7] how little you see of the Ox; pray mind the Obscurity they are both placed in: It hangs in a strong Light, or else one might look ten times upon the Picture without observing them: Behold these Pillars of the *Corinthian* Order, how lofty they are, and what an Effect they have, what a noble Space, what an *Area* here is! How nobly every thing concurs to express the majestick Grandeur of the Subject, and strikes the Soul with Awe and Admiration at the same time!

Ful. Pray Cousin, has good Sense ever any Share in the Judgment which your Men of true Taste form about Pictures?

Hor. Madam!

Ful. I beg pardon, Sir, if I have offended: but to me it seems strange to hear such Commendation given to a Painter, for turning the Stable of a Country Inn into a Palace of extraordinary Magnificence: This is a great deal worse than *Swift*'s Metamorphosis of

Philemon and *Baucis* ; for there some Shew of Resemblance is kept in the Changes.[1]

Hor. In a Country Stable, Madam, there is nothing but Filth and Nastiness, or vile abject Things not fit to be seen, at least not capable of entertaining Persons of Quality.

Ful. The *Dutch* Picture in the next Room has nothing that is offensive : but an *Augean* Stable, even before *Hercules* had clean'd it, would be less shocking [8] to me than those | fluted Pillars ; for no body can please my Eye that affronts my Understanding : When I desire a Man to paint a considerable History, which every body knows to have been transacted at a Country Inn, does he not strangely impose upon me, because he understands Architecture, to draw me a Room that might have serv'd for a great Hall or Banquetting-house to any *Roman* Emperor ? Besides that the poor and abject State in which our Saviour chose to appear at his coming into the World, is the most material Circumstance of the History : it contains an excellent Moral against vain Pomp, and is the strongest Persuasive to Humility, which in the *Italian* are more than lost.

Hor. Indeed, Madam, Experience is against you ; and it is certain, that even among the Vulgar the Representations of mean and abject Things, and such as they are familiar with, have not that Effect, and either breed Contempt, or are Insignificant : whereas vast Piles, stately Buildings, Roofs of uncommon Height, surprizing Ornaments, and all the Archi-

[1] In this poem, when the cottage of Philemon and Baucis is changed into a church,

The groaning - chair began to crawl,
Like an huge snail, half up the wall ;
There stuck aloft in public view,

And with small change, a pulpit grew. . . .

A bedstead of the antique mode,
Compact of timber many a load,
Such as our ancestors did use,
Was metamorphos'd into pews ;
Which still their ancient nature keep
By lodging folk disposed to sleep.

tecture of the grand Taste, are the fittest to raise Devotion and inspire Men with Veneration and a Religious Awe for the Places that have these Excellencies to boast of. Is there ever a Meeting-house or Barn to be compared to a fine Cathedral, for this purpose?

Ful. I believe there is a Mechanical Way of raising Devotion in silly superstitious Crea-|tures; but an [9] attentive Contemplation on the Works of God, I am sure ——

Cleo. Pray, Cousin, say no more in Defence of your low Taste : The Painter has nothing to do with the Truth of the History; his Business is to express the Dignity of the Subject, and in Compliment to his Judges, never to forget the Excellency of our Species : All his Art and good Sense must be employ'd in raising that to the highest pitch : Great Masters don't paint for the common People, but for Persons of refin'd Understanding : What you complain of is the Effect of the good Manners and Complaisance of the Painter. When he had drawn the Infant and the *Madona*, he thought the least glimpse of the Ox and the Ass would be sufficient to acquaint you with the History : They who want more fescuing and a broader Explanation he don't desire his Picture should ever be shewn to; for the rest, he entertains you with nothing but what is Noble and worthy your Attention : You see he is an Architect, and compleatly skill'd in Perspective, and he shews you how finely he can round a Pillar, and that both the Depth and the Height of Space [a] may be drawn on a Flat, with all the other Wonders he performs by his Skill in that inconceivable Mystery of Light and Shadows.

| *Ful.* Why then is it pretended that Painting is an [10] Imitation of Nature?

Cleo. At first setting out a Scholar is to copy things exactly as he sees them; but from a great Master,

[a] Space] a Space *30*

when he is left to his own Invention, it is expected he should take the Perfections of Nature, and not paint it as it is, but as we would wish it to be. *Zeuxis,* to draw a Goddess, took five beautiful Women, from which he cull'd what was most graceful in each.

Ful. Still every Grace he painted was taken from Nature.

Cleo. That's true; but he left Nature her Rubbish, and imitated nothing but what was excellent, which made the *Assemblage* superior to any thing in Nature. *Demetrius* was tax'd for being too Natural; *Dionysius* was also blamed for drawing Men like us. Nearer our times, *Michael Angelo* was esteem'd too Natural, and *Lysippus* of old upbraided the common sort of Sculptors for making Men such as they were found in Nature.

Ful. Are these things real?

Cleo. You may read it your self in *Graham's* Preface to *The Art of Painting:* [1] the Book is above in the Library.

Hor. These Things may seem strange to you, Madam, but they are of immense Use to the Publick: The higher we can carry the Excellency of our Species, the more those beautiful Images will fill noble Minds [11] | with worthy and suitable Ideas of their own Dignity, that will seldom fail of spurring them on to Virtue and Heroick Actions. There is a Grandeur to be express'd in Things that far surpasses the Beauties of simple Nature. You take Delight in Opera's, Madam, I don't question; you must have minded the noble

[1] Richard Graham contributed not a preface, but a supplement, to Du Fresnoy's Latin poem, which Dryden translated in 1695 under the title of *The Art of Painting.* The preface, called 'A Parallel of Poetry and Painting', was by Dryden. It is from this preface that Mandeville almost literally cited the material in Cleomenes' preceding speech (see Dryden, *Works,* ed. Scott-Saintsbury, xvii. 293-4).

Manner and Stateliness beyond Nature, which every thing there is executed with. What gentle Touches, what slight and yet majestick Motions are made use of to express the most boisterous Passions! As the Subject is always lofty, so no Posture is to be chosen but what is Serious and Significant as well as Comely and Agreeable; should the Actions there be represented as they are in common Life, they would ruin the Sublime, and at once rob you of all your Pleasure.

Ful. I never expected any thing Natural at an Opera; but as Persons of Distinction resort thither, and every body comes dress'd, it is a sort of Employment, and I seldom miss a Night, because it is the Fashion to go: Besides, the Royal Family, and the Monarch himself, generally honouring them with their Presence, it is almost become a Duty to attend them, as much as it is to go to Court.[1] What diverts me there is the Company, the Lights, the Musick, the Scenes, and other Decorations: but as I understand but very few Words of *Italian*, so what | is most [12] admired in the *Recitativo*[2] is lost upon me, which makes the acting Part to me rather ridiculous than ——

Hor. Ridiculous, Madam! for Heaven's sake ——

Ful. I beg pardon, Sir, for the Expression. I never laught at an Opera in my Life; but I confess, as to the Entertainment it self, that a good Play is infinitely more diverting to me; and I prefer any thing that informs my Understanding beyond all the Recreations

[1] George II was a Händelian, and allowed the composer, then conducting a season at the King's Theatre, a pension, as George I had done. In addition, Queen Caroline had long been Händel's patroness, and he was the princesses' music-master.

[2] There were two kinds of *recitativo* in Mandeville's day: the *recitativo secco*, which was accompanied by the harpsichord, and the more effective *recitativo stromentato*, accompanied by orchestra. Splendid contemporary examples of the latter are 'Alma del gran Pompeo', from Händel's *Giulio Cesare*, and 'Deeper and deeper still', from his *Jephthah*.

which either my Eyes or my Ears can be regal'd with.[1]

Hor. I am sorry to hear a Lady of your good Sense make such a Choice. Have you no Taste for Musick, Madam?

Ful. I named that as part of my Diversion.

Cleo. My Cousin plays very well upon the Harpsicord herself.

Ful. I love to hear good Musick; but it does not throw me into those Raptures, I hear others speak of.

Hor. Nothing certainly can elevate the Mind beyond a fine Consort: It seems to disengage the Soul from the Body, and lift it up to Heaven. It is in this Situation, that we are most capable of receiving extraordinary Impressions: When the Instruments cease, our Temper is subdued, and beautiful Action joyns with the skilful Voice in setting before us in a transcendent Light, the Heroick Labours we are [13] come to admire, and which the Word | *Opera* imports. The powerful Harmony between the engaging Sounds and speaking Gestures invades the Heart, and forcibly inspires us with those noble Sentiments, which to entertain the most expressive Words can only attempt to persuade us. Few Comedies are tollerable, and in the best of them, if the Levity of the Expressions does not corrupt, the Meanness of the Subject must debase the Manners; at least to Persons of Quality. In Tragedies the Style is more sublime, and the Subjects generally great; but all violent Passions, and even the Representations of them, ruffle and discompose the Mind: Besides, when Men endeavour to express Things strongly, and they are acted to the Life, it

---

[1] In this satire on the conventions forbidding realism in the arts Mandeville may have been not only indirectly preparing the defence of his psychological and moral realism, but vindicating the realistic homeliness of his style, which had been attacked, e. g., by Dennis, who called it ' barbarous ' (*Vice and Luxury Public Mischiefs*, p. xvii). Mandeville, who cited Dennis's abuse (*Letter to Dion*, p. 46), was sensitive on this score (cf. above, i. 105, *n.* 1).

often happens that the Images do Mischief, because they are too moving, and that the Action is faulty for being too natural; and Experience teaches us, that in unguarded Minds, by those Pathetick Performances, Flames are often rais'd that are prejudicial to Virtue. The Play-houses themselves are far from being inviting, much less the Companies, at least the greatest part of them that frequent them, some of which are almost of the lowest Rank of all. The Disgusts that Persons of the least Elegance receive from these People are many; besides the ill Scents and unseemly Sights one meets with of careless Rakes and impudent Wenches, that, having paid their Mony, reckon themselves to be all upon the Level with every Bo-|dy [14] there; the Oaths, Scurrilities and vile Jests one is often obliged to hear, without resenting them; and the odd mixture of high and low that are all partaking of the same Diversion, without Regard to Dress or Quality, are all very offensive; and it cannot but be very disagreeable to polite People to be in the same Crowd with a Variety of Persons, some of them below Mediocrity, that pay no Deference to one another. At the Opera every thing charms and concurs to make Happiness compleat. The Sweetness of Voice in the first place, and the solemn Composure of the Action, serve to mitigate and allay every Passion; it is the Gentleness of them, and the calm Serenity of the Mind, that make us amiable, and bring us the nearest to the Perfection of Angels; whereas the Violence of the Passions, in which the Corruption of the Heart chiefly consists, dethrones our Reason, and renders us most like unto Savages. It is incredible, how prone we are to Imitation, and how strangely, unknown to ourselves, we are shaped and fashioned after the Models and Examples that are often set before us. No Anger nor Jealousy are ever to be seen at an Opera that distort the Features, no Flames that are noxious, nor is any Love represented in them, that is not pure

and next to Zeraphick; and it is impossible for the
Remembrance to carry any thing away from them,
[15] that can sully the Imagination. *Secondly,* The | Com-
pany is of another sort: the Place it self is a Security
to Peace, as well as every ones Honour, and it is
impossible to name another, where blooming Innocence and irresistible Beauty stand in so little need of
Guardians. Here we are sure never to meet with
Petulancy or ill Manners, and to be free from immodest
Ribaldry, Libertine Wit, and detestable Satyr. If
you will mind, on the one hand, the Richness and
Splendour of Dress, and the Quality of the Persons
that appear in them, the Variety of Colours, and the
Lustre of the Fair in a spacious Theatre, well illumi-
nated and adorn'd; and on the ᵃ other, the grave
Deportment of the Assembly, and the Consciousness,
that appears in every Countenance, of the Respect they
owe to each other, you will be forced to confess, that
upon Earth there can not be a Pastime more agreeable :
Believe me, Madam, there is no Place, where both
Sexes have such Opportunities of imbibing exalted
Sentiments, and raising themselves above the Vulgar,
as they have at the Opera; and there is no other sort
of Diversion or Assembly from the frequenting of
which young Persons of Quality can have equal Hopes
of forming their Manners, and contracting a strong
and lasting Habit of Virtue.

Ful. You have said more in Commendation of
Operas, *Horatio,* than I ever heard or thought of
before; and I think every Body who loves that
[16] Diversion is highly obliged | to you. The *grand Gout,*
I believe, is a great help in Panegyrick, especially,
where it is an Incivility strictly to examine and over-
curiously to look into Matters.

Cleo. What say you now *Fulvia* of Nature and good
Sense, are they not quite beat out o' Doors?

Ful. I have heard nothing yet, to make me out of

ᵃ the *om.* 29

Conceit with good Sense ; tho' what you insinuated of Nature, as if it was not to be imitated in Painting, is an Opinion, I must confess, which hitherto I more admire at, than I can approve of it.

Hor. I would never recommend any thing, Madam, that is repugnant to good Sense : but *Cleomenes* must have some Design in over-acting the Part he pretends to have chosen. What he said about Painting is very true, whether he spoke it in Jest or in Earnest ; but he talks so diametrically opposite to the Opinion which he is known every where to defend of late, that I don't know what to make of him.

Ful. I am convinced of the Narrowness of my own Understanding, and am going to visit some Persons, with whom I shall be more upon the Level.

Hor. You'll give me Leave to wait upon you to your Coach, Madam.------ Pray, *Cleomenes*, what is it you have got in your Head?

Cleo. Nothing at all : I told you before, that I was so entirely recover'd from my Fol-|ly, that few People [17] went my Lengths. What Jealousy you entertain of me I don't know ; but I find my self much improv'd in the Social System. Formerly I thought, that Chief Ministers, and all those at the Helm of Affairs, acted from Principles of Avarice and Ambition ; that in all the Pains they took, and even in the Slaveries they underwent for the Publick Good, they had their private Ends, and that they were supported in the Fatigue by secret Enjoyments they were unwilling to own. It is not a Month ago, that I imagin'd that the inward Care and real Sollicitude of all great Men Center'd within themselves ; and that to enrich themselves, acquire Titles of Honour, and raise their Families on the one hand, and to have Opportunities on the other of displaying a judicious Fancy in all the Elegant Comforts of Life, and establishing, without the least Trouble of Self-denial, the Reputation of being wise, humane and munificent, were the Things,

which, besides the Satisfaction there is in Superiority
and the Pleasure of governing, all Candidates to high
Offices and great Posts proposed to themselves, from
the Places they sued for; I was so narrow-minded
that I could not conceive how a Man would ever
voluntarily submit to be a Slave but to serve himself.
But I have abandon'd that ill-natur'd way of judging :
I plainly perceive the Publick Good, in all the Designs
[18] of Politicians, the social Virtues shine in | every Action,
and I find that the national Interest ᵃ is the Compass
that all Statesmen steer by.

Hor. That's more than I can prove; but certainly
there have been such Men, there have been Patriots,
that without selfish Views have taken incredible Pains
for their Country's Welfare : Nay, there are Men
now that would do the same, if they were employ'd;
and we have had Princes that have neglected their
Ease and Pleasure, and sacrificed their Quiet, to promote the Prosperity and encrease the Wealth and
Honour of the Kingdom, and had nothing so much
at Heart as the Happiness of their Subjects.

Cleo. No Disaffection, I beg of you. The Difference
between past and present Times, and Persons in and
out of Places, is perhaps clearer to you than it is to
me; but it is many Years ago, you know, that it has
been agreed between us never to enter into Party
Disputes : What I desire your Attention to is my
Reformation, which you seem to doubt of, and the
great Change that is wrought in me. The Religion of
most Kings and other high Potentates, I formerly
had but a slender Opinion of, but now I measure
their Piety by what they say of it themselves to their
Subjects.

Hor. That's very kindly done.

Cleo. By thinking meanly of things, I once had
strange blundering Notions concerning Foreign Wars :
[19] I thought that many of them | arose from trifling
Causes, magnify'd by Politicians for their own Ends;

ᵃ Intrest 29

that the most ruinous Misunderstandings between States and Kingdoms might spring from the hidden Malice, Folly, or Caprice of one Man ; that many of them had been owing to the private Quarrels, Piques, Resentments, and the Haughtiness of the chief Ministers of the respective Nations, that were the Sufferers ; and that what is call'd Personal Hatred between Princes seldom was more at first, than either an open or secret Animosity which the two great Favorites of those Courts had against one another : But now I have learn'd to derive those things from higher Causes. I am reconciled likewise to the Luxury of the Voluptuous, which I used to be offended at, because now I am convinced that the Money of most rich Men is laid out with the social Design of promoting Arts and Sciences, and that in the most expensive Undertakings their principal Aim is the Employment of the Poor.

Hor. These are Lengths indeed.

Cleo. I have a strong Aversion to Satyr, and detest it every whit as much as you do : The most instructive Writings to understand the World, and penetrate into the Heart of Man, I take to be Addresses, Epitaphs, Dedications, and above all the Preambles to Patents, of which I am making a large Collection.

Hor. A very useful Undertaking !

| *Cleo.* But to remove all your Doubts of my Con- [20] version, I'll shew you some easy Rules I have laid down for young Beginners.

Hor. What to do?

Cleo. To judge of Mens Actions by the lovely System of Lord *Shaftsbury*, in a Manner diametrically opposite to that of *the Fable of the Bees.*

Hor. I don't understand you.

Cleo. You will presently. I have call'd them Rules, but they are rather Examples from which the Rules are to be gather'd : As for instance, If we see an industrious poor Woman, who has pinch'd her Belly,

and gone in Rags for a considerable time to save forty
Shillings, part with her Money to put out her Son
at six Years of Age to a Chimney-sweeper ; to judge
of her charitably according to the System of the Social
Virtues we must imagine, That tho' she never paid
for the sweeping of a Chimney in her Life, she knows
by Experience that for want of this necessary Cleanli-
ness the Broth has been often spoyl'd, and many
a Chimney has been set o' Fire, and therefore to do
good in her Generation, as far as she is able, she gives
up her All, both Offspring and Estate, to assist in
preventing the several Mischiefs that are often occasion'd by great Quantities of Soot disregarded ; and,
free from Selfishness, sacrifices her only Son to
the most wretched Employment for the Publick
Welfare.

[21] | *Hor.* You don't vy I see with Lord *Shaftsbury*, for
Loftiness of Subjects.

Cleo. When in a Starry Night with Amazement we
behold the Glory of the Firmament, nothing is more
obvious than that the whole, the beautiful *All*, must
be the Workmanship of one great Architect of Power
and Wisdom stupendious ; and it is as evident, that
every thing in the Universe is a constituent Part of
one entire Fabrick.[1]

Hor. Would you make a Jest of this too?

Cleo. Far from it : they are awful Truths, of which

---

[1] A parody of the extremities
of Shaftesbury's rhetoric, which
did not shrink from flights like
' O mighty Nature ! wise substitute of Providence! impowered
creatress ! Or thou impowering
Deity, supreme creator ! Thee
I invoke, and thee alone adore.
To thee this solitude, this place,
these rural meditations are sacred ;
whilst thus inspired with harmony
of thought, though unconfined
by words, and in loose numbers,
I sing of Nature's order in
created beings, and celebrate the
beauties which resolve in thee,
the source and principle of all
beauty and perfection ' (*Characteristics*, ed. Robertson, 1900,
ii. 98, in ' The Moralists ').
' The Moralists ' contains the
most exaggerated examples of
Shaftesbury's rhetoric.

I am as much convinced as I am of my own Existence ; but I was going to name the Consequences, which Lord *Shaftsbury* draws from them, in order to demonstrate to you, that I am a Convert and a punctual [a] Observer of his Lordship's Instructions, and that in my Judgment on the poor Woman's Conduct, there is nothing that is not entirely agreeable to the generous way of thinking set forth and recommended in the *Characteristicks*.[1]

Hor. Is it possible a Man should read such a Book, and make no better use of it ! I desire you would name the Consequences you speak of.

Cleo. As that Infinity of luminous Bodies, however different in Magnitude, Velocity, and the Figures they describe in their Courses, concur all of them to make up the Universe, so this little Spot we inhabit is likewise a Com-|pound of Air, Water, Fire, Minerals, [22] Vegetables and living Creatures, which, tho' vastly differing from one another in their Nature, do altogether make up the Body of this terraqueous Globe.

[a] punctual] very punctual 30

[1] Shaftesbury's philosophy need hardly have committed him to the contention that the old woman was conscious and careful of the social implications of her conduct. It committed him only to the position that unless thus conscious she was not virtuous. Shaftesbury held ' that in a sensible creature that which is not done through any affection at all makes neither good nor ill in the nature of that creature, who then only is supposed good when the good or ill of the system to which he has relation is the immediate object of some passion or affection moving him ' (*Characteristics*, ed. Robertson, 1900, i. 247). And he continues, ' And in this case alone it is we call any creature worthy or virtuous, when it can have the notion of a public interest, and can attain the speculation or science of what is morally good or ill, admirable or blamable, right or wrong. For though we may vulgarly call an ill horse vicious, yet we never say of a good one . . . that he is worthy or virtuous ' (i. 252).

AlthoughMandeville somewhat misunderstood Shaftesbury, he was, however, right in affirming the fundamental opposition between their thought ; see above, i. lxxii–lxxv.

Hor. This is very right, and in the same manner as our whole Species is composed of many Nations of different Religions, Forms of Government, Interests and Manners that divide and share the Earth between them, so the civil Society in every Nation consists in great Multitudes of both Sexes, that widely differing from each other in Age, Constitution, Strength, Temper, Wisdom and Possessions, all help to make up one Body Politick.

Cleo. The same exactly which I would have said : Now, pray Sir, is not the great End of Men's forming themselves into such Societies, mutual Happiness ; I mean, do not all individual Persons, from being thus combined, propose to themselves a more comfortable Condition of Life, than human Creatures, if they were to live like other wild Animals, without Tie or Dependance, could enjoy in a free and savage State?

Hor. This certainly is not only the End, but the End which is every where attain'd to by Government and Society, in some Degree or other。

Cleo. Hence it must follow that it is always wrong for Men to pursue Gain or Pleasure, by Means that [23] are visibly detrimental to the ci-|vil Society, and that Creatures, who can do this, must be narrow-soul'd, short-sighted, selfish People ; whereas wise Men never look upon themselves as individual Persons, without considering the Whole, of which they are but trifling Parts in respect to Bulk, and are incapable of receiving any Satisfaction from Things that interfere with the Publick Welfare. This being undeniably true, ought not all private Advantage to give way to this general Interest; and ought it not to be every one's Endeavour, to encrease this common Stock of Happiness ; and, in order to it, do what he can to render himself a serviceable and useful Member of that whole Body which he belongs to?

Hor. What of all this?

Cleo. Has not my poor Woman, in what I have

related of her, acted in Conformity to this Social System?

Hor. Can any one in his Senses imagine, that an indigent thoughtless Wretch, without Sense or Education, should ever act from such generous Principles?

Cleo. Poor I told you the Woman was, and I won't insist upon her Education; but as for her being thoughtless and void of Sense, you'll give me leave to say, that it is an Aspersion, for which you have no manner of Foundation; and from the Account I have given of her, nothing can be gather'd but that she was | a considerate, virtuous, wise Woman, in Poverty. [24]

Hor. I suppose you would persuade me, that you are in Earnest.

Cleo. I am much more so than you imagine: and say once more, that in the Example I have given, I have trod exactly in my Lord *Shaftsbury*'s Steps, and closely follow'd the Social System. If I have committed any Error, shew it me.

Hor. Did that Author ever meddle with any thing so low and pitiful?

Cleo. There can be nothing mean in noble Actions, whoever the Persons are that perform them : But if the Vulgar are to be all excluded from the Social Virtues, what Rule or Instruction shall the labouring Poor, which are by far the greatest part of the Nation, have left them to walk by, when the *Characteristicks* have made a Jest of all reveal'd Religion, especially the Christian? But if you despise the Poor and Illiterate; I can in the same Method judge of Men in higher Stations. Let the Enemies to the Social System behold the venerable Counsellor, now grown eminent for his Wealth, that at his great Age continues sweltering at the Bar to plead the doubtful Cause, and regardless of his Dinner shortens his own Life in endeavouring to secure the Possessions of others. How conspicuous is the Benevolence of the Physician to | his Kind, who, from Morning till Night [25] visiting the Sick, keeps several Sets of Horses to be more serviceable to many, and still grudges himself the time for the necessary Functions of Life ! In the same manner the indefatigable Clergyman, who with his Ministry supplies a very large Parish already, sollicites with Zeal to be as useful and beneficent to another, tho' fifty of his Order yet unemploy'd offer their Service for the same Purpose.

Hor. I perceive your Drift : From the strain'd Panegyricks you labour at, you would form Arguments *ad absurdum :* The Banter is ingenious enough, and at proper times might serve to raise a Laugh ; but then you must own likewise, that those study'd Encomiums will not bear to be seriously examin'd into. When we consider that the great Business as well as perpetual Sollicitude of the Poor are to supply their immediate Wants, and keep themselves from starving, and that their Children are a Burden to them, which they groan under, and desire to be deliver'd from by all possible Means, that are not clashing with the low involuntary Affection which Nature forces them to have for their Offspring : When, I say, we consider this, the Virtues of your industrious Woman [a] make no great Figure. The Publick Spirit likewise, and the generous Principles, your Sagacity has found out in the three Faculties, [26] to which Men are | brought up for a Livelihood, seem to be very far fetch'd. Fame, Wealth and Greatness every Body knows are the Things that all Lawyers and Physicians aim at, that are any ways considerable : That many of them entirely devote themselves to their Practice, with incredible Patience and Assiduity every Age can witness ; but whatever Labour or Fatigue they submit to, the Motives of their Actions are as conspicuous as their Callings themselves.

Cleo. Are they not beneficial to Mankind, and of Use to the Publick?

---

[a] Woman *om. 30*

Hor. I don't deny that ; we often receive inestimable Benefits from them, and the good ones in either Profession are not only useful, but very necessary to the Society : But tho' there are several that sacrifice their whole Lives, and all the Comforts of them, to their Business, there is not one of them that would take a quarter of the Pains he now is at, if without taking any he could acquire the same Money, Reputation, and other Advantages that may accrue to him from the Esteem or Gratitude of those whom he has been serviceable to ; and I don't believe, there is an eminent Man among them that would not own this, if the Question was put to him. Therefore when Ambition and the Love of Money are the avow'd Principles Men act from, it is very silly to ascribe Virtues to them, which they themselves pretend to lay no manner of | claim to. But your Encomium [27] upon the Parson is the merriest Jest of all : I have heard many Excuses made, and some of them very frivolous, for the Covetousness of Priests ; but what you have pick'd out in their Praise is more extraordinary than any Thing I ever met with ; and the most partial Advocate and Admirer of the Clergy never yet discover'd before your self a great Virtue in their Hunting after Pluralities, when they were well provided for themselves, and many others for want of Employ were ready to starve.

Cleo. But if there be any Reality in the Social System, it would be better for the Publick if Men in all Professions were to act from those generous Principles ; and you'll allow that the Society would be the Gainers, if the Generality in the three Faculties would mind others more and themselves less than they do now.

Hor. I don't know that ; and considering what Slavery some Lawyers, as well as Physicians, undergo, I much question whether it would be possible for them to exert themselves in the same manner, tho' they would, if the constant Baits and Refreshments of large Fees did not help to support Human Nature, by continually stimulating this darling Passion.

Cleo. Indeed, *Horatio*, this is a stronger Argument [28] against the Social System, and | more injurious to it, than any thing that has been said by the Author whom you have exclaim'd against with so much Bitterness.

Hor. I deny that : I don't conclude from the Selfishness in some, that there is no Virtue in others.

Cleo. Nor he neither, and you very much wrong him if you assert that he ever did.

Hor. I refuse to commend what is not Praiseworthy; but as bad as Mankind are, Virtue has an Existence as well as Vice, tho' it is more scarce.

Cleo. What you said last no body ever contradicted ; but I don't know what you would be at : Does not the Lord *Shaftsbury* endeavour to do Good, and promote the Social Virtues, and am I not doing the very same? Suppose me to be in the wrong in the favourable Constructions I have made of Things, still it is to be wish'd for at least, that Men had a greater Regard to the Publick Welfare, less Fondness for their Private Interest, and more Charity for their Neighbours, than the generality of them have.

Hor. To be wish'd for perhaps it may be, but what Probability is there that this ever will come to pass?

Cleo. And unless that can come to pass, it is the idlest Thing in the World to discourse upon, and demonstrate the Excellency of Virtue ; what signifies [29] it to set forth the | Beauty of it, unless it was possible that Men should fall in Love with it?

Hor. If Virtue was never recommended, Men might grow worse than they are.

Cleo. Then by the same Reason, if it was recommended more, Men might grow better than they are. But I see perfectly well the Reason of these Shifts and Evasions you make use of against your Opinion : You find your self under a Necessity of allowing my Panegyricks, as you call them, to be just; or finding the same Fault with most of my Lord *Shaftsbury*'s; and you would do neither if you could help it : From Mens preferring Company to Solitude, his Lordship pretends to prove the Love and Natural Affection we have for our own Species : If this was examin'd into with the same Strictness as you have done every Thing I have said in behalf of the three Faculties, I believe that the Solidity of the Consequences would be pretty equal in both. But I stick to my Text, and stand up for the Social Virtues : The noble Author of that System had a most charitable Opinion of his Species, and extoll'd the Dignity of it in an extraordinary manner, and why my Imitation of him should be call'd a Banter I see no Reason. He certainly wrote with a good Design, and endeavour'd to inspire his Readers with refin'd Notions, and a Publick Spirit abstract from Religion : The World enjoys the | Fruits of his [30] Labours, but the Advantage that is justly expected from his Writings can never be universally felt, before that Publick Spirit, which he recommended, comes down to the meanest Tradesmen, whom you would endeavour to exclude from the generous Sentiments and noble Principles that are already so visible in many. I am now thinking on two sorts of People that stand very much in need of, and yet hardly ever meet with, one another : This Misfortune must have caused such a Chasm in the Band of Society, that no Depth of Thought or Happiness of Contrivance could have fill'd up the Vacuity, if a most tender Regard for the Commonwealth, and the height of Benevolence did not influence and oblige others, mere strangers to those People, and commonly Men of small Education, to assist them with their good Offices, and stop up the Gap. Many ingenious Workmen in obscure Dwellings would be starv'd in spight of Industry, only for want of knowing where to sell the Product of their Labour, if there were not others to dispose of it for them :

And again, the Rich and Extravagant are daily furnish'd with an infinite Variety of superfluous Knicknacks and elaborate Trifles, every one of them invented to gratify either a needless Curiosity, or else Wantonness and Folly; and which they would never have thought of, much less wanted, had they never seen [31] | or known where to buy them. What a Blessing then to the Publick is the Social Toyman, who lays out a considerable Estate to gratify the Desires of these two different Classes of People? He procures Food and Raiment for the deserving Poor, and searches with great Diligence after the most skillful Artificers, that no Man shall be able to produce better Workmanship than himself: with study'd Civilities and a serene Countenance he entertains the greatest Strangers; and, often speaking to them first, kindly offers to guess at their Wants: He confines not his Attendance to a few stated Hours, but waits their Leisure all Day long in an open Shop, where he bears the Summer's Heat and Winter's Cold with equal Chearfulness. What a beautiful Prospect is here of Natural Affection to our Kind! For if He acts from that Principle, who only furnishes us with Necessaries of Life, certainly He shews a more superlative Love and Indulgence to his Species, who will not suffer the most whimsical of it to be an Hour destitute of what he shall fancy, even Things the most unnecessary.

Hor. You have made the most of it indeed, but are you not tired yet with these Fooleries your self?

Cleo. What Fault do you find with these kind Constructions; do they detract from the Dignity of our Species?

[32] | *Hor.* I admire your Invention, and thus much I will own, that by over-acting the Part in that extravagant Manner, you have set the Social System in a more disadvantageous Light than ever I had consider'd it before: But the best Things, you know, may be ridicul'd.

DIALOGUE.

Cleo. Whether I know that or not, Lord *Shaftsbury* has flatly denied it ; and takes Joke and Banter to be the best and surest Touchstone to prove the Worth of Things :[1] It is his Opinion, that no Ridicule can be fasten'd upon what is really great and good ; his Lordship has made use of that Test to try the Scriptures and the Christian Religion by, and expos'd them because it seems they could not stand it.

Hor. He has exposed Superstition and the miserable Notions the Vulgar were taught to have of God ; but no Man ever had more Sublime Idea's of the Supreme Being and the Universe than himself.

Cleo. You are convinc'd, that what I charge him with is true.

Hor. I don't pretend to defend every Syllable that noble Lord has wrote. His Style is engaging, his Language polite, his Reasoning strong ; many of his Thoughts are beautifully express'd, and his Images, for the greatest Part, inimitably fine. I may be pleased with an Author, without obliging my self to answer every Cavil that shall be made against | him. [33] As to what you call your Imitation of him, I have no Taste in Burlesque : but the Laugh you would raise might be turn'd upon you with less Trouble than you seem to have taken. Pray when you consider the hard and dirty Labours that are perform'd to supply the Mob with the vast Quantities of strong Beer they swill, don't you discover Social Virtue in a Drayman?

Cleo. Yes, and in a Dray-horse too ; at least as well as I can in some great Men, who yet would be very angry should we refuse to believe, that the most selfish Actions of theirs, if the Society receiv'd but the least Benefit from them, were chiefly owing to Principles of Virtue, and a generous Regard to the Publick.

---

[1] See his *Freedom of Wit and Humour* (*Characteristics*, ed. Robertson, i. 43–99), where his thesis is, largely, ' Grimace and tone are mighty helps to imposture . . . . a subject which would not bear raillery was suspicious . . . (i. 52).

Do you believe that in the Choice of a *Pope* the greatest
Dependance of the Cardinals, and what they principally rely upon, is the Influence of the Holy Ghost?

Hor. No more than I do Transubstantiation.

Cleo. But if you had been brought up a *Roman*
Catholick, you would believe both.

Hor. I don't know that.

Cleo. You would, if you was sincere in your Religion,
as thousands of them are, that are no more destitute
of Reason and good Sense than you or I.

Hor. I have nothing to say as to that : there are
many Things incomprehensible, that yet are certainly
[34] true : These are pro-|perly the Objects of Faith ;
and therefore when Matters are above my Capacity,
and really surpass my Understanding, I am silent, and
submit with great Humility : but I will swallow
nothing which I plainly apprehend to be contrary to
my Reason, and is directly clashing with my Senses.

Cleo. If you believe a Providence, what Demonstration can you have, that God does not direct Men in
an Affair of higher Importance to all Christendom
than any other you can name?

Hor. This is an ensnaring, and a very unfair Question. Providence superintends and governs every
Thing without Exception. To defend my Negative
and give a Reason for my Unbelief, it is sufficient, if
I prove, that all the Instruments and the Means they
make use of in those Elections are visibly human and
mundane, and many of them unwarrantable and
wicked.

Cleo. Not all the Means ; because every Day they
have Prayers, and solemnly invoke the Divine Assistance.

Hor. But what Stress they lay upon it may be easily
gather'd from the rest of their Behaviour. The Court
of *Rome* is without dispute the greatest Academy of
refin'd Politicks, and the best School to learn the Art
of Caballing : there ordinary Cunning and known
Stratagems are counted Rusticity, and Designs are

pursued through all the Mazes of | human Subtlety. [35]
Genius there must give way to Finesse, as Strength
does to Art in wrestling; and a certain Skill, some
Men have in concealing their Capacities from others,
is of far greater Use with them, than real Knowledge
or the soundest Understanding. In the Sacred College,
where every Thing is *auro venale*, Truth and Justice
bear the lowest Price : Cardinal *Palavicini*[1] and other
Jesuits that have been the stanch Advocates of the
Papal Authority, have own'd with Ostentation the
Politia Religiosa della chiésa,[2] and not hid from us the
Virtues and Accomplishments, that were only valuable
among the *Purpurati*,[3] in whose Judgment Over-
reaching at any rate is the highest Honour, and to be
outwitted, tho' by the basest Artifice, the greatest
Shame. In Conclaves more especially nothing is
carried on without Tricks and Intrigue, and in them
the Heart of Man is so deep and so dark an Abyss
that the finest Air of Dissimulation is sometimes found
to have been insincere, and Men often deceive one
another by counterfeiting Hypocrisy. And is it credible
that Holiness, Religion, or the least Concern for
Spirituals, should have any Share in the Plots, Machina-
tions, Brigues[4] and Contrivances of a Society, of
which each Member, besides the Gratification of his
own Passions, has nothing at Heart but the Interest
of his Party, right or wrong, and to distress every
Faction that opposes it?

[1] Compare Bayle, *Miscellaneous Reflections* (1708) i. 227: '... the celebrated Cardinal *Pallavicin* has most learnedly and piously prov'd, the Catholick Church ought to be on the foot of Temporal Power. . . .'
In his *Free Thoughts* (1729), p. 147, Mandeville cited Palla-vicini's *Istoria del Concilio di Trento*. But this does not mean that Mandeville had read Palla-vicini, for the reference is taken almost literally from the 1710 English translation of Bayle's *Dictionnaire*, art. ' Leo X ', *n.* A.

[2] A chapter heading in Mande-ville's *Free Thoughts* reads *Of the Politicks of the Church*—the same thing.

[3] Cardinals.   [4] Factions.

[36] | *Cleo.* These Sentiments confirm to me, what I have often heard, that Renegades are the most cruel Enemies.

Hor. Was ever I a *Roman* Catholick?

Cleo. I mean from the Social System, of which you have been the most strenuous Asserter; and now no Man can judge of Actions more severely, and indeed less charitably, than yourself, especially of the poor Cardinals. I little thought, if once I quitted the Scheme of Deformity, to have found an Adversary in you; but we have both changed Sides, it seems.

Hor. Much alike, I believe.

Cleo. Nay, what could any body think to hear me making the kindest Interpretations of Things that can be imagin'd, and yourself doing quite the Reverse?

Hor. What ignorant People, that knew neither of us, might have done, I don't know: but it has been very manifest from our Discourse, that you have maintain'd your Cause by endeavouring to shew the Absurdity of the contrary Side, and that I have defended mine by letting you see, that we were not such Fools as you would represent us to be. I had taken a Resolution never to engage with you on this Topick, but you see I have broke it: I hate to be thought uncivil; it was mere Complaisance drew me in; tho' I am not sorry that we talk'd of it so much as we did, because I found your Opinion less dangerous [37] than | I imagin'd: you have own'd the Existence of Virtue, and that there are Men who act from it as a Principle, both which I thought you denied: but I would not have you flatter yourself, that you deceiv'd me by hanging out false Colours.

Cleo. I did not lay on the Disguise so thick, as not to have you see through it, nor would I ever have discours'd upon this Subject with any body, who could have been so easily imposed upon. I know you to be a Man of very good Sense and sound Judgment; and it is for that very Reason I so heartily wish, you would suffer me to explain my self, and demonstrate to you how small the Difference is between us, which you imagine to be so considerable : There is not a Man in the World, in whose Opinion I would less pass for an ill Man than in yours ; but I am so scrupulously fearful of offending you, that I never dared to touch upon some Points, unless you had given me leave. Yield something to our Friendship, and condescend for once to read *the Fable of the Bees* for my Sake : It's a handsome Volume : you love Books : I have one extremely well bound ; do ; let me, suffer me to make you a Present of it.

Hor. I am no Bigot, *Cleomenes* ; but I am a Man of Honour, and you know of strict Honour : I cannot endure to hear that ridicul'd, and the least Attempt of it chafes my Blood : Honour is the strongest and noblest | Tye of Society by far, and therefore, believe [38] me, can never be innocently sported with. It is a Thing so solid and awful, as well as serious, that it can at no Time become the Object of Mirth or Diversion ; and it is impossible for any Pleasantry to be so ingenious, or any Jest so witty, that I could bear with it on that Head. Perhaps I am singular in this, and, if you will, in the wrong : be that as it will, all I can say is, *Je n'entens pas Raillerie la dessus* ; [1] and therefore no *Fable of the Bees* for me, if we are to remain Friends : I have heard enough of that.

Cleo. Pray, *Horatio*, can there be Honour without Justice?

Hor. No : Who affirms there can?

Cleo. Have you not own'd, that you have thought worse of me, than now you find me to deserve? No Men, nor their Works, ought to be condemn'd upon Hearsays, and bare Surmises, much less upon the Accusations of their Enemies, without being examin'd into.

Hor. There you are in the right : I heartily beg

[1] Cf. Molière's ' Nous n'entendons point raillerie sur les matières de l'honneur . . . ' (*George Dandin* i. iv).

your Pardon, and to attone for the wrong I have done you, say what you please, I'll hear it with Patience, be it never so shocking ; but I beg of you be serious.

Cleo. I have nothing to say to you, that is distastful, much less shocking : all I desire is to convince you, that I am neither so ill-natured nor uncharitable, in my Opinion of Mankind, as you take me to be ; and [39] that the | Notions I entertain of the Worth of Things will not differ much from yours, when both come to be look'd into. Do but consider what we have been doing : I have endeavour'd to set every thing in the handsomest Light I could think of ; you say, to ridicule the Social System ; I own it ; now reflect on your own Conduct, which has been to shew the Folly of my strain'd Panegyricks, and replace Things in that natural View, which all just, knowing Men would certainly behold them in. This is very well done : but it is contrary to the Scheme you pretended to maintain ; and if you judge of all Actions in the same Manner, there's an End of the Social System ; or at least it will be evident, that it is a Theory never to be put into Practice. You argue for the Generality of Men, that they are possess'd of these Virtues, but when we come to Particulars you can find none ; I have tried you every where : you are as little satisfied with Persons of the highest Rank, as you are with them of the lowest, and you count it ridiculous to think better of the midling People. Is this otherwise than standing up for the Goodness of a Design, at the same time you confess, that it never was, or ever can be executed? What sort of People are they, and where must we look for them, whom you will own to act from those Principles of Virtue?

[40] | *Hor.* Are there not in all Countries Men of Birth and ample Fortune, that would not accept of Places, tho' they were offer'd, that are generous and beneficent, and mind nothing but what is great and noble?

Cleo. Yes : But examine their Conduct, look into

their Lives, and scan their Actions with as little Indulgence as you did those of the Cardinals, or the Lawyers and Physicians, and then see what Figure their Virtues will make beyond those of the poor industrious Woman. There is, generally speaking, less Truth in Panegyricks than there is in Satyrs. When all our Senses are soothed, when we have no Distemper of Body or Mind to disturb us, and meet with nothing that is disagreeable, we are pleased with our Being : it is in this Situation, that we are most apt to mistake outward Appearances for Realities, and judge of Things more favourably than they deserve. Remember, *Horatio*, how feelingly you spoke half an Hour ago in Commendation of Opera's : Your Soul seem'd to be lifted up whilst you was thinking on the many Charms you find in them. I have nothing to say against the Elegancy of the Diversion, or the Politeness of those that frequent them : but I am afraid you lost yourself in the Contemplation of the lovely Idea, when you asserted that they were the most proper Means to contract a strong and lasting Habit of Virtue :[1] do you think that among the same Num-|ber of People there is more real Virtue at an [41] Opera, than there is at a Bear-garden?

Hor. What a Comparison !

Cleo. I am very serious.

Hor. The Noise of Dogs and Bulls and Bears make a fine Harmony !

Cleo. It is impossible you should mistake me, and you know very well, that it is not the different Pleasures of those two Places I would compare together. The Things you mention'd are the least to be complain'd of : The continual Sounds of Oaths and Imprecations, the frequent Repetitions of the Word *Lie*, and other more filthy Expressions, the Lowdness and Dissonance of many strain'd and untuneful Voices, are a perfect Torment to a delicate Ear. The Frowsiness of the

[1] See *Fable* ii. 40.

Place, and the ill Scents of different kinds, are a perpetual Nuisance ; but in all Mob Meetings----

Hor. L'*odorat souffre beaucoup.*

Cleo. The Entertainment in general is abominable, and all the Senses suffer. I allow all this. The greasy Heads, some of them bloody, the jarring Looks, and threatning, wild, and horrid Aspects, that one meets with in those ever-restless Assemblies, must be very shocking to the Sight, and so indeed is every thing else that can be seen among a rude and ragged Multitude that are cover'd with Dirt, and have in none of their Pastimes one Action that is inoffensive : But [42] after all, Vice and what is | criminal are not to be confounded with Roughness and want of Manners, no more than Politeness and an artful Behaviour ought to be with Virtue or Religion. To tell a premeditated Falshood in order to do Mischief, is a greater Sin, than to give a Man the Lie, who speaks an Untruth ; and it is possible, that a Person may suffer greater Damage and more Injury to his Ruin from Slander in the low Whisper of a secret Enemy, than he could have receiv'd from all the dreadful Swearing and Cursing the most noisy Antagonist could pelt him with. Incontinence, and Adultery it self, Persons of Quality are not more free from all over Christendom, than the meaner People : But if there are some Vices, which the Vulgar are more guilty of than the better sort, there are others the Reverse. Envy, Detraction, and the Spirit of Revenge, are more raging and mischievous in Courts than they are in Cottages. Excess of Vanity and hurtful Ambition are unknown among the Poor ; they are seldom tainted with Avarice, with Irreligion never ; and they have much less Opportunity of robbing the Publick than their Betters. There are few Persons of Distinction, whom you are not acquainted with : I desire, you would seriously reflect on the Lives of as many as you can think of, and next Opera Night on the Virtues of the Assembly.

| *Hor.* You make me laugh. There is a good deal [43] in what you say; and I am persuaded, all is not Gold that glisters. Would you add any more?

Cleo. Since you have given me Leave to talk, and you are such a patient Hearer, I would not slip the Opportunity of laying before you some things of high Concern, that perhaps you never consider'd in the Light, which you shall own yourself they ought to be seen in.

Hor. I am sorry to leave you; but I have really Business that must be done to-night : It is about my Law-suit, and I have stay'd beyond my time already : But if you will come and eat a Bit of Mutton with me to-morrow, I'll see no body but your self, and we'll converse as long as you please.

Cleo. With all my Heart. I'll not fail to wait on you.

THE SECOND

DIALOGUE

BETWEEN

Horatio and *Cleomenes.*

H O R A T I O.

HE Discourse we had Yesterday, has made a great Impression upon me ; you said several Things, that were very entertaining, and some which I shall not easily forget : I don't remember, I ever look'd into myself so much as I have done since last Night after I left you.

Cleo. To do that faithfully, is a more difficult and a severer Task, than is commonly imagin'd. When Yesterday I ask'd you, where and among what sort of People we were to look for those, whom you would allow to act from Principles of Virtue, you named a Class, among whom I have found very agreeable [45] Characters of Men, that yet all have their | Failings : If these could be left out, and the best were pick'd and cull'd from the different good Qualities that are to be seen in several, the Compound would make a very handsome Picture.

Hor. To finish it well every way would be a great Master-piece.

Cleo. That I shan't attempt : But I don't think it would be very difficult to make a little Sketch of it, that yet should exceed Nature, and be a better Pattern for Imitation than any can be shewn alive. I have a Mind to try : the very Thought enlivens me. How charming is the Portrait of a complete Gentleman, and how ravishing is the Figure which a Person of great Birth and Fortune, to whom Nature has been no Niggard, makes, when he understands the World, and is throughly well bred !

Hor. I think them so, I can assure you, whether you are in Jest or in Earnest.

Cleo. How entirely well hid are his greatest Imperfections ! Tho' Money is his Idol, and he is covetous in his Heart, yet his inward Avarice is forc'd to give way to his outward Liberality, and an open Generosity shines through all his Actions.

Hor. There lies your Fault : It is this I cannot endure in you.

Cleo. What's the matter?

Hor. I know what you are about, you are going to give me the *Caricatura* of a Gentle-|man, under pre- [46] tence of drawing his Portrait.

Cleo. You wrong me, I have no such Thought.

Hor. But why is it impossible for Human Nature ever to be good? Instead of leaving out, you put in Failings without the least Grounds or Colour. When Things have a handsome Appearance every way, what Reason have you to suspect them still to be bad? How came you to know, and which way have you discover'd, Imperfections that are entirely well hid ; and why should you suppose a Person to be covetous in his Heart, and that Money is his Idol, when you own yourself that he never shews it, and that an open

Generosity shines through all his Actions? This is monstrous.[1]

Cleo. I have made no such Supposition of any Man, and I protest to you, that, in what I said, I had no other Meaning than to observe, that whatever Frailties and natural Infirmities Persons might be conscious of within, good Sense and good Manners were capable, and, without any other Assistance, sufficient to keep them out of Sight : But your Questions are very seasonable, and since you have started this, I will be very open to you, and acquaint you before-hand with my Design of the Description I am going to make ; and the Use I intend it for ; which in short is, to demonstrate to you, That a most beautiful Super-
[47] |structure may be rais'd upon a rotten and despicable Foundation. You'll understand me better presently.

Hor. But how do you know a Foundation to be rotten that supports the Building, and is wholly conceal'd from you?

Cleo. Have Patience, and I promise you, that I shall take nothing for granted, which you shall not allow of yourself.

Hor. Stick close to that, and I desire no more : Now say what you will.

Cleo. The true Object of Pride or Vain-glory is the Opinion of others ; and the most superlative Wish, which a Man possess'd, and entirely fill'd with it can make, is, that he may be well thought of, applauded, and admired by the whole World, not only in the present, but all future Ages. This Passion is generally exploded, but it is incredible, how many strange and widely different Miracles are and may be perform'd by the force of it ; as Persons differ in Circumstances and Inclinations. In the first place, there is no Danger so great, but by the help of his Pride a Man may

---

[1] That of two possible inter-pretations Mandeville always arbitrarily chose the uncharitable one was a common objection, as in Fiddes, *General Treatise of Morality*, 1724 (p. xx), which Mandeville cites (*Letter to Dion*, p. 46). Cf. below, ii. 406.

slight and confront it ; nor any manner of Death so terrible, but with the same Assistance, he may court, and if he has a firm Constitution, undergo it with Alacrity. In the second, there are no good Offices or Duties, either to others or ourselves, that *Cicero* has spoke of, nor any Instances of Benevolence, Humanity, or other Social Virtue, that | Lord *Shaftsbury* has [48] hinted at, but a Man of good Sense and Knowledge may learn to practise them from no better Principle than Vain-glory, if it be strong enough to subdue and keep under all other Passions, that may thwart and interfere with his Design.

Hor. Shall I allow all this?

Cleo. Yes.

Hor. When?

Cleo. Before we part.

Hor. Very well.

Cleo. Men of tolerable Parts in plentiful Circumstances, that were artfully educated, and are not singular in their Temper, can hardly fail of a genteel Behaviour : The more Pride they have and the greater Value they set on the Esteem of others, the more they'll make it their Study, to render themselves acceptable to all they converse with ; and they'll take uncommon Pains to conceal and stifle in their Bosoms every thing, which their good Sense tells them ought not to be seen or understood.

Hor. I must interrupt you, and cannot suffer you to go on thus. What is all this but the old Story over again, that every Thing is Pride, and all we see, Hypocrisy, without Proof or Argument? Nothing in the World is more false, than what you have advanced now ; for according to that, the most noble, the most gallant, and the best-bred Man would be the proudest ; which is so clashing | with daily experience, that the [49] very reverse is true. Pride and Insolence are no where more common than among Upstarts ; Men of no Family, that raise Estates out of nothing, and the most ordinary People, that having had no Education, are puff'd up with their Fortune, whenever they are lifted up above Mediocrity, and from mean Stations advanced to Posts of Honour : Whereas no Men upon Earth, generally speaking, are more Courteous, Humane, or Polite than Persons of high Birth, that enjoy the large Possessions, and known Seats of their Ancestors ; Men illustrious by Descent, that have been used to Grandeur and Titles of Honour from their Infancy, and receiv'd an Education suitable to their Quality. I don't believe there ever was a Nation, that were not Savages, in which the Youth of both Sexes were not expressly taught never to be Proud or Haughty : Did you ever know a School, a Tutor, or a Parent, that did not continually inculcate to those under their Care to be civil and obliging ; nay, does not the word *Mannerly* itself import as much?

Cleo. I beg of you let us be calm, and speak with exactness. The Doctrine of good Manners furnishes us with a thousand Lessons against the various Appearances and outward Symptoms of Pride, but it has not one Precept against the Passion it self.[1]

Hor. How is that?

[50] | *Cleo.* No, not one against the Passion it self ; the Conquest of it is never attempted, nor talk'd of in a Gentleman's Education, where Men are to be continually inspired and kept warm with the Sense of their Honour, and the inward Value they must put upon themselves on all Emergencies.

Hor. This is worth Consideration, and requires time to be examin'd into ; but where is your fine Gentleman, the Picture you promis'd?

Cleo. I am ready, and shall begin with his Dwelling : Tho' he has several noble Seats in different Counties,[a] yet I shall only take notice of his chief Mansion-house, that bears the Name, and does the Honours of the Family : this is amply Magnificent, and yet Commodious to Admiration. His Gardens are very extensive, and contain an infinite variety of pleasing Objects :

ᵃ Countries *30*   [1] Cf. *Fable* i. 72.

they are divided into many Branches for divers Purposes, and every where fill'd with Improvements of Art upon Nature; yet a beautiful Order and happy Contrivance are conspicuous through every Part; and tho' nothing is omitted to render them Stately and Delightful; the whole is laid out to the best Advantage. Within Doors every Thing bespeaks the Grandeur and Judgment of the Master; and as no Cost is spared any where to procure Beauty or Conveniency, so you see none impertinently lavish'd. All his Plate | and Furniture are completely fine, and you [51] see nothing but what is fashionable. He has no Pictures but of the most eminent Hands: The Rarities he shews are really such; he hoards up no Trifles, nor offers any thing to your Sight that is shocking: But the several Collections he has of this sort are agreeable as well as extraordinary, and rather valuable than large: But Curiosities and Wealth are not confin'd to his Cabinet; the Marble and Sculpture that are display'd up and down are a Treasure themselves; and there is abundance of admirable Gilding and excellent Carving to be seen in many Places. What has been laid out on the great Hall and one Gallery would be a considerable Estate; and there is a Salloon and a Staircase not inferior to either: These are all very spacious and lofty; the Architecture of them is of the best Taste, and the Decorations surprising. Throughout the whole there appears a delicate mixture and astonishing Variety of lively Embellishments, the Splendor of which, join'd to a perfect Cleanliness, no where neglected, are highly entertaining to the most careless and least observng Eye; whilst the Exactness of the Workmanship bestow'd on every Part of the meanest Utensil, gives a more solid Satisfaction, and is ravishing to the Curious. But the greatest Excellency in this Model of Perfection is this; that as in the most ordina-|ry [52] Rooms there is nothing wanting for their Purpose, and the least Passage is handsomly finish'd; so in those of the greatest *Eclat* there is nothing overcharg'd, nor any Part of them incumbred with Ornaments.

Hor. This is a study'd Piece ; but I don't like it the worse for it, pray go on.

Cleo. I have thought of it before, I own. His Equipage is rich and well chosen, and there is nothing to be seen about him that Art or Expence, within the Compass of Reason, could make better. At his own Table his Looks are ever Jovial, and his Heart seems to be as open as his Countenance. His chief Business there is to take care of others without being troublesome, and all his Happiness seems to consist in being able to please his Friends : In his greatest Mirth he is wanting in Respect to no Man, and never makes use of Abbreviations in Names, or unhandsome Familiarities with the meanest of his Guests. To every one that speaks to him he gives an obliging Attention, and seems never to disregard any Thing but what is said in Commendation of his Fare : He never interrupts any Discourse but what is made in his Praise, and seldom assents to any Encomiums, tho' the most equitable, that are made on any thing that is His. When he is abroad he never spies Faults, and whatever is amiss, he either says nothing ; or, in answer [53] to the Com-|plaints and Uneasiness of others, gives every thing the best-natur'd turn it can bear ; but he seldom leaves a House before he finds out something to extoll in it without wronging his Judgment. His Conversation is always facetious and goodhumour'd, but as solid as it is diverting. He never utters a Syllable that has the least Tincture of Obscenity or Prophaneness ; nor ever made a Jest that was offensive.

Hor. Very fine !

Cleo. He seems to be entirely free from Bigotry and Superstition, avoids all Disputes about Religion ; but goes constantly to Church, and is seldom absent from his Family-Devotions.

Hor. A very godly Gentleman !

Cleo. I expected we should differ there.

Hor. I don't find fault. Proceed, pray.

Cleo. As he is a Man of Erudition himself, so he is a Promoter of Arts and Sciences ; he is a Friend to Merit, a Rewarder of Industry, and a profess'd Enemy to nothing but Immorality and Oppression. Tho' no Man's Table is better furnish'd, nor Cellars better stored ; he is temperate in his Eating, and never commits excess in Drinking : Tho' he has an exquisite Palate, he always prefers wholesome Meats to those that are delicious only, and never indulges his Appetite in any thing that might probably be prejudicial to his Health.

| *Hor.* Admirably good !   [54]

Cleo. As he is in all other Things, so he is elegant in his Cloaths, and has often new ones : Neatness he prefers to Finery in his own Dress, but his Retinue is rich. He seldom wears Gold or Silver himself, but on very solemn Occasions, in Compliment to others ; and to demonstrate that these pompous Habits are made for no other purpose, he is never seen twice in the same ; but having appear'd in them one day, he gives them away the next. Tho' of every thing he has the best of the sort, and might be call'd curious in Apparel ; yet he leaves the Care of it to others ; and no Man has his Cloaths put on better that seems so little to regard them.

Hor. Perfectly right ; to be well dress'd is a necessary Article, and yet to be sollicitous about it is below a Person of Quality.

Cleo. Therefore he has a Domestick of good Taste, a judicious Man, who saves him that trouble, and the Management likewise of his Lace and Linnen is the Province of a skilful Woman. His Language is courtly, but natural and intelligible ; it is neither low nor bombastick, and ever free from pedantick and vulgar Expressions. All his Motions are Genteel without

Affectation ; his Mein is rather Sedate than Airy, and his Manner Noble : for tho' he is ever Civil and [55] Condescending, and no Man less | Arrogant, yet in all his Carriage there is something gracefully Majestick ; and as there is nothing mean in his Humility, so his Loftiness has nothing disobliging.

Hor. Prodigiously good !

Cleo. He is charitable to the Poor, his House is never shut to Strangers, and all his Neighbours he counts to be his Friends. He is a Father to his Tenants, and looks upon their Welfare as inseparable from his Interest. No Man is less uneasy at little Offences, or more ready to forgive all Trespasses without Design. The Injuries that are suffer'd from other Landlords he turns into Benefits ; and whatever Damages, great or small, are sustain'd on his Account, either from his Diversions or otherwise, he doubly makes good. He takes care to be early inform'd of such Losses, and commonly repairs them before they are complain'd of.

Hor. Oh rare Humanity ; hearken ye Fox-hunters !

Cleo. He never chides any of his People, yet no Man is better serv'd ; and tho' nothing is wanting in his House-keeping, and his Family is very numerous, yet the Regularity of it is no less remarkable, than the Plenty they live in. His Orders he will have strictly obey'd, but his Commands are always reasonable, and he never speaks to the meanest Footman without Regard to Humanity. Extraordinary Diligence in [56] Servants, and all laud-|able Actions he takes notice of himself, and often commends them to their Faces ; but leaves it to his Steward to reprove or dismiss those he dislikes.

Hor. Well judg'd.

Cleo. Whoever lives with him is taken care of in Sickness as well as in Health. The Wages he gives are above double those of other Masters, and he often makes Presents to those, that are more than ordinary observing and industrious to please : but he suffers no body to take a Penny of his Friends or others, that come to his House on any Account whatever. Many Faults are conniv'd at, or pardon'd for the first time, but a Breach of this Order is ever attended with the Loss of their Places, as soon as it is found out ; and there is a Premium for the Discovery.

Hor. This is the only exceptionable thing in my Opinion that I have heard yet.

Cleo. I wonder at that : Why so, pray?

Hor. In the first place, it is very difficult to enforce Obedience to such a Command ; Secondly, if it could be executed, it would be of little use ; unless it could be made general, which is impossible : and therefore I look upon the Attempt of introducing this Maxim to be singular and fantastical. It would please Misers and others, that would never follow the Example at Home ; but it would take away from generous Men a handsome Opportunity of shewing their liberal and beneficent | Disposition : besides, it would manifestly [57] make ones House too open to all sorts of People.

Cleo. Ways might be found to prevent that ; but then it would be a Blessing, and do great Kindness to Men of Parts and Education, that have little to spare, to many of whom this Money to Servants is a very grievous Burden.

Hor. What you mention is the only thing that can be said for it, and I own, of great Weight : But I beg your Pardon for interrupting you.

Cleo. In all his Dealings he is punctual and just. As he has an immense Estate, so he has good Managers to take care of it : But tho' all his Accounts are very neatly kept, yet he makes it part of his Business to look them over himself. He suffers no Tradesman's Bill to lie by unexamin'd, and tho' he meddles not with his ready Cash himself, yet he is a quick and chearful, as well as an exact Pay-master ; and the only Singularity he is guilty of, is, that he never will owe any thing on a New-Year's Day.

Hor. I like that very well.

Cleo. He is affable with Discretion, of easy Access, and never ruffled with Passion. To sum up all, no Man seems to be less elevated with his Condition than himself ; and in the full Enjoyment of so many personal Accomplishments, as well as other Possessions, his [58] Modesty is equal to the rest of his Happi-|ness ; and in the midst of the Pomp and Distinction he lives in, he never appears to be entertain'd with his Greatness, but rather unacquainted with the Things he excels in.

Hor. It is an admirable Character, and pleases me exceedingly ; but I will freely own to you, that I should have been more highly delighted with the Description, if I had not known your Design, and the Use you intend to make of it ; which, I think, is barbarous : to raise so fine, so elegant, and so complete an Edifice, in order to throw it down, is taking great Pains to shew ones Skill in doing Mischief. I have observ'd the several Places where you left room for Evasions, and sapping the Foundation you have built upon. *His Heart seems to be as open* ; and *He never appears to be entertain'd with his Greatness.*[1] I am persuaded, that, where-ever you have put in this *seeming* and *appearing*, you have done it designedly, and with an Intent to make use of them as so many Back-doors to creep out at. I could never have taken Notice of these Things, if you had not acquainted me with your Intention before-hand.

Cleo. I have made use of the Caution you speak of : But with no other View than to avoid just Censure, and prevent your accusing me of Incorrectness, or judging with too much Precipitation ; if it should be proved afterwards, that this Gentleman had acted [59] from an ill Principle, which is the thing I own I | pur-pos'd to convince you of ; but seeing, that it would be unpleasant to you, I'll be satisfied with having given you some small Entertainment in the Descrip-

---

[1] See *Fable* ii. 68 and above.

tion, and for the rest, I give you Leave to think me in the Wrong.

Hor. Why so? I thought the Character was made and contriv'd on purpose for my Instruction.

Cleo. I don't pretend to instruct you : I would have offer'd something, and appeal'd to your Judgment [a] ; but I have been mistaken, and plainly see my Error. Both last Night and now, when we began our Discourse, I took you to be in another Disposition of thinking, than I perceive you are. You spoke of an Impression that had been made upon you, and of looking into your self, and gave some other Hints, which too rashly I misconstrued in my Favour ; but I have found since, that you are as warm as ever against the Sentiments I profess myself to be of ; and therefore I'll desist. I expect no Pleasure from any Triumph, and I know nothing, that would vex me more, than the Thoughts of disobliging you. Pray let us do in this as we do in another matter of Importance, never touch upon it : Friends in Prudence should avoid all Subjects in which they are known essentially to differ. Believe me, *Horatio*, if it was in my Power to divert or give you any Pleasure, I would grudge no Pains to compass that End : But to make you uneasy, is a thing that I shall never be know-|ingly [60] guilty of, and I beg a thousand Pardons for having said so much both Yesterday and To-day. Have you heard any thing from *Gibraltar?*[1]

Hor. I am ashamed of my Weakness and your Civility : You have not been mistaken in the Hints you speak of ; what you have said has certainly made a great Impression upon me, and I have endeavour'd to examine myself : But, as you say, it is a severe Task to do it faithfully. I desired you to dine with me on purpose, that we might talk of these Things.

[a] Jndgment 29

[1] From Feb. 1727 to Mar. 1728 Gibraltar was fruitlessly besieged by Spain. During or slightly after that period, therefore, Mandeville was writing the second dialogue.

It is I that have offended, and it is I that ought to ask
Pardon for the ill Manners I have been guilty of :
But you know the Principles I have always adhered to ;
it is impossible to recede from them at once. I see
great Difficulties, and now and then a Glimpse of
Truth, that makes me start : I sometimes feel great
Struggles within ; but I have been so used to derive
all Actions that are really good from laudable Motives,
that as soon as I return to my accustom'd way of
thinking, it carries all before it. Pray bear with my
Infirmities. I am in Love with your fine Gentleman,
and I confess, I cannot see how a Person so universally
good, so far remote from all Selfishness, can act in
such an extraordinary manner every way, but from
Principles of Virtue and Religion. Where is there
such a Landlord in the World? If I am in an Error,
[61] I shall be glad to be undeceiv'd. Pray | inform me,
and say what you will, I promise you to keep my
Temper, and, I beg of you, speak your Mind with
Freedom.

Cleo. You have bid me before say what I would,
and when I did, you seem'd displeas'd ; but since you
command me, I will try once more.----- Whether
there is or ever was such a Man as I have describ'd
in the World, is not very material : But I will easily
allow that most People would think it less difficult, to
conceive one, than to imagine, that such a clear and
beautiful Stream could flow from so mean and muddy
a Spring as an excessive Thirst after Praise, and an
immoderate Desire of general Applause from the most
knowing Judges : Yet it is certain, that great Parts
and extraordinary Riches may compass all this in
a Man, who is not deform'd, and has had a refin'd
Education ; and that there are many Persons naturally
no better than thousand others ; who by the Helps
mention'd might attain to those good Qualities and
Accomplishments ; If they had but Resolution and
Perseverance enough, to render every Appetite and

every Faculty subservient to that one predominant Passion, which, if continually gratify'd, will always enable them to govern, and, if requir'd, to subdue all the rest without Exception, even in the most difficult Cases.

Hor. To enter into an Argument, concerning the Possibility of what you say, might occasion a long Dispute; but the Probability, I | think, is very clear [62] against you, and if there was such a Man, it would be much more credible, that he acted from the Excellency of his Nature, in which so many Virtues and rare Endowments were assembled, than that all his good Qualities sprung from vicious Motives. If Pride could be the Cause of all this, the Effect of it would sometimes appear in others : According to your System, there is no scarcity of it, and there are Men of great Parts and prodigious Estates all over *Europe :* Why are there not several such Patterns to be seen up and down, as you have drawn us one; and why is it so very seldom, that many Virtues and good Qualities are seen to meet in one Individual?

Cleo. Why so few Persons, tho' there are so many Men of immense Fortune, ever arrive at any thing like this high pitch of Accomplishments, there are several Reasons that are very obvious. In the first place, Men differ in Temperament : Some are naturally of an active, stirring; others of an indolent, quiet Disposition; some of a bold, others of a meek Spirit. In the second, it is to be consider'd, that this Temperament in Men come to Maturity is more or less conspicuous, according as it has been either check'd or encourag'd by Education. Thirdly, that on these two depend the different Perception Men have of Happiness, according to which the Love of Glory determines them different ways. Some think | it the greatest Felicity to govern and rule over [63] others : Some take the Praise of Bravery and Undauntedness in Dangers to be the most valuable :

Others, Erudition, and to be a celebrated Author :
So that, tho' they all love Glory, they set out differently
to acquire it. But a Man, who hates a Bustle, and is
naturally of a quiet, easy Temper, and which has been
encouraged in him by Education, it is very likely
might think nothing more desirable than the Character
of a Fine Gentleman ; and if he did, I dare say, that
he would endeavour to behave himself pretty near
the Pattern I have given you ; I say pretty near,
because I may have been mistaken in some Things,
and as I have not touch'd upon every thing, some will
say, that I have left out several necessary ones : But
in the main I believe, that in the Country and Age
we live in, the Qualifications I have named would get
a Man the Reputation I have supposed him to desire.

Hor. Without doubt. I make no manner of scruple
about what you said last, and I told you before that
it was an admirable Character, and pleas'd me exceedingly. That I took Notice of your making your
Gentleman so very Godly as you did, was because it
is not common, but I intended it not as a Reflection.
One thing indeed there was in which I differ'd from
you ; but that was merely speculative ; and, since
[64] I have reflected on what | you answered me, I don't
know, but I may be in the wrong, as I should certainly
believe myself to be, if there really was such a Man,
and he was of the contrary Opinion : To such a fine
Genius I would pay an uncommon Deference, and
with great Readiness submit my Understanding to his
superiour Capacity. But the Reasons you give, why
those Effects, which you ascribe to Pride, are not
more common, the Cause being so universal, I think
are insufficient. That Men are prompted to follow
different Ends, as their Inclinations differ, I can easily
allow ; but there are great Numbers of rich Men that
are likewise of a quiet and indolent Disposition, and
moreover very desirous of being thought fine Gentlemen : How comes it, that among so many Persons of

high Birth, princely Estates and the most refin'd Education, as there are in Christendom, that study, travel, and take great Pains to be well-accomplish'd, there is not one, to whom all the good Qualities and every thing you named could be applied without Flattery?

Cleo. It is very possible, that thousands may aim at this, and not one of them succeed to that Degree : in some perhaps the predominant Passion is not strong enough entirely to subdue the rest : Love or Covetousness may divert others : Drinking, Gaming may draw away many, and break in upon their Resolution ; they may not have strength to persevere in a Design, and steadily to pursue the same | Ends ; or they may want [65] a true Taste and Knowledge of what is esteem'd by Men of Judgment ; or lastly they may not be so thoroughly well-bred as is required to conceal themselves on all Emergencies : For the Practical Part of Dissimulation is infinitely more difficult than the Theory ; and any one of these Obstacles is sufficient to spoil all, and hinder the finishing of such a Piece.

Hor. I shall not dispute that with you : But all this while you have proved nothing, nor given the least Reason why you should imagine, that a Man of a Character, to all outward Appearance so bright and beautiful, acted from vicious Motives. You would not condemn him without so much as naming the Cause why you suspect him.

Cleo. By no means ; nor have I advanced any thing, that is ill-natured or uncharitable : For I have not said, that if I found a Gentleman in Possession of all the Things I mention'd, I would give his rare Endowments this Turn, and think all his Perfections derived from no better Stock than an extraordinary Love of Glory. What I argue for, and insist upon, is, the Possibility that all these Things might be perform'd by a Man from no other Views, and with no other Helps, than those I have named : Nay, I believe moreover, that a Gentleman so accomplished, all his Knowledge and great Parts notwithstanding, may himself be [66] ignorant, or at least | not well assured of the Motive he acts from.

Hor. This is more unintelligible than any thing you have said yet ; Why will you heap Difficulties upon one another, without solving any? I desire you would clear up this last Paradox, before you do any thing else.

Cleo. In order to obey you, I must put you in mind of what happens in early Education, by the first Rudiments of which Infants are taught, in the Choice of Actions to prefer the Precepts of others, to the Dictates of their own Inclinations ; which in short is no more than doing as they are bid. To gain this Point, Punishments and Rewards are not neglected, and many different Methods are made use of ; but it is certain, that nothing proves more often effectual for this Purpose, or has a greater Influence upon Children, than the Handle that is made of Shame ; which, tho' a natural Passion, they would not be sensible of so soon, if we did not artfully rouze and stir it up in them, before they can speak or go : By which means, their Judgments being then weak, we may teach them to be asham'd of what we please, as soon as we can perceive them to be any ways affected with the Passion itself. But as the fear of Shame is very insignificant, where there is but little Pride ; so it is impossible to augment the first, without encreasing the latter in the same Proportion.

[67] | *Hor.* I should have thought that this Encrease of Pride would render Children more stubborn and less docile.

Cleo. You judge right, it would so ; and must have been a great Hindrance to good Manners, till Experience taught Men, that, tho' Pride was not to be destroy'd by Force, it might be govern'd by Stratagem, and that the best way to manage it, is by playing the

Passion against itself. Hence it is that in an artful Education we are allow'd to place as much Pride as we please in our Dexterity of concealing it.[1] I do not suppose, that this covering ourselves, notwithstanding the Pride we take in it, is perform'd without a Difficulty that is plainly felt, and perhaps very unpleasant at first ; but this wears off as we grow up ; and when a Man has behaved himself with so much Prudence as I have describ'd, lived up to the strictest Rules of good Breeding for many Years, and has gain'd the Esteem of all that know him, when his [a] noble and polite Manner is become habitual to him, it is possible, he may in time forget the Principle he set out with, and become ignorant, or at least insensible of the hidden Spring, that gives Life and Motion to all his Actions.

Hor. I am convinc'd of the great Use that may be made of Pride, if you will call it so ; but I am not satisfied yet, how a Man of so much Sense, Knowledge and Penetration, one that understands himself so entirely well, | should be ignorant of his own Heart, [68] and the Motives he acts from. What is it that induces you to believe this, besides the Possibility of his Forgetfulness?

Cleo. I have two Reasons for it, which I desire may be seriously consider'd. The first is, that in what relates to ourselves, especially our own Worth and Excellency [b], Pride blinds the Understanding in Men of Sense and great Parts as well as in others, and the greater Value we may reasonably set upon ourselves, the fitter we are to swallow the grossest Flatteries in spight of all our Knowledge and Abilities in other Matters : Witness *Alexander the Great,* whose vast Genius could not hinder him from doubting seriously, whether he was a God or not.[2] My second Reason will prove to us ; that, if the Person in question was capable of examining himself, it is yet highly impro-

---

[a] this *30*   [b] Exellency *29*
[1] Cf. *Fable* i. 79.   [2] See Plutarch's *Life.*

bable, that he would ever set about it : For it must
be granted, that in order to search into ourselves, it is
required, we should be willing as well as able ; and
we have all the Reason in the World to think, that
there is nothing, which a very proud Man of such
high Qualifications would avoid more carefully, than
such an Enquiry : Because for all other Acts of Self-
denial he is repaid in his darling Passion ; but this
alone is really mortifying, and the only Sacrifice of his
Quiet, for which he can have no Equivalent. If the
Hearts of the best and sincerest Men are corrupt and
[69] deceit-|ful, what Condition must theirs be in, whose
whole Life is one continued Scene of Hypocrisy !
Therefore enquiring within, and boldly searching into
ones own Bosom, must be the most shocking Employment, that a Man can give his Mind to, whose greatest
Pleasure consists in secretly admiring himself. It
would be ill Manners after this to appeal to your self ;
but the Severity of the Task . . . .

Hor. Say no more, I yield this Point, tho' I own,
I cannot conceive what Advantage you can expect
from it : For, instead of removing, it will rather help
to encrease the grand Difficulty, which is to prove,
that this complete Person you have describ'd, acts
from a vicious Motive : And if that be not your
Design, I cannot see what you drive at.

Cleo. I told you it was.

Hor. You must have a prodigious Sagacity in detect-
ing abstruse Matters beyond other Men.

Cleo. You wonder, I know, which way I arrogate
to my self such a superlative Degree of Penetration,
as to know an artful cunning Man better than he does
himself, and how I dare pretend to enter and look
into a Heart, which I have own'd to be completely
well conceal'd from all the World; which in strictness
is an Impossibility, and consequently not to be bragg'd
of but by a Coxcomb.

Hor. You may treat yourself as you please, I have

said no such thing; but I own that I | long to see it [70] proved, that you have this Capacity. I remember the Character very well : Notwithstanding the Precautions you have taken, it is very full : I told you before, that where Things have a handsome Appearance every way, there can be no just Cause to suspect them. I'll stick close to that ; your Gentleman is all of a piece : You shall alter nothing, either by retracting any of the good Qualities you have given him, or making Additions that are either clashing with, or unsuitable to what you have allow'd already.

Cleo. I shall attempt neither : And without that decisive Tryals may be made, by which it will plainly appear, whether a Person acts from inward Goodness and a Principle of Religion, or only from a Motive of Vain-glory; and, in the latter Case, there is an infallible way of dragging the lurking Fiend from his darkest Recesses into a glaring Light, where all the World shall know him.

Hor. I don't think my self a Match for you in Argument; but I have a great Mind to be your Gentleman's Advocate against all your Infallibility : I never liked a Cause better in my Life. Come, I undertake to defend him in all the Suppositions you can make, that are reasonable, and consistent with what you have said before.

Cleo. Very well : Let us suppose what may happen to the most inoffensive, the most prudent and best-bred Man ; that our fine Gen-|tleman differs in [71] Opinion before Company, with another, who is his Equal in Birth and Quality, but not so much Master over his outward Behaviour, and less guarded in his Conduct : Let this Adversary, *mal a propos*, grow warm, and seem to be wanting in the Respect that is due to the other, and reflect on his Honour in ambiguous Terms. What is your Client to do?

Hor. Immediately to ask for an Explanation.

Cleo. Which if the hot Man disregards with Scorn, or flatly refuses to give, Satisfaction must be demanded, and tilt they must.

Hor. You are too hasty : It happen'd before Company; in such Cases, Friends or any Gentlemen present, should interpose and take care, that, if threatning Words ensue, they are by the civil Authority both put under Arrest, and before they came to uncourteous Language, they ought to have been parted by friendly Force, if it were possible. After that, Overtures may be made of Reconciliation with the nicest Regard to the Point of Honour.

Cleo. I don't ask for Directions to prevent a Quarrel ; what you say may be done, or it may not be done : The good Offices of Friends may succeed, and they may not succeed. I am to make what Suppositions I think fit within the Verge of Possibility, so they are [72] reasonable and consistent with the Character I | have drawn : Can we not suppose these two Persons in such a Situation, that you yourself would advise your Friend to send his Adversary a Challenge?

Hor. Without doubt such a thing may happen.

Cleo. That's enough. After that a Duel must ensue ; in which, without determining any thing, the Fine Gentleman, we'll say, behaves himself with the utmost Gallantry.

Hor. To have expected or suppos'd otherwise would have been unreasonable.

Cleo. You see therefore how fair I am. But what is it, pray, that so suddenly disposes a courteous sweet-temper'd Man, for so small an Evil, to seek a Remedy of that extreme Violence? but above all, what is it, that buoys up and supports him against the Fear of Death? for there lies the greatest Difficulty.

Hor. His natural Courage and Intrepidity, built on the Innocence of his Life, and the Rectitude of his Manners.

Cleo. But what makes so just and prudent a Man, that has the Good of Society so much at Heart, act knowingly against the Laws of his Country?

Hor. The strict Obedience he pays to the Laws of Honour, which are superior to all others.

DIALOGUE. 83

Cleo. If Men of Honour would act consistently, they ought all to be *Roman* Catholicks.

| *Hor.* Why, pray? [73]

Cleo. Because they prefer oral Tradition to all written Laws : For no body can tell, when, in what King's or Emperor's Reign, in what Country or by what Authority these Laws of Honour were first enacted : It is very strange they should be of such Force.

Hor. They are [a] wrote and engraved in every one's Breast that is a Man of Honour : there is no denying of it, you are conscious of it your self, every body feels it within.

Cleo. Let them be wrote or engraved where-ever you please, they are directly opposite to and clashing with the Laws of God ; and if the Gentleman I described [b] was as sincere in his Religion, as he appear'd to be, he must have been of an Opinion contrary to yours ; for Christians of all Persuasions are unanimous in allowing the Divine Laws to be far above all other ; and that all other Considerations ought to give Way to them. How, and under what Pretence can a Christian, who is a Man of Sense, submit or agree to Laws that prescribe Revenge, and countenance Murder ; both which are so expressly forbid by the Precepts of his Religion?

Hor. I am no Casuist : But you know, that what I say is true ; and that among Persons of Honour a Man would be laugh'd at, that should make such a Scruple. Not but that I think killing a Man to be a great Sin, | where it can be help'd ; and that all [74] prudent Men ought to avoid the Occasion, as much as it is in their Power : He is highly blameable who is the first Aggressor and gives the Affront ; and whoever enters upon it out of Levity, or seeks a Quarrel out of Wantonness, ought to be hang'd : No body would chuse it, who is not a Fool ; and yet, when it is [c] forc'd upon one, all the Wisdom in the World cannot teach him how to avoid it. It has been my Case, you

---

[a] were *33*   [b] descibed *29*   [c] it is] is it *29*

F 2

know : I shall never forget the Reluctancy I had against it ; but Necessity has no Law.

Cleo. I saw you that very Morning, and you seem'd to be sedate and void of Passion : You could have no Concern.

Hor. It is silly to shew any at such Times ; but I know best what I felt ; the Struggle I had within was unspeakable : It is a terrible Thing. I would then have given a considerable Part of my Estate, that the Thing which forc'd me into it had not happen'd, and yet upon less Provocation I would act the same Part again to-morrow.

Cleo. Do you remember what your Concern was chiefly about ?

Hor. How can you ask ? It is an Affair of the highest Importance, that can occur in Life ; I was no Boy ; it was after we came from *Italy*, I was in my nine and twentieth Year, had very good Acquaintance, and was not ill receiv'd : A Man of that Age, in [75] | Health and Vigour, who has seven thousand a Year, and the Prospect of being a Peer of *England*, has no Reason to quarrel with the World, or wish himself out of it. It is a very great Hazard a Man runs in a Duel ; besides the Remorse and Uneasiness one must feel as long as he lives, if he has the Misfortune of killing his Adversary. It is impossible to reflect on all these Things, and at the same Time resolve to run those Hazards, (tho' there are other Considerations of still greater Moment) without being under a prodigious Concern.

Cleo. You say nothing about the Sin.

Hor. The Thoughts of that, without doubt, are a great Addition ; but the other Things are so weighty of themselves, that a Man's Condition at such a Time is very perplex'd without further Reflection.

Cleo. You have now a very fine Opportunity, *Horatio*, of looking into your Heart, and, with a little of my Assistance, examining yourself. If you can condescend to this, I promise you, that you shall make great Discoveries, and be convinc'd of Truths you are now unwilling to believe. A Lover of Justice and Probity, as you are, ought not to be fond of a Road of Thinking, where he is always forc'd to skulk, and never dares to meet with Light or Reason. Will you suffer me to ask you some Questions, and will | you [76] answer them directly and in good Humour?

Hor. I will, without Reserve.

Cleo. Do you remember the Storm upon the Coast of *Genoa?*

Hor. Going to *Naples?* very well; it makes me cold to think of it.

Cleo. Was you afraid?

Hor. Never more in my Life. I hate that fickle Element, I can't endure the Sea.

Cleo. What was you afraid of?

Hor. That's a pretty Question : Do you think a young Fellow of six and twenty, as I was then, and in my Circumstances, had a great Mind to be drown'd? The Captain himself said we were in Danger.

Cleo. But neither he nor any body else discover'd half so much Fear and Anxiety as you did.

Hor. There was no body there, yourself excepted, that had half a quarter so much to lose as I had : Besides, they are used to the Sea; Storms are familiar to them.[1] I had never been at Sea before, but that fine Afternoon we cross'd from *Dover* to *Calais.*

[1] Cf. the *Virgin Unmask'd* (1724), p. 25 : 'The Sailor in a Storm shews less Concern, and seems to be braver than the Soldier ; not because he has more Courage, or fears Death less than the other, but because the Dangers of the Sea are more familiar to him.'

La Rochefoucauld wrote (maxim 215, *Œuvres,* ed. Gilbert and Gourdault), ' Il s'en trouve à qui l'habitude des moindres périls affermit le courage, et les prépare à s'exposer à de plus grands. Il y en a qui sont braves à coups d'épée, et craignent les coups de mousquet; d'autres sont assurés aux coups de mousquet, et appréhendent de se battre à coups d'épée.' Cf. also Aristotle, *Nic. Ethics* iii. vi. 9–10, and Charron, *De la Sagesse,* bk. 3, ch. 19.

Cleo. Want of Knowledge and Experience may make Men apprehend Danger where there is none ; but real Dangers, when they are known to be such, try the natural Courage of all Men ; whether they have been used to them or not : Sailors are as unwilling to lose their Lives as other People.

[77] | *Hor.* I am not ashamed to own, that I am a great Coward at Sea : Give me *Terra Firma*, and then ——

Cleo. Six or seven Months after you fought that Duel, I remember you had the Small-Pox ; you was then very much afraid of dying.

Hor. Not without a Cause.

Cleo. I heard your Physicians say, that the violent Apprehension you was under, hinder'd your Sleep, increased your Fever, and was as mischievous to you as the Distemper itself.

Hor. That was a terrible Time ; I'm glad it is over : I had a Sister died of it. Before I had it, I was in perpetual Dread of it, and many Times to hear it named only has made me uneasy.

Cleo. Natural Courage is a general Armour against the Fear of Death, whatever Shape that appears in, *Si fractus illabatur orbis.*[1] It supports a Man in tempestuous Seas, and in a burning Fever, whilst he is in his Senses, as well as in a Siege before a Town, or in a Duel with Seconds.

Hor. What ! you are going to shew me, that I have no Courage.

Cleo. Far from it ; it would be ridiculous to doubt a Man's Bravery, that has shewn it in such an extraordinary manner as you have done more than once : What I question is the Epithet you join'd to it at [78] first, the Word | *natural* ; for there is a great Difference between that and *artificial* Courage.

Hor. That's a Chicane I won't enter into : But I am not of your Opinion, as to what you said before. A Gentleman is not required to shew his Bravery, but

[1] Horace, *Carmina* III. iii. 7.

where his Honour is concern'd ; and if he dares to fight for his King, his Friend, his Mistress, and every thing where his Reputation is engaged, you shall think of him what you please for the rest. Besides that in Sickness and other Dangers, as well as Afflictions, where the Hand of God is plainly to be seen, Courage and Intrepidity are impious as well as impertinent. Undauntedness in Chastisements is a Kind of Rebellion : It is waging War with Heaven, which none but Atheists and Free-Thinkers would be guilty of ; it is only they that can glory in Impenitence, and talk of dying hard. All others, that have any Sense of Religion, desire to repent before they go out of the World : The best of us don't always live, as we could wish to die.

Cleo. I am very glad to hear you are so religious : But don't you perceive yet, how inconsistent you are with yourself ; how can a Man sincerely wish to repent, that willfully plunges himself into a mortal Sin, and an Action where he runs a greater and more immediate Hazard of his Life, than he could have done in almost any other ; without Force or Necessity ?

| *Hor.* I have over and over own'd to you that [79] Duelling is a Sin ; and, unless a Man is forced to it by Necessity, I believe, a mortal one : But this was not my Case, and therefore I hope God will forgive me : Let them look to it that make a Sport of it. But when a Man comes to an Action with the utmost Reluctancy, and what he does is not possibly to be avoided, I think he then may justly be said to be forc'd to it, and to act from Necessity. You may blame the rigorous Laws of Honour and the Tyranny of Custom, but a Man that will live in the World must and is bound to obey them. Would not you do it yourself ?

Cleo. Don't ask me what I would do : The Question is, what every body ought to do. Can a Man

believe the Bible, and at the same Time apprehend
a Tyrant more crafty or malicious, more unrelenting
or inhuman than the Devil, or a Mischief worse than
Hell, and Pains either more exquisite or more durable
than Torments unspeakable and yet everlasting? You
don't answer. What Evil is it? think of it, and tell
me what dismal Thing it is you apprehend, should
you neglect those Laws, and despise that Tyrant :
what Calamity could befall you? Let me know the
worst that can be fear'd.

Hor. Would you be posted for a Coward?

Cleo. For what? for not daring to violate all human
and divine Laws?

[80] | *Hor.* Strictly speaking you are in the right, it is
unanswerable ; But who will consider Things in that
Light?

Cleo. All good Christians.

Hor. Where are they then? for all Mankind in
general would despise and laugh at a Man, who should
move those Scruples. I have heard and seen Clergymen themselves in Company shew their Contempt of
Poltrons, whatever they might talk or recommend in
the Pulpit. Entirely to quit the World, and at once
to renounce the Conversation of all Persons that are
valuable in it, is a terrible Thing to resolve upon.
Would you become a Town and Table-talk? could
you submit to be the Jest and Scorn of Publick-
Houses, Stage Coaches, and Market-Places? Is not
this the certain Fate of a Man, who should refuse to
fight, or bear an Affront without Resentment? Be
just, *Cleomenes* ; is it to be avoided? Must he not
be made a common Laughing-stock, be pointed at in
the Streets, and serve for Diversion to the very
Children, to Link-boys and Hackney Coachmen? Is
it a Thought to be born with Patience?

Cleo. How come you now to have such an anxious
Regard for what may be the Opinion of the Vulgar,
whom at other Times you so heartily despise?

Hor. All this is Reasoning, and you know the Thing will not bear it : How can you be so cruel?

| *Cleo.* How can you be so backward in discovering [81] and owning the Passion, that is so conspicuously the Occasion of all this, the palpable and only Cause of the Uneasiness we feel at the Thoughts of being despis'd?

Hor. I am not sensible of any ; and I declare to you, that I feel nothing that moves me to speak as I do, but the Sense and Principle of Honour within me.

Cleo. Do you think that the lowest of the Mob, and the Scum of the People, are possess'd of any Part of this Principle?

Hor. No, indeed.

Cleo. Or that among the highest Quality Infants can be affected with it before they are two Years old?

Hor. Ridiculous.

Cleo. If neither of these are affected with it, then Honour should be either adventitious, and acquir'd by Culture ; or, if contain'd in the Blood of those that are nobly born, imperceptible 'till the Years of Discretion ; and neither of them can be said of the Principle, the palpable Cause I speak of. For we plainly see on the one hand, that Scorn and Ridicule are intollerable to the poorest Wretches, and that there is no Beggar so mean or miserable, that Contempt will never offend him : On the other, that human Creatures are so early influenced by the Sense of Shame, that Children, by being laugh'd at and made a Jest of, may be set a crying before they can well | speak or go. Whatever therefore this mighty Prin- [82] ciple is, it is born with us, and belongs to our Nature : Are you unacquainted with the proper, genuine, homely Name of it?

Hor. I know you call it Pride. I won't dispute with you about Principles and Origins of Things ; but that high Value which Men of Honour set upon themselves as such, and which is no more than what is due to the Dignity of our Nature, when well cultivated, is the Foundation of their Character, and a Support to them in all Difficulties, that is of great Use to the Society. The Desire likewise of being thought well of, and the Love of Praise and even of Glory are commendable Qualities, that are beneficial to the Publick. The Truth of this is manifest in the Reverse; all shameless People that are below Infamy, and matter not what is said or thought of them, these, we see, no body can trust; they stick at nothing, and if they can but avoid Death, Pain, and penal Laws, are always ready to execute all manner of Mischief, their Selfishness or any brutal Appetite shall prompt them to, without Regard to the Opinion of others: Such are justly call'd Men of no Principles, because they have nothing of any Strength within, that can either spur them on to brave and virtuous Actions, or restrain them from Villainy and Baseness.

[83] | *Cleo.* The first Part of your Assertion is very true, when that high Value, that Desire and that Love are kept within the Bounds of Reason : But in the second there is a Mistake; those, whom we call Shameless, are not more destitute of Pride than their Betters. Remember what I have said of Education, and the Power of it; you may add Inclinations, Knowledge, and Circumstances; for as Men differ in all these, so they are differently influenced and wrought upon by all the Passions. There is nothing that some Men may not be taught to be ashamed of. The same Passion, that makes the well-bred Man and prudent Officer value and secretly admire themselves for the Honour and Fidelity they display, may make the Rake and Scoundrel brag of their Vices and boast of their Impudence.

Hor. I cannot comprehend, how a Man of Honour, and one that has none, should both act from the same Principle.

Cleo. This is not more strange, than that Self-love may make a Man destroy himself, yet nothing is more true; and it is as certain, that some Men indulge their Pride in being shameless. To understand human Nature requires Study and Application, as well as Penetration and Sagacity. All Passions and Instincts in general were given to all Animals for some wise End, tending to the Preservation and Happiness either of themselves or | their Species : It is our Duty to [84] hinder them from being detrimental or offensive to any Part of the Society; but why should we be ashamed of having them? The Instinct of high Value, which every Individual has for himself, is a very useful Passion : but a Passion it is, and though I could demonstrate, that we should be miserable Creatures without it, yet, when it is excessive, it often is the Cause of endless Mischiefs.

Hor. But in well-bred People it never is excessive.

Cleo. You mean the Excess of it never appears outwardly : But we ought never to judge of its Height or Strength from what we can discover of the Passion itself, but from the Effects it produces : It often is most superlative, where it is most conceal'd ; and nothing increases and influences it more, than what is call'd a refin'd Education, and a continual Commerce with the *Beau monde :* The only Thing, that can subdue or any ways curb it, is a strict Adherence to the Christian Religion.

Hor. Why do you so much insist upon it, that this Principle, this Value Men set upon themselves, is a Passion? And why will you chuse to call it Pride rather than Honour?

Cleo. For very good Reasons. Fixing this Principle in human Nature, in the first place, takes away all Ambiguity : Who is a Man of Honour, and who is not, is often a disputable | Point ; and, among those, [85] that are allow'd to be such, the several Degrees of Strictness in complying with the Rules of it, make great Difference in the Principle itself. But a Passion that is born with us is unalterable, and Part of our

Frame, whether it exerts itself or not : The Essence of it is the same, which Way soever it is taught to turn. Honour is the undoubted Offspring of Pride, but the same Cause produces not always the same Effect. All the Vulgar, Children, Savages and many others that are not affected with any Sense of Honour, have all of them Pride, as is evident from the Symptoms. Secondly, it helps us to explain the Phænomena that occur in Quarrels and Affronts, and the Behaviour of Men of Honour on these Occasions, which cannot be accounted for any other Way. But what moves me to it most of all, is the prodigious Force and exorbitant Power of this Principle of Self-Esteem, where it has been long gratify'd and encourag'd. You remember the Concern you was under, when you had that Duel upon your Hands, and the great Reluctancy you felt in doing what you did ; you knew it to be a Crime, and at the same Time had a strong Aversion to it ; What secret Power was it, that subdued your Will and gain'd the Victory over that great Reluctancy you felt against it? You call it Honour, and the too strict though unavoidable Adherence to the [86] Rules of it : But Men ne-|ver commit Violence upon themselves but in struggling with the Passions that are innate and natural to them. Honour is acquir'd, and the Rules of it are taught : Nothing adventitious, that some are possess'd and others destitute of, could raise such intestine Wars and dire Commotions within us ; and therefore whatever is the Cause, that can thus divide us against ourselves, and, as it were, rend human Nature in twain, must be Part of us ; and to speak without Disguise, the Struggle in your Breast was between the Fear of Shame and the Fear of Death ; had this latter not been so considerable, your Struggle would have been less : Still the first conquered, because it was strongest ; but if your Fear of Shame had been inferior to that of Death, you would have reason'd otherwise, and found out some Means or other to have avoided Fighting.

Hor. This is a strange Anatomy of human Nature.

Cleo. Yet, for want of making Use of it, the Subject we are upon is not rightly understood by many ; and Men have discours'd very inconsistently on Duelling. A Divine who wrote a Dialogue to explode that Practice,[1] said, that those, who were guilty of it, had mistaken Notions of, and went by false Rules of Honour ; for which my Friend justly ridicul'd him ; saying, *You may as well deny, that it is the Fashion what you see every body wear,* | *as to say, that demanding* [87] *and giving Satisfaction is against the Law of true Honour.*[2] Had that Man understood human Nature, he could not have committed such a Blunder : But when once he took it for granted, that Honour is a just and good Principle, without enquiring into the Cause of it among the Passions, it is impossible he should have accounted for Duelling, in a Christian pretending to act from such a Principle ; and therefore in another Place, with the same Justice, he said, that a Man who had accepted a Challenge was not qualify'd to make his Will, because he was not *Compos Mentis :*[3] He might with greater Shew of Reason have said, that he was bewitch'd.

Hor. Why so?

Cleo. Because People out of their Wits, as they think at Random, so commonly they act and talk incoherently ; but when a Man of known Sobriety, and who shews no manner of Discomposure, discourses and behaves himself in every thing, as he is used to do ; and moreover, reasons on Points of great Nicety with the utmost Accuracy, it is impossible we should

[1] See Jeremy Collier's dialogue *Of Duelling,* in *Essays upon Several Moral Subjects.* Cf. below, *n.* 3.

[2] See *Fable* i. 219.

[3] In his dialogue, *Of Duelling,* Collier wrote : ' If you design to make your *Will,* you are out : For to do that to any Purpose, a Man must be *sound in Mind and Memory* ; which is none of your Case. For the Business you are going about [duelling], is sufficient to prove you *Non Compos* ' (*Essays upon Several Moral Subjects,* ed. 1703, p. 114).

take him to be either a Fool or a Madman ; and when such a Person in an Affair of the highest Importance acts so diametrically against his Interest, that a Child can see it ; and with Deliberation pursues his own Destruction, those who believe that there are malignant Spirits of that Power, would rather imagine, that [88] | he was led away by some Enchantment, and over-rul'd by the Enemy of Mankind, than they would fancy a palpable Absurdity : But even the Supposition of that is not sufficient to solve the Difficulty, without the Help of that strange Anatomy. For what Spell or Witchcraft is there, by the Delusion of which a Man of Understanding shall, keeping his Senses, mistake an imaginary Duty for an unavoidable Necessity to break all real Obligations? But let us wave all Ties of Religion as well as human Laws, and the Person we speak of be a profess'd *Epicure*, that has no Thoughts of Futurity ; what violent Power of Darkness is it, that can force and compel a peaceable quiet Man, neither inured to Hardship, nor valiant by Nature, to quit his beloved Ease and Security ; and seemingly by Choice go ᵃ fight in cold Blood for his Life, with this comfortable Reflection, that nothing forfeits it so certainly as the entire Defeat of his Enemy?

Hor. As to the Law and the Punishment, Persons of Quality have little to fear of that.

Cleo. You can't say that in *France*,¹ nor the Seven Provinces.² But Men of Honour, that are of much lower Ranks, decline Duelling no more than those of the highest Quality. How many Examples have we, even here, of gallant Men, that have suffer'd for it, either by Exile or the Hangman ! A Man of Honour

---

ᵃ to 33

¹ In his *Origin of Honour* (pp. 64 sqq.) Mandeville devotes a score of pages to a discussion of the effectiveness of the endeavours of Henry IV and Louis XIV to abolish duelling.

² Of the Netherlands.

must fear nothing : Do but consider | every Obstacle, [89] which this Principle of Self-Esteem has conquer'd at one Time or other ; and then tell me whether it must not be something more than Magick, by the Fascination of which, a Man of Taste and Judgment, in Health and Vigour, as well as the Flower of his Age, can be tempted and actually drawn from the Embraces of a Wife he loves, and the Endearments of hopeful Children, from polite Conversation and the Charms of Friendship, from the fairest Possessions and the happy Enjoyment of all worldly Pleasures, to an unwarrantable Combat, of which the Victor must be exposed, either to an ignominious Death or perpetual Banishment.

Hor. When Things are set in this Light I confess it is very unaccountable : but will your System explain this ; can you make it clear your self?

Cleo. Immediately, as the Sun : If you will but observe two things, that must necessarily follow, and are manifest from what I have demonstrated already. The first is, that the fear of Shame in general is a matter of Caprice, that varies with Modes and Customs, and may be fix'd on different Objects, according to the different Lessons we have receiv'd, and the Precepts we are imbued with ; and that this is the Reason, why this fear of Shame, as it is either well or ill-placed, sometimes produces very good effects, and at others is the cause of the most enormous Crimes. Se-|condly, that, tho' Shame is a real Passion, the [90] Evil to be fear'd from it is altogether imaginary, and has no Existence but in our own Reflection on the Opinion of others.

Hor. But there are real and substantial Mischiefs which a Man may draw upon himself, by misbehaving in Point of Honour ; it may ruin his Fortune and all hopes of Preferment : An Officer may be broken for putting up an Affront : No Body will serve with a Coward, and who will employ him?

Cleo. What you urge is altogether out of the Question; at least it was in your own case; you had nothing to dread or apprehend but the bare Opinion of Men. Besides, when the fear of Shame is superior to that of Death, it is likewise superior to, and outweighs all other Considerations; as has been sufficiently proved : But when the fear of Shame is not violent enough to curb the fear of Death, nothing else can; and whenever the fear of Death is stronger than that of Shame, there is no Consideration that will make a Man fight in cold Blood, or comply with any of the Laws of Honour, where Life is at Stake. Therefore whoever acts from the fear of Shame as a Motive, in sending and accepting of Challenges, must be sensible on the one hand; that the Mischiefs he apprehends, should he disobey the Tyrant, can only be the Off-spring of his own Thoughts; and on the other, that if he could [91] be persuaded any ways | to lessen the great Esteem and high Value he sets upon himself, his Dread of Shame would likewise palpably diminish. From all which it is most evident, that the grand Cause of this Distraction, the powerful Enchanter we are seeking after, is Pride, Excess of Pride, that highest Pitch of Self-Esteem, to which some Men may be wound up by an artful Education, and the perpetual Flatteries bestow'd upon our Species, and the Excellencies of our Nature. This is the Sorcerer, that is able to divert all other Passions from their natural Objects, and make a rational Creature ashamed of what is most agreeable to his Inclination as well as his Duty; both which the Duellist owns, that he has knowingly acted against.

Hor. What a wonderful Machine, what an heterogeneous Compound is Man ! You have almost conquer'd me.

Cleo. I aim at no Victory, all I wish for is to do you Service, in undeceiving you.

Hor. What is the Reason that in the same Person

the fear of Death should be so glaringly conspicuous in Sickness, or a Storm, and so entirely well hid in a Duel, and all military Engagements? Pray solve that too.

Cleo. I will as well as I can : On all Emergencies where Reputation is thought to be concern'd, the fear of Shame is effectually rous'd in Men of Honour, and immediately their Pride rushes in to their Assistance, and summons all their Strength to fortify and sup- |port them in concealing the fear of Death; by [92] which extraordinary Efforts, the latter, that is the fear of Death, is altogether stifled, or at least kept out of Sight, and remains undiscover'd. But in all other Perils, in which they don't think their Honour engaged, their Pride lies dormant. And thus the fear of Death being check'd by nothing, appears without Disguise. That this is the Reason, is manifest from the different Behaviour that is observ'd in Men of Honour, according as they are either Pretenders to Christianity or tainted with Irreligion ; for there are of both Sorts ; and you shall see, most commonly at least, that your *Esprits forts,* and those who would be thought to disbelieve a future State, (I speak of Men of Honour) shew the greatest Calmness and Intrepidity in the same Dangers, where the pretended Believers among them appear to be the most ruffled and pusillanimous.

Hor. But why Pretended Believers? at that rate there are no Christians among the Men of Honour.

Cleo. I don't see how they can be real Believers.

Hor. Why so?

Cleo. For the same Reason that a *Roman Catholick* cannot be a good Subject always to be depended upon, in a Protestant, or indeed any other Country, but the Dominions of his Holiness. No Sovereign can confide with Safety in a Man's Allegiance, who owns and | pays Homage to another Superior Power upon Earth. [93] I am sure, you understand me.

Hor. Too well.

Cleo. You may yoke a Knight with a Prebendary, and put them together into the same Stall; but Honour and the Christian Religion make no Couple, *nec in unâ sede morantur,*[1] any more than Majesty and Love. Look back on your own Conduct, and you shall find, that what you said of the Hand of God[2] was only a Shift, an Evasion, you made to serve your then present Purpose. On another Occasion,[3] you had said Yesterday yourself, that Providence superintends and governs every thing without Exception; you must therefore have known, that the Hand of God is as much to be seen in one common Accident in Life, and in one Misfortune, as it is in another, that is not more extraordinary. A severe Fit of Sickness may be less fatal, than a slight Skirmish between two hostile Parties; and among Men of Honour there is often as much Danger in a Quarrel about nothing, as there can be in the most violent Storm. It is impossible therefore that a Man of Sense, who has a solid Principle to go by, should in one sort of Danger think it Impiety not to shew Fear, and in another be ashamed to be thought to have any. Do but consider your own Inconsistency with yourself. At one time, to justify your fear of Death, when Pride is absent, you [94] become religious on a sudden, and your Consci-|ence then is so tenderly scrupulous, that to be undaunted under Chastisements from the Almighty, seems no less to you than waging War with Heaven; and at another, when Honour calls, you dare not only knowingly and wilfully break the most positive Command of God, but likewise to own; that the greatest Calamity, which, in your Opinion, can befall you, is, that the World should believe, or but suspect of you, that you had any Scruple about it. I defy the Wit of Man to carry the Affront to the Divine Majesty higher. Barely to deny his Being is not half so daring,

---

[1] Ovid, *Metamorphoses* ii. 846.   [2] See *Fable* ii. 87.
[3] See *Fable* ii. 54.

as it is to do this after you have own'd him to exist. No Atheism----

Hor. Hold, *Cleomenes*; I can no longer resist the Force of Truth, and I am resolved to be better acquainted with myself for the future. Let me become your Pupil.

Cleo. Don't banter me, *Horatio*; I don't pretend to instruct a Man of your Knowledge; but if you will take my Advice, search into yourself with Care and Boldness, and at your Leisure peruse the Book I recommended.

Hor. I promise you, I will, and shall be glad to accept of the handsome Present I refus'd : Pray send a Servant with it to Morrow-morning.

Cleo. It's a Trifle. You had better let one of yours go with me now ; I shall drive Home directly.

Hor. I understand your Scruple. It shall be as you please.

THE THIRD

DIALOGUE

BETWEEN

Horatio and *Cleomenes.*

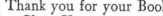

H O R A T I O.

Thank you for your Book.

Cleo. Your Acceptance of it I acknowledge as a great Favour.

Hor. I confess that once I thought no body could have per-suaded me to read it; but you managed me very skilfully, and nothing could have convinced me so well as the Instance of Duelling: The Argument *a majori ad minus* struck me, without your mentioning it. A Passion that can subdue the fear of Death may blind a Man's Understanding, and do almost every thing else.

Cleo. It is incredible, what strange, various, un-accountable and contradictory Forms we may be shaped into by a Passion, that is not to be gratify'd without being conceal'd, and never enjoy'd with [96] greater Ecstasy than | when we are most fully per-suaded, that it is well hid: and therefore there is no

Benevolence or good Nature, no amiable Quality, or social Virtue, that may not be counterfeited by it; and in short no Atchievment good or bad, that the human Body or Mind are capable of, which it may not seem to perform. As to its blinding and infatuating the Persons possess'd with it to a high Degree, there is no Doubt of it : for what Strength of Reason, I pray, what Judgment or Penetration has the greatest Genius, if he pretends to any Religion, to boast of; after he has own'd himself to have been more terrify'd by groundless Apprehensions, and an imaginary Evil from vain impotent Men, whom he has never injured, than he was alarm'd with the just Fears of a real Punishment from an all-wise and omnipotent God, whom he has highly offended? [a]

Hor. But your Friend makes no such Religious Reflections : he actually speaks in Favour of Duelling.

Cleo. What, because he would have the Laws against it as severe as possible, and no Body pardon'd without Exception that offends that way?

Hor. That indeed seems to discourage it ; but he shews the Necessity of keeping up that Custom, to polish and brighten Society in general.

Cleo. Don't you see the Irony there?

| *Hor.* No indeed : he plainly demonstrates the [97] Usefulness of it, gives as good Reasons as it is possible to invent, and shews how much Conversation would suffer if that Practice was abolished.

Cleo. Can you think a Man serious on a Subject, when he leaves it in the manner he does?

Hor. I don't remember that.

Cleo. Here is the Book : I'll look for the Passage —— Pray read this.

Hor. It is strange that a Nation should grudge to see perhaps half a dozen Men sacrificed in a Twelve-month to obtain so valuable a Blessing, as the Politeness of Manners, the Pleasure of Conversation, and the Happiness of Company in general, that is often so willing to expose,

[a] offended ?] offended.? 29

and *sometimes loses as many thousands in a few Hours,*
without knowing whether it will do any good or not.[1]
This indeed seems to be said with a Sneer : but in what
goes before he is very serious.

Cleo. He is so, when he says that the Practice of
Duelling, that is the keeping up of the Fashion of it,
contributes to the Politeness of Manners and Pleasure
of Conversation, and this is very true ; but that
Politeness itself, and that Pleasure, are the Things he
laughs at and exposes throughout his Book.

Hor. But who knows, what to make of a Man, who
recommends a thing very seriously in one Page, and
ridicules it in the next?

[98] | *Cleo.* It is his Opinion, that there is no solid
Principle to go by but the Christian Religion, and
that few embrace it with Sincerity : Always look upon
him in this View, and you'll never find him inconsistent with himself. Whenever at first sight he seems
to be so, look again, and upon nearer Enquiry you'll
find ; that he is only pointing at or labouring, to
detect the Inconsistency of others with the Principles
they pretend to.

Hor. He seems to have nothing less at Heart than
Religion.

Cleo. That's true, and if he had appear'd otherwise,
he would never have been read by the People whom
he design'd his Book for, the Modern Deists [2] and all
the *Beau Monde :* It is those he wants to come at.
To the first he sets forth the Origin and Insufficiency
of Virtue, and their own Insincerity in the Practice of
it : To the rest he shews the Folly of Vice and Pleasure,
the Vanity of Worldly Greatness, and the Hypocrisy
of all those Divines, who pretending to preach the
Gospel, give and take Allowances that are inconsistent
with, and quite contrary to the Precepts of it.

[1] *Fable* i. 220.
[2] Mandeville's own definition
of a deist runs : 'HE who believes,
in the common acceptation, that
there is a GOD, and that the world
is rul'd by providence, but has no
faith in any thing reveal'd to us,
is a deist . . .' (*Free Thoughts,* ed.
1729, p. 3). Cf. above, i. xxxix–
xli.

Hor. But this is not the Opinion the World has of the Book, it is commonly imagin'd, that it is wrote for the Encouragement of Vice, and to debauch the Nation.[1]

Cleo. Have you found any such thing in it?

Hor. To speak my Conscience, I must confess, I have not : Vice is expos'd in it, and | laugh'd at ; [99] but it ridicules War and martial Courage, as well as Honour and every thing else.

Cleo. Pardon me, Religion is ridiculed in no part of it.

Hor. But if it is a good Book, why then are so many of the Clergy so much against it as they are?

Cleo. For the Reason I have given you : My Friend has expos'd their Lives, but he has done it in such a Manner, that no Body can say he has wrong'd them, or treated them harshly. People are never more vex'd, than when the thing that offends them, is what they must not complain of : They give the Book an ill Name, because they are angry, but it is not their Interest, to tell you the true Reason why they are so. I could draw you a Parallel Case that would clear up this Matter, if you would have Patience to hear me, which, as you are a great Admirer of Opera's, I can hardly expect.

Hor. Any thing to be inform'd.

Cleo. I always had such an Aversion to Eunuchs, as no fine singing or acting of any of them has yet been able to conquer ; when I hear a Feminine Voice, I look for a Petticoat ; and I perfectly loath the sight of those Sexless Animals. Suppose that a Man with the same Dislike to them had Wit at will, and a Mind to lash that abominable piece of Luxury, by which Men are taught [a] in Cold Blood to spoil Males for Diversion, and out of Wantonness | to make waste of [100] their own Species. In order to this, we'll say, he takes a Handle from the Operation itself ; he describes and

[a] thought *29, 33* ; taught *29 Errata*

[1] See the Grand Jury's presentment, *Fable* i. 385.

treats it in the most inoffensive Manner ; then shews
the narrow Bounds of human Knowledge, and the
small Assistance we can have, either from Dissection
or Philosophy, or any part of the Mathematicks to
trace and penetrate into the Cause *a Priori*, why this
destroying of Manhood should have that surprizing
Effect upon the Voice ; and afterwards demonstrates,
how sure we are *a Posteriori*, that it has a considerable
Influence, not only on the *Pharinx*, the Glands and
Muscles of the Throat, but likewise the Windpipe,
and the Lungs themselves, and in short on the whole
Mass of Blood, and consequently all the Juices of the
Body, and every Fibre in it. He might say likewise,
that no Honey, no Preparations of Sugar, Raisins, or
Sperma Ceti; no Emulsions, Lozenges or other
Medicines, cooling or balsamick ; no Bleeding, no
Temperance or Choice in Eatables ; no Abstinence
from Women, from Wine, and every thing that is hot,
sharp or spirituous, were of that Efficacy to preserve,
sweeten and strengthen the Voice ; he might insist
upon it, that nothing could do this so effectually as
Castration. For a Blind to his main Scope, and to
amuse his Readers, he might speak of this Practice,
as made use of for other Purposes ; that it had been
[101] inflicted as a solemn Punishment for analogous | Crimes;
that others had voluntarily submitted to it, to preserve
Health and prolong Life ; whilst the *Romans* by
Cæsar's Testimony thought it more cruel than Death,
morte gravius.[1] How it had been used sometimes by
way of Revenge ; and then say something in Pity of
poor *Abelard* ; at other times for Precaution ; and
then relate the Story of *Combabus* and *Stratonice :*[2]
with Scraps from *Martial*, *Juvenal*, and other Poets,
he might interlard it, and from a thousand pleasant

[1] See Pseudo-Caesar, *Bellum Alexandrinum* 70.
[2] See Pseudo-Lucian, *De Syria Dea* 17 sqq. The story is found also in Bayle's *Dictionary* (art. ' Combabus '), from which Mandeville may well have derived it.

Things that have been said on the Subject, he might pick out the most diverting to embellish the whole. His Design being Satyr, he would blame our Fondness for these *Castrati*, and ridicule the Age in which a brave *English* Nobleman and a General Officer serves his Country at the hazard of his Life, a whole Twelvemonth, for less Pay than an *Italian* No-man of Scoundrel Extraction receives for now and then singing a Song in great Safety, during only the Winter Season.[1] He would laugh at the Caresses and the Court that are made to them by Persons of the first Quality, who prostitute their Familiarity with these most abject Wretches, and misplace the Honour and Civilities only due to their Equals, on Things that are no part of the Creation, and owe their Being to the Surgeon ; Animals so contemptible, that they can curse their Maker without Ingratitude. If he should call this Book, *the Eunuch is the Man* ; as soon | as I heard the [102] Title, before I saw the Book, I should understand by it, that Eunuchs were now esteem'd, that they were in Fashion and in the Publick Favour, and considering that a Eunuch is in Reality not a Man, I should think it was a Banter upon Eunuchs, or a Satyr against those, who had a greater Value for them than they deserv'd. But if the Gentlemen of the Academy of Musick,[2] displeas'd at the Freedom they were treated with, should take it ill, that a paultry Scribler should

---

[1] The rage for these *castrati* is epitomized in a lady's remark about one of them, ' One God, one Farinelli ' (cf. Hogarth's *Rake's Progress* and John Hawkins, *General History of . . . Music,* ed. 1776, v. 321, *n*.). Farinelli managed to make £5,000 a year. On returning to Italy, he built a villa with his savings, and called it the ' English Folly '.

[2] The Royal Academy of Music was founded in 1720 for the maintenance of Italian opera. The composers Buononcini and Ariosti came to England under its auspices ; and works by them and Händel, Scarlatti, and others were performed with magnificent casts at the King's Theatre in the Haymarket. Personal animosities and financial ill success caused the lapse of the society in 1728 after a last performance 1 June (C. Burney, *General History of Music,* ed. 1776–89, iv. 337).

interfere and pretend to censure their Diversion, as well they might; if they should be very angry, and study to do him a Mischief, and accordingly, not having much to say in Behalf of Eunuchs, not touch upon any thing the Author had said against their Pleasure, but represent him to the World as an Advocate for Castration, and endeavour to draw the publick *Odium* upon him by Quotations taken from him proper for that purpose, it would not be difficult to raise a Clamour against the Author, or find a grand Jury to present his Book.

Hor. The *Simile* holds very well as to the Injustice of the Accusation, and the Insincerity of the Complaint; but is it as true, that Luxury will render a Nation flourishing, and that private Vices are publick Benefits, as that Castration preserves and strengthens the Voice?

Cleo. With the Restrictions my Friend requires, [103] I believe it is, and the Cases are ex-|actly alike. Nothing is more effectual to preserve, mend and strengthen a fine Voice in Youth than Castration: The Question is not, whether this is true, but whether it is eligible; whether a fine Voice is an Equivalent for the Loss, and whether a Man would prefer the Satisfaction of singing, and the Advantages that may accrue from it, to the Comforts of Marriage, and the Pleasure of Posterity, of which Enjoyments it destroys the Possibility. In like manner, my Friend demonstrates in the first place, that the National Happiness which the Generality wish and pray for, is Wealth and Power, Glory and Worldly Greatness; to live in Ease, in Affluence and Splendour at Home, and to be fear'd, courted and esteem'd Abroad: In the second, that such a Felicity is not to be attain'd to without Avarice, Profuseness, Pride, Envy, Ambition and other Vices. The latter being made evident beyond Contradiction, the Question is not, whether it is true, but whether this Happiness is worth having at the Rate it is only to be had at, and whether any thing ought to be wish'd for, which a Nation cannot enjoy, unless the Generality of them are vicious. This he offers to the Consideration of *Christians*, and Men who pretend to have renounc'd the World with all the Pomp and Vanity of it.

Hor. How does it appear that the Author addresses himself to such?

| *Cleo.* From his writing it in *English*, and publish- [104] ing it in *London*. But have you read it through yet?

Hor. Twice : There are many things I like very well, but I am not pleas'd with the whole.

Cleo. What Objections have you against it?

Hor. It has diminish'd the Pleasure I had in reading a much better Book. Lord *Shaftsbury* is my favourite Author : I can take Delight in Enthusiasm ᵃ ; ¹ but the Charms of it cease as soon as I am told what it is I enjoy. Since we are such odd Creatures, why should we not make the most of it?

Cleo. I thought you was resolv'd to be better acquainted with yourself, and to search into your Heart with Care and Boldness.

Hor. That's a cruel Thing ; I tried it three times since I saw you last, till it put me into a Sweat, and then I was forced to leave off.²

Cleo. You should try again, and use yourself by

ᵃ Euthusiasm 29

¹ Besides the derogatory sense of 'fanaticism', which he, with the majority of his contemporaries, had given the word (e.g., in *Characteristics*, ed. Robertson, 1900, i. 37), Shaftesbury used 'enthusiasm' to denote love of the beauty of nature's harmony and, indeed, 'all sound love and admiration' ; and he declared all exalted endeavour a manifestation of this 'enthusiasm' (*Characteristics* ii. 129).

² The difficulty of self-knowledge was a commonplace, but a genuine psychological analysis of the causes for this such as is offered throughout the *Fable* was comparatively rare. Among writers who announced the pains of introspection somewhat in Mandeville's spirit were Nicole (*Essais de Morale*, Paris, 1714, iii. 3), Fontenelle (*Œuvres*, Paris, 1790, i. 278), Abbadie (*L'Art de se connoitre soy-meme*, The Hague, 1711, ii. 237), and J. F. Bernard (*Reflexions Morales*, Amsterdam, 1716, pref., sign. *3ᵛ.

Degrees to think abstractly, and then the Book will be a great Help to you.

Hor. To confound me it will: It makes a Jest of all Politeness and good Manners.

Cleo. Excuse me, Sir, it only tells us, what they are.

Hor. It tells us, that all good Manners consist in flattering the Pride of others, and concealing our own.[1] Is not that a horrid Thing?

Cleo. But is it not true?

[105] |*Hor.* As soon as I had read that Passage, it struck me: Down I laid the Book, and try'd in above fifty Instances, sometimes of Civility, and sometimes of ill Manners, whether it would answer or not, and I profess that it held good in every one.

Cleo. And so it would if you try'd till Doomsday.

Hor. But is not that provoking? I'd give a hundred Guineas with all my Heart, that I did not know it. I can't endure to see so much of my own Nakedness.

Cleo. I never met with such an open Enmity to Truth in a Man of Honour before.

Hor. You shall be as severe upon me as you please; what I say is fact. But since I am got in so far, I must go through with it now: There are fifty Things that I want to be inform'd about.

Cleo. Name them, pray; if I can be of any Service to you, I shall reckon it as a great Honour; I am perfectly well acquainted with the Author's Sentiments.

Hor. I have twenty Questions to ask about Pride, and I don't know where to begin. There's another thing I don't understand; which is, that there can be no Virtue without Self-denial.

Cleo. This was the Opinion of all the Ancients, Lord *Shaftsbury* was the first that maintain'd the contrary.[2]

[106] |*Hor.* But are there no Persons in the World that are good by Choice?

[1] Cf., for instance, *Fable* i. 76–9.　　[2] Cf. *Fable* i. 323.

Cleo. Yes, but then they are directed in that Choice by Reason and Experience, and not by Nature, I mean, not by untaught Nature : But there is an Ambiguity in the Word Good which I would avoid ; let us stick to that of Virtuous, and then I affirm, that no Action is such, which does not suppose and point at some Conquest or other, some Victory great or small over untaught Nature ; otherwise the Epithet is improper.

Hor. But if by the help of a careful Education this Victory is obtain'd, when we are young, may we not be virtuous afterwards voluntarily and with Pleasure?

Cleo. Yes, if it really was obtain'd : But how shall we be sure of this, and what Reason have we to believe that it ever was? When it is evident, that from our Infancy, instead of endeavouring to conquer our Appetites, we have always been taught, and have taken pains ourselves to conceal them ; and we are conscious within, that, whatever Alterations have been made in our Manners and our Circumstances, the Passions themselves always remain'd? The System, that Virtue requires no Self-denial, is, as my Friend has justly observ'd, a vast Inlet to Hypocrisy : [1] It will on all Accounts furnish Men with a more obvious Handle, and a greater Opportunity of counterfeiting the Love of Society and Regard to the | Publick, than [107] ever they could have receiv'd from the contrary Doctrine, *viz.* That there is no Merit but in the Conquest of the Passions, nor any Virtue without apparent Self-denial. Let us ask those, that have had long Experience and are well skill'd in human Affairs, whether they have found the Generality of Men such impartial Judges of themselves, as never to think better of their own Worth than it deserv'd, or so candid in the Acknowledgment of their hidden Faults and Slips, they could never be convinc'd of, that there is no fear, they should ever stifle or deny them. Where is the Man, that has at no time covered his Failings, and

[1] Cf. *Fable* i. 331.

skreened himself with false Appearances, or never pretended to act from Principles of Social Virtue, and his Regard to others, when he knew in his Heart, that his greatest Care had been to oblige himself? The best of us sometimes receive Applause, without undeceiving those who give it ; tho' at the same time we are conscious that the Actions, for which we suffer ourselves to be thought well of, are the Result of a powerful Frailty in our Nature, that has often been prejudicial to us, and which we have wish'd a thousand times in vain, that we could have conquer'd. The same Motives may produce very different Actions, as Men differ in Temper and Circumstances. Persons of an easy Fortune may appear virtuous, from the same [108] turn of Mind that would shew their | Frailty if they were poor. If we would know the World, we must look into it. You take no Delight in the Occurrences of low Life ; but if we always remain among Persons of Quality, and extend our Enquiries no farther, the Transactions there will not furnish us with a sufficient Knowledge of every thing that belongs to our Nature. There are among the midling People Men of low Circumstances tolerably [a] well educated, that set out with the same Stock of Virtues and Vices, and tho' equally qualify'd, meet with very different Success ; visibly owing to the Difference in their Temper. Let us take a View of two Persons bred to the same Business, that have nothing but their Parts, and the World before them, launching out with the same Helps and Disadvantages : Let there be no difference between them, but in their Temper ; the one active, and the other indolent. The latter will never get an Estate by his own Industry, tho' his Profession be gainful, and himself Master of it. Chance, or some uncommon Accident, may be the Occasion of great Alterations in him, but without that he will hardly ever raise himself to Mediocrity.[b] Unless his Pride affects him in

[a] tolleraby *29*   [b] Medicority *29*

an extraordinary Manner, he must always be poor,
and nothing but some Share of Vanity can hinder
him from being despicably so. If he be a Man of
Sense he'll be strictly honest, and a midling Stock of
Covetousness will never di-|vert him from it. In the [109]
active stirring Man, that is easily reconcil'd to the
Bustle of the World, we shall discover quite different
Symptoms under the same Circumstances ; and a very
little Avarice will egg him on to pursue his Aim with
Eagerness and Assiduity : Small Scruples are no
Opposition to him ; where Sincerity [a] will not serve
he uses Artifice ; and in compassing his Ends the
greatest use he will make of his good Sense will be, to
preserve as much as is possible the Appearance of
Honesty ; when his Interest obliges him to deviate
from it. To get Wealth, or even a Livelihood by
Arts and Sciences, it is not sufficient to understand [b]
them : It is a Duty incumbent on all Men, who have
their Maintenance to seek, to make known and forward
themselves in the World, as far as Decency allows of,
without bragging of themselves, or doing Prejudice to
others : Here the indolent Man is very deficient and
wanting to himself ; but seldom will own his Fault,
and often blames the Publick for not making use of
him, and encouraging that Merit, which they never
were acquainted with, and himself perhaps took
Pleasure to conceal : and tho' you convince him of
his Error, and that he has neglected even the most
warrantable Methods of solliciting Employment, he'll
endeavour to colour over his Frailty with the Appearance of Virtue ; and what is altogether owing to his
too easy Temper, and an | excessive Fondness for the [110]
Calmness of his Mind, he'll ascribe to his Modesty
and the great Aversion he has to Impudence and Boast-
ing. The Man of a contrary Temper trusts not to
his Merit only, or the setting it off to the best Advantage ; he takes Pains to heighten it in the Opinion of
others, and make his Abilities seem greater than he

[a] Sincerity] Sincerity, *29*   [b] underderstand *29*

knows them to be. As it is counted Folly for a Man to proclaim his own Excellencies, and speak magnificently of himself, so his chief Business is to seek Acquaintance, and make Friends on purpose to do it for him : All other Passions he sacrifices to his Ambition, he laughs at Disappointments, is inured to Refusals, and no Repulse dismays him : This renders the whole Man always flexible to his Interest ; he can defraud his Body of Necessaries, and allow no Tranquility to his Mind ; and counterfeit, if it will serve his Turn, Temperance, Chastity, Compassion, and Piety itself without one Grain of Virtue or Religion ; his Endeavours to advance his Fortune *per fas & nefas* are always restless, and have no Bounds ; but where he is oblig'd to act openly, and has reason to fear the Censure of the World. It is very diverting to see, how, in the different Persons I speak of, natural Temper will warp and model the very Passions to its own Biass : Pride, for Example, has not the same, but almost a quite contrary Effect on the one to what [111] it has on the other : The | stirring active Man it makes in love with Finery, Cloaths, Furniture, Equipages, Building, and every thing his Superiors enjoy : the other it renders sullen, and perhaps morose ; and if he has Wit prone to Satyr, tho' he be otherwise a good-natur'd Man. Self-love in every Individual ever bestirs itself in soothing and flattering the darling Inclination ; always turning from us the dismal Side of the Prospect ; and the indolent Man in such Circumstances, finding nothing pleasing without, turns his View inward upon himself ; and there looking on every Thing with great Indulgence, admires and takes delight in his own Parts, whether natural or acquired : hence he is easily induced to despise all others, who have not the same good Qualifications, especially the Powerful and Wealthy, whom yet he never hates or envies with any Violence ; because that would ruffle his Temper. All things that are difficult he looks upon as impossible, which makes him despair of meliorating his Condition; and as he has no Possessions, and his Gettings will but just maintain him in a low Station of Life, so his good Sense, if he would enjoy so much as the Appearance of Happiness, must necessarily put him upon two Things; to be frugal, and pretend to have no value for Riches; for by neglecting either, he must be blown up, and his Frailty unavoidably discover'd.

| *Hor.* I am pleas'd with your Observations, and the [112] Knowledge you display of Mankind; but pray is not the Frugality you now speak of ª a Virtue?

Cleo. I think not.

Hor. Where there is but a small Income, Frugality is built upon Reason; and in this Case there is an apparent Self-denial, without which an indolent Man that has no value for Money cannot be frugal; and when we see indolent Men, that have no regard for Wealth, reduced to Beggery, as it often happens, it is most commonly for want of this Virtue.

Cleo. I told you before, that the indolent Man, setting out as he did, would be poor; and that nothing but some Share of Vanity could hinder him from being despicably so. A strong fear of Shame may gain so much upon the Indolence of a Man of Sense, that he'll bestir himself sufficiently to escape Contempt; but it will hardly make him do any more; therefore he embraces Frugality, as being instrumental and assisting to him in procuring his *summum bonum*, the darling Quiet of his easy Mind; whereas the active Man with the same Share of Vanity would do any Thing rather than submit to the same Frugality, unless his Avarice forc'd him to it. Frugality is no Virtue, when it is imposed upon us by any of the Passions, and the Contempt of Riches is seldom sincere. I have known Men of plentiful Estates, that on Ac-|count of Posterity, or [113] other warrantable Views of employing their Money,

ª of *add. 30*

were saving and more penurious, than they would
have been if their Wealth had been greater : but
I never yet found a frugal Man, without Avarice or
Necessity. And again, there are innumerable Spend-
thrifts, lavish and extravagant to a high degree, who
seem not to have the least Regard to Money, whilst
they have any to fling away : but these Wretches are
the least capable of bearing Poverty of any, and the
Money once gone, hourly discover, how uneasy, im-
patient and miserable they are without it. But what
several in all ages have made pretence to, the Contempt
of Riches, is more scarce than is commonly imagin'd.
To see a Man of a very good Estate, in Health and
Strength of Body and Mind, one that has no reason
to complain of the World or Fortune, actually despise
both, and embrace a voluntary Poverty for a laudable
Purpose, is a great Rarity. I know but one in all
Antiquity, to whom all this may be applied with
strictness of Truth.

Hor. Who is that, pray?

Cleo. Anaxagoras of *Clazomene* in *Ionia :* he was
very rich, of noble Extraction, and admired for his
great Capacity : he divided and gave away his Estate
among his Relations, and refus'd to meddle with the
Administration of Publick Affairs that was offer'd
him, for no other Reason, than that he might have
[114] more | Leisure for Contemplation on the Works of
Nature, and the Study of Philosophy.

Hor. To me it seems to be more difficult to be
virtuous without Money, than with : it is senseless for
a Man to be poor, when he can help it, and if I saw
any body chuse it when he might as lawfully be rich,
I would think him to be distracted.

Cleo. But you would not think him so, if you saw
him sell his Estate and give the Money to the Poor :
you know where that was required.

Hor. It is not required of us.

Cleo. Perhaps not : but what say you to renouncing

the World, and the Solemn Promise we have made of it?

Hor. In a literal Sense that is impossible, unless we go out of it; and therefore I don't think, that to renounce the World signifies any more, than not to comply with the vicious, wicked part of it.

Cleo. I did not expect a more rigid Construction from you, tho' it is certain, that Wealth and Power are great Snares, and strong Impediments to all christian Virtue : but the generality of Mankind, that have any thing to lose, are of your Opinion ; and let us bar Saints and Madmen, we shall find everywhere, that those who pretend to undervalue, and are always haranguing against, Wealth, are generally poor and indolent. But who can blame | them? They act in [115] their own defence : no body that could help it would ever be laugh'd at ; for it must be own'd, that of all the Hardships of Poverty it is that, which is the most intollerable.

> *Nil habet infelix Paupertas durius in se,*
> *Quam quod ridiculos homines faciat.---* [1]

In the very Satisfaction that is enjoy'd by those, who excel in, or are possess'd of things valuable, there is interwoven a spice of Contempt for others, that are destitute of them, which nothing keeps from publick View, but a Mixture of Pity and good Manners. Whoever denies this let them consult within, and examine whether it is not the same with Happiness, as what *Seneca* says of the Reverse, *nemo est miser nisi comparatus.*[2] The Contempt and Ridicule I speak of is, without doubt, what all Men of Sense and Education endeavour to avoid, or disappoint. Now look upon the Behaviour of the two contrary Tempers before us, and mind how differently they set about this Task, every one suitably to his own Inclination. The Man of Action, you see, leaves no Stone unturn'd

---

[1] Cf. Juvenal, *Satires* iii. 152.   [2] Seneca, *Troades* 1033.

to acquire *quod oportet habere :* but this is impossible
for the indolent ; he can't stir ; his Idol ties him
down hand and foot ; and therefore the easiest, and
indeed the only thing he has left, is to quarrel with
the World, and find out Arguments to depreciate
what others value themselves upon.

[116] | *Hor.* I now plainly see, how Pride and good Sense
must put an indolent Man, that is poor, upon Frugality;
and likewise the Reason, why they will make him affect
to be content, and seem pleased with his low Condition : for if he won't be frugal, Want and Misery
are at the Door ; and if he shews any Fondness for
Riches, or a more ample way of living, he loses the
only Plea he has for his darling Frailty, and immediately
he'll be ask'd, why he don't exert himself in a better
Manner, and he'll be continually told of the Opportunities he neglects.

Cleo. It is evident then, that the true Reasons, why
Men speak against things, are not always writ upon
their Foreheads.

Hor. But after all this quiet easy Temper, this
Indolence you talk of, is it ª not what in plain *English*
we call Laziness?

Cleo. Not at all ; it implies no Sloth, or Aversion
to Labour : an indolent Man may be very diligent,
tho' he cannot be industrious : he will take up with
things below him, if they come in his way ; he'll
work in a Garret, or any where else, remote from
Publick View, with Patience and Assiduity, but he
knows not, how to sollicit and teaze others to employ
him, or demand his due of a shuffling, designing Master,
that is either difficult of Access, or tenacious of his
Money : if he be a Man of Letters he'll study hard
for a Livelihood, but generally parts with his Labours
[117] at a dis-|advantage, and will knowingly sell them at
an Under-rate to an obscure Man, who offers to
purchase, rather than bear the Insults of haughty

ª is it] it is *33*

Booksellers, and be plagued with the sordid Language of the Trade. An indolent Man may by chance meet with a Person of Quality, that takes a fancy to him; but he will never get a Patron by his own Address; neither will he ever be the better for it, when he has one, further than the unask'd-for Bounty, and down-right Generosity of his Benefactor make him. As he speaks for himself with Reluctancy, and is always afraid of asking Favours, so for Benefits receiv'd he shews no other Gratitude, than what the natural Emotions of his Heart suggest to him. The striving, active Man studies all the winning Ways to ingratiate himself, and hunts after Patrons with Design and Sagacity: whilst they are beneficial to him, he affects a perpetual Sense of Thankfulness; but all his Acknow-ledgments of past Obligations he turns into Sollicita-tions for fresh Favours: his Complaisance may be engaging, and his Flattery ingenious, but the Heart is untouch'd: he has neither Leisure nor the Power to love his Benefactors: the eldest he has he will always sacrifize to a new one, and he has no other Esteem for the Fortune, the Greatness, or the Credit of a Patron, than as he can make them subservient either to raise or maintain his own. From all this, and a little Attention on human | Affairs, we may [118] easily perceive, in the first place, that the Man of Action, and an enterprizing Temper, in following the Dictates of his Nature, must meet with more Rubs and Obstacles infinitely, than the indolent, and a Multitude of strong Temptations to deviate from the Rules of strict Virtue, which hardly ever come in the other's way; that in many Circumstances he'll be forc'd to commit such Actions, for which, all his Skill and Prudence notwithstanding, he will by some body or other deservedly be thought to be an ill Man; and that to end with a tolerable Reputation, after a long Course of Life, he must have had a great deal of good Fortune as well as Cunning. Secondly, that

the indolent Man may indulge his Inclinations, and be
as sensual as his Circumstances will let him, with little
Offence or Disturbance to his Neighbour ; that the
excessive Value he sets upon the Tranquility of his
Mind, and the grand Aversion he has to part with it,
must prove a strong Curb to every Passion, that comes
uppermost ; none of which by this means can ever
affect him in any high degree, and consequently that
the Corruption of his Heart remaining, he may with
little Art and no great Trouble acquire many amiable
Qualities, that shall have all the Appearances of Social
Virtues, whilst nothing extraordinary befalls him. As
to his Contempt of the World, the indolent Man
[119] perhaps will scorn to make his court | and cringe to
a haughty Favourite, that will browbeat him at first ;
but he'll run with Joy to a rich Nobleman, that he is
sure will receive him with Kindness and Humanity :
With him he'll partake without Reluctancy of all the
elegant Comforts of Life, that are offer'd, the most
expensive not excepted : Would you try him further,
confer upon him Honour and Wealth in Abundance.
If this Change in his Fortune stirs up no Vice, that
lay dormant before, as it may by rendring him either
covetous or extravagant, he will soon conform himself to the fashionable World : Perhaps he'll be a kind
Master, an indulgent Father, a benevolent Neighbour,
munificent to Merit that pleases him, a Patron to
Virtue, and a Well-wisher to his Country ; but for
the rest he'll take all the Pleasure he is capable of
enjoying ; stifle no Passion he can calmly gratify, and
in the midst of a luxurious Plenty laugh heartily at
Frugality and the Contempt of Riches and Greatness,
he profess'd in his Poverty ; and chearfully own the
Futility of those Pretences.

Hor. I am convinc'd that in the Opinion of Virtue's
requiring Self-denial there is greater Certainty, and
Hypocrites have less Latitude than in the contrary
System.

Cleo. Whoever follows his own Inclinations, be they never so kind, beneficent, or humane, never quarrels with any Vice, but what is clashing with his Tempera-ment and Na-|ture ; whereas those, who act from [120] a Principle of Virtue take always Reason for their Guide, and combat without Exception every Passion, that hinders them from their Duty ! The indolent Man will never deny a just Debt ; but, if it be large, he will not give himself the trouble, which, poor as he is, he might and ought to take to discharge it, or at least satisfy his Creditor ; unless he is often dunn'd or threaten'd to be sued for it. He will not be a litigious Neighbour, nor make Mischief among his Acquaintance ; but he will never serve his Friend, or his Country, at the Expence of his Quiet. He will not be rapacious, oppress the Poor, or commit vile Actions for Lucre ; but then he will never exert himself and be at the pains, another would take on all Opportunities, to maintain a large Family, make Pro-vision for Children, and promote his Kindred and Relations ; and his darling Frailty will incapacitate him from doing a thousand things for the Benefit of the Society, which with the same Parts and Oppor-tunities he might and would have done, had he been of another Temper.

Hor. Your Observations are very curious, and, as far as I can judge from what I have seen myself, very just and natural.

Cleo. Every body knows that there is no Virtue so often counterfeited as Charity, and yet so little Regard have the generality of Men to Truth ; that, how gross and barefaced soever | the Deceit is in Pretences of [121] this Nature, the World never fails of being angry with, and hating those who detect or take notice of the Fraud. It is possible, that, with blind Fortune on his side, a mean Shopkeeper, by driving a Trade prejudicial to his Country on the one hand, and grind-ing on all Occasions the Face of the Poor on the other, may accumulate great Wealth; which in process of time, by continual scraping and sordid saving, may be raised into an exorbitant and [a] unheard-of Estate for a Tradesman. Should such a one, when old and decrepit, lay out the greatest part of his immense Riches in the building, or largely endowing an Hospital, and I was thoroughly acquainted with his Temper and Manners, I could have no Opinion of his Virtue, tho' he parted with the Money, whilst he was yet alive; more especially, if I was assured, that in his Last Will he had been highly unjust, and had not only left unrewarded several, whom he had great Obligations to, but likewise defrauded others, to whom in his Conscience, he knew that he was and would die actually indebted. I desire you to tell me, what Name, knowing all I have said to be true, you would give to this extraordinary Gift, this mighty Donation![1]

Hor. I am of Opinion, that when an Action of our Neighbour may admit of different Constructions, it is our Duty to side with and embrace the most favourable.

[122] | *Cleo.* The most favourable Construction,[b] with all my Heart: But what is that to the Purpose, when all the straining in the World cannot make it a good one? I don't mean the thing it self, but the Principle it came from, the inward Motive of the Mind, that put him upon performing it, for it is that which in a free Agent I call the Action: And therefore call it what you please, and judge as charitably of it as you can, what can you say of it?

Hor. He might have had several Motives, which I don't pretend to determine; but it is an admirable Contrivance of being extremely beneficial to all Posterity in this Land, a noble Provision, that will perpetually relieve, and be an unspeakable Comfort to a multitude of miserable People; and it is not only a prodigious, but likewise a well-concerted Bounty,

[a] an *30*   [b] Constructions *30*

[1] Cf. *Fable* i. 261-5.

that was wanting, and for which in after-Ages thousands of poor Wretches will have reason to bless his Memory, when every Body else shall have neglected them.

Cleo. All that I have nothing against; and if you would add more, I shan't dispute it with you, as long as you confine your Praises to the Endowment it self, and the Benefit the Publick is like to receive from it. But to ascribe it to, or suggest that it was derived from a Publick Spirit in the Man, a generous Sense of Humanity and Benevolence to his Kind, a liberal Heart, or any other Virtue or good Quality, which it is manifest the Donor was | an utter Stranger to, is [123] the utmost Absurdity in an intelligent Creature, and can proceed from no other Cause than either a wilful wronging of his own Understanding, or else Ignorance and Folly.

Hor. I am persuaded, that many Actions are put off for virtuous, that are not so; and that according as Men differ in natural Temper, and turn of Mind, so they are differently influenc'd by the same Passions : I believe likewise that these last are born with us, and belong to our Nature, that some of them are in us, or at least the Seeds of them, before we perceive them : But since they are in every Individual, how comes it that Pride is more predominant in some than it is in others? For from what you have demonstrated already it must follow, that one Person is more affected with the Passion within than another ; I mean, that one Man has actually a greater Share of Pride than another, as well among the artful that are dextrous in concealing it, as among the Ill-bred that openly shew it.

Cleo. What belongs to our Nature, all Men may justly be said to have actually or virtually in them at their Birth ; and whatever is not born with us, either the thing it self, or that which afterwards produces it, cannot be said to belong to our Nature : But as we differ in our Faces and Stature, so we do in other things, that are more remote from Sight : But all

[124] these depend only upon the different Frame, | the inward Formation of either the Solids or the Fluids ; and there are Vices of Complexion, that are peculiar, some to the Pale and Phlegmatick, others to the Sanguine and Cholerick:[1] Some are more lustful, others more fearful in their Nature, than the Generality are : But I believe of Man, generally speaking, what my Friend has observ'd of other Creatures, that the best of the Kind, I mean the best form'd within, such as have the finest natural Parts, are born with the greatest Aptitude to be proud ; but I am convinced, that the difference there is in Men, as to the Degrees of their Pride, is more owing to Circumstances and Education, than any thing in their Formation. Where Passions are most gratify'd and least controul'd, the Indulgence makes them stronger ; whereas those Persons, that have been kept under, and whose Thoughts have never been at Liberty to rove beyond the first Necessaries of Life ; such as have not been suffer'd or had no Opportunity to gratify this Passion, have commonly the least share of it. But whatever Portion of Pride a Man may feel in his Heart, the quicker his Parts are, the better his Understanding is, and the more Experience he has, the more plainly he'll perceive the Aversion which all Men have to those, that discover their Pride : And the sooner Persons are imbued with good Manners, the sooner they grow perfect in concealing that Passion. Men [125] of mean Birth | and Education, that have been kept in great Subjection, and consequently had no great Opportunities to exert their Pride, if ever they come to command others, have a sort of Revenge mix'd with that Passion, which makes it often very mischievous, especially in Places where they have no Superiours or Equals, before whom they are obliged to conceal the odious Passion.

Hor. Do you think Women have more Pride from Nature than Men?

[1] Cf. above, i. 144, *n.* 1.

Cleo. I believe not : but they have a great deal more from Education.

Hor. I don't see the Reason : for among the better sort, the Sons, especially the eldest, have as many Ornaments and fine Things given them from their Infancy to stir up their Pride, as the Daughters.

Cleo. But among People equally well-educated, the Ladies have more Flattery bestow'd upon them, than the Gentlemen, and it begins sooner.

Hor. But why should Pride be more encouraged in Women than in Men?

Cleo. For the same reason, that it is encouraged in Soldiers, more than it is in other People ; to encrease their Fear of Shame, which makes them always mindful of their Honour.

Hor. But to keep both to their respective Duties, why must a Lady have more Pride than a Gentleman?

| *Cleo.* Because the Lady is in the greatest Danger [126] of straying from it : She has a Passion within, that may begin to affect her at twelve or thirteen, and perhaps sooner, and she has all the Temptations of the Men to withstand besides : She has all the Artillery of our Sex to fear ; a Seducer of uncommon Address and resistless Charms may court her to what Nature prompts and sollicites her to do ; he may add great Promises, actual Bribes ; this may be done in the Dark, and when no Body is by to dissuade her. Gentlemen very seldom have occasion to shew their Courage before they are six [a] or seventeen Years of Age, and rarely so soon : They are not put to the Tryal, till by conversing with Men of Honour, they are confirm'd in their Pride : In the Affair of a Quarrel they have their Friends to consult, and these are so many Witnesses of their Behaviour, that awe them to their Duty, and in a manner oblige them to obey the Laws of Honour : All these things conspire to encrease their Fear of Shame ; and if they can but render that

---

[a] sixteen *30*

Superiour to the Fear of Death, their Business is done ; they have no Pleasure to expect from breaking the Rules of Honour, nor any crafty Tempter that sollicites them to be Cowards. That Pride, which is the Cause of Honour in Men, only regards their Courage ; and if they can but appear to be brave, [127] and will but follow the fashionable Rules of | manly Honour, they may indulge all other Appetites, and brag of Incontinence without Reproach : The Pride likewise that produces Honour in Women has no other Object than their Chastity ; and whilst they keep that Jewel entire, they can apprehend no Shame : Tenderness and Delicacy are a Compliment to them ; and there is no Fear of Danger so ridiculous, but they may own it with Ostentation. But notwithstanding the Weakness of their Frame, and the Softness in which Women are generally educated, if overcome by chance they have sinn'd in private, what real Hazards will they not run, what Torments will they not stifle, and what Crimes will they not commit, to hide from the World that Frailty, which they were taught to be most ashamed of !

Hor. It is certain, that we seldom hear of Publick Prostitutes, and such as have lost their Shame, that they murder their Infants, tho' they are otherwise the most abandon'd Wretches : I took notice of this in *the Fable of the Bees*,[1] and it is very remarkable.

Cleo. It contains a plain Demonstration, that the same Passion may produce either a palpable Good or a palpable Evil in the same Person, according as Self-love and his present Circumstances shall direct ; and that the same Fear of Shame, that makes Men sometimes appear so highly virtuous, may at others oblige [128] them to commit the most heinous Crimes : | That therefore Honour is not founded upon any Principle, either of real Virtue or true Religion, must be obvious to all that will but mind what sort of People they are,

[1] *Fable* i. 75–6.

that are the greatest Votaries of that Idol, and the different Duties it requires in the two Sexes : In the first place the Worshippers of Honour are the vain and voluptuous, the strict Observers of Modes and Fashions, that take Delight in Pomp and Luxury, and enjoy as much of the World as they are able : In the second, the Word itself, I mean the Sense of it, is so whimsical, and there is such a prodigious difference in the Signification of it, according as the Attribute is differently applied, either to a Man or to a Woman, that neither of them shall forfeit their Honour ; tho' each should be guilty, and openly boast of what would be the other's greatest Shame.

Hor. I am sorry that I cannot charge you with Injustice ; but it is very strange ; that to encourage and industriously encrease Pride in a refined Education, should be the most proper means to make Men sollicitous in concealing the outward Appearances of it.

Cleo. Yet nothing is more true : but where Pride is so much indulged, and yet to be so carefully kept from all human View, as it is in Persons of Honour of both Sexes, it would be impossible for mortal Strength to endure the Restraint, if Men could not be taught to play the Passion against itself, and were not | allow'd to change the natural Home-bred Symptoms of it, for artificial Foreign ones. [129]

Hor. By playing the Passion against itself, I know you mean placing a secret Pride in concealing the barefac'd Signs of it : But I don't rightly understand what you mean by changing the Symptoms of it.

Cleo. When a Man exults in his Pride, and gives a loose to that Passion, the Marks of it are as visible in his Countenance, his Mien, his Gate, and Behaviour, as they are in a prancing Horse, or a strutting Turkey-cock. These are all very odious ; every one feeling the same Principle within, which is the Cause of those Symptoms ; and, Man being endued with Speech, all the open Expressions, the same Passion can suggest to him, must for the same Reason be equally displeasing : These therefore have in all Societies been strictly prohibited by common Consent, in the very Infancy of good Manners ; and Men have been taught, in the room of them, to substitute other Symptoms, equally evident with the first, but less offensive, and more beneficial to others.

Hor. Which are they?

Cleo. Fine Cloaths, and other Ornaments about them, the Cleanliness observed about their Persons, the Submission that is required of Servants, costly Equipages, Furniture, Buildings, Titles of Honour, and every thing that Men can acquire to make them-[130]selves esteem'd | by others, without discovering any of the Symptoms that are forbid : upon a Satiety of enjoying these, they are allow'd likewise to have the Vapours and be whimsical, tho' otherwise they are known to be in Health and of good Sense.

Hor. But since the Pride of others is displeasing to us in every Shape, and these latter Symptoms, you say, are equally evident with the first, what is got by the Change?

Cleo. A great deal : When Pride is designedly express'd in Looks and Gestures, either in a wild or tame Man, it is known by all human Creatures that see it ; it is the same, when vented in Words, by every Body that understands the Language they are spoken in. These are Marks and Tokens, that are all the World over the same : no Body shews them, but to have them seen and understood, and few Persons ever display them without designing that Offence to others, which they never fail to give ; whereas the other Symptoms may be denied to be what they are ; and many Pretences, that they are deriv'd from other Motives, may be made for them, which the same good Manners teach us never to refute, nor easily to disbelieve : In the very Excuses, that are made for them there is a Condescension, that satisfies and pleases us.

In those that are altogether destitute of the Opportunities to display the Symptoms of Pride that are allow'd of, the least Portion of that Passion is a trou-|blesome, tho' often an unknown Guest; for [131] in them it is easily turn'd into Envy and Malice, and on the least Provocation it sallies out in those Disguises, and is often the Cause of Cruelty, and there never was a Mischief committed by Mobs or Multitudes, which this Passion had not a hand in : Whereas the more room Men have to vent and gratify the Passion in the warrantable ways, the more easy it is for them to stifle the odious Part of Pride, and seem to be wholly free from it.

Hor. I see very well, that real Virtue requires a Conquest over untaught Nature, and that the Christian Religion demands a still stricter Self-denial : It likewise is evident, that to make ourselves acceptable to an omniscient Power, nothing is more necessary than Sincerity, and that the Heart should be pure ; but setting aside sacred Matters and a future State, don't you think, that this Complaisance and easy Construction of one another's Actions do a great deal of Good upon Earth ; and don't you believe, that good Manners and Politeness make Men more happy, and their Lives more comfortable in this World, than any thing else could make them without those Arts?

Cleo. If you will set aside what ought to employ our first Care, and be our greatest Concern ; and Men will have no Value for that Felicity and Peace of Mind, which can only arise from a Consciousness of being good, | it is certain [a], that in a great Nation, and [132] among a flourishing People, whose highest Wishes seem to be Ease and Luxury, the upper Part could not, without those Arts, enjoy so much of the World as that can afford ; and that none stand more in need of them than the voluptuous Men of Parts, that will joyn worldly Prudence to Sensuality, and make it their chief Study to refine upon Pleasure.

[a] certan 29

Hor. When I had the Honour of your Company at my House, you said, that no body knew, when or where, nor in what King's or Emperor's Reign the Laws of Honour were enacted ; pray, can you inform me, when or which Way, what we call good Manners or Politeness, came into the World? What Moralist or Politician was it, that could teach Men to be proud of hiding their Pride?

Cleo. The restless Industry of Man to supply his Wants, and his constant Endeavours to meliorate his Condition upon Earth, have produced and brought to Perfection many useful Arts and Sciences, of which the Beginnings are of uncertain Æra's, and to which we can assign no other Causes, than human Sagacity in general, and the joynt Labour of many Ages, in which Men have always employ'd themselves in studying and contriving Ways and Means to sooth their [133] various Appetites, and make the best of their | Infirmities. Whence had we the first Rudiments of Architecture ; how came Sculpture and Painting to be what they have been these many hundred Years ; and who taught every Nation the respective Languages they speak now? When I have a Mind to dive into the Origin of any Maxim or political Invention, for the Use of Society in general, I don't trouble my Head with enquiring after the Time or Country, in which it was first heard of, nor what others have wrote or said about it ; but I go directly to the Fountain Head, human Nature itself, and look for the Frailty or Defect in Man, that is remedy'd or supply'd ᵃ by that Invention : When Things are very obscure, I sometimes make Use of Conjectures to find my Way.

Hor. Do you argue, or pretend to prove any thing from those Conjectures?

Cleo. No ; I never reason but from the plain Observations which every body may make on Man, the *Phænomena* that appear in the lesser World.

Hor. You have, without doubt, thought on this

ᵃ suplpy'd 29

DIALOGUE. 129

Subject before now; would you communicate to me some of your Guesses?

Cleo. With abundance of Pleasure.

Hor. You'll give me Leave, now and then, when Things are not clear to me, to put in a Word for Information's Sake.

Cleo. I desire you would : You will oblige me with it. That Self-love was given to all | Animals, at least, [134] the most perfect, for Self-Preservation, is not disputed ; but as no Creature can love what it dislikes, it is necessary, moreover, that every one should have a real liking to its own Being, superior to what they have to any other. I am of Opinion, begging Pardon for the Novelty, that if this Liking was not always permanent, the Love, which all Creatures have for themselves, could not be so unalterable as we see it is.

Hor. What Reason have you to suppose this Liking, which Creatures have for themselves, to be distinct from Self-love ; since the one plainly comprehends the other? [1]

[1] It is very possible that the distinction Mandeville here makes was the result of certain criticisms by Bishop Butler which appeared in 1726 between the publication of the two parts of the *Fable*. Butler very ably attacked Mandeville's theory that all conduct is motivated by self-love (without, however, referring specifically to Mandeville) : 'The principle we call self-love never seeks any thing external for the sake of the thing, but only as a means of happiness or good : particular affections rest in the external things themselves. . . . *Such affections are not to be resolved into self-love.* . . . And if, because every particular affection is a man's own, and the pleasure arising from its gratification his own pleasure . . . such particular affection must be called self-love ; according to this way of speaking, no creature whatever can possibly act but merely from self-love ; and every action and every affection whatever is to be resolved up into this one principle. But then this is not the language of mankind : or if it were, we should want words to express the difference, between the principle of an action, proceeding from cool consideration that it will be to my own advantage ; and an action, suppose of revenge, or of friendship, by which a man runs upon certain ruin, to do evil or good to another. It is manifest the principles of these

2522.2   I

Cleo. I will endeavour to explain myself better. I fancy, that, to encrease the Care in Creatures to preserve themselves, Nature has given them an Instinct, by which every Individual values itself above its real Worth; this in us, I mean, in Man, seems to be accompany'd with a Diffidence, arising from a Consciousness, or at least an Apprehension, that we do over-value ourselves : It is this that makes us so fond of the Approbation, Liking and Assent of others; because they strengthen and confirm us in the good Opinion we have of ourselves. The Reasons why this Self-liking, give me Leave to call it so, is not plainly to be seen in all Animals that are of the same Degree of Perfection, are many. Some want Ornaments, and consequently the Means to express it ; others are too [135] stupid | and listless : It is to be consider'd likewise, that Creatures, which are always in the same Circumstances, and meet with little Variation in their Way of Living, have neither Opportunity nor Temptation to shew it ; that the more Mettle and Liveliness Creatures have, the more visible this Liking is ; and that in those of the same kind, the greater Spirit they are of, and the more they excel in the Perfections of

actions are totally different, and so want different words to be distinguished by : all that they agree in is, that they both proceed from, and are done to gratify an inclination in a man's self' (*Works*, ed. Gladstone, 1896, ii. 187–8, in Sermon 11 ; cf. also Sermon 1). Mandeville's distinction between self-love and self-liking offers an answer of a kind to all of Butler's objections. First, it offers the new word demanded by Butler of those who, like Mandeville, call all emotions selfish because they are ' a man's own '. Secondly, it affords an explanation of how self-love may dictate an action to one's own disadvantage (see below, ii. 135–6). And, finally, it can be used to show how the emotions and affections which Butler discriminated from self-love derive their motive force from self-regard (see below, ii. 132–6). That Mandeville's argument here fits so pat to Butler's objections (and they were not common) raises at least the supposition that Mandeville had them in mind.

In his *Origin of Honour* (1732), pp. 3–13, Mandeville again explains his distinction between self-love and self-liking.

their Species, the fonder they are of shewing it : In most Birds it is evident, especially in those that have extraordinary Finery to display : In a Horse it is more conspicuous than in any other irrational Creature : It is most apparent in the swiftest, the strongest, the most healthy and vigorous ; and may be encreas'd in that Animal by additional Ornaments, and the Presence of Man, whom he knows, to clean, take Care of, and delight in him. It is not improbable, that this great Liking, which Creatures have for their own Individuals, is the Principle on which the Love to their Species is built : Cows and Sheep, too dull and liveless ᵃ to make any Demonstration of this Liking, yet herd and feed together, each with his own Species ; because no others are so like themselves : By this they seem to know likewise, that they have the same Interest, and the same Enemies ; Cows have often been seen to joyn in a common Defence against Wolves : Birds of a Feather flock together ; and I dare say, that | the [136] Screech Owl likes her own Note, better than that of the Nightingale.

Hor. Montain seems to have been somewhat of your Opinion, when he fancy'd ; that if Brutes were to paint the Deity, they would all draw him of their own Species.¹ But what you call Self-liking is evidently Pride.

Cleo. I believe it is, or at least the Cause of it.² I believe, moreover, that many Creatures shew this Liking, when, for want of understanding them, we

ᵃ lifeless 33

¹ Montaigne's opnion derives from Xenophanes, as Montaigne himself mentions ; see *Essais* (Bordeaux, 1906–20) ii. 269–70.
² Resuming this same discussion in his *Origin of Honour* (1732), Mandeville adds :
'*Cleo.* . . . When this Self-liking is excessive, and so openly shewn as to give Offense to others, I know very well it is counted a Vice and call'd Pride : But when it is kept out of Sight . . . it has no Name, tho' Men act from that and from no other Principle.
'*Hor.* When what you call Self-liking, that just Esteem which Men have naturally for themselves, is moderate, and spurs

don't perceive it : When a Cat washes her Face, and a Dog licks himself clean, they adorn themselves as much as it is in their Power. Man himself in a savage State, feeding on Nuts and Acorns, and destitute of all outward Ornaments, would have infinitely less Temptation, as well as Opportunity, of shewing this Liking of himself, than he has when civiliz'd ; yet if a hundred Males of the first, all equally free, were together, within less than half an Hour, this Liking in question, though their Bellies were full, would appear in the Desire of Superiority, that would be shewn among them ; and the most vigorous, either in Strength or Understanding, or both, would be the first, that would display it : If, as suppos'd, they were all untaught, this would breed Contention, and there would certainly be War before there could be any Agreement among them ; unless one of them had [137] some one | or more visible Excellencies above the rest. I said *Males*, and *their Bellies full* ; because if they had Women among them, or wanted Food, their Quarrel might begin on another Account.

Hor. This is thinking abstractly indeed : But do you think, that two or three hundred single Savages, Men and Women, that never had been under any Subjection, and were above twenty Years of Age, could ever establish a Society, and be united into one Body ; if, without being acquainted with one another, they should meet by chance?

Cleo. No more, I believe, than so many Horses : But Societies never were made that Way. It is possible, that several Families of Savages might unite, and the Heads of them agree upon some sort of Government or other, for their common Good : But among them it is certain likewise ; that, though Superiority was

them on to good Actions, it is very laudable, and is call'd the Love of Praise or a Desire of the Applause of others. Why can't you take up with either of these Names? ' *Cleo.* Because I would not confound the Effect with the Cause ' (pp. 3-4).

tollerably well settled, and every Male had Females
enough, Strength and Prowess in this unciviliz'd State
would be infinitely more valued than Understanding;
I mean in the Men; for the Women will always prize
themselves for what they see the Men admire in them :
Hence it would follow, that the Women would value
themselves, and envy one another for being handsome; and that the ugly and deform'd, and all those
that were least favour'd by Nature, would be the first,
that would fly to Art and additio-|nal Ornaments : [138]
Seeing that this made them more agreeable to the Men,
it would soon be follow'd by the rest, and in a little
Time they would strive to outdo one another, as much
as their Circumstances would allow of; and it is
possible, that a Woman with a very handsome Nose
might envy her Neighbour with a much worse, for
having a Ring thro' it.

Hor. You take great Delight in dwelling on the
Behaviour of Savages; What relation has this to
Politeness?

Cleo. The Seeds of it are lodg'd in this Self-love
and Self-liking, which I have spoke of; as will soon
appear, if we consider what would be the Consequence
of them in the Affair of Self-preservation, and a
Creature endued with Understanding, Speech, and
Risibility. Self-love would first make it scrape together
every thing it wanted for Sustenance, provide against
the Injuries of the Air, and do every thing to make
itself and young Ones secure. Self-liking would make
it seek for Opportunities, by Gestures, Looks, and
Sounds, to display the Value it has for itself, superiour
to what it has for others; an untaught Man would
desire every body that came near him, to agree with
him in the Opinion of his superiour Worth, and be
angry, as far as his Fear would let him, with all that
should refuse it : He would be highly delighted with,
and love every body, whom he thought to | have [139]
a good Opinion of him, especially those, that by

Words or Gestures should own it to his Face : Whenever he met with any visible Marks in others of Inferiority to himself, he would laugh,[1] and do the same at their Misfortunes, as far as his own Pity would give him Leave, and he would insult every body that would let him.

Hor. This Self-liking, you say, was given to Creatures for Self-preservation ; I should think rather that it is hurtful to Men, because it must make them odious to one another ; and I cannot see what Benefit they can receive from it, either in a savage or a civiliz'd State : Is there any Instance of its doing any good?

Cleo. I wonder to hear you ask that Question. Have you forgot the many Virtues which I have demonstrated [a], may be counterfeited to gain Applause, and the good Qualities a Man of Sense in great Fortune may acquire, by the sole Help and Instigation of his Pride?

Hor. I beg your Pardon ; yet what you say only regards Man in the Society, and after he has been perfectly well educated : What Advantage is it to him as a single Creature? Self-love I can plainly see induces him to labour for his Maintenance and Safety, and makes him fond of every thing which he imagines to tend to his Preservation : But what good does the Self-liking to him?

[140] | *Cleo.* If I should tell you, that the inward Pleasure and Satisfaction a Man receives from the Gratification of that Passion, is a Cordial that contributes to his Health, you would laugh at me, and think it far fetch'd.

Hor. Perhaps not ; but I would set against it the many sharp Vexations and heart-breaking Sorrows, that Men suffer on the score of this Passion, from Disgraces, Disappointments, and other Misfortunes,

---

[a] demonstated 29

[1] This is an adaptation of Hobbes's theory of laughter, for a discussion of which see below, ii. 156, *n*. 1.

which, I believe, have sent Millions to their Graves, much sooner, than they would have gone, if their Pride had less affected them.

Cleo. I have nothing against what you say : But this is no Proof, that the Passion itself was not given to Man for Self-preservation ; and it only lays open to us the Precariousness of sublunary Happiness, and the wretched Condition of Mortals. There is nothing created that is always a Blessing ; the Rain and Sunshine themselves, to which all earthly Comforts are owing, have been the Causes of innumerable Calamities. All Animals of Prey, and thousand others, hunt after Food with the Hazard of their Lives, and the greater Part of them perish in their Pursuits after Sustenance. Plenty itself is not less fatal to some, than Want is to others ; and of our own Species, every opulent Nation has had great Numbers, that in full Safety from all other Dangers, have destroy'd themselves by Excesses of Eating and Drinking : Yet nothing is more | certain, than that Hunger and Thirst [141] were given to Creatures to make them sollicitous after, and crave those Necessaries, without which it would be impossible for them to subsist.

Hor. Still I can see no Advantage accruing from this Self-liking to Man, consider'd as a single Creature, which can induce me to believe, that Nature should have given it us for Self-preservation. What you have alledg'd is obscure ; can you name a Benefit every individual Person receives from that Principle within him, that is manifest, and clearly to be understood?

Cleo. Since it has been in Disgrace, and every body disowns the Passion, it seldom is seen in its proper Colours, and disguises itself in a thousand different Shapes : we are often affected with it, when we have not the least Suspicion of it ; but it seems to be that, which continually furnishes us with that Relish we have for Life, even when it is not worth having. Whilst Men are pleas'd, Self-liking has every Moment a considerable Share, tho' unknown, in procuring the

Satisfaction they enjoy. It is so necessary to the Well-being of those that have been used to indulge it; that they can taste no Pleasure without it, and such is the deference, and the submissive Veneration they pay to it, that they are deaf to the loudest Calls of Nature, and will rebuke the strongest Appetites [142] that should pretend to | be gratify'd at the Expence of that Passion. It doubles our Happiness in Prosperity, and buoys us up against the Frowns of adverse Fortune. It is the Mother of Hopes, and the End as well as the Foundation of our best Wishes : It is the strongest Armour against Despair, and as long as we can like any ways our Situation, either in regard to present Circumstances, or the Prospect before us, we take care of ourselves ; and no Man can resolve upon Suicide, whilst Self-liking lasts : but as soon as that is over, all our Hopes are extinct, and we can form no Wishes but for the Dissolution of our Frame : till at last our Being becomes so intollerable to us, that Self-love prompts us to make an end of it, and seek Refuge in Death.

Hor. You mean Self-hatred; for you have said your self, that a Creature cannot love what it dislikes.

Cleo. If you turn the Prospect, you are in the right ; but this only proves to us what I have often hinted at, that Man is made up of Contrarieties ; otherwise nothing seems to be more certain, than that whoever kills himself by Choice, must do it to avoid something, which he dreads more than that Death which he chuses. Therefore, how absurd soever a Person's Reasoning may be, there is in all Suicide a palpable Intention of Kindness to ones self.

[143] | *Hor.* I must own that your Observations are entertaining. I am very well pleas'd with your Discourse, and I see an agreeable Glimmering of Probability that runs through it ; but you have said nothing that comes up to a half Proof on the Side of your Conjecture, if it be seriously consider'd.

Cleo. I told you before that I would lay no Stress upon, nor draw any Conclusions from it : But whatever Nature's Design was in bestowing this Self-liking on Creatures ; and, whether it has been given to other Animals besides ourselves or not, it is certain, that in our own Species every individual Person likes himself better than he does any other.

Hor. It may be so, generally speaking ; but that it is not universally true, I can assure you, from my own Experience ; for I have often wish'd myself to be Count *Theodati*, whom you knew at *Rome*.

Cleo. He was a very fine Person indeed, and extremely well accomplish'd ; and therefore you wish'd to be such another, which is all you could mean. *Celia* has a very handsome Face, fine Eyes, fine Teeth ; but she has red Hair, and is ill made ; therefore she wishes for *Chloe*'s Hair and *Bellinda*'s Shape ; but she would still remain *Celia*.

Hor. But I wish'd, that I might have been that Person, that very *Theodati*.

Cleo. That is impossible.[1]

| *Hor.* What, is it impossible to wish it ! [144]

Cleo. Yes, to wish it ; unless you wish'd for Annihilation at the same time. It is that *Self* we wish well to ; and therefore we cannot wish for any Change in ourselves, but with a Proviso, that that τò self, that Part of us, that wishes, should still remain : for take away that Consciousness you had of yourself, whilst you was wishing, and tell me pray, what part of you it is, that could be the better for the Alteration you wish'd for ?

Hor. I believe you are in the right. No Man can wish but to enjoy something, which no Part of that same Man could do, if he was entirely another.

Cleo. That *He* itself, the Person wishing, must be destroy'd before the Change could be entire.

---

[1] Cf. Abbadie, *L'Art de se connoitre soy-meme* (The Hague, 1711) ii. 436 : '. . . c'en est une extrememem difficile de vouloir serieusement être autre qu'on n'est.'

Hor. But when shall we come to the Origin of
Politeness?

Cleo. We are at it now, and we need not look for it
any further than in the Self-liking, which I have
demonstrated every individual Man to be possess'd of.
Do but consider these two things; first, that from
the Nature of that Passion it must follow, that all
untaught Men will ever be hateful to one another in
Conversation, where neither Interest nor Superiority
are consider'd : for if of two Equals one only values
himself more by half, than he does the other ; tho'
that other should value the first equally with himself,
[145] they would | both be dissatisfied, if their Thoughts
were known to each other : but if both valued themselves more by half, than they did each other, the
difference between them would still be greater, and
a Declaration of their Sentiments would render them
both insufferable to each other ; which among unciviliz'd Men would happen every Moment, because
without a Mixture of Art and Trouble, the outward
Symptoms of that Passion are not to be stifled. The
second Thing I would have you consider, is, the Effect
which in all human Probability this Inconveniency,
arising from self-liking, would have upon Creatures,
endued with a great Share of Understanding, that are
fond of their Ease to the last degree, and as industrious
to procure it. These two Things, I say, do but duely
weigh, and you shall find, that the Disturbance and
Uneasiness, that must be caused by Self-liking, whatever Strugglings and unsuccessful Tryals to remedy
them might precede, must necessarily produce at
long run, what we call good Manners and Politeness.

Hor. I understand you, I believe. Everybody, in
this undisciplin'd State, being affected with the high
Value he has for himself, and displaying the most
natural Symptoms, which you have describ'd, they
would all be offended at the barefac'd Pride of their
Neighbours : and it is impossible, that this should

continue long among rational Creatures, but the
repeated | Experience of the Uneasiness they received [146]
from such Behaviour, would make some of them reflect
on the Cause of it ; which, in tract of time, would make
them find out, that their own barefaced Pride must be
as offensive to others, as that of others is to themselves.

Cleo. What you say is certainly the Philosophical
Reason of the Alterations, that are made in the
Behaviour of Men, by their being civiliz'd : but all
this is done without reflection, and Men by degrees,
and great Length of Time, fall as it were into these
Things spontaneously.

Hor. How is that possible, when it must cost them
Trouble, and there is a palpable Self-denial to be seen
in the Restraint they put upon themselves?

Cleo. In the Pursuit of Self-preservation, Men
discover a restless Endeavour to make themselves easy,
which insensibly teaches them to avoid Mischief on
all Emergencies : and when human Creatures [a] once
submit to Government, and are used to live under
the Restraint of Laws, it is incredible, how many
useful Cautions, Shifts, and Stratagems, they will
learn to practise by Experience and Imitation, from
conversing together ; without being aware of the
natural Causes, that oblige them to act as they do,
viz. The Passions within, that, unknown to themselves, govern their Will and direct their Behaviour.

| *Hor.* You'll make Men as mere Machines as *Cartes* [147]
does Brutes.

Cleo. I have no such Design : [1] but I am of Opinion,

[a] Crearures 29

[1] Cleomenes' reply is an eva-
sion. Although Mandeville believed that animals feel and think
(see *Fable* i. 181 and ii. 166), he
none the less held the doctrine
that they are automata. What
he repudiated is only the Carte-
sian aspect of the doctrine ;

Mandeville differed from Descartes in contending, first, that
the automata have feeling, and,
secondly, that men as well as
animals are machines. What
Mandeville held was not,
' Brutes are like men ; therefore
they are not automata ', but

that Men find out the use of their Limbs by Instinct, as much as Brutes do the use of theirs ; and that, without knowing any thing of Geometry or Arithmetick, even Children may learn to perform Actions, that seem to bespeak great Skill in Mechanicks, and a considerable Depth of Thought and Ingenuity in the Contrivance besides.

Hor. What Actions are they, which you judge this from?

Cleo. The advantageous Postures, which they'll chuse in resisting Force, in pulling, pushing, or otherwise removing Weight; from their Slight and Dexterity in throwing Stones, and other *Projectils*, and the stupendious Cunning made use of in Leaping.

Hor. What stupendious Cunning, I pray?

Cleo. When Men would leap or jump a great way, you know, they take a Run before they throw themselves off the Ground. It is certain, that by this Means they jump further, and with greater Force than they could do otherwise : the Reason likewise is very plain. The Body partakes of, and is moved by, two Motions ; and the Velocity, imprest upon it by leaping, must be added to so much, as it retained of the Velocity it was put into by running : Whereas the Body of a Person who takes his Leap, as he is [148] standing | still, has no other Motion, than what is

' Brutes are like men ; consequently these animal automata feel '. In thus refusing to separate man from the animals (see above, i. 44, *n.* 2) and declaring the equal automatism of man and brute, Mandeville was in accord with Gassendi : ' Fiunt omnia, *inquis* [Descartes], in brutis impulsione cæcâ spirituum cæterorumque organorum : eo modo, quo in horologio machinâve aliâ peraguntur motus. Sed . . . *asserine*

potest vel actiones sensuum, vel quas passiones animæ dicunt, exseri in brutis cæco impetu, non exseri verò in nobis ? ' (Gassendi, in Descartes, *Œuvres*, Paris, 1897–1910, vii. 269–70, in *Meditationes de Prima Philosophia, Objectiones Quintæ* ii. 7).

For a remarkable discussion of human automatism, anticipating modern psychology, see Mandeville's *Free Thoughts* (1729), pp. 96–100.

receiv'd from the muscular Strength exerted in the Act of Leaping. See a thousand Boys, as well as Men, jump, and they'll all make use of this Stratagem : but you won't find one of them, that does it knowingly for that Reason. What I have said of this Stratagem made use of in Leaping, I desire you would apply to the Doctrine of good Manners, which is taught and practised by Millions, who never thought on the Origin of Politeness, or so much as knew the real Benefit it is of to Society. The most crafty and designing will every where be the first, that for Interest-sake will learn to conceal this Passion of Pride, and in a little time no body will shew the least Symptom of it, whilst he is asking Favours, or stands in need of Help.

Hor. That rational Creatures should do all this, without thinking or knowing what they were about, is inconceivable. Bodily Motion is one thing, and the Exercise of the Understanding is another ; and therefore agreeable Postures, a graceful Mein, an easy Carriage, and a genteel outward Behaviour, in general, may be learn'd and contracted perhaps without much Thought ; but good Manners are to be observ'd every where, in speaking, writing, and ordering Actions to be perform'd by others.

Cleo. To Men who never turn'd their Thoughts that way, it certainly is almost in-|conceivable to [149] what prodigious Height, from next to nothing, some Arts may be and have been raised by human Industry and Application, by the uninterrupted Labour, and joint Experience of many Ages, tho' none but Men of ordinary Capacity should ever be employ'd in them. What a Noble as well as Beautiful, what a glorious Machine is a First-Rate Man of War, when she is under Sail, well rigg'd, and well mann'd ! As in Bulk and Weight it is vastly superior to any other moveable Body of human Invention, so there is no other that has an equal Variety of differently surprizing

Contrivances to boast of. There are many Sets of Hands in the Nation, that, not wanting proper Materials, would be able in less than half a Year to produce, fit out, and navigate a First-Rate : yet it is certain, that this Task would be impracticable, if it was not divided and subdivided into a great Variety of different Labours ; [1] and it is as certain, that none of these Labours require any other, than working Men of ordinary Capacities.

Hor. What would you infer from this?

Cleo. That we often ascribe to the Excellency of Man's Genius, and the Depth of his Penetration, what is in Reality owing to length of Time, and the Experience of many Generations, all of them very little differing from one another in natural Parts and Sagacity. And to know what it must have cost to [150] bring that Art of making Ships [2] for | different Pur-

---

[1] Allusions to division of labour were common throughout antiquity (see Trever, *History of Greek Economic Thought*, Chicago, 1916), but rarely accompanied with much consciousness of the economic implications of the fact. Plato's *Republic* 369–71 and 433 A and Xenophon's *Cyropaedia* VIII. ii. 5–6 are perhaps the most analytical. In modern times, Petty is the earliest author whom I have found to develop the consequences of this division fully enough to deserve being credited with what we now term the division of labour theory. In his *Political Arithmetick* (published 1690, but written and circulated in manuscript long before) there is a definite statement of the division of labour theory (*Economic Writings*, ed. Hull, 1899, i. 260) ; and an equally clear exposition will be found in his *Another Essay in Political Arithmetick*, 1683

(*Economic Writings* ii. 473). The anonymous *Considerations on the East-India Trade*, 1701, contains a still more definite statement of the theory, together with a very able elaboration of it (see *Select Collection of Early English Tracts on Commerce*, ed. Political Economy Club, 1856, pp. 591–3). Compare, also, the slighter anticipation by Locke (*Of Civil Government* II. v. 43) and by Simon Clement (*Discourse of the General Notions of Money*, ed. 1695, ch. I).—For the influence of Mandeville in giving currency to the division of labour theory see above, i. cxxxiv–cxxxv.

[2] The anonymous author of *Considerations on the East-India Trade*, who had anticipated Mandeville in 1701 in the exposition of the division of labour theory, also used ship-construction to illustrate his point (see *Select Collection of Early English Tracts*

poses, to the Perfection in which it is now, we are only to consider in the first place; that many considerable Improvements have been made in it within these fifty years and less; and in the Second, that the Inhabitants of this Island did build and make use of Ships eighteen hundred Years ago, and that from that time to this, they have never been without.

Hor. Which all together make a strong Proof of the slow Progress that Art has made, to be what it is.

Cleo. The Chevalier *Reneau* has wrote a Book, in which he shews the Mechanism of Sailing, and accounts mathematically for every thing that belongs to the working and steering of a Ship.[1] I am persuaded, that neither the first Inventors of Ships and Sailing, or those, who have made Improvements since in any Part of them, ever dream'd of those Reasons, any more than now the rudest and most illiterate of the vulgar do, when they are made Sailors, which Time and Practice will do in Spight of their Teeth. We have thousands of them, that were first haul'd on board and detain'd against their Wills, and yet in less than three Years time knew every Rope and every Pully in the Ship, and without the least Scrap of Mathematicks had learn'd the Management, as well as Use of them, much better than the greatest Mathematician could have done in all his Life-time, if he had ne-|ver been at [151] Sea. The Book I mention'd, among other curious Things, demonstrates what Angle the Rudder must make with the Keel, to render its Influence upon the Ship the most powerful. This has its Merit; but a Lad of Fifteen, who has serv'd a Year of his Time on board of a Hoy, knows every thing that is useful in this Demonstration practically. Seeing the Poop always answering the Motion of the Helm, he only minds the latter, without making the least Reflection

on *Commerce*, ed. Political Economy Club, 1856, p. 592).

[1] See the *Théorie de la Manœuvre des Vaisseaux*, Paris, 1689, by Bernard Renau d'Éliçagaray (1652–1719), a leading designer of vessels and naval commander.

on the Rudder, 'till in a Year or two more his Knowledge in sailing, and Capacity of steering his Vessel become so habitual to him, that he guides her as he does his own Body, by Instinct, tho' he is half a-sleep, or thinking on quite another thing.

Hor. If, as you said, and which I now believe to be true, the People, who first invented, and afterwards improved upon Ships and Sailing, never dream'd of those Reasons of Monsieur *Reneau,* it is impossible, that they should have acted from them, as Motives that induced them *a priori,* to put their Inventions and Improvements in practice, with Knowledge and Design; which, I suppose, is what you intended to prove.

Cleo. It is ; and I verily believe, not only that the raw Beginners, who made the first Essays in either Art, good Manners as well as Sailing, were ignorant of the true Cause, the real Foundation those Arts are [152] built upon in | Nature ; but likewise that, even now both Arts are brought to great Perfection, the greatest Part of those that are most expert, and daily making Improvements in them, know as little of the *Rationale* of them, as their Predecessors did at first : tho' I believe at the same time Monsieur *Reneau*'s Reasons to be very just, and yours as good as his ; that is, I believe, that there is as much Truth and Solidity in your accounting for the Origin of good Manners, as there is in his for the Management of Ships. They are very seldom the same Sort of People, those that invent Arts, and Improvements in them, and those that enquire into the Reason of Things : this latter is most commonly practis'd by such, as are idle and indolent, that are fond of Retirement, hate Business, and take delight in Speculation: whereas none succeed oftener in the first, than active, stirring, and laborious Men, such as will put their Hand to the Plough, try Experiments, and give all their Attention to what they are about.

Hor. It is commonly imagin'd, that speculative Men are best at Invention of all sorts.

Cleo. Yet it is a Mistake. Soap-boyling, Grain-

dying, and other Trades and Mysteries, are from mean
Beginnings brought to great Perfection; but the
many Improvements, that can be remembred to have
been made in them, have for the Generality been
owing to Persons, who either were brought up to, or
| had long practis'd and been conversant in those [153]
Trades, and not to great Proficients in Chymistry or
other Parts of Philosophy, whom one would naturally
expect those Things from. In some of these Arts,
especially Grain or Scarlet-dying, there are Processes
really astonishing; and by the Mixture of various
Ingredients, by Fire and Fermentation, several Operations are perform'd, which the most sagacious Naturalist
cannot account for by any System yet known ; a certain
Sign, that they were not invented by reasoning
a Priori. When once the Generality begin to conceal
the high Value they have for themselves, Men must
become more tolerable to one another. Now new
Improvements must be made every Day, 'till some of
them grow impudent enough, not only to deny the
high Value they have for themselves, but likewise to
pretend that they have greater Value for others, than
they have for themselves.[1] This will bring in Complaisance, and now Flattery will rush in upon them
like a Torrent. As soon as they are arrived at this
Pitch of Insincerity, they will find the Benefit of it,
and teach it their Children. The Passion of Shame
is so general, and so early discover'd in all human
Creatures, that no Nation can be so stupid, as to be
long without observing and making use of it accordingly. The same may be said of the Credulity of
Infants, which is very inviting to many good Pur-
poses. The Knowledge of | Parents is communicated [154]
to their Off-spring, and every one's Experience in Life,
being added to what he learn'd in his Youth, every
Generation after this must be better taught than the

---

[1] Cf. Esprit, *La Fausseté des
Vertus Humaines* (1678) i. 449:
'. . . il [man] a porté sa fausseté
au comble de l'impudence lors
qu'il a osé dire qu'il est desinte-
ressé. . . .'

preceding; by which Means, in two or three Centuries, good Manners must be brought to great Perfection.

Hor. When they are thus far advanced, it is easy to conceive the rest : For Improvements, I suppose, are made in good Manners, as they are in all other Arts and Sciences. But to commence from Savages, Men I believe would make but a small Progress in good Manners the first three hundred Years. The *Romans*, who had a much better Beginning, had been a Nation above six Centuries, and were almost Masters of the World, before they could be said to be a polite People. What I am most astonish'd at, and which I am now convinc'd of, is, that the Basis of all this Machinery is Pride. Another thing I wonder at is, that you chose to speak of a Nation, that enter'd upon good Manners before they had any Notions of Virtue or Religion, which I believe there never was in the World.

Cleo. Pardon me, *Horatio* ; I have no where insinuated that they had none, but I had no reason to mention them. In the first place, you ask'd my Opinion concerning the use of Politeness in this World, abstract from the Considerations of a future [155] State : Secondly, | the Art of good Manners has nothing to do with Virtue or Religion, tho' it seldom clashes with either. It is a Science that is ever built on the same steady Principle in our Nature, whatever the Age or the Climate may be, in which it is practis'd.

Hor. How can any thing be said not to clash with Virtue or Religion, that has nothing to do with either, and consequently disclaims both?

Cleo. This I confess seems to be a Paradox ; yet it is true. The Doctrine of good Manners teaches Men to speak well of all Virtues, but requires no more of them in any Age, or Country, than the outward Appearance of those in Fashion. And as to Sacred Matters, it is every where satisfied with a [a] seeming Conformity in outward Worship ; for all the Religions

[a] a *om. 30*

in the Universe are equally agreeable to good Manners, where they are national ; and pray what Opinion must we say a Teacher to be of, to whom all Opinions are probable alike ? All the Precepts of good Manners throughout the World have the same Tendency, and are no more than the various Methods of making ourselves acceptable to others, with as little Prejudice to ourselves as is possible : by which Artifice we assist one another in the Enjoyments of Life, and refining upon Pleasure ; and every individual Person is rendred more happy by it, in the Fruition of all the good Things he can purchase, than he | could have been [156] without such Behaviour. I mean happy, in the Sense of the Voluptuous. Let us look back on old *Greece*, the *Roman* Empire, or the great Eastern Nations, that flourish'd before them, and we shall find, that Luxury and Politeness ever grew up together, and were never enjoy'd asunder : that Comfort and Delight upon Earth have always employ'd the Wishes of the *Beau Monde* ; and that, as their chief Study and greatest Sollicitude, to outward Appearance, have ever been directed to obtain Happiness in this World, so what would become of them in the next seems, to the naked Eye, always to have been the least of their Concern.

Hor. I thank you for your Lecture : you have satisfied me in several Things, which I had intended to ask : but you have said some others, that I must have time to consider ; after which I am resolved to wait upon you again, for I begin to believe, that concerning the Knowledge of ourselves most Books are either very defective or very deceitful.

Cleo. There is not a more copious nor a more faithful Volume than human Nature, to those who will diligently peruse it ; and I sincerely believe, that I have discover'd nothing to you, which, if you had thought of it with Attention, you would not have found out yourself. But I shall never be better pleas'd with myself, than when I can contribute to any Entertainment you shall think diverting.

THE FOURTH

DIALOGUE

BETWEEN

Horatio and *Cleomenes.*

C L E O M E N E S.

 OUR Servant.

Hor. What say you now, *Cleomenes*; is [a] not this without
Ceremony?

Cleo. You are very obliging.

Hor. When they told me where
you was, I would suffer no body
to tell you, who it was that wanted
you, or to come up with me.

Cleo. This is friendly indeed!

Hor. You see what a Proficient I am : in a little
Time you'll teach me to lay aside all good Manners.

Cleo. You make a fine Tutor of me.

Hor. You'll pardon me, I know : This Study of
yours is a very pretty Place.

| *Cleo.* I like it, because the Sun never enters it.

Hor. A very pretty Room !

Cleo. Shall we sit down in it? it is the coolest Room
in the House.

[a] is] is it *29–33*

*H*or. With all my Heart.

Cleo. I was in Hopes to have seen you before now : you have taken a long time to consider.

Hor. Just eight Days.

Cleo. Have you thought on the Novelty I started?

Hor. I have, and think it not void of Probability ; for that there are no innate Idea's,[1] and Men come into the World without any Knowledge at all, I am convinc'd of, and therefore it is evident to me, that all Arts and Sciences must once have had a Beginning in some body's Brain, whatever Oblivion that may now be lost in. I have thought twenty times, since I saw you last, on the Origin of good Manners, and what a pleasant Scene it would be to a Man, who is tolerably well versed in the World, to see among a rude Nation those first Essays they made of concealing their Pride from one another.

Cleo. You see by this, that it is chiefly the Novelty of Things, that strikes, as well in begetting our Aversion, as in gaining our Approbation ; and that we may look upon many indifferently, when they come to be fami-|liar to us, tho' they were shocking when they [159] were new. You are now diverting yourself with a Truth, which eight Days ago you would have given an hundred Guineas not to have known.

Hor. I begin to believe there is nothing so absurd, that it would appear to us to be such, if we had been accustom'd to it very young.

Cleo. In a tolerable Education we are so industriously and so assiduously instructed, from our most early Infancy, in the Ceremonies of bowing, and pulling off Hats, and other Rules of Behaviour ; that even before we are Men we hardly look upon a mannerly Deportment as a Thing acquired, or think Conversation to

---

[1] In place of the theory of innate ideas Mandeville offers the counter-speculation (*Fable* i. 281) that we are born with ' the Seeds of every Passion . . . innate to us ', the trend of these passions determining the ideas which we shall form.

be a Science. Thousand things are call'd easy and natural in Postures and Motions, as well as Speaking and Writing, that have caus'd infinite Pains to others as well as ourselves, and which we know to be the Product of Art. What aukward Lumps have I known, which the Dancing-master has put Limbs to !

Hor. Yesterday morning, as I sate musing by myself, an Expression of yours, which I did not so much reflect upon at first, when I heard it, came in to my Head, and made me smile. Speaking of the Rudiments of good Manners in an infant Nation, when they once enter'd upon concealing their Pride, you said, that Improvements would be made every Day, *'till some of them grew impudent enough, not only* [160] *to deny the high Value they had for them-|selves, but likewise to pretend that they had greater Value for others, than they had for themselves.*[1]

Cleo. It is certain, that this every where must have been the Fore-runner of Flattery.

Hor. When you talk of Flattery and Impudence, what do you think of the first Man that had the Face to tell his Equal, that he was his humble Servant?

Cleo. If that had been a new Compliment, I should have wonder'd much more at the Simplicity of the proud Man that swallow'd, than I would have done at the Impudence of the Knave that made it.

Hor. It certainly once was new : Which pray do you believe more antient, pulling off the Hat, or saying, Your humble Servant?

Cleo. They are both of them *Gothick* and modern.

Hor. I believe pulling off the Hat was first, it being the Emblem of Liberty.

Cleo. I don't think so : for he who pull'd off his Hat the first time, could not have been understood ; if saying *Your Servant* had not been practis'd : and to shew Respect, a Man as well might have pull'd off one of his Shoes, as his Hat ; if saying, Your Servant,

[1] *Fable* ii. 145.

had not been an establish'd and well-known Compliment.

Hor. So he might, as you say, and had a better Authority for the first, than he could have for the latter.

| *Cleo.* And to this Day, taking off the Hat is a dumb [161] Shew of a known Civility in Words : Mind now the Power of Custom, and imbibed Notions. We both laugh at this *Gothick* Absurdity, and are well assured, that it must have had its Origin from the basest Flattery : yet neither of us, walking with our Hats on, could meet an Acquaintance with whom we are not very familiar, without shewing this Piece of Civility ; nay, it would be a Pain to us not to do it. But we have no Reason to think, that the Compliment of saying, *Your Servant,* began among Equals ; but rather that, Flatterers having given it to Princes, it grew afterwards more common : for all those Postures and Flexions of Body and Limbs, had in all Probability their Rise from the Adulation that was paid to Conquerors and Tyrants ; who, having every Body to fear, were always alarm'd at the least Shadow of Opposition, and never better pleas'd than with submissive and defenceless Postures : and you see, that they have all a Tendency that Way ; they promise Security, and are silent Endeavours to ease and rid them, not only of their Fears, but likewise every Suspicion of Harm approaching them : such as lying prostrate on our Faces, touching the Ground with our Heads, kneeling, bowing low, laying our Hands upon our Breasts, or holding them behind us, folding our Arms together, and all the Cringes that can be made to demonstrate, | that we neither indulge our Ease, nor stand upon [162] our Guard. These are evident Signs and convincing Proofs to a Superior, that we have a mean Opinion of ourselves in respect to him, that we are at his Mercy, and have no Thought to resist, much less to attack him ; and therefore it is highly probable, that saying,

Your Servant, and pulling off the Hat, were at first Demonstrations of Obedience to those that claim'd it.

Hor. Which in Tract of Time became more familiar, and were made use of reciprocally in the way of Civility.

Cleo. I believe so ; for as good Manners encrease, we see, that the highest Compliments are made common, and new ones to Superiors [a] invented instead of them.

Hor. So the Word *Grace*, which not long ago was a Title, that none but our Kings and Queens were honoured with, is devolved upon Archbishops and Dukes.

Cleo. It was the same with *Highness*, which is now given to the Children, and even the Grandchildren of Kings.

Hor. The Dignity, that is annex'd to the Significa-tion of the Word *Lord*, has been better preserv'd with us, than in most Countries : In *Spanish*, *Italian*, *High* and *Low-Dutch*, it is prostituted to almost every Body.

Cleo. It has had better Fate in *France* ; where likewise the Word *Sire* has lost nothing of its Majesty, [163] and is only used to the Monarch: | whereas with us it is a Compliment of Address, that may be made to a Cobler, as well as to a King.

Hor. Whatever Alterations may be made in the Sense of Words, by Time ; yet, as the World grows more polish'd, Flattery becomes less bare-faced, and the Design of it upon Man's Pride is better disguis'd than it was formerly. To praise a Man to his Face, was very common among the Ancients : Considering Humility to be a Virtue particularly required of Christians, I have often wonder'd how the Fathers of the Church could suffer those Acclamations and Applauses, that were made to them whilst they were preaching ; and which, tho' some of them spoke against them, many of them appear to have been extremely fond of.

[a] Supeririors 29

Cleo. Human Nature is always the same ; where Men exert themselves to the utmost, and take un-common Pains, that spend and waste the Spirits, those Applauses are very reviving : The Fathers, who spoke against them, spoke chiefly against the Abuse of them.

Hor. It must have been very odd to hear People bawling out, as often the greatest Part of an Audience did, *Sophos, divinitus, non potest melius, mirabiliter, acriter, ingeniose :* They told the Preachers likewise that they were Orthodox, and sometimes call'd them, *Apostolus decimus tertius.*

| *Cleo.* These Words at the end of a Period might [164] have pass'd, but the Repetitions of them were often so loud and so general ; and the Noise they made with their Hands and Feet, so disturbing in and out of Season ; that they could not hear a quarter of the Sermon : Yet several Fathers own'd that it was highly delightful, and soothing human Frailty.

Hor. The Behaviour at Churches is more decent, as it is now.

Cleo. Since Paganism has been quite extinct in the old Western World, the Zeal of Christians is much diminish'd from what it was, when they had many Opposers : [1] The want of Fervency had a great hand in abolishing that Fashion.

Hor. But whether it was the Fashion, or not, it must always have been shocking.

Cleo. Do you think, that the repeated Acclamations, the Clapping, Stamping, and the most extravagant Tokens of Applause, that are now used at our several Theatres, were ever shocking to a favorite Actor ; or that the Huzzah's of the Mob, or the hideous Shouts of Soldiers, were ever shocking to Persons of the highest Distinction, to whose Honour they were made?

Hor. I have known Princes that were very much tired with them.

[1] Cf. *Fable* i. 94.

Cleo. When they had too much of them; but never at first. In working a Machine, we ought to [165] have Regard to the Strength of its | Frame : Limited Creatures are not susceptible of infinite Delight ; therefore we see, that a Pleasure protracted beyond its due Bounds becomes a Pain : But where the Custom of the Country is not broken in upon, no Noise, that is palpably made in our Praise, and which we may hear with Decency, can ever be ungrateful, if it don't out-last a reasonable Time : But there is no Cordial so sovereign, that it may not become offensive, by being taken to excess.

Hor. And the sweeter and more delicious Liquors are, the sooner they become fulsom, and the less fit they are to sit by.

Cleo. Your Simile is not amiss ; and the same Acclamations that are ravishing to a Man at first, and perhaps continue to give him an unspeakable Delight for eight or nine Minutes, may become more moderately pleasing, indifferent, cloying, troublesome, and even so offensive as to create Pain, all in less than three Hours ; if they were to continue so long without Intermission.

Hor. There must be great Witchcraft in Sounds, that they should have such different Effects upon us, as we often see they have.

Cleo. The Pleasure we receive from Acclamations, is not in the Hearing ; but proceeds from the Opinion we form of the Cause, that produces those Sounds, the Approbation of others. At the Theatres all over *Italy* you have heard, that, when the whole [166] Audience | demands Silence and Attention, which there is an establish'd Mark of Benevolence and Applause, the Noise they make comes very near, and is hardly to be distinguish'd from, our Hissing, which with us is the plainest Token of Dislike and Contempt : And without doubt the Cat-calls to affront *Faustina* were far more agreeable to *Cozzoni*, than the most artful Sounds she ever heard from her Triumphant Rival.[1]

Hor. That was abominable !

Cleo. The *Turks* shew their Respects to their Sovereigns by a profound Silence, which is strictly kept throughout the *Seraglio*, and still more religiously observed the nearer you come to the *Sultan*'s Apartment.

Hor. This latter is certainly the politer way of gratifying one's Pride.

Cleo. All that depends upon Mode and Custom.

Hor. But the Offerings, that are made to a Man's Pride in Silence, may be enjoy'd without the loss of his Hearing, which the other cannot.

Cleo. That is a Trifle, in the Gratification of that Passion : We never enjoy higher Pleasure, from the Appetite we would indulge, than when we feel nothing from any other.

Hor. But Silence expresses greater Homage and deeper Veneration, than Noise.

Cleo. It is good to sooth the Pride of a Drone ; but an active Man loves to have that | Passion rous'd, and [167] as it were kept awake, whilst it is gratify'd ; and Approbation from Noise is more unquestionable than the other : However I won't determine between

---

[1] Francesca Cuzzoni was for a while Händel's mainstay, making her début in his *Ottone*. Later, partly because he wearied of the tantrums that finally led her to poison her husband, Händel engaged Faustina Bordoni as her colleague. Cuzzoni was not, however, subdued by the presence of a rival, though their first joint appearance—May 1726, in Händel's *Alessandro*—was amicable. The public immediately espoused the cause of either one singer or the other. Lady Pembroke, backed Cuzzoni, and Lady Burlington, Faustina. The factions grew so heated, finally, that each side not only applauded its favourite, but would not suffer the other to be heard. There were riots in the theatre, the press was flooded with controversy, and Faustina and Cuzzoni furnished a climax by tearing each other's hair out on the stage ; or, rather, Händel furnished the climax, by a bankruptcy due partly to the scandal (cf. Streatfeild's *Handel*, ed. 1909, pp. 98-104).

them ; much may be said on both sides. The *Greeks* and *Romans* used Sounds, to stir up Men to noble Actions, with great Success ; and the Silence observed among the *Ottomans* has kept them very well in the slavish Submission, which their Sovereigns require of them : Perhaps the one does better where absolute Power is lodg'd in one Person, and the other where there is some Shew of Liberty. Both are proper Tools to flatter the Pride of Man, when they are understood and made use of as such. I have known a very brave Man used to the Shouts of War, and highly delighted with loud Applause, be very angry with his Butler, for making a little ratling with his Plates.

Hor. An old Aunt of mine th' other Day turn'd away a very clever Fellow, for not walking upon his Toes ; and I must own myself, that the stamping of Footmen, and all unmannerly Loudness of Servants, are very offensive to me ; tho' I never enter'd into the Reason of it before now. In our last Conversation, when you describ'd the Symptoms of Self-liking, and what the Behaviour would be of an unciviliz'd Man, you named Laughing : I know it is one of the Characteristicks of our Species : Pray do you take that to be likewise the Result of Pride?

[168] | *Cleo.* *Hobbes* is of that Opinion,[1] and in most

---

[1] Cf. *English Works*, ed. Molesworth, iv. 45–7, in *Human Nature* : 'That it [the passion of laughter] consisteth in *wit*, or, as they call it, in the *jest*, experience confuteth : for men laugh at mischances and indecencies, wherein there lieth no wit nor jest at all. And forasmuch as the same thing is no more ridiculous when it groweth stale or usual, . . . it must be *new* and *unexpected*. Men laugh often . . . at their *own* actions performed never so little beyond their own expectations ; as also at their own *jests* : and in this case it is manifest, that the passion of laughter proceedeth from a *sudden conception* of some *ability* in himself that laugheth. Also men laugh at the *infirmities* of others, by comparison wherewith their own abilities are set off and illustrated. . . . I may therefore conclude, that the passion of laughter is nothing else but *sudden glory* arising from some sudden *conception* of some *eminency* in ourselves, by *comparison*

Instances it might be derived from thence ; but there are some *Phænomena*[a] not to be explain'd by that *Hypothesis* ; therefore I would chuse to say, that Laughter is a Mechanical Motion, which we are naturally thrown into, when we are unaccountably pleas'd. When our Pride is feelingly gratify'd ; when we hear or see any thing which we admire or approve of ; or when we are indulging any other Passion or Appetite, and the Reason why we are pleas'd, seems to be just and worthy, we are then far from laughing : But when Things or Actions are odd and out of the way, and happen to please us, when we can give no just Reason why they should do so, it is then, generally speaking, that they make us laugh.

Hor. I would rather side with what you said was *Hobbes*'s Opinion : For the Things we commonly laugh at are such, as are some way or other mortifying, unbecoming, or prejudicial to others.

Cleo. But what will you say to Tickling, which will make an Infant laugh that is deaf and blind?

Hor. Can you account for that, by your System?

Cleo. Not to my Satisfaction ; but I'll tell you what might be said for it. We know by Experience, that the smoother, the softer, and the more sensible the Skin is, the more ticklish Persons are, generally speaking : We know | likewise, that Things rough, [169] sharp and hard when they touch the Skin are displeasing to us, even before they give Pain ; and that on the contrary every thing, apply'd to the Skin, that

[a] *Phænomena* 29.

with the *infirmity* of others, or with our own formerly. . . . It is no wonder therefore that men take heinously to be laughed at or derided, that is, triumphed over.'

In his objection to Hobbes's theory Mandeville somewhat misses Hobbes's real point. Hobbes is explaining, not the phenomenon of laughter itself, but the ' passion of laughter ', by which he obviously intends the sensation of the comic, something with which the laughter which proceeds from tickling has nothing to do.

Cureau de la Chambre had considered the relation of tickling to laughter (*Les Characteres des Passions*, ed. 1662, i. 197-9).

is soft and smooth, and not otherwise offensive, is delightful. It is possible, that gentle Touches being impress'd on several nervous Filaments at once, every one of them producing a pleasing Sensation, may create that confus'd Pleasure, which is the Occasion of Laughter.

Hor. But how come you to think of Mechanick Motion, in the Pleasure of a free Agent?

Cleo. Whatever free Agency we may pretend to in the forming of Ideas, the Effect of them upon the Body is independent of the Will. Nothing is more directly opposite to laughing than frowning : The one draws Wrinkles in the Forehead, knits the Brows, and keeps the Mouth shut : The other does quite the reverse ; *exporrigere frontem*,[1] you know, is a Latin Phrase for being merry. In sighing, the Muscles of the Belly and Breast are pull'd inward, and the Diaphragm is pull'd upward more than ordinary ; and we seem to endeavour, tho' in vain, to squeeze and compress the Heart, whilst we draw in our Breath in a forcible manner ; and when in that squeezing Posture we have taken in as much Air, as we can contain, we throw it out with the same Violence we [170] suck'd it in with, and at | the same time give a sudden Relaxation to all the Muscles we employ'd before. Nature certainly design'd this for something in the Labour for Self-preservation, which she forces upon us. How mechanically do all Creatures that can make any Sound cry out, and complain in great Afflictions, as well as Pain and imminent Danger ! In great Torments the Efforts of Nature are so violent that way, that to disappoint her, and prevent the Discovery of what we feel, by Sounds, and which she bids us make, we are forc'd to draw our Mouth into a Purse, or else suck in our Breath, bite our Lips, or squeeze them

[1] Terence (*Adelphi* 839) has 'Exporge [short form of *exporrige*] frontem', and Horace, 'explicuere frontem' (*Carmina* III. xxix. 16).

close together, and use the most effectual Means to hinder the Air from coming out. In Grief we sigh, in Mirth we laugh : In the latter, little Stress is laid upon the Respiration, and this is perform'd with less Regularity than it is at any other time ; all the Muscles without and every thing within feel loose, and seem to have no other Motion, than what is communicated to them by the convulsive Shakes of Laughter.

Hor. I have seen People laugh till they lost all their Strength.

Cleo. How much is all this the Reverse of what we observe in sighing ! When Pain or depth of Woe make us cry out, the Mouth is drawn round, or at least into an Oval ; the Lips are thrusted forward without touching each other, and the Tongue is pull'd in, which is the Reason that all Nations, when they exclaim, cry, *Oh !*

| *Hor.* Why, pray ?   [171]

Cleo. Because whilst the Mouth, Lips, and Tongue remain in those Postures, they can sound no other Vowel, and no Consonant at all. In laughing, the Lips are pull'd back, and strain'd to draw the Mouth in its fullest Length.

Hor. I would not have you lay great Stress upon that, for it is the same in Weeping, which is an undoubted Sign of Sorrow.

Cleo. In great Afflictions, where the Heart is oppress'd, and Anxieties, which we endeavour to resist, few People can weep ; but when they do, it removes the Oppression, and sensibly relieves them : For then their Resistance is gone, and Weeping in Distress is not so much a Sign of Sorrow, as it is an Indication, that we can bear our Sorrow no longer ; and therefore it is counted unmanly to weep, because it seems to give up our Strength, and is a kind of yielding to our Grief. But the Action of Weeping itself is not more peculiar to Grief, than it is to Joy,

in adult People; and there are Men, who shew great
Fortitude in Afflictions, and bear the greatest Misfortunes with dry Eyes, that will cry heartily at
a moving Scene in a Play. Some are easily wrought
upon by one thing, others are sooner affected with
another; but whatever touches us so forcibly, as to
overwhelm the Mind, prompts us to weep, and is the
[172] mechanical Cause of Tears; and therefore, be-|sides
Grief, Joy, and Pity, there are other things no way
relating to ourselves, that may have this Effect upon
us; such as the Relations of surprizing Events and
sudden Turns of Providence in behalf of Merit;
Instances of Heroism, of Generosity; in Love, in
Friendship, in an Enemy; or the hearing or reading
of noble Thoughts and Sentiments of Humanity;
more especially, if these Things are convey'd to us
suddenly, in an agreeable manner, and unlook'd for,
as well as lively Expressions. We shall observe likewise, that none are more subject to this Frailty of
shedding Tears on such foreign Accounts, than Persons
of Ingenuity and quick Apprehension; and those
among them that are most benevolent, generous and
open-hearted; whereas the Dull and Stupid, the
Cruel, Selfish, and Designing, are very seldom troubled
with it. Weeping therefore, in earnest, is always
a sure and involuntary Demonstration that something
strikes and overcomes the Mind, whatever that be
which affects it. We find likewise, that outward
Violence, as sharp Winds and Smoak, the *Effluvia* of
Onions, and other volatile Salts, *&c.* have the same
Effect upon the external Fibres of the lachrymal Ducts
and Glands, that are exposed, which the sudden
Swelling and Pressure of the Spirits [a] has upon those
within. The Divine Wisdom is in nothing more
conspicuous, than in the infinite Variety of living
[173] Creatures of different Constructi-|on; every part of
them being contriv'd with stupendious Skill, and fitted

[a] Spiris *29*

with the utmost Accuracy for the different Purposes they were design'd for : The human Body, above all, is a most astonishing Master-piece of Art : The Anatomist may have a perfect Knowledge of all the Bones and their Ligaments, the Muscles and their Tendons, and be able to dissect every Nerve and every Membrane with great Exactness ; the Naturalist likewise may dive a great Way into the inward Oeconomy, and different Symptoms of Health and Sickness : They may all approve of, and admire the curious Machine ; but no Man can have a tolerable Idea of the Contrivance, the Art, and the Beauty of the Workmanship itself, even in those Things he can see, without being likewise vers'd in Geometry and Mechanicks.

Hor. How long is it ago that Mathematicks were brought into Physick? That Art, I have heard, is brought to great Certainty by them.

Cleo. What you speak of is quite another thing. Mathematicks never had, nor ever can have, any thing to do with Physick; if you mean by it the Art of Curing the Sick. The Structure and Motions of the Body, may, perhaps, be mechanically accounted for, and all Fluids are under the Laws of *Hydrostaticks* : [1] But we can have no Help from any Part of the Mechanicks, in the Discovery of | Things, infinitely [174] remote from Sight, and entirely unknown as to their Shapes and Bulks. Physicians, with the rest of Mankind, are wholly ignorant of the first Principles and

[1] This passage is paralleled by a discussion in Mandeville's *Treatise* (1730), pp. 172–83: '... The Branch of Physick in which I have asserted the Study of Mathematicks to be of no Use, was the Practice it self, the Cure of Diseases. But to speak mechanically of the Structure of Animals or the Motion of the Muscles, and to calculate the Weight that is equivalent to the Force they exert, are Tasks that require mathematical Knowledge. All Fluids likewise are subject to the Laws of Hydrostaticks ' (pp. 178–9).

Perhaps the greatest of the ' mathematical doctors ' against whom Mandeville is arguing was Archibald Pitcairne. It is possible that Mandeville met this very doctor, for Pitcairne taught at Leyden the year after Mandeville took his degree of M.D. there.

constituent Parts of Things, in which all the Virtues
and Properties of them consist; and this, as well of
the Blood and other Juices of the Body, as the Simples,
and consequently all the Medicines they make use of.
There is no Art that has less Certainty than theirs,
and the most valuable Knowledge in it arises from
Observation, and is such; as a Man of Parts and
Application, who has fitted himself for that Study,
can only be possess'd of, after a long and judicious
Experience.[1]   But the Pretence to Mathematicks, or
the Usefulness of it in the Cure of Diseases, is a Cheat,
and as errant a Piece of Quackery as a Stage and
a *Merry Andrew*.

Hor. But since there is so much Skill display'd in
the Bones, Muscles, and grosser Parts, is it not reasonable to think, that there is no less Art bestow'd on
those that are beyond the Reach of our Senses?

Cleo. I no ways doubt it : Microscopes have open'd
a new World to us, and I am far from thinking, that
Nature should leave off her Work, where we can trace
her no further.   I am persuaded that our Thoughts,
and the Affections of the Mind, have a more certain
and more mechanical Influence upon several Parts of
[175] the Body, than has been hitherto, or in | all human
Probability, ever will be discovered.   The visible
Effect they have on the Eyes, and Muscles of the Face,
must shew the least attentive, the Reason I have for
this Assertion.   When in Mens Company we are upon
our Guard, and would preserve our Dignity, the Lips
are shut and the Jaws meet; the Muscles of the
Mouth are gently braced, and the rest all over the
Face are kept firmly in their Places : Turn away from
these into another Room, where you meet with a fine
young Lady that is affable and easy; immediately,
before you think on it, your Countenance will be
strangely alter'd; and without being conscious of
having done any thing to your Face, you'll have quite

---

[1] This is a dominant conception in Mandeville's *Treatise*.

another Look; and every body, that has observ'd you, will discover in it more Sweetness and less Severity than you had the Moment before. When we suffer the lower Jaw to sink down, the Mouth opens a little : If in this Posture we look strait before us, without fixing our Eyes on any thing, we may imitate the Countenance of a Natural; by dropping, as it were, our Features, and laying no Stress on any Muscle of the Face. Infants, before they have learn'd to swallow their Spittle, generally keep their Mouths open, and are always drivelling : In them, before they shew any Understanding, and whilst it is yet very confus'd, the Muscles of the Face are, as it were, relax'd, the lower Jaw falls down, and the Fibres of | the Lips are [176] unbraced ; at least, these *Phænomena* we observe in them, during that Time, more often than we do afterwards. In extreme old Age, when People begin to doat, these [a] Symptoms return ; and in most Idiots they continue to be observ'd, as long as they live : Hence it is that we say, that a Man wants a Slabbering-Bibb, when he behaves very sillily, or talks like a natural Fool. When we reflect on all this, on the one hand, and consider on the other, that none are less prone to Anger than Idiots, and no Creatures are less affected with Pride, I would ask, whether there is not some Degree of Self-liking, that mechanically influences, and seems to assist us, in the decent Wearing of our Faces.

Hor. I cannot resolve you ; what I know very well is, that by these Conjectures on the Mechanism of Man, I find my Understanding very little inform'd : I wonder how we came upon the Subject.

Cleo. You enquired into the Origin of Risibility, which no body can give an Account of, with any Certainty ; and in such Cases every body is at liberty to make Guesses, so they draw no Conclusions from them, to the Prejudice of any thing better establish'd. But the chief Design I had in giving you these indi-

[a] those 30

L 2

gested Thoughts, was to hint to you, how really mysterious the Works of Nature are; I mean, how [177] replete they are every where, | with a Power glaringly conspicuous, and yet incomprehensible beyond all human Reach; in order to demonstrate, that more useful Knowledge may be acquired from unwearied Observation, judicious Experience, and arguing from Facts *à posteriori*, than from the haughty Attempts of entring into first Causes, and reasoning *à priori*. I don't believe there is a Man in the World of that Sagacity, if he was wholly unacquainted with the Nature of a Spring-Watch, that he would ever find out by dint of Penetration the Cause of its Motion, if he was never to see the Inside: But every middling Capacity may be certain, by seeing only the Outside, that its pointing at the Hour, and keeping to Time, proceed from the Exactness of some curious Workmanship that's hid; and that the Motion of the Hands, what Number of Resorts [1] soever it is communicated by, is originally owing to something else that first moves within. In the same manner we are sure that, as the Effects of Thought upon the Body are palpable, several Motions are produced by it, by contact, and consequently mechanically: But the Parts, the Instruments which that Operation is perform'd with, are so immensely far remote from our Senses, and the Swiftness of the Action is so prodigious, that it infinitely surpasses our Capacity to trace them.

[178] | *Hor.* But is not Thinking the Business of the Soul? What has Mechanism to do with that?

Cleo. The Soul, whilst in the Body, cannot be said to think, otherwise than an Architect is said to build a House, where the Carpenters, Bricklayers, &c. do the Work, which he chalks out and superintends.

Hor. Which Part of the Brain do you think the Soul to be more immediately lodg'd in; or do you take it to be diffused through the whole?

[1] Springs.

Cleo. I know nothing of it more than what I have told you already.

Hor. I plainly feel that this Operation of Thinking is a Labour, or at least something that is transacting, in my Head, and not in my Leg nor my Arm : What Insight or real Knowledge have we from Anatomy concerning it?

Cleo. None at all *à priori :* The most consummate Anatomist knows no more of it than a Butcher's Prentice. We may admire the curious Duplicate of Coats,[1] and close Embroidery of Veins and Arteries that environ the Brain : But when dissecting it we have viewed the several Pairs of Nerves with their Origin, and taken Notice of some Glands of various Shapes and Sizes, which differing from the Brain in Substance, could not but rush in View ; when these, I say, have been | taken Notice of, and distinguish'd [179] by different Names, some of them not very pertinent, and less polite, the best Naturalist must acknowledge, that even of these large visible Parts there are but few, the Nerves and Blood-Vessels excepted, at the Use of which he can give any tollerable Guesses : But as to the mysterious Structure of the Brain itself, and the more abstruse Oeconomy of it, that he knows nothing ; but that the whole seems to be a medullary Substance, compactly treasur'd up in infinite Millions of imperceptible Cells, that dispos'd in an unconceivable Order, are cluster'd together in a perplexing Variety of Folds and Windings. He'll add, perhaps, that it is reasonable to think, this to be the capacious Exchequer of human Knowledge, in which the faithful Senses deposite the vast Treasure of Images, constantly, as through their Organs they receive them : That it is the Office in which the Spirits are separated from the Blood, and afterwards sublim'd and volatiliz'd into Particles hardly corporeal ; and that the most minute

---

[1] The *dura mater* and *pia mater*, two of the membranes enveloping the brain.

of these are always, either searching for, or variously
disposing the Images retain'd, and shooting through
the infinite Meanders of that wonderful Substance,
employ themselves, without ceasing, in that inexplicable Performance, the Contemplation of which fills
the most exalted Genius with Amazement.

[180] | *Hor.* These are very airy Conjectures, but nothing
of all this can be proved ; the Smallness of the Parts,
you'll say, is the Reason ; but if greater Improvements were made in Optick Glasses, and Microscopes
could be invented that magnify'd Objects three or
four Millions of Times more than they do now, then
certainly those minute Particles, so immensely remote
from the Senses you speak of, might be observed, if
that which does the Work is corporeal at all.

   Cleo. That such Improvements are impossible, is
demonstrable ; but if it was not, even then we could
have little Help from Anatomy. The Brain of an
Animal cannot be look'd and search'd into whilst it
is alive. Should you take the main Spring out of
a Watch, and leave the Barrel that contain'd it, standing empty, it would be impossible to find out what it
had been that made it exert itself, whilst it shew'd
the Time. We might examine all the Wheels, and
every other Part belonging, either to the *Movement* or
the *Motion*, and, perhaps, find out the Use of them,
in relation to the Turning of the Hands ; but the first
Cause of this Labour would remain a Mystery for ever.

   Hor. The main Spring in us is the Soul, which is
immaterial and immortal : But what is that to other
Creatures that have a Brain like ours, and no such
[181] immortal Substance distinct | from Body? Don't you
believe that Dogs and Horses think?

   Cleo. I believe they do, though in a Degree of
Perfection far inferior to us.[1]

[1] This was the position taken
by Gassendi in opposition to
Descartes. Descartes had argued,
' Et cecy ne tesmoigne pas seulement que les bestes ont moins
de raison que les hommes, mais
qu'elles n'en ont point du tout '
(*Œuvres*, Paris, 1897–1910, vi.

Hor. What is it, that superintends Thought in them? where must we look for it? which is the main Spring?

Cleo. I can answer you no otherwise, than Life.

Hor. What is Life?

Cleo. Every body understands the Meaning of the Word, though, perhaps, no body knows the Principle of Life, that Part which gives Motion to all the rest.

Hor. Where Men are certain that the Truth of a Thing is not to be known, they will always differ, and endeavour to impose upon one another.

Cleo. Whilst there are Fools and Knaves they will : But I have not impos'd upon you : What I said of the Labour of the Brain, I told you, was a Conjecture, which I recommend no farther to you than you shall think it probable. You ought to expect no Demonstration of a Thing, that from its Nature can admit of none. When the Breath is gone, and the Circulation ceas'd, the Inside of an Animal is vastly different from what it was whilst the Lungs play'd, and the Blood and Juices were in full Motion through every Part of it. You have seen those Engines that raise Water by the Help of Fire ; the Steam | you know, is [182] that which forces it up ;[1] it is as impossible to see the volatile Particles that perform the Labour of the Brain, when the Creature is dead, as in the Engine it would be to see the Steam, (which yet does all the Work) when the Fire is out and the Water cold. Yet

58, in *Discours de la Methode*, pt. 5). To this Gassendi replied, 'Ratione, *inquis,* carent bruta. Sed nimirum carent humanâ, non suâ' (in Descartes, *Œuvres* vii. 270–1, in *Meditationes de Prima Philosophia, Objectiones Quintæ* ii. 7). Another noteworthy discussion as to the rationality of animals took place between Cureau de la Chambre and Pierre Chanet, the former arguing for the rationality of beasts in his *Quelle est la Con-*noissance des Bestes (in *Les Characteres des Passions*, 1645, vol. 2) and *Traité de la Connoissance des Animaux*(1648). Others who believed that animals think were Montaigne, Charron, La Mothe le Vayer, and Bayle (cf. above, i. 44, n. 2).

[1] Mandeville was writing at a time when the steam-engine first became really practicable in England.

if this Engine was shewn to a Man when it was not at Work, and it was explain'd to him, which Way it rais'd the Water, it would be a strange Incredulity, or great Dullness of Apprehension, not to believe it ; if he knew perfectly well, that by Heat, Liquids may be rarified into Vapour.

Hor. But don't you think there is a Difference in Souls, and are they all equally good or equally bad?

Cleo. We have some tolerable Ideas of Matter and Motion ; or, at least, of what we mean by them, and therefore we may form Idea's of Things corporeal, though they are beyond the Reach of our Senses; and we can conceive any Portion of Matter a thousand times less than our Eyes, even by the Help of the best Microscopes, are able to see it : But the Soul is altogether incomprehensible, and we can determine but little about it, that is not reveal'd to us. I believe that the Difference of Capacities in Men depends upon, and is entirely owing to, the Difference there is between them, either in the Fabrick itself, that is, the greater or lesser Exactness in the Composure of their Frame, [183] or else in the Use that | is made of it. The Brain of a Child, newly born, is *Charte Blanche* ; [1] and, as you have hinted very justly, we have no Ideas, which we are not obliged for to our Senses. I make no question, but that in this Rummaging of the Spirits through the Brain, in hunting after, joyning, separating, changing, and compounding of Ideas with inconceivable Swiftness, under the Superintendency of the Soul, the Action of Thinking consists. The best Thing, therefore, we can do to Infants after the first Month, besides feeding and keeping them from Harm, is to make them take in Ideas, beginning by the two most useful Senses, the Sight and Hearing ; and dispose them to set about this Labour of the Brain, and by

---

[1] Cf. Locke's theory that we are born quite empty of all knowledge—our minds a *tabula* *rasa*—achieving our knowledge from experience.

our Example, encourage them to imitate us in Thinking; which, on their Side, is very poorly perform'd at first. Therefore the more an Infant, in Health, is talk'd to, and jumbl'd about, the better it is for it, at least, for the first two Years; and for its Attendance in this early Education, to the wisest Matron in the World, I would prefer an active young Wench, whose Tongue never stands still, that should run about, and never cease diverting and playing with it whilst it was awake; and where People can afford it, two or three of them, to relieve one another when they are tired, are better than one.

| *Hor.* Then you think Children reap great Benefit [184] from the non-sensical Chat of Nurses?

Cleo. It is of inestimable Use to them, and teaches them to think, as well as speak, much sooner and better, than with equal aptitude of Parts they would do without. The Business is to make them exert those Faculties, and keep Infants continually employ'd about them; for the time which is lost then, is never to be retriev'd.

Hor. Yet we seldom remember any thing of what we saw or heard, before we were two Years old : then what would be lost, if Children should not hear all that Impertinence?

Cleo. As Iron is to be hammer'd whilst it is hot and ductile, so Children are to be taught when they are young : as the Flesh and every Tube and Membrane about them, are then tenderer, and will yield sooner to slight Impressions, than afterwards; so many of their Bones are but Cartilages, and the Brain itself is much softer, and in a manner fluid : This is the Reason, that it cannot so well retain the Images it receives, as it does afterwards, when the Substance of it comes to be of a better Consistence. But as the first Images are lost, so they are continually succeeded by new ones; and the Brain at first serves as a Slate to Cypher, or a Sampler to work upon. What Infants should chiefly learn, is the Performance itself, the

[185] Exercise of Thinking, and to con-|tract a Habit of disposing, and with Ease and Agility managing the Images retain'd, to the Purpose intended : which is never attain'd better than whilst the Matter is yielding, and the Organs are most flexible and supple. So they but exercise themselves in thinking and speaking, it is no Matter what they think on, or what they say, that is inoffensive. In sprightly Infants we soon see by their Eyes the Efforts they are making to imitate us, before they are able ; and that they try at this Exercise of the Brain, and make Essays to think, as well as they do, to hammer out Words, we may know from the Incoherence of their Actions, and the strange Absurdities they utter : but as there are more Degrees of Thinking well, than there are of Speaking plain, the first is of the greatest Consequence.

Hor. I wonder you should talk of teaching, and lay so great a Stress on a thing that comes so naturally to us, as Thinking : no Action is perform'd with greater Velocity by every Body : *as quick as Thought,* is a Proverb, and in less than a Moment a stupid Peasant may remove his Ideas from *London* to *Japan,* as easily as the greatest Wit.

Cleo. Yet there is nothing, in which Men differ so immensely from one another, as they do in the Exercise of this Faculty : the differences between them in Height, Bulk, Strength, and Beauty, are trifling, in Comparison to that which I speak of ; and there is [186] nothing in the | World more valuable, or more plainly perceptible in Persons, than a happy Dexterity of Thinking. Two Men may have equal Knowledge, and yet the one shall speak as well off-hand, as the other can after two Hours Study.

Hor. I take it for granted, that no Man would study two Hours for a Speech, if he knew how to make it in less ; and therefore I can't see what Reason you have, to suppose two such Persons to be of equal Knowledge.

Cleo. There is a double Meaning in the Word, *knowing*, which you seem not to attend to. There is a great Difference between knowing a Violin when you see it, and knowing how to play upon it. The Knowledge I speak of is of the first sort ; and if you consider it in that Sense, you must be of my Opinion ; for no Study can fetch any thing out of the Brain that is not there. Suppose you conceive a short Epistle in three Minutes, which another, who can make Letters and join them together as fast as your self, is yet an Hour about, tho' both of you write the same thing : it is plain to me, that the slow Person knows as much as you do ; at least it does not appear that he knows less : he has receiv'd the same Images, but he cannot come at them, or at least not dispose them in that order, so soon as yourself. When we see two Exercises of equal Goodness, either in prose or verse ; if the one is made *ex tempore*, and we are sure of it, and the other has cost two Days Labour, | the Author of the first is [187] a Person of finer natural Parts than the other, tho' their Knowledge, for ought we know, is the same : you see then the Difference between Knowledge, as it signifies the Treasure of Images receiv'd, and Knowledge, or rather Skill, to find out those Images when we want them, and work them readily to our Purpose.

Hor. When we know a Thing, and cannot readily think of it, or bring it to mind, I thought that was the Fault of the Memory.

Cleo. So it may be in part : but there are Men of prodigious Reading, that have likewise great Memories, who judge ill, and seldom say any thing *a propos*, or say it when it is too late. Among the *helluones librorum*, the Cormorants of Books, there are wretched Reasoners, that have canine Appetites, and no Digestion. What Numbers of learned Fools do we not meet with in large Libraries ; from whose Works it is evident, that Knowledge must have lain in their Heads, as Furniture at an Upholder's ; and the Treasure of the Brain was a Burden to them, instead of an Ornament ! All this proceeds from a Defect in the Faculty of Thinking ; an Unskilfulness, and want of Aptitude in managing, to the best Advantage, the Idea's we have receiv'd. We see others, on the contrary, that have very fine Sense, and no Litterature at all. The generality of Women are quicker of Invention, and more ready at [188] Repartee, than the Men, | with equal Helps of Education ; ¹ and it is surprizing to see, what a considerable Figure some of them make in Conversation, when we consider the small Opportunities they have had of acquiring Knowledge.

Hor. But sound Judgment is a great Rarity among them.

Cleo. Only for want of Practice, Application and Assiduity. Thinking on abstruse Matters, is not their Province in Life ; and the Stations they are commonly placed in, find them other Employment : but there is no Labour of the Brain, which Women are not as capable of performing, at least, as well as the Men, with the same Assistance, if they set about, and persevere in it : sound Judgment is no more than the Result of that Labour : he that uses himself to take Things to Pieces, to compare them together, to consider them abstractly and impartially ; that is, he, who of two Propositions he is to examine, seems not to care which is true ; he that lays the whole Stress of his Mind on every Part alike, and puts the same Thing in all the Views it can be seen in : he, I say, that employs himself most often in this Exercise, is most likely, *cæteris paribus,* to acquire what we call a sound Judgment. The Workmanship in the Make of Women seems to be more elegant, and better finish'd : the Features are more delicate, the Voice is

¹ The equality, if not superiority, of women was not an uncommon contention at the time. Defoe, for instance, argued much like Mandeville in the *Essay upon Projects* (in the early part of the section on an academy for women).—Compare the feministic passage in Mandeville's *Virgin Unmask'd* (1724), pp. 115–16, beginning, 'They [the men] have enslaved our Sex....'

sweeter, the whole Outside of them is more curiously wove, than they | are in Men ; and the difference in [189] the Skin between theirs and ours is the same, as there is between fine Cloth and coarse. There is no Reason to imagine, that Nature should have been more neglectful of them out of Sight, than she has where we can trace her ; and not have taken the same Care of them in the Formation of the Brain, as to the Nicety of the Structure, and superior Accuracy in the Fabrick, which is so visible in the rest of their Frame.

Hor. Beauty is their Attribute, as Strength is ours.

Cleo. How minute soever those Particles of the Brain are, that contain the several Images, and are assisting in the Operation of Thinking, there must be a difference in the Justness, the Symmetry, and Exactness of them, between one Person and another, as well as there is in the grosser Parts : what the Women excel us in then, is the Goodness of the Instrument, either in the Harmony, or Pliableness of the Organs, which must be very material in the Art of Thinking, and is the only thing that deserves the Name of Natural Parts ; since the Aptitude I have spoke of, depending upon Exercise, is notoriously acquired.

Hor. As the Workmanship in the Brain is rather more curious in Women than it is in Men, so in Sheep and Oxen, Dogs and Horses, I suppose it is infinitely coarser.

| *Cleo.* We have no Reason to think otherwise.   [190]

Hor. But after all, that Self, that Part of us that wills and wishes, that chuses one thing rather than another, must be incorporeal : For if it is Matter, it must either be one single Particle, which I can almost feel it is not, or a Combination of many, which is more than inconceivable.

Cleo. I don't deny what you say ; and that the Principle of Thought and Action is inexplicable in all Creatures, I have hinted already : But its being incorporeal does not mend the Matter, as to the Difficulty of explaining or conceiving it. That there must be

a mutual Contact between this Principle, whatever it
is, and the Body itself, is what we are certain of
à posteriori ; and a reciprocal Action upon each other,
between an immaterial Substance and Matter, is as
incomprehensible to human Capacity, as that Thought
should be the Result of Matter and Motion.

Hor. Tho' many other Animals seem to be endued
with Thought, there is no Creature we are acquainted
with, besides Man, that shews or seems to feel, a Consciousness of his Thinking.

Cleo. It is not easy to determine what Instincts,
Properties or Capacities other Creatures are either
possess'd or destitute of, when those Qualifications fall
not under our Senses : But it is highly probable that
[191] the principal | and most necessary Parts of the Machine
are less elaborate in Animals, that attain to all the
Perfection they are capable of, in three, four, five, or
six Years at furthest, than they are in a Creature that
hardly comes to Maturity, its full Growth and Strength,
in five and twenty. The Consciousness of a Man of
fifty, that he is the same Man that did such a thing
at twenty, and was once the Boy that had such and
such Masters, depends wholly upon the Memory, and
can never be traced to the Bottom : I mean, that no
Man remembers any thing of himself, or what was
transacted before he was two Years old, when he was
but a Novice in the Art of Thinking, and the Brain
was not yet of a due Consistence to retain long the
Images it receiv'd : But this Remembrance, how far
soever it may reach, gives us no greater Surety of our
selves, than we should have of another that had been
brought up with us, and never above a Week or
a Month out of Sight. A Mother, when her Son is
thirty Years old, has more Reason to know that he
is the same whom she brought into the World, than
himself ; and such a one, who daily minds her Son,
and remembers the Alterations of his Features from
time to time, is more certain of him that he was not

chang'd in the Cradle, than she can be of herself. So that all we can know of this Consciousness is, that it consists in, or is the Result of, the running and rummaging of the Spirits through | all the Mazes of the [192] Brain, and their looking there for Facts concerning ourselves : He that has lost his Memory, tho' otherwise in perfect Health, can't think better than a Fool, and is no more conscious that he is the same he was a Year ago, than he is of a Man whom he has known but a Fortnight. There are several Degrees of losing our Memory, but he who has entirely lost it becomes, *ipso facto*, an Idiot.

Hor. I am conscious of having been the Occasion of our rambling a great way from the Subject we were upon, but I don't repent of it : What you have said of the OEconomy of the Brain, and the Mechanical Influence of Thought upon the grosser Parts, is a noble Theme for Contemplation, on the infinite unutterable Wisdom, with which the various Instincts are so visibly planted in all Animals, to fit them for the respective Purposes they were design'd for ; and every Appetite is so wonderfully interwove with the very Substance of their Frame. Nothing could be more seasonable, after you had shew'd me the Origin of Politeness, and in the Management of Self-liking set forth the Excellency of our Species beyond all other Animals, so conspicuous in the superlative Docility and indefatigable Industry ; by which all Multitudes are capable of drawing innumerable Benefits, as well for the Ease and Comfort, as the Welfare and Safety of congregate Bodies, from a most stub- | born and an unconquerable Passion, which in its [193] Nature seems to be destructive to Sociableness and Society, and never fails, in untaught Men, to render them insufferable to one another.

Cleo. By the same Method of reasoning from Facts *à posteriori*, that has laid open to us the Nature and Usefulness of Self-liking, all the rest of the Passions may easily be accounted for, and become intelligible. It is evident, that the Necessaries of Life stand not every where ready dish'd up before all Creatures ; therefore they have Instincts, that prompt them to look out for those Necessaries, and teach them how to come at them. The Zeal and Alacrity to gratify their Appetites is always proportion'd to the Strength, and the Degree of Force, with which those Instincts work upon every Creature : But considering the Disposition of things upon Earth, and the multiplicity of Animals, that have all their own Wants to supply, it must be obvious that these Attempts of Creatures, to obey the different Calls of Nature, will be often oppos'd and frustrated ; and that, in many Animals, they would seldom meet with Success; if every Individual was not endued with a Passion that, summoning all his Strength, inspired him with a transporting Eagerness to overcome the Obstacles that hinder him in his great Work of Self-Preservation. The Passion I describe is call'd Anger. How a Creature [194] possess'd of | this Passion and Self-liking, when he sees others enjoy what he wants, should be affected with Envy, can likewise be no Mystery. After Labour, the most savage and the most industrious Creature seeks Rest : Hence we learn that all of them are furnish'd, more or less, with a Love of Ease ; [a] Exerting their Strength tires them ; and the loss of Spirits, Experience teaches us, is best repair'd by Food and Sleep. We see that Creatures, who in their way of living must meet with the greatest Opposition, have the greatest share of Anger, and are born with offensive Arms. If this Anger was to employ a Creature always, without Consideration of the Danger he exposed himself to, he would soon be destroy'd : For this Reason they are all endued with Fear; and the Lion himself turns Tail, if the Hunters are arm'd, and too numerous. From what we observe in the Behaviour of Brutes, we have Reason to think, that among the more perfect

[a] Ease ;] Ease : 29[b]

Animals, those of the same Species have a Capacity on many Occasions, to make their Wants known to one another; and we are sure of several, not only that they understand one another, but likewise that they may be made to understand us. In comparing our Species with that of other Animals, when we consider the Make of Man, and the Qualifications that are obvious in him, his superior ᵃ Capacity in the Faculties of thinking and reflecting, beyond other Creatures, his being capable of learn-|ing to speak, and the Useful- [195] ness of his Hands and Fingers, there is no room to doubt, that he is more fit for Society than any other Animal we know.

Hor. Since you wholly reject my Lord *Shaftsbury*'s System, I wish you would give me your Opinion at large concerning Society, and the Sociableness of Man ; and I will hearken to you with great Attention.

Cleo. The Cause of Sociableness in Man, that is his Fitness for Society, is no such abstruse Matter : A Person of midling Capacity, that has some Experience, and a tolerable Knowledge of human Nature, may soon find it out, if his Desire of knowing the Truth be sincere, and he will look for it without Prepossession ; but most People that have treated on this Subject had a Turn to serve, and a Cause in View which they were resolved to maintain. It is very unworthy of a Philosopher to say, as *Hobbes* did, that Man is born unfit for Society, and alledge no better Reason for it, than the Incapacity that Infants come into the World with ;¹ but some of his Adversaries have as far overshot the Mark, when they asserted, that every thing which Men can attain to, ought to be esteem'd as a Cause of his Fitness for Society.

Hor. But is there in the Mind of Man a natural Affection, that prompts him to love his Species, beyond what other Animals have for theirs ; or are

ᵃ superiour 29ᵇ

¹ See Hobbes's note to the words 'born fit' in his *Philosophical* *Elements of a True Citizen* (*English Works*, ed. Molesworth, ii. 2).

[196] we born with Hatred and Aver-|sion, that makes us Wolves and Bears, to one another?

Cleo. I believe neither. From what appears to us in human Affairs, and the Works of Nature, we have more Reason to imagine that the Desire as well as Aptness of Man to associate, do not proceed from his Love to others, than we have to believe that a mutual Affection of the Planets to one another, superiour to what they feel to Stars more remote, is not the true Cause why they keep always moving together in the same solar System.

Hor. You don't believe that the Stars have any Love for one another, I am sure : Then why, *more Reason?*

Cleo. Because there are no *Phænomena,* plainly to contradict this Love of the Planets ; and we meet with Thousands every Day to convince us, that Man centers every thing in himself, and neither loves nor hates, but for his own Sake. Every Individual is a little World by itself, and all Creatures, as far as their Understanding and Abilities will let them, endeavour to make that Self happy : This in all of them is the continual Labour, and seems to be the whole Design of Life. Hence it follows, that in the Choice of Things Men must be determin'd by the Perception they have of Happiness ; and no Person can commit or set about an Action, which at that then present time seems not to be the best to him.

[197] | *Hor.* What will you say then to, *video meliora proboque, deteriora sequor?* [1]

Cleo. That only shews the Turpitude of our Inclinations. But Men may say what they please : Every Motion in a free Agent which he does not approve of, is either convulsive, or it is not his ; I speak of those that are subject to the Will. When two Things are left to a Person's Choice, it is a Demonstration, that he thinks That most eligible which he chuses, how contradictory, impertinent or pernicious soever his

[1] Ovid, *Metamorphoses* vii. 20–1.

Reason for chusing it may be : Without this there could be no voluntary *Suicide*; and it would be Injustice to punish Men for their Crimes.

Hor. I believe every Body endeavours to be pleas'd ; but it is inconceivable that Creatures of the same Species should differ so much from one another, as Men do in their Notions of Pleasure ; and that some of them should take Delight in what is the greatest Aversion to others : All aim at Happiness, but the Question is, where it is to be found.

Cleo. It is with complete Felicity in this World, as it is with the Philosopher's Stone : Both have been sought after many different Ways, by wise Men as well as Fools, tho' neither of them has been obtain'd hitherto : But in searching after either, diligent Enquirers have often stumbled by Chance on useful Discoveries of Things they did not look for, and which human Sagacity labouring with De-|sign [198] *à priori* never would have detected. Multitudes of our Species may, in any habitable part of the Globe, assist one another in a common Defence, and be rais'd into a Body politick, in which Men shall live comfortably together for many Centuries, without being acquainted with a thousand things, that if known would every one of them be instrumental to render the Happiness of the Publick more complete, according to the common Notions, Men have of Happiness. In one part of the World we have found great and flourishing Nations that knew nothing of Ships ; and in others, Traffick by Sea had been in use above two thousand Years, and Navigation had receiv'd innumerable Improvements, before they knew, how to sail by the help of the Loadstone : It would be ridiculous to alledge this piece of Knowledge, either as a Reason, why Man first chose to go to Sea, or as an Argument to prove his natural Capacity for Maritime Affairs. To raise a Garden, it is necessary that we should have a Soil, and a Climate fit for that Purpose : When we

M 2

have these, we want nothing besides Patience, but the Seeds of Vegetables, and proper Culture. Fine Walks and Canals, Statues, Summer-houses, Fountains and Caskades are great Improvements on the Delights of Nature ; but they are not essential to the Existence of a Garden. All Nations must have had mean [199] Beginnings ; and it is in those, the Infancy of | them, that the Sociableness of Man is as conspicuous as it can be ever after. Man is call'd a Sociable Creature chiefly for two Reasons ; First, because it is commonly imagin'd, that he is naturally more fond, and desirous of Society, than any other Creature. Secondly, because it is manifest, that associating in Men turns to better Account, than it possibly could do in other Animals, if they were to attempt it.

Hor. But why do you say of the first, that it is commonly imagin'd : is it not true then?

Cleo. I have a very good Reason for this Caution. All Men born in Society are certainly more desirous of it, than any other Animal ; but whether Man be naturally so, that's a Question : But, if he was, it is no Excellency, nothing to brag of : The Love Man has for his Ease and Security, and his perpetual Desire of meliorating his Condition, must be sufficient Motives to make him fond of Society ; considering the necessitous and helpless Condition of his Nature.

Hor. Don't you fall into the same Error, which you say *Hobbes* has been guilty of, when you talk of Man's necessitous and helpless Condition?

Cleo. Not at all ; I speak of Men and Women full grown ; and the more extensive their Knowledge is, the higher their Quality, and the greater their Possessions are, the more necessitous and helpless they are in [200] their Nature. | A Nobleman of 25 or 30 Thousand Pounds a Year, that has three or four Coaches and Six, and above fifty People to serve him, is in his Person consider'd singly, abstract from what he possesses, more necessitous than an obscure Man, that has but fifty Pounds a Year, and is used to walk a-foot : So a Lady, who never stuck a Pin in herself, and is dress'd and undress'd from Head to Foot like a jointed [a] Baby [1], by her Woman and the Assistance of another Maid or two, is a more helpless Creature than *Doll* the Dairy-Maid, who all the Winter long dresses herself in the Dark, in less time than the other bestows in placing of her Patches.

Hor. But is the Desire of meliorating our Condition, which you named, so general, that no Man is without it?

Cleo. Not one that can be call'd a sociable Creature ; and I believe this to be as much a Characteristick of our Species, as any can be named : For there is not a Man in the World, educated in Society, who, if he could compass it by wishing, would not have something added to, taken from, or alter'd in his Person, Possessions, Circumstances, or any part of the Society he belongs to. This is what is not to be perceiv'd in any Creature but Man ; whose great Industry in supplying what he calls his Wants, could never have been known so well as it is, if it had not been for the Unreasonableness, as well as Multiplicity, of his Desires. From all which it is manifest, that the [201] most civiliz'd People stand most in need of Society, and consequently none less than Savages. The second Reason for which I said Man was call'd Sociable, is, that associating together turn'd to better Account in our Species, than it would do in any other, if they were to try it. To find out the Reason of this, we must search into humane Nature for such Qualifications as we excel all other Animals in, and which the Generality of Men are endued with, taught or untaught : But in doing this, we should neglect nothing that is observable in them, from their most early Youth to their extreme old Age.

Hor. I can't see, why you use this Precaution, of taking in the whole Age of Man ; would it not be

[a] joynted 29[b]   [1] Doll.

sufficient to mind those Qualifications which he is possess'd of, when he is come to the height of Maturity, or his greatest Perfection?

Cleo. A considerable part of what is call'd Docility in Creatures, depends upon the Pliableness of the Parts, and their Fitness to be moved with Facility, which are either entirely lost, or very much impair'd, when they are full grown. There is nothing in which our Species so far surpasses all others, than in the Capacity of acquiring the Faculty of Thinking and Speaking well : That this is a peculiar Property belonging to our Nature is very certain, yet it is as [202] manifest, that this Capaci-|ty vanishes, when we come to Maturity, if till then it has been neglected. The Term of Life likewise, that is commonly enjoy'd by our Species, being longer than it is in most other Animals, we have a Prerogative above them in point of Time ; and Man has a greater Opportunity of advancing in Wisdom, though not to be acquired but by his own Experience, than a Creature that lives but half his Age, though it had the same Capacity. A Man of threescore, *cæteris paribus*, knows better what is to be embraced or avoided in Life, than a Man of thirty. What *Mitio*, in excusing the Follies of Youth, said to his Brother *Demea*, in the *Adelphi*, *ad omnia alia Ætate sapimus rectius*,[1] holds among Savages, as well as among Philosophers. It is the Concurrence of these, with other Properties, that together compose the Sociableness of Man.

Hor. But why may not the Love of our Species be named, as one of these Properties?

Cleo. First, because, as I have said already, it does not appear, that we have it beyond other Animals : Secondly, because it is out of the Question : For if

---

[1] See line 832 of Terence's comedy. This line is also quoted by Mandeville in his *Treatise* (1730), p. 212, where, in a note, he translates it, ' *At another Age that in all things we can act with Prudence* '.

we examine into the Nature of all Bodies Politick, we shall find, that no Dependance is ever had, or Stress laid on any such Affection, either for the Raising or Maintaining of them.

| *Hor.* But the Epithet itself, the Signification of [203] the Word, imports this Love to one another ; as is manifest from the contrary. One who loves Solitude, is averse to Company ; or of a singular, reserv'd, and sullen Temper, is the very Reverse of a Sociable Man.

Cleo. When we compare some Men to others, the Word, I own, is often used in that Sense : But when we speak of a Quality peculiar to our Species, and say, that Man is a Sociable Creature, the Word implies no more, than that in our Nature we have a certain Fitness, by which great Multitudes of us co-operating, may be united and form'd into one Body ; that endued with, and able to make Use of, the Strength, Skill, and Prudence of every Individual, shall govern itself, and act on all Emergencies, as if it was animated by one Soul, and actuated by one Will. I am willing to allow, that among the Motives, that prompt Man to enter into Society, there is a Desire which he has naturally after Company ; but he has it for his own Sake, in hopes of being the better for it ; and he would never wish for, either Company or any thing else, but for some Advantage or other he proposes to himself from it. What I deny is, that Man naturally has such a Desire, out of a Fondness to his Species, superiour to what other Animals have for theirs. It is a Compliment which we commonly pay to ourselves, but there is no more Reality in it, than | in our [204] being one another's humble Servants ; and I insist upon it, that this pretended Love of our Species, and natural Affection we are said to have for one another, beyond other Animals, is neither instrumental to the Erecting of Societies, nor ever trusted to in our prudent Commerce with one another, when associated, any more than if it had no Existence. The undoubted

Basis of all Societies is Government : This Truth, well examin'd into, will furnish us with all the Reasons of Man's Excellency, as to Sociableness. It is evident from it, that Creatures, to be rais'd into a Community, must, in the first Place, be governable : This is a Qualification that requires Fear, and some degree of Understanding ; for a Creature not susceptible of Fear, is never to be govern'd ; and the more Sense and Courage it has, the more refractory and untractable it will be, without the Influence of that useful Passion : And again, Fear without Understanding puts Creatures only upon avoiding the Danger dreaded, without considering what will become of themselves afterwards : So wild Birds will beat out their Brains against the Cage, before they will save their Lives by eating.[a] There is great Difference between being submissive, and being governable ; for he who barely submits to another, only embraces what he dislikes, to shun what he dislikes more ; and we may be very [205] submissive, and be of no Use to the Per-|son we submit to : But to be governable, implies an Endeavour to please, and a Willingness to exert ourselves in behalf of the Person that governs : But Love beginning every where at Home, no Creature can labour for others, and be easy long, whilst Self is wholly out of the Question : Therefore a Creature is then truly governable, when, reconcil'd to Submission, it has learn'd to construe his Servitude to his own Advantage ; and rests satisfy'd with the Account it finds for itself, in the Labour it performs for others. Several kinds[b] of Animals are, or may, with little Trouble, be made thus governable ; but there is not one Creature so tame, that it can be made to serve its own Species, but Man ; yet without this he could never have been made sociable.

Hor. But was not Man, by Nature, designed for Society?

[a] eating.] eating, *29*   [b] kind *30*

DIALOGUE. 185

Cleo. We know from Revelation that Man was made for Society.

Hor. But if it had not been reveal'd, or you had been a *Chinese*, or a *Mexican*, what would you answer me as a Philosopher?

Cleo. That Nature had design'd Man for Society, as she has made Grapes for Wine.

Hor. To make Wine is an Invention of Man, as it is to press Oil from Olives and other Vegetables, and to make Ropes of Hemp.

Cleo. And so it is to form a Society of independent Multitudes; and there is nothing that requires greater Skill.

‖ *Hor.* But is not the Sociableness of Man the Work [206] of Nature, or rather of the Author of Nature, Divine Providence?[1]

Cleo. Without doubt : But so is the innate Virtue and peculiar Aptitude of every thing; that Grapes are fit to make Wine, and Barley and Water to make other Liquors, is the Work of Providence ; but it is

---

[1] This passage seems intended as an answer to critics like William Law (cf. below, ii. 197, *n.* 3, and 401–6), who asserted the divine origin of morality and society against Mandeville's argument that morality and society are the results of human endeavour, are based on human imperfections, and are merely for human convenience. In his *Origin of Honour* (1732) Mandeville once more argued against the divine origin of virtue: 'There is no Virtue that has a Name, but it curbs, regulates, or subdues some Passion that is peculiar to Humane Nature ; and therefore to say, that God has all the Virtues in the highest Perfection . . . is an Expression accom-modated to vulgar Capacities. . . . For as God has not a Body, nor any Thing that is Corporeal belonging to his Essence, so he is entirely free from Passions and Frailties. With what Propriety then can we attribute any Thing to him that was invented, or at least signifies a Strength or Ability to conquer or govern Passions and Frailties? The Holiness of God, and all his Perfections . . . belong to his Nature ; and there is no Virtue but what is acquired. . . . 'I recommend the fore-going Paragraph to the Consideration of the Advocates for the Eternity and Divine Original of Virtue . . .' (pp. ix–x).

human Sagacity that finds out the Uses we make of them : All the other Capacities of Man likewise, as well as his Sociableness, are evidently derived from God, who made him : Every thing therefore that our Industry can produce or compass, is originally owing to the Author of our Being. But when we speak of the Works of Nature, to distinguish them from those of Art, we mean such, as were brought forth without our Concurrence. So Nature in due Season produces Peas ; but in *England* you cannot have them green in *January*, without Art and uncommon Industry. What Nature designs, she executes herself : There are Creatures, of whom it is visible, that Nature has design'd them for Society, as is most obvious in Bees, to whom she has given Instincts for that purpose, as appears from the Effects. We owe our Being, and every thing else, to the great Author of the Universe ; but as Societies cannot subsist without his preserving Power, so they cannot exist without the Concurrence of human Wisdom : All of them must have a Depend-
[207] ance, either on mutual | Compact, or the Force of the Strong, exerting itself upon the Patience of the Weak. The Difference between the Works of Art, and those of Nature, is so immense, that it is impossible not to know them asunder. Knowing, *à priori*, belongs to God only, and Divine Wisdom acts with an original Certainty, of which, what we call Demonstration, is but an imperfect, borrow'd Copy. Amongst the Works of Nature, therefore, we see no Tryals nor Essays ; they are all compleat, and such as she would have them, at the first Production ; and, where she has not been interrupted, highly finish'd, beyond the Reach of our Understanding, as well as Senses. Wretched Man, on the contrary, is sure of nothing, his own Existence not excepted, but from reasoning *à posteriori*. The Consequence of this is, that the Works of Art and human Invention are all very lame and defective, and most of them pitifully mean at

first : Our Knowledge is advanced by slow Degrees, and some Arts and Sciences require the Experience of many Ages, before they can be brought to any tolerable Perfection. Have we any Reason to imagine, that the Society of Bees, that sent forth the first Swarm, made worse Wax or Honey than any of their Posterity have produced since? And again, the Laws of Nature are fix'd and unalterable : In all her Orders and Regulations there is a Stabi-|lity, no where to be [208] met with in Things of human Contrivance and Approbation ;

Quid placet aut odio est, quod non mutabile credas? [1]

Is it probable, that amongst the Bees, there has ever been any other Form of Government, than what every Swarm submits to now? What an infinite Variety of Speculations, what ridiculous Schemes have not been proposed amongst Men, on the Subject of Government ; what Dissentions in Opinion, and what fatal Quarrels has it not been the Occasion of ! And, which is the best Form of it, is a Question to this Day undecided. The Projects, good and bad, that have been stated for the Benefit, and more happy Establishment of Society, are innumerable ; but how short-sighted is our Sagacity, how fallible human Judgment ! What has seem'd highly advantageous to Mankind in one Age, has often been found, to be evidently detrimental by the succeeding ; and even among Contemporaries, what is rever'd in one Country, is the Abomination of another. What Changes have ever Bees made in their Furniture or Architecture? Have they ever made Cells that were not Sexangular, or added any Tools to those which Nature furnish'd them with at the Beginning? What mighty Structures have been rais'd, what prodigious Works have been per-|form'd by the great Nations of the World ! [209] Toward all these Nature has only found Materials ;

[1] Horace, *Epistles* ii. i. 101.

the Quarry yields Marble, but it is the Sculptor that makes a Statue of it. To have the infinite Variety of Iron Tools that have been invented, Nature has given us nothing but the Oar, which she has hid in the Bowels of the Earth.

Hor. But the Capacity of the Workmen, the Inventors of Arts, and those that improved them, has had a great Share in bringing those Labours to Perfection ; and their Genius they had from Nature.

Cleo. So far as it depended upon the Make of their Frame, the Accuracy of the Machine, they had, and no further ; but this I have allow'd already ; and if you remember what I have said on this Head, you will find, that the Part, which Nature contributed toward the Skill and Patience of every single Person, that had a Hand in those Works, was very inconsiderable.

Hor. If I have not misunderstood you, you would insinuate two Things : First, that the Fitness of Man for Society, beyond other Animals, is something real ; but that it is hardly perceptible in Individuals, before great Numbers of them are joyn'd together, and artfully manag'd. Secondly, that this real Something, this Sociableness, is a Compound, that consists in a Concurrence of several Things, and not in any one [210] palpable Qua-|lity, that Man is endued with, and Brutes are destitute of.

Cleo. You are perfectly right : Every Grape contains a small Quantity of Juice, and when great Heaps of them are squeez'd together, they yield a Liquor, which by skillful Management may be made into Wine : But if we consider, how necessary Fermentation is to the Vinosity of the Liquor, I mean, how essential it is to its being Wine ; it will be evident to us, that without great Impropriety of Speech, it cannot be said, that in every Grape there is Wine.

Hor. Vinosity, so far as it is the Effect of Fermentation, is adventitious ; and what none of the Grapes could ever have receiv'd, whilst they remain'd single ;

and therefore, if you would compare the Sociableness of Man to the Vinosity of Wine, you must shew me, that in Society there is an Equivalent for Fermentation ; I mean, something that individual Persons are not actually possess'd of, whilst they remain single, and which, likewise, is palpably adventitious to Multitudes, when joyn'd together ; in the same manner as Fermentation is to the Juice of Grapes, and as necessary and essential to the compleating of Society, as that is, that same Fermentation, to procure the Vinosity of Wine.

Cleo. Such an Equivalent is demonstrable in mutual Commerce : for if we examine every Faculty and Qualification, from and for which | we judge and [211] pronounce Man to be a sociable Creature beyond other Animals, we shall find, that a very considerable, if not the greatest Part of the Attribute is acquired, and comes upon Multitudes, from their conversing with one another. *Fabricando fabri fimus.* Men become sociable, by living together in Society. Natural Affection prompts all Mothers to take Care of the Offspring they dare own ; so far as to feed and keep them from Harm, whilst they are helpless : but where People are poor, and the Women have no Leisure to indulge themselves in the various Expressions of their Fondness for their Infants, which fondling of them ever encreases, they are often very remiss in tending and playing with them ; and the more healthy and quiet such Children are, the more they are neglected. This want of pratling to, and stirring up the Spirits in Babes, is often the principal Cause of an invincible Stupidity, as well as Ignorance, when they are grown up ; and we often ascribe to natural Incapacity, what is altogether owing to the Neglect of this early Instruction. We have so few Examples of human Creatures, that never convers'd with their own Species, that it is hard to guess, what Man would be, entirely untaught ; but we have good Reason to believe, that

the Faculty of Thinking would be very imperfect in
such a one, if we consider ; that the greatest Docility
[212] can be of no | use to a Creature, whilst it has nothing
to imitate, nor any body to teach it.

Hor. Philosophers therefore are very wisely employ'd
when they discourse about the Laws of Nature ; and
pretend to determine, what a Man in the State of
Nature would think, and which way he would reason,
concerning himself and the Creation, uninstructed.

Cleo. Thinking, and Reasoning justly, as Mr. *Lock*
has rightly observed, require Time and Practice.[1]
Those that have not used themselves to thinking, but
just on their present Necessities, make poor Work of
it, when they try beyond that. In remote Parts, and
such as are least inhabited, we shall find our Species
come nearer the State of Nature, than it does in and
near great Cities and considerable Towns, even in the
most civiliz'd Nations. Among the most ignorant of
such People, you may learn the Truth of my Assertion ;
talk to them about any thing, that requires abstract
Thinking, and there is not one in Fifty that will
understand you, any more than a Horse would ; and
yet many of them are useful Labourers, and cunning
enough to tell Lies, and deceive. Man is a rational
Creature, but he is not endued with Reason when he
comes into the World ; nor can he afterwards put it
on when he pleases, at once, as he may a Garment.
Speech likewise is a Characteristick of our Species, but
[213] no Man is born with it ; | and a dozen Generations
proceeding from two Savages would not produce any
tolerable Language ;[2] nor have we reason to believe,
that a Man could be taught to speak after Five and
Twenty, if he had never heard others before that time.

Hor. The Necessity of teaching, whilst the Organs
are supple, and easily yield to Impression, which you

[1] See *Of the Conduct of the Understanding* (*Works*, ed. 1823, iii. 214) : ' As it is in the body, so it is in the mind ; practice makes it what it is. . . .'

[2] Cf. below, ii. 288, *n.* I.

have spoke of before, I believe is of great Weight, both in Speaking and Thinking : but could a Dog, or a Monkey, ever be taught to speak?

Cleo. I believe not ; but I don't think, that Creatures of another Species had ever the Pains bestow'd upon them, that some Children have, before they can pronounce one Word. Another thing to be consider'd is, that tho' some Animals perhaps live longer than we do, there is no Species that remains young so long as ours ; and besides what we owe to the superior Aptitude to learn, which we have from the great Accuracy of our Frame and inward Structure, we are not a little indebted for our Docility, to the Slowness and long Gradation of our Encrease, before we are full grown : the Organs in other Creatures grow stiff, before ours are come to half their Perfection.

Hor. So that in the Compliment we make to our Species, of its being endued with Speech and Sociableness, there is no other Reality; than that by Care and Industry Men may be taught | to speak, and be made sociable, [214] if the Discipline begins when they are ª very young.

Cleo. Not otherwise. A thousand of our Species all grown up, that is above Five and Twenty, could never be made sociable, if they had been brought up wild, and were all Strangers to one another.

Hor. I believe they could not be civilis'd, if their Education began so late.

Cleo. But I mean barely sociable, as it is the Epithet peculiar to Man ; that is, it would be impossible by Art to govern them, any more than so many wild Horses, unless you had two or three times that Number to watch and keep them in awe. Therefore it is highly probable, that most Societies, and Beginnings of Nations, were form'd in the Manner Sir *William Temple* supposes it ; but nothing near so fast : and I wonder how a Man of his unquestionable good Sense could form an Idea of Justice, Prudence, and Wisdom,

ª are] are are *29*

in an untaught Creature ; or think of a civilis'd Man,
before there was any Civil Society, and even before
Men had commenc'd to associate.

Hor. I have read it, I am sure, but I don't remember
what it is you mean.

Cleo. He is just behind you : the third Shelf from
the Bottom ; the first Volume : pray reach it me, it
is worth your hearing.--- It is in his Essay on Government.[1] Here it is. *For if we consider Man multiplying*
[215] *his Kind by the | Birth of many Children, and his Cares
by providing even necessary Food for them, 'till they are
able to do it for themselves (which happens much later to
the Generations of Men, and makes a much longer
Dependence of Children upon Parents, than we can
observe among any other Creatures;) if we consider, not
only the Cares, but the Industry he is forc'd to, for the
necessary Sustenance of his helpless Brood, either in
gathering the natural Fruits, or raising those which are
purchas'd with Labour and Toil : if he be forced for
Supply of this Stock, to catch the tamer Creatures, and
hunt the wilder, sometimes to exercise his Courage in
defending his little Family, and fighting with the strong
and savage Beasts, (that would prey upon him, as he
does upon the weak and the mild :) if we suppose him
disposing with Discretion and Order, whatever he gets
among his Children, according to each of their Hunger
or Need ; sometimes laying up for to-morrow, what was
more than enough for to-day ; at other times pinching
himself, rather than suffering any of them should
want.──*

Hor. This Man is no Savage, or untaught Creature ;
he is fit to be a Justice of Peace.

Cleo. Pray let me go on, I shall only read this
Paragraph : *and as each of them grows up, and able to
share in the common Support, teaching them, both by
Lesson and Example, what he is now to do, as the Son of
his Family, and what hereafter, as the Father of another ;*

---

[1] See *An Essay upon the
Original and Nature of Govern-* ment in *Works of Sir William
Temple* (1814) i. 11-12.

instructing them all, what Qualities are good, and what are | ill, for their Health and Life, or common Society [216] *(which will certainly comprehend whatever is generally esteem'd Virtue or Vice among Men) cherishing and encouraging Dispositions to the good, disfavouring and punishing those to the ill : And lastly, among the various Accidents of Life, lifting up his Eyes to Heaven, when the Earth affords him no Relief; and having Recourse to a higher and a greater Nature, whenever he finds the Frailty of his own : we must needs conclude, that the Children of this Man cannot fail of being bred up with a great Opinion of his Wisdom, his Goodness, his Valour, and his Piety. And if they see constant Plenty in the Family, they believe well of his Fortune too.*

Hor. Did this Man spring out of the Earth, I wonder, or did he drop from the Sky?

Cleo. There is no manner of Absurdity in supposing-----

Hor. The Discussion of this would too far engage us : I am sure, I have tired you already with my Impertinence.

Cleo. You have pleas'd me extremely : the Questions you have ask'd, have all been very pertinent, and such as every Man of Sense would make, that had not made it his Business to think on these Things. I read that Passage on purpose to you, to make some use of it ; but if you are weary of the Subject, I will not trespass upon your Patience any longer.

Hor. You mistake me ; I begin to be fond of the Subject : but before we talk of it any | further, I have [217] a mind to run over that Essay again ; it is a great while since I read it, and after that I shall be glad to resume the Discourse ; the sooner the better. I know you are a Lover of fine Fruit, if you'll dine with me to-morrow, I'll give you an *Ananas.*

Cleo. I love your Company so well, that I can refuse no Opportunity of enjoying it.

Hor. A Revoir then.

Cleo. Your Servant.

THE FIFTH

DIALOGUE

BETWEEN

Horatio and *Cleomenes.*

CLEOMENES.

T excells every thing ; it is extremely rich without being luscious,
and I know nothing, to which I
can compare the Taste of it : to
me it seems to be a Collection of
different fine Flavours, that puts
me in mind of several delicious
Fruits, which yet are all out-
done by it.

Hor. I am glad it pleas'd you.

Cleo. The Scent of it likewise is wonderfully reviving. As you was paring it, a Fragrancy I thought
perfum'd the Room that was perfectly Cordial.

Hor. The Inside of the Rind has an Oyliness of no
disagreeable Smell, that upon handling of it sticks to
ones Fingers for a consider-|able time ; for tho' now
I have wash'd and wiped my Hands, the Flavour of it
will not be entirely gone from them by to-morrow
Morning.

Cleo. This was the third I ever tasted, of our own

Growth : the Production of them in these Northern
Climates, is no small Instance of human Industry,
and our Improvements in Gard'ning. It is very
elegant to enjoy the wholsome Air of temperate
Regions, and at the same time be able to raise Fruit
to its highest Maturity, that naturally requires the
Sun of the Torrid Zone.

Hor. It is easy enough to procure Heat, but the
great Art consists in finding out, and regulating the
Degrees of it at pleasure ; without which it would
be impossible to ripen an *Ananas* here ; and to compass this with that Exactness, as it is done by the Help
of *Thermometers*, was certainly a fine Invention.——

Cleo. I don't care to drink any more.

Hor. Just as you please : otherwise I was going to
name a Health, which would not have come *mal a propos.*

Cleo. Whose is that, pray?

Hor. I was thinking on the Man, to whom we are
in a great measure obliged for the Production and
Culture of the *Exotick*, we were speaking of, in this
Kingdom ; Sir *Matthew Decker :* [1] the first *Ananas*,
or Pine-apple, that was brought to Perfection in
England, grew in his Garden at *Richmond*.

| *Cleo.* With all my Heart ; let us finish with that ; [220]
he is a Beneficent, and, I believe, a very honest Man.

Hor. It would not be easy to name another, who
with the same Knowledge of the World, and Capacity
of getting Money, is equally disinterested and inoffensive. ——

Cleo. Have you consider'd the Things we discoursed
of Yesterday ?

Hor. I have thought on nothing else, since I saw
you : This Morning I went through the whole Essay,
and with more Attention than I did formerly : I like

[1] A contemporary and countryman of Mandeville, who established himself as a merchant in
London in 1702. He was made a
baronet in 1716.—From the tone
of this passage I conjecture a
friendship between Mandeville
and his fellow-Dutchman Decker.

it very well; only that Passage which you read Yesterday, and some others to the same Purpose, I cannot [a] reconcile with the Account we have of Man's Origin from the Bible: [1] Since all are Descendants of *Adam*, and consequently of *Noah* and his Posterity: [2]

[a] can't *30*

[1] In the following attempt to reconcile Genesis with the *Fable* there is far more than at present appears on the surface. Mandeville is constantly either stating or suggesting objections to Scripture current in his day; and, if my reasoning above (ii. 21, *n.* 2) is correct, his answers to these objections are insincere and disingenuous. In the notes to pp. 196–8, and 237, *n.* 1, I have attempted to indicate possible sources for Mandeville's objections and replies.

[2] Mandeville here, I believe, wished to suggest to the reader the current objections that all men were *not* the descendants of Adam and Noah. In the well-known *Theory of the Earth* (ed. 1697, bk. 2, p. 185) Thomas Burnet wrote, ' For I do not see any necessity of deducing all Mankind from *Noah* after the Flood : If *America* was peopled before, it might continue so ; not but that the Flood was universal. But ... Providence ..., as we may reasonably suppose, made provision to save a remnant in every Continent, that the race of Mankind might not be quite extinct in any of them.' And Sir Thomas Browne considered a suggestion which could also be used to argue that some men were not descended from Noah—

that the Flood was ' particular ' (*Works*, ed. Wilkin, 1852, ii. 352–3, in *Religio Medici*)—a theory expounded also in Isaac de la Peyrère's *Theological Systeme upon that Presupposition, that Men were before Adam* (1655), p. 244. Stillingfleet combated the contention that all men were not Noah's posterity (*Origines Sacræ*, Oxford, 1836, ii. 161).—The objection against the universal fatherhood of Adam was notorious. A heresy which had been charged to Giordano Bruno (J. M. Robertson, *History of Freethought*, ed. 1906, ii. 66), in Mandeville's time it found perhaps its best-known exposition in the tracts composing La Peyrère's *Men before Adam* (*Præadamitæ*). The gist of La Peyrère's contention was '... That the men of the first Creation [the Gentiles] were created long before *Adam*, who according to my supposition is Author of the Linage of the Jews [only] ' (*Theological Systeme*, p. 130). That Adam was not the first man had been held also by Charles Blount (*Miscellaneous Works*, ed. 1695, pp. 220–1, in *Oracles of Reason*). Knowledge of this heresy was spread by the many attempts to answer it. William Nichols carefully rehearsed La Peyrère's arguments before attacking them (*Conference with a Theist*, ed.

how came Savages into the World? [1]

Cleo. The History of the World, as to very ancient Times, is very imperfect : [2] What Devastations have been made by War, by Pestilence, and by Famine ; what Distress some Men have been drove to, and how strangely our Race has been dispers'd and scatter'd over the Earth, since the Flood, we don't know.

Hor. But Persons that are well instructed themselves, never fail of teaching their Children ; and we have no Reason to think, that knowing, civiliz'd Men, as the Sons of *Noah* were, should have neglected their Offspring ; but it is altogether incredible, as all are De-|scendants from them, that succeeding Genera- [221] tions, instead of encreasing in Experience, and Wisdom, should learn backward, and still more and more abandon their Broods, in such a manner, as to degenerate at last to what you call the State of Nature.[3]

1723, i. 93–7) ; Philippe le Prieur and Claude Dormay wrote books in answer to the *Præadamitæ* ; Stillingfleet attacked it (*Origines Sacræ* ii. 137 sqq.) ; and he referred to La Peyrère's ' very many not unlearned adversaries ' (ii. 141). Some of these are named in Moréri's *Grand Diction-naire Historique* (ed. 1707, art. ' Peirere '), which also records the notoriety of the *Præadamitæ*. Gui Patin praised the work (*Lettres*, ed. Reveillé-Parise, 1846, ii. 175 and 264).

[1] This query must have had some circulation as a criticism of the belief that Adam was our common progenitor, for William Nichols attacked a variety of it in his *Conference with a Theist* (1723) i. 74–7.

[2] Stillingfleet had defended the credibility of Scripture by impugning the sufficiency of ancient

history (*Origines Sacræ*, Oxford, 1836, bk. 1, ch. 1), and Thomas Burnet also announced the inadequacy of ancient accounts (*Theory of the Earth*, ed. 1697, bk. 2, pp. 187–91).

[3] This was William Law's argument in his *Remarks upon a Late Book, Entituled, the Fable of the Bees* (ed. 1724, pp. 10–11) :

' To defend your Account of the Origin of Morality, you suppose Man in a State of Nature, savage and brutal, without any Notions of Morality or Ideas of Religion.

' Now this very Supposition, is so far from being any Apology for you, that it enhances your Accusation : For you suppose such a State of Nature, (as you call it) as the Scripture makes it morally impossible, that Men should ever have been in.

' When *Noah*'s Family came

Cleo. Whether you intend this as a *Sarcasm* or not, I don't know ; but you have rais'd no Difficulty that can render the Truth of the sacred History suspected. Holy Writ has acquainted us with the miraculous Origin of our Species, and the small Remainder of it after the Deluge : But it is far from informing us of all the Revolutions, that have happen'd among Mankind since : The Old Testament hardly touches upon any Particulars, that had no Relation to the *Jews* ; [1] neither does *Moses* pretend to give a full Account of every thing that happen'd to, or was transacted by, our first Parents : He names none of *Adam*'s Daughters, and takes no Notice of several Things, that must have happen'd in the Beginning of the World ; as is evident from *Cain*'s building a City,[2] and several other Circumstances ; from which it is plain, that *Moses* meddled with nothing but what was material, and to his Purpose ; which in that part of his History was to trace the Descent of the Patriarchs, from the first Man. But that there are Savages, is certain : Most Nations of *Europe* have met with wild Men and Women in

out of the Ark, we presume, they were as well educated in the Principles of Virtue and moral Wisdom, as any People were ever since ; at least we are sure they were well instructed in the true Religion.

' There was therefore a Time, when all the People in the World were well vers'd in moral Virtue, and worship'd God according to the true Religion.

' He therefore that gives a *later* Account of the Origin of moral Virtue, gives a *false* Account of it.

' Now as all parts of the World were by degrees inhabited, by the Descendants of such Ancestors, as were well instructed both in Religion and Morality, it is

morally impossible that there should be any Nation of the World, amongst whom there was no Remains of Morality, no Instances of Virtue, no Principles of Religion deriv'd from their Ancestors.'—Cf. below, ii. 401–6.

[1] This was one of the arguments considered by Stillingfleet in answer to La Peyrère's *Præadamitæ* (*Origines Sacræ*, Oxford, 1836, ii. 139 and 141).

[2] The irreconcilability of the story of Cain with Genesis if Adam is believed the sole father of mankind had been urged by La Peyrère, who instanced this very detail of Cain's building a city (*Theological Systeme*, ed. 1655, proeme, signn. F–Fᵛ).

DIALOGUE. 199

several Parts of the World, that were ignorant | of the [222]
use of Letters, and among whom they could observe
no Rule or Government.

Hor. That there are Savages, I don't question; and
from the great Number of Slaves, that are yearly
fetch'd from *Africa*,[1] it is manifest, that in some Parts
there must be vast Swarms of People, that have not
yet made a great hand of their Sociableness : But how
to derive them all from the Sons of *Noah*, I own, is
past my Skill.

Cleo. You'll find it as difficult to account for the
loss of the many fine Arts, and useful Inventions of
the Ancients, which the World has certainly sustain'd.
But the Fault I find with Sir *William Temple*, is in
the Character of his Savage. Just Reasoning, and such
an orderly way of proceeding, as he makes him act in,
are unnatural to a wild Man : In such a one, the
Passions must be boisterous, and continually jostling
and succeeding one another ; no untaught Man could
have a regular way of thinking, or pursue any one
Design with Steadiness.

Hor. You have strange Notions of our Species :
But has not a Man, by the time that he comes to
Maturity, some Notions of Right and Wrong, that are
natural?

Cleo. Before I answer your Question, I would have
you consider, that among Savages, there must be
always a great difference, as to the Wildness or Tame-
ness of them. All Creatures naturally love their
Offspring, whilst | they are helpless, and so does Man : [223]
But in the Savage State Men are more liable to
Accidents and Misfortunes, than they are in Society,
as to the rearing of their young ones ; and therefore
the Children of Savages must very often be put to

---

[1] One of the treaties signed
at Utrecht in 1713, the Asiento,
gave England the right to provide
slaves for the Spanish colonies
in America. This, of course,
plunged England heavily into
slave-trading.

their Shifts, so as hardly to remember, by the time that they are grown up, that they had any Parents. If this happens too early, and they are dropt or lost, before they are four or five Years of Age, they must perish ; either die for want, or be devour'd by Beasts of Prey, unless some other Creature takes care of them. Those Orphans that survive, and become their own Masters very young, must, when they are come to Maturity, be much wilder than others, that have lived many Years under the Tuition of Parents.

Hor. But would not the wildest Man, you can imagine, have from Nature some Thoughts of Justice and Injustice?

Cleo. Such a one, I believe, would naturally, without much Thinking in the Case, take every thing to be his own, that he could lay his Hands on.

Hor. Then they would soon be undeceiv'd, if two or three of them met together.

Cleo. That they would soon disagree and quarrel, is highly probable ; but I don't believe, they ever would be undeceiv'd.

Hor. At this Rate, Men could never be form'd into an aggregate Body : How came Society into the World?

[224] | *Cleo.* As I told you, from private Families ; but not without great Difficulty, and the Concurrence of many favourable Accidents ; and many Generations may pass, before there is any Likelihood of their being form'd into a Society.

Hor. That Men are form'd into Societies, we see : But if they are all born with that false Notion, and they can never be undeceiv'd, which way do you account for it?

Cleo. My Opinion concerning this Matter, is this. Self-preservation bids all Creatures gratify their Appetites, and that of propagating his Kind never fails to affect a Man in Health, many Years before he comes to his full Growth. If a wild Man and a wild Woman

DIALOGUE. 201

should meet very young, and live together for fifty Years undisturb'd, in a mild wholesome Climate, where there is plenty of Provisions, they might see a prodigious Number of Descendants : For in the wild State of Nature, Man multiplies his Kind much faster, than can be allow'd of in any regular Society : No Male at fourteen would be long without a Female, if he could get one ; and no Female of Twelve would be refractory, if applied to ; or remain long uncourted, if there were Men.

Hor. Considering, that Consanguinity would be no Bar among these People, the Progeny of two Savages might soon amount to Hundreds : All this I can grant you ; but as Pa-|rents, no better qualify'd, [225] could teach their Children but little, it would be impossible for them to govern these Sons and Daughters, when they grew up ; if none of them had any Notions of Right or Wrong : and Society is as far off as ever ; the false Principle, which you say all Men are born with, is an Obstacle never to be surmounted.

Cleo. From that false Principle, as you call it, the Right, Men naturally claim to every thing they can get, it must follow, that Man will look upon his Children as his Property, and make such use of them as is most consistent with his Interest.

Hor. What is the Interest of a wild Man, that pursues nothing with Steadiness?

Cleo. The Demand of the predominant Passion, for the time it lasts.

Hor. That may change every Moment, and such Children would be miserably managed.

Cleo. That's true ; but still managed they would be ; I mean, they would be kept under, and forc'd to do as they were bid, at least till they were strong enough to resist. Natural Affection would prompt a wild Man to love, and cherish his Child ; it would make him provide Food and other Necessaries for his Son, till he was ten or twelve Years old, or perhaps longer : But this Affection is not the only Passion, he has to gratify ; if his Son provokes him by Stubborness, or doing otherwise than he would have him, this Love [226] is | suspended ; and if his Displeasure be strong enough to raise his Anger, which is as natural to him as any other Passion, it is ten to one, but he'll knock him down : If he hurts him very much, and the Condition, he has put his Son in, moves his Pity, his Anger will cease ; and, natural Affection returning, he'll fondle him again, and be sorry for what he has done. Now if we consider, that all Creatures hate and endeavour to avoid Pain, and that Benefits beget Love in all that receive them, we shall find, that the Consequence of this Management would be ; that the Savage Child would learn to love and fear his Father : These two Passions, together with the Esteem, which we naturally have for every thing that far excels us, will seldom fail of producing that Compound, which we call Reverence.[1]

Hor. I have it now ; you have open'd my Eyes, and I see the Origin of Society, as plain as I do that Table.

Cleo. I am afraid the Prospect is not so clear yet, as you imagine.

Hor. Why so ? The grand Obstacles are remov'd : Untaught Men, it is true, when they are grown up, are never to be govern'd ; and our Subjection is never sincere, where the Superiority of the Governour is not very apparent : But both these are obviated ; the Reverence we have for a Person, when we are young, is easily continued as long as we live ; and [227] where Authority is once acknowledg'd, | and that Acknowledgment well establish'd, it cannot be a difficult Matter to govern. If thus a Man may keep up

[1] Compare Descartes' definition : ' La Veneration ou le Respect est une inclination de l'âme, non seulement à estimer l'object qu'elle revere, mais aussi à se soumetre à luy avec quelque crainte . . .' (*Passions de l'Âme,* pt. 3, art. 162).

his Authority over his Children, he'll do it still with
greater Ease over his Grand-Children : For a Child,
that has the least Reverence for his Parents, will
seldom refuse Homage to the Person, to whom he
sees his Father pay it. Besides, a Man's Pride would be
a sufficient Motive for him to maintain the Authority
once gain'd; and, if some of his Progeny proved
Refractory, he would leave no Stone unturn'd, by the
help of the rest to reduce the Disobedient. The old
Man being dead, the Authority from him would
devolve upon the eldest of his Children, and so on.

Cleo. I thought you would go on too fast. If the
wild Man had understood the Nature of Things, and
been endued with general Knowledge, and a Language
ready made, as *Adam* was by Miracle, what you say,
might have been easy ; but an ignorant Creature, that
knows nothing, but what his own Experience has
taught him, is no more fit to govern, than he is fit to
teach the Mathematicks.

Hor. He would not have above one or two Children
to govern at first, and his Experience would encrease
by degrees, as well as his Family : This would require
no such consummate Knowledge.

Cleo. I don't say it would : An ordinary Capacity,
of a Man tollerably well educated, | would be sufficient [228]
to begin with ; but a Man who never had been taught
to curb any of his Passions, would be very unfit for
such a Task. He would make his Children, as soon as
they were able, assist him in getting Food, and teach
them, how and where to procure it. Savage Children,
as they got Strength, would endeavour to imitate every
Action they saw their Parents do, and every Sound
they heard them make ; but all the Instructions they
receiv'd would be confin'd to Things immediately
necessary. Savage Parents would often take Offence
at their Children, as they grew up, without a Cause ;
and as these encreas'd in Years, so natural Affection
would decrease in the other. The Consequence would

be, that the Children would often suffer for Failings that were not their own. Savages would often discover Faults in the Conduct of what was past ; but they would not be able to establish Rules for future Behaviour, which they would approve of themselves for any Continuance ; and Want of Foresight would be an inexhaustible Fund for Changes in their Resolutions. The Savage's Wife, as well as himself, would be highly pleas'd to see their Daughters impregnated, and bring forth ; and they would both take great Delight in their Grand-Children.

Hor. I thought, that in all Creatures the natural Affection of Parents had been confin'd to their own young ones.

[229] | *Cleo.* It is so in all but Man ; there is no Species but ours, that are so conceited of themselves, as to imagine every thing to be theirs. The Desire of Dominion is a never-failing Consequence of the Pride, that is common to all Men ; and which the Brat of a Savage is as much born with, as the Son of an Emperour. This good Opinion, we have of ourselves, makes Men not only claim a Right to their Children, but likewise imagine, that they have a great Share of Jurisdiction over their Grand-Children. The young ones of other Animals, as soon as they can help themselves, are free ; but the Authority, which Parents pretend to have over their Children, never ceases : How general and unreasonable this eternal Claim is naturally in the Heart of Man, we may learn from the Laws ; which, to prevent the Usurpation of Parents, and rescue Children from their Dominion, every civil Society is forc'd to make ; limiting paternal Authority to a certain Term of Years. Our Savage Pair would have a double Title to their Grand-Children, from their undoubted Property in each Parent of them ; and all the Progeny being sprung from their own Sons and Daughters, without Intermixture of Foreign Blood, they would look upon the

whole Race to be their natural Vassals; and I am persuaded, that the more Knowledge and Capacity of reasoning this first Couple acquired, the more just and | unquestionable their Sovereignty over all their [230] Descendants would appear to them, tho' they should live to see the fifth or sixth Generation.

Hor. Is it not strange, that Nature should send us all into the World with a visible Desire after Government, and no Capacity for it at all?

Cleo. What seems strange to you, is an undeniable Instance of Divine Wisdom : For if all had not been born with this Desire, all must have been destitute of it ; and Multitudes could never have been form'd into Societies, if some of them had not been possessed of this Thirst of Dominion. Creatures may commit Force upon themselves, they may learn to warp their natural Appetites, and divert them from their proper Objects ; but peculiar Instincts, that belong to a whole Species, are never to be acquir'd by Art or Discipline ; and those that are born without them, must remain destitute of them for ever. Ducks run to the Water, as soon as they are hatch'd, but you can never make a Chicken swim, any more than you can teach it to suck.

Hor. I understand you very well. If Pride had not been innate to all Men, none of them could ever have been ambitious : And as to the Capacity of Governing, Experience shews us, that it is to be acquired ; but how to bring Society into the World, I know no more than the wild Man himself. What you | have [231] suggested to me, of his Unskilfulness, and want of Power to govern himself, has quite destroy'd all the Hopes I had conceiv'd of Society, from this Family. But would Religion have no Influence upon them? Pray, how came that into the World?

Cleo. From God, by Miracle.

Hor. *Obscurum per obscurius.* I don't understand Miracles, that break in upon, and subvert the Order of Nature; and I have no Notion of Things that come to pass, *en dépît de bon sens,* and are such ; that judging from sound Reason and known Experience, all wise Men would think themselves mathematically sure, that they could never happen.

Cleo. It is certain, that by the Word Miracle, is meant, an Interposition of the Divine Power, when it deviates from the common Course of Nature.

Hor. As when Matters, easily combustible, remain whole and untouch'd, in the Midst of a Fire, fiercely burning ; or Lions in Vigour, industriously kept hungry, forbear eating what they are most greedy after.[1] These Miracles are strange Things.

Cleo. They are not pretended to be otherwise ; the Etymology of the Word imports it ; but it is almost as unaccountable, that Men should disbelieve them, and pretend to be of a Religion, that is altogether built upon Miracles.

[232] | *Hor.* But when I ask'd you that general Question, why did you confine yourself to reveal'd Religion?

Cleo. Because nothing, in my Opinion, deserves the Name of Religion, that has not been reveal'd : The Jewish was the first that was national, and the Christian the next.

Hor. But *Abraham, Noah,* and *Adam* himself were no *Jews,* and yet they had Religion.

Cleo. No other, than what was reveal'd to them. God appear'd to our first Parents, and gave them Commands, immediately after he had created them : The same Intercourse was continued between the Supream Being and the Patriarchs ; but the Father of *Abraham* was an Idolater.

Hor. But the *Ægyptians,* the *Greeks,* and the *Romans* had Religion, as well as the *Jews.*

Cleo. Their gross Idolatry, and abominable Worship, I call Superstition.

Hor. You may be as partial as you please, but they

---

[1] See Dan. iii. 19–27 and vi. 16–23.

all call'd their Worship Religion, as well as we do ours. You say, Man brings nothing with him, but his Passions; and when I ask'd you, how Religion came into the World, I meant, what is there in Man's Nature, that is not acquired, from which he has a Tendency to Religion; what is it, that disposes him to it?

Cleo. Fear.

| *Hor.* How! *Primus in orbe Deos fecit Timor:* [1] [233] Are you of that Opinion?

Cleo. No Man upon Earth less: But that noted *Epicurean* Axiom, which irreligious Men are so fond of, is a very poor one; and it is silly, as well as impious, to say, that Fear made a God; you may as justly say, that Fear made Grass, or the Sun and the Moon: But when I am speaking of Savages, it is not clashing, either with good Sense, nor the Christian Religion, to assert; that, whilst such Men are ignorant of the true Deity, and yet very defective in the Art of Thinking and Reasoning, Fear is the Passion, that first gives them an Opportunity of entertaining some glimmering Notions of an invisible Power; [2] which afterwards, as

[1] See Statius, *Thebaid* iii. 661, and Petronius Arbiter, *Fragmenta* xxvii. 1.

[2] With this compare Hobbes's definition: '*Fear* of power invisible, feigned by the mind, or imagined from tales publicly allowed, RELIGION; not allowed, SUPERSTITION. And when the power imagined, is truly such as we imagine, TRUE RELIGION' (*English Works*, ed. Molesworth, iii. 45, in *Leviathan* i. 6; cf. also *Works* iii. 95).—In his *Origin of Honour* (1732), Mandeville thus develops the text to which this is a note: ' I have told you already, in our Fifth Conversation, how this Aversion to

Evil, and Endeavour to shun it, this Principle of Fear, would always naturally dispose Human Creatures to suspect the Existence of an intelligent Cause that is invisible, whenever any Evil happen'd to them, which came they knew not whence, and of which the Author was not to be seen. If you remember what I said then, the Reasons why no Nations can be govern'd without Religion, will be obvious. Every Individual, whether he is a Savage, or is born in a Civil Society, is persuaded within, that there is such an invisible Cause; and should any Mortal contradict this, no Multitude would

by Practice and Experience they grow greater Proficients, and become more perfect in the Labour of the Brain, and the Exercise of their highest Faculty, will infallibly lead them to the certain Knowledge of an infinite and eternal Being ; whose Power and Wisdom will always appear the greater, and more stupendious to them, the more they themselves advance in Knowledge and Penetration ; though both should be carried on to a much higher Pitch, than it is possible for our limited Nature ever to arrive at.

Hor. I beg your Pardon for suspecting you ; though I am glad it gave you an Opportunity of explaining [234] yourself. The Word *Fear,* | without any Addition, sounded very harsh ; and even now I cannot conceive, how an invisible Cause should become the Object of a Man's Fear, that should be so entirely untaught, as you have made the first Savage : Which Way can any thing invisible, and that affects none of the Senses, make an Impression upon a wild Creature ?

Cleo. Every Mischief and every Disaster that happens to him, of which the Cause is not very plain and obvious ; excessive Heat and Cold ; Wet and Drought, that are offensive ; Thunder and Lightning, even when they do no visible Hurt ; Noises in the dark, Obscurity itself, and every thing that is frightful and unknown, are all administring and contributing to the Establishment of this Fear. The wildest Man, that can be conceiv'd, by the time that he came to Maturity, would be wise enough to know, that Fruits and other Eatables are not to be had, either always, or every where : This would naturally put him upon hoarding, when he had good Store : His Provision might be spoil'd by the Rain ; he would see that Trees were

believe a Word of what he said. Whereas, on the other Hand, if a Ruler humours this Fear, and puts it out of all Doubt, that there is such an invisible Cause, he may say of it what he pleases ; and no Multitude, that was never taught any Thing to the contrary, will ever dispute it with him ' (pp. 21–2).

blasted, and yielded not always the same Plenty :
He might not always be in Health, or his young ones
might grow sick, and die, without any Wounds or
external Force to be seen. Some of these Accidents
might at first escape his Attention, or only alarm his
weak Understanding, without occasioning much Re-
flecti-|on for some Time ; but as they came often, [235]
he would certainly begin to suspect some invisible
Cause ; and, as his Experience encreased, be confirm'd
in his Suspicion. It is likewise highly probable, that
a Variety of different Sufferings, would make him
apprehend several such Causes ; and at last induce
him to believe, that there was a great Number of
them, which he had to fear. What would very much
contribute to this credulous Disposition, and naturally
lead him into such a Belief, is a false Notion, we imbibe
very early, and which we may observe in Infants, as
soon as by their Looks, their Gestures, and the Signs
they make, they begin to be intelligible to us.

Hor. What is that, pray?

Cleo. All young Children seem to imagine, that
every thing thinks and feels in the same Manner as
they do themselves : And, that they generally have
this wrong Opinion of Things inanimate, is evident,
from a common Practice among them ; whenever they
labour under any Misfortune, which their own Wildness, and want of Care have drawn upon them. In all
such Cases, you see them angry at and strike, a Table,
a Chair, the Floor, or any thing else, that can seem to
have been accessary to their hurting themselves, or
the Production of any other Blunder, they have committed. Nurses, we see, in Compliance to their
Frailty, seem to en-|tertain the same ridiculous Senti- [236]
ments ; and actually appease wrathful Brats, by
pretending to take their Part : Thus you'll often see
them very serious, in scolding at and beating, either
the real Object of the Baby's Indignation, or something else, on which the Blame of what has happen'd,

may be thrown, with any Shew of Probability. It is
not to be imagin'd, that this natural Folly should be
so easily cured in a Child, that is destitute of all
Instruction and Commerce with his own Species, as it
is in those, that are brought up in Society, and hourly
improv'd by conversing with others, that are wiser
than themselves; and I am persuaded, that a wild
Man would never get entirely rid of it, whilst he
lived.

Hor. I cannot think so meanly of human Understanding.

Cleo. Whence came the *Dryades* and *Hama-
Dryades?* how came it ever to be thought impious,
to cut down, or even to wound, large venerable Oaks,
or other stately Trees; and what Root did the
Divinity spring from, which the Vulgar, among the
ancient Heathens, apprehended to be in Rivers and
Fountains?

Hor. From the Roguery of designing Priests, and
other Impostors, that invented those Lies, and made
Fables for their own Advantage.

Cleo. But still it must have been want of Under-
[237] standing; and a Tincture, some Re-|mainder of that
Folly, which is discover'd in young Children, that
could induce, or would suffer Men to believe those
Fables. Unless Fools actually had Frailties, Knaves
could not make Use of them.

Hor. There may be something in it; but, be that
as it will, you have own'd, that Man naturally loves
those he receives Benefits from; therefore, how comes
it; that Man, finding all the good Things he enjoys,
to proceed from an invisible Cause, his Gratitude
should not sooner prompt him to be religious, than
his Fear?

Cleo. There are several substantial Reasons, why it
does not. Man takes every thing to be his own, which
he has from Nature : Sowing and Reaping, he thinks,
deserve a Crop, and whatever he has the least Hand

in, is always reckon'd to be his. Every Art, and every Invention, as soon as we know them, are our Right and Property; and whatever we perform by the Assistance of them, is, by the Courtesy of the Species to itself, deem'd to be our own. We make Use of Fermentation, and all the Chymistry of Nature, without thinking ourselves beholden to any thing, but our own Knowledge. She that churns ᵃ the Cream, makes the Butter; without enquiring into the Power, by which the thin lymphatick Particles are forced to separate themselves, and slide away from the more unctious. In brewing, baking, cooking, and | almost [238] every thing we have a Hand in, Nature is the Drudge, that makes all the Alterations, and does the principal Work; yet all, forsooth, is our own. From all which it is manifest; that Man, who is naturally for making every thing centre in himself, must, in his wild State, have a great Tendency, and be very prone to look upon every thing, he enjoys, as his due; and every thing he meddles with, as his own Performance. It requires Knowledge and Reflection; and a Man must be pretty far advanced in the Art of thinking justly, and reasoning consequentially, before he can, from his own Light, and without being taught, be sensible of his Obligations to God. The less a Man knows, and the more shallow his Understanding is, the less he is capable, either of enlarging his Prospect of Things, or drawing Consequences from the little which he does know. Raw, ignorant, and untaught Men, fix their Eyes on what is immediately before, and seldom look further than, as it is vulgarly express'd, the length of their Noses. The wild Man, if Gratitude moved him, would much sooner pay·his Respects to the Tree, he gathers his Nuts from, than he would think of an Acknowledgment to him who had planted it; and there is no Property so well establish'd, but a civiliz'd Man would suspect his Title to it sooner,

ᵃ churms 29

O 2

than a wild one would question the Sovereignty he [239] has over his own Breath. | Another Reason, why Fear is an elder Motive to Religion, than Gratitude, is, that an untaught Man would never suspect ; that the same Cause, which he receiv'd Good from, would ever do him Hurt ; and Evil, without doubt, would always gain his Attention first.

Hor. Men, indeed, seem to remember one ill Turn, that is serv'd them, better than ten good ones ; one Month's Sickness, better than ten Years Health.

Cleo. In all the Labours of Self-preservation, Man is intent on avoiding what is hurtful to him ; but in the Enjoyment of what is pleasant, his Thoughts are relax'd, and he is void of Care : he can swallow a thousand Delights, one after another, without asking Questions ; but the least Evil makes him inquisitive, whence it came, in order to shun it. It is very material, therefore, to know the Cause of Evil ; but to know that of Good, which is always welcome, is of little Use ; that is, such a Knowledge seems not to promise any Addition to his Happiness. When a Man once apprehends such an invisible Enemy, it is reasonable to think, that he would be glad to appease, and make him his Friend, if he could find him out ; it is highly probable, likewise, that in order to this, he would search, investigate, and look every where about him ; and that finding all his Enquiries upon Earth in vain, he would lift up his Eyes to the Sky.

[240] | *Hor.* And so a wild Man might ; and look down and up again, long enough, before he would be the wiser. I can easily conceive, that a Creature must labour under great Perplexities, when it actually fears something, of which it knows, neither what it is, nor where it is ; and that, though a Man had all the Reason in the World to think it invisible, he would still be more afraid of it in the Dark, than when he could see.

Cleo. Whilst a Man is but an imperfect Thinker,

and wholly employ'd in furthering Self-preservation, in the most simple manner; and removing the immediate Obstacles he meets with, in that Pursuit, this Affair, perhaps, affects him but little; but when he comes to be a tollerable Reasoner, and has Leisure to reflect, it must produce strange Chimera's and Surmises; and a wild Couple would not converse together long, before they would endeavour to express their Minds to one another, concerning this Matter; and, as in Time they would invent and agree upon certain Sounds of Distinction for several Things, of which the Idea's would often occur; so I believe, that this invisible Cause would be one of the first, which they would coin a Name for. A wild Man and a wild Woman would not take less Care of their helpless Brood, than other Animals; and it is not to be imagin'd, but the Children that were brought up by them, tho' without In-|struction or Discipline, would, [241] before they were ten Years old, observe in their Parents this Fear of an invisible Cause : It is incredible likewise; considering, how much Men differ from one another in Features, Complexion, and Temper, that all should form the same Idea of this Cause; from whence it would follow, that as soon as any considerable Number of Men could intelligibly converse together, it would appear, that there were different Opinions among them, concerning the invisible Cause : The Fear and Acknowledgment of it being universal, and Man always attributing his own Passions to every thing, which he conceives to think, every body would be sollicitous to avoid the Hatred and Ill-will, and, if it was possible, to gain the Friendship of such a Power. If we consider these Things, and what we know of the Nature of Man, it is hardly to be conceiv'd, that any considerable Number of our Species could have any Intercourse together long, in Peace or otherwise, but willful Lies would be rais'd, concerning this Power, and some would pretend to have seen or heard it.

How different Opinions about invisible Power, may, by the Malice and Deceit of Impostors, be made the Occasion of mortal Enmity among Multitudes, is easily accounted for. If we want Rain very much, and I can be persuaded, that it is your Fault we have [242] none, there needs no greater Cause to | quarrel ; and nothing has happen'd in the World, of Priestcraft or Inhumanity, Folly or Abomination, on religious Accounts, that cannot be solved or explained, with the least Trouble, from these *Data*, and the Principle of Fear.

Hor. I think I must yield to you, that the first Motive of Religion, among Savages, was Fear ; but you must allow me, in your Turn, that from the general Thankfulness, that Nations have always paid to their Gods, for signal Benefits and Success ; the many Hecatombs that have been offer'd after Victories ; and the various Institutions of Games and Festivals ; it is evident, that, when Men came to be wiser, and more civiliz'd, the greatest Part of their Religion was built upon Gratitude.

Cleo. You labour hard, I see, to vindicate the Honour of our Species ; but we have no such Cause to boast of it ; and I shall demonstrate to you, that a well-weigh'd Consideration, and a thorough Understanding of our Nature, will give us much less Reason to exult in our Pride, than it will furnish us with, for the Exercise of our Humility. In the first place, there is no Difference between the original Nature of a Savage, and that of a civiliz'd Man : They are both born with Fear ; and neither of them, if they have their Senses about them, can live many Years, but an invisible Power, will, at one Time or other, become [243] | the Object of that Fear ; and this will happen to every Man, whether he be wild and alone, or in Society, and under the best Discipline. We know by Experience, that Empires, States, and Kingdoms, may excell in Arts and Sciences, Politeness, and all worldly

DIALOGUE. 215

Wisdom, and at the same time be Slaves to the grossest Idolatry, and submit to all the Inconsistencies of a false Religion. The most civiliz'd People have been as foolish and absurd in Sacred Worship, as it is possible for any Savages to be; and the first have often been guilty of study'd Cruelties, which the latter would never have thought of. The *Carthaginians* were a subtle flourishing People, an opulent and formidable Nation, and *Hannibal* had half conquer'd the *Romans,* when still to their Idols they sacrific'd the Children of their chief Nobility. And as to private Persons, there are innumerable Instances in the most polite Ages of Men of Sense and Virtue, that have entertain'd the most miserable, unworthy, and extravagant Notions of the Supreme Being. What confus'd and unaccountable Apprehensions must not some Men have had of Providence, to act as they did! *Alexander Severus,* who succeeded *Heliogabalus,* was a great Reformer of Abuses, and thought to be as good a Prince, as his Predecessor was a bad one : In his Palace he had an Oratory, a Cabinet set aside for his private Devotion, where he had the | Images of *Apollonius Thyanæus,*[1] [244] *Orpheus, Abraham, Jesus Christ,* and such like Gods, says his Historian. What makes you smile?

Hor. To think how industrious Priests are in concealing a Man's Failings, when they would have you think well of him. What you say of *Severus,* I had read before ; when looking, one Day, for something in *Moreri,* I happen'd to cast my Eye on the Article of that Emperour,[2] where no Mention is made, either of *Orpheus* or *Apollonius :* Which, remembring the Passage in *Lampridius,*[3] I wonder'd at ; and thinking

---

[1] A great myth grew up about this Greek reformer and philosopher. He was credited with having raised the dead, and was supposed to have escaped the persecution of both Nero and Domitian by miraculous means.

[2] See Moréri's *Grand Dictionnaire Historique* (1702) i. 109.

[3] See the Life of Severus in the *Scriptores Historiae Augustae* 29.

that I might have been mistaken, I again consulted that Author, where I found it, as you have related it. I don't question, but *Moreri* left this out, on purpose to repay the Civilities of the Emperour to the Christians, whom he tells us, *Severus* had been very favourable to.

Cleo. That's not impossible, in a *Roman* Catholick. But what I would speak to, in the second place, is the Festivals you mention'd, the Hecatombs after Victories, and the general Thankfulness of Nations to their Gods. I desire, you would consider, that in sacred Matters, as well as all human Affairs, there are Rites and Ceremonies, and many Demonstrations of Respect to be seen, that to outward Appearance seem to proceed from Gratitude, which upon due Examination will be found to have been originally the Result of Fear. [245] At what time the Floral Games were first | instituted, is not well known ; [1] but they never were celebrated every Year constantly, before a very unseasonable Spring put the Senate upon the Decree, that made them annual. To make up the true Compound of Reverence or Veneration, Love and Esteem are as necessary Ingredients as Fear ; but the latter alone is capable of making Men counterfeit both the former ; as is evident from the Duties, that are outwardly paid to Tyrants, at the same time that inwardly they are execrated and hated. Idolaters have always behaved themselves to every invisible Cause they adored, as

---

[1] According to tradition, they were instituted in 238 B.C., by order of the Sibylline books. At first, they were held irregularly, and, probably, only in the country ; it is not even certain that they were always, in the beginning, dedicated to Flora, the flower-goddess. But, finally, they extended to the cities, and took the form of a six-day festival lasting from 28 April to 3 May. In 173 B.C., the blossoms that year having suffered from the weather, they were made a regular institution. Their nature was extremely licentious.—In his *Free Thoughts* (1729), pp. 189-91, Mandeville gives, concerning these games, some information derived from the first article on Flora in Bayle's *Dictionary*.

Men do to a lawless arbitrary Power; when they reckon it as captious, haughty, and unreasonable, as they allow it to be sovereign, unlimited, and irresistible. What Motive could the frequent Repetitions of the same Solemnities spring from, whenever it was suspected, that the least holy Trifle had been omitted? You know, how often the same Farce was once acted over again, because after every Performance, there was still room to apprehend, that some thing had been neglected. Do but consult, I beg of you, and call to mind your own Reading; cast your Eyes on the infinite Variety of Ideas, Men have form'd to themselves, and the vast Multitude of Divisions they have made of the invisible Cause, which every one imagines to influence human Affairs : Run over the History of all Ages ; look into every considerable Nation, their Streights | and Calamities, as well as [246] Victories and Successes ; the Lives of great Generals, and other famous Men, their adverse Fortune and Prosperity : Mind at which times their Devotion was most fervent ; when Oracles were most consulted, and on what Accounts the Gods were most frequently address'd. Do but calmly consider every thing, you can remember, relating to Superstition, whether grave, ridiculous, or execrable ; and you will find in the first place ; that the Heathens, and all that have been ignorant of the true Deity, tho' many of them were Persons otherwise of great Knowledge, fine Understanding, and tried Probity, have represented their Gods, not as wise, benign, equitable, and merciful ; but on the contrary, as passionate, revengeful, capricious, and unrelenting Beings ; not to mention the abominable Vices, and gross Immoralities, the Vulgar were taught to ascribe to them : In the second, that for every one Instance, that Men have address'd themselves to an invisible Cause, from a Principle of Gratitude, there are a thousand in every false Religion to convince you, that Divine Worship, and Men's

Submission to Heaven, have always proceeded from
their Fear. The Word Religion itself, and the Fear
of God, are synonimous ; and had Man's Acknowledg-
ment been originally founded in Love, as it is in Fear,
the Craft of Impostors could have made no Advantage
[247] of the Passion ; and all their boasted | Acquaintance
with Gods and Goddesses, would have been useless to
them, if Men had worship'd the Immortal Powers, as
they call'd their Idols, out of Gratitude.

Hor. All Lawgivers and Leaders of People gain'd
their Point, and acquired what they expected from
those Pretences, which is Reverence ; and which to
produce, you have own'd yourself, Love and Esteem
to be as requisite as Fear.

Cleo. But from the Laws they imposed on Men,
and the Punishments they annex'd to the Breach and
Neglect of them, it is easily seen which of the Ingredients they most relied upon.

Hor. It would be difficult to name a King, or other
great Man in very ancient times, who attempted to
govern any Infant Nation, that laid no Claim to some
Commerce or other with an invisible Power, either
held by himself or his Ancestors. Between them and
Moses, there is no other difference, than that he alone
was a true Prophet, and really inspired, and all the
rest were Impostors.

Cleo. What would you infer from this?

Hor. That we can say no more for ourselves, than
what Men of all Parties and Persuasions have done in
all Ages, every one for their Cause, *viz.* That they
alone were in the Right, and all that differ'd from
them in the Wrong.

[248] | *Cleo.* Is it not sufficient, that we can say this of
ourselves, with Truth and Justice, after the strictest
Examination ; when no other Cause can stand any
Test, or bear the least Enquiry? A Man may relate
Miracles, that never were wrought, and give an
Account of Things that never happen'd ; but a

thousand Years hence, all knowing Men will agree, that no Body could have wrote Sir *Isaac Newton's* *Principia*, unless he had been a great Mathematician. When *Moses* acquainted the *Israelites*, with what had been reveal'd to him, he told them a Truth, which no Body then upon Earth knew but himself.

Hor. You mean the Unity of God, and his being the Author of the Universe.

Cleo. I do so.

Hor. But is not every Man of Sense, capable of knowing this from his Reason?

Cleo. Yes, when the Art of Reasoning consequentially is come to that Perfection, which it has been arrived at these several hundred Years, and himself has been led into the Method of thinking justly. Every common Saylor could steer a Course through the midst of the Ocean, as soon as the Use of the Loadstone and the Mariners Compass were invented. But before that, the most expert Navigator would have trembled at the Thoughts of such an Enterprise. When *Moses* acquainted and imbued the Posterity of *Jacob* with this sublime and important Truth, they were | de- [249] generated into Slaves, attach'd to the Superstition of the Country they dwell'd in ; and the *Ægyptians* their Masters, tho' they were great Proficients in many Arts and Sciences, and more deeply skill'd in the Mysteries of Nature than any other Nation then was, had the most abject and abominable Notions of the Deity, which it is possible to conceive ; and no Savages could have exceeded their Ignorance and Stupidity, as to the supreme Being, the invisible Cause that governs the World. He taught the *Israelites*, *à priori* ; and their Children, before they were nine or ten Years old, knew, what the greatest Philosophers did not attain to, by the Light of Nature, till many Ages after.

Hor. The Advocates for the Ancients will never allow, that any modern Philosophers have either thought or reason'd better, than Men did in former Ages.

Cleo. Let them believe their Eyes : What you say, every Man of Sense may know, by his own Reason, was in the Beginning of Christianity contested, and denied with Zeal and Vehemence by the greatest Men in *Rome.* *Celsus, Symmachus, Porphyry, Hierocles,*[1] and other famous Rhetoricians, and Men of unquestionable good Sense, wrote in Defence of Idolatry, and strenuously maintained the Plurality and Multiplicity of their Gods. *Moses* lived above fifteen hundred Years before the Reign of *Augustus.* If in a Place, [250] where I was ve-|ry well assured, that no Body understood any thing of colouring or drawing, a Man should tell me, that he had acquired the Art of Painting by Inspiration, I should be more ready to laugh at him, than to believe him ; but if I saw him draw several fine Portraicts, before my Face, my Unbelief would cease, and I should think it ridiculous, any longer to suspect his Veracity. All the Accounts that other Lawgivers and Founders of Nations have given of the Deities, which they or their Predecessors convers'd with, contain'd Idea's that were unworthy of the Divine Being ; and by the Light of Nature only, it is easily prov'd, that they must have been false : But the Image which *Moses* gave the *Jews* of the Supreme Being, that he was One, and had made Heaven and Earth, will stand all Tests, and is a Truth that will outlast the World. Thus, I think, I have fully proved

[1] *The True Word,* published in 248 A.D., seventy years after its composition, an attack on Christianity, is Celsus's chief claim to fame.—Quintus Aurelius Symmachus (*c.* 345–410), a prominent political figure, was banished by Gratian for the importunateness of his defence of paganism.—Porphyry was a Greek scholar, historian, and follower of Plotinus, of the third century A.D. He attacked Christianity in his κατὰ Χριστιανῶν, in fifteen books, only fragments of which are now extant.—Hierocles is said to have instigated the persecution of Christians under Galerius in 303 A.D., and published a now lost work against them.

on the one hand, that all true Religion must be reveal'd, and could not have come into the World without Miracle; and on the other, that what all Men are born with towards Religion, before they receive any Instruction, is Fear.

Hor. You have convinced me many ways, that we are poor Creatures, by Nature; but I can't help strugling against those mortifying Truths, when I hear them started first. I long to hear the Origin of Society, and I continually retard your Account of it myself, with new Questions.

| *Cleo.* Do you remember where we left off? [251]

Hor. I don't think we have made any Progress yet; for we have nothing towards it but a wild Man, and a wild Woman; with some Children and Grandchildren, which they are not able either to teach or to govern.

Cleo. I thought that the Introduction of the Reverence, which the wildest Son must feel more or less for the most Savage Father, if he stays with him, had been a considerable Step.

Hor. I thought so too, till you destroy'd the Hopes I had conceiv'd of it, yourself, by shewing me the Incapacity of Savage Parents to make use of it : And since we are still as far from the Origin of Society as ever we were, or ever can be, in my Opinion ; I desire, that before you proceed to that main Point, you would answer what you have put off once already, which is my Question concerning the Notions of Right and Wrong : I cannot be easy, before I have your Sentiments on this Head.

Cleo. Your Demand is very reasonable, and I will satisfy you as well as I can. A Man of Sense, Learning and Experience, that has been well educated, will always find out the difference between Right and Wrong in things diametrically opposite ; and there are certain Facts, which he will always condemn, and others which he will always approve of : To kill

[252] a Member of the same Society, that has | not offended us, or to rob him, will always be bad ; and to cure the Sick, and be beneficent to the Publick, he will always pronounce to be good Actions in themselves : and for a Man to do as he would be done by, he will always say is a good Rule in Life ; and not only Men of great Accomplishments, and such as have learn'd to think abstractly, but all Men of midling Capacities, that have been brought up in Society, will agree in this, in all Countries, and in all Ages. Nothing likewise seems more true to all, that have made any tolerable use of their Faculty of Thinking, than that out of the Society, before any Division was made, either by Contract or otherwise, all Men would have an equal Right to the Earth : But do you believe, that our wild Man, if he had never seen any other human Creature but his Savage Consort, and his Progeny, would ever have entertain'd the same Notions of Right and Wrong?

Hor. Hardly ; his small Capacity in the Art of Reasoning, would hinder him from doing it so justly ; and the Power he found he had over his Children would render him very arbitrary.

Cleo. But without that Incapacity, suppose that at threescore he was by a Miracle to receive a fine Judgment, and the Faculty of Thinking, and Reasoning consequentially, in as great a Perfection, as the wisest Man ever had it ; do you think, he'd ever alter his [253] No-|tion, of the Right he had to every thing he could manage ; or have other Sentiments in Relation to himself, and his Progeny, than from his Behaviour it appear'd he entertain'd, when he seem'd to act almost altogether by Instinct?

Hor. Without doubt : For if Judgment and Reason were given him, what could hinder him from making use of those Faculties, as well as others do?

Cleo. You seem not to consider, that no Man can reason but *à posteriori*, from something that he knows, or supposes to be true : What I said of the difference between Right and Wrong, I spoke of Persons, who remembred their Education, and lived in Society ; or at least such, as plainly saw others of their own Species, that were independent of them, and either their Equals or Superiours.

Hor. I begin to believe you are in the Right : But at second Thoughts, why might not a Man with great Justice think himself the Sovereign of a Place, where he knew no human Creature but his own Wife, and the Descendents of both?

Cleo. With all my Heart : But may there not be an hundred such Savages in the World with large Families, that might never meet, nor ever hear of one another?

Hor. A thousand, if you will, and then there would be so many natural Sovereigns.

| *Cleo.* Very well : what I would have you observe, [254] is, that there are things, which are commonly esteem'd to be eternal Truths, that an hundred or a thousand People of fine Sense and Judgment, could have no Notion of. What if it should be true, that every Man is born with this domineering Spirit, and that we cannot be cured of it, but by our Commerce with others, and the Experience of Facts, by which we are convinc'd, that we have no such Right? Let us examine a Man's whole Life, from his Infancy to his Grave, and see, which of the two seems to be most natural to him ; a Desire of Superiority, and grasping every thing to himself ; or a Tendency to act according to the reasonable Notions of Right and Wrong ; and we shall find, that in his early Youth the first is very conspicuous ; that nothing appears of the second before he has receiv'd some Instructions, and that this latter will always have less Influence upon his Actions, the more uncivilis'd he remains : From whence I infer, that the Notions of Right and Wrong are acquired ; for if they were as natural, or if they affected us, as

early as the Opinion, or rather the Instinct we are born with, of taking every thing to be our own, no Child would ever cry for his eldest Brother's Playthings.

Hor. I think, there is no Right more natural, nor [255] more reasonable, than that which | Men have over their Children; and what we owe our Parents can never be repaid.

Cleo. The Obligations we have to good Parents, for their Care and Education, is certainly very great.

Hor. That's the least. We are indebted to them for our Being; we might be educated by an hundred others, but without them, we could never have existed.

Cleo. So we could have no Malt Liquor, without the Ground that bears the Barley : I know no Obligations for Benefits that never were intended. Should a Man see a fine Parcel of Cherries, be tempted to eat, and devour them accordingly with great Satisfaction : It is possible, he might swallow some of the Stones, which we know by Experience don't digest : If twelve or fourteen Months after, he should find a little Sprig of a Cherry-tree growing in a Field, where no Body would expect it : If he recollected the time, he had been there before, it is not improbable, that he might guess at the true Reason how it came there. It is possible likewise, that for Curiosity's sake, this Man might take up this Plant, and take Care of it; I am well assured, that whatever became of it afterwards, the Right he would have to it from the Merit of his Action, would be the same, which a Savage would have to his Child.[1]

---

[1] Cf. Swift, *Gulliver's Travels*, in *Prose Works*, ed. Temple Scott, viii. 61–2 : '. . . the Lilliputians will needs have it, that men and women are joined together like other animals, by the motives of concupiscence; and that their tenderness towards their young proceeds from the like natural principle : for which reason they will never allow, that a child is under any obligation to his father for begetting him, or to his mother for bringing him into the world. . . .'

Hor. I think, there would be a vast Difference between the one and the other : The | Cherry-stone [256] was never part of himself, nor mix'd with his Blood.

Cleo. Pardon me ; all the difference, as vast as you take it to be, can only consist in this, that the Cherry-stone was not Part of the Man, who swallow'd it, so long, nor receiv'd so great an Alteration in its Figure, whilst it was, as some other things, which the Savage swallow'd, were, and receiv'd in their Figure, whilst they stay'd with him.

Hor. But he that swallow'd the Cherry-stone, did nothing to it; it produced a Plant as a Vegetable, which it might have done as well without his swallowing it.

Cleo. That's true ; and I own, that as to the Cause to which the Plant owes its Existence, you are in the right : But I plainly spoke as to the Merit of the Action, which in either Case could only proceed from their Intentions, as free Agents ; and the Savage might, and would in all Probability act, with as little Design to get a Child, as the other had eat Cherries in order to plant a Tree. It is commonly said, that our Children are our own Flesh and Blood : But this way of speaking is strangely figurative. However, allow it to be just, tho' Rhetoriciens have no Name for it ; what does it prove, what Benevolence in us, what Kindness to others, in the Intention?

Hor. You shall say what you please, but I think, that nothing can endear Children to | their Parents [257] more, than the Reflection, that they are their own Flesh and Blood.

Cleo. I am of your Opinion ; and it is a plain Demonstration of the superlative Value, we have for our own selves, and every thing that comes from us, if it be good, and counted laudable ; whereas other things, that are offensive, tho' equally our own, are in Compliment to ourselves industriously conceal'd ; and as soon as it is agreed upon that any thing is unseemly, and rather a Disgrace to us than otherwise,

presently it becomes ill Manners to name, or so much
as to hint at it. The Contents of the Stomach are
variously disposed of, but we have no hand in that;
and whether they go to the Blood, or elsewhere, the
last thing we did to them voluntarily, and with our
Knowledge, was swallowing them; and whatever is
afterwards perform'd by the Animal Oeconomy, a Man
contributes no more to, than he does to the going of
his Watch. This is another Instance of the unjust
Claim we lay to every Performance, we are but in the
least concern'd in, if good comes of it, tho' Nature
does all the Work; but whoever places a Merit in his
prolifick Faculty, ought likewise to expect the Blame,
when he has the Stone, or a Fever. Without this
violent Principle of innate Folly, no rational Creature
would value himself on his free Agency, and at the
same time accept of Applause for Actions that are
[258] visibly independent | of his Will. Life in all Creatures
is a compound Action, but the Share they have in it
themselves, is only passive. We are forc'd to breathe,
before we know it; and our Continuance palpably
depends upon the Guardianship, and perpetual Tute-
lage of Nature; whilst every part of her Works,
ourselves not excepted, is an impenetrable Secret [1] to
us, that eludes all Enquiries. Nature furnishes us
with all the Substance of our Food herself, nor does
she trust to our Wisdom for an Appetite to crave it;
to chew it, she teaches us by Instinct, and bribes us
to it by Pleasure. This seeming to be an Action of
Choice, and ourselves being conscious of the Performance, we perhaps may be said to have a part in it;
but the Moment after, Nature resumes her Care, and,
again withdrawn from our Knowledge, preserves us
in a mysterious manner, without any Help or Concurrence of ours, that we are sensible of. Since then
the Management of what we have eat and drank,

[1] Compare Bayle's *Dictionary*, art. 'Pyrrho', *n.* B: '. . . Nature is
an impenetrable Abyss. . . .'

remains entirely under the Direction of Nature, what Honour or Shame ought we to receive from any part of the Product, whether it is to serve as a doubtful Means toward Generation, or yields to Vegetation a less fallible Assistance? It is Nature that prompts us to propagate, as well as to eat ; and a Savage Man multiplies his Kind by Instinct, as other Animals do, without more Thought or Design of preserving his Species, than a new-born Infant | has of keeping itself [259] alive, in the Action of Sucking.

Hor. Yet Nature gave the different Instincts to both, for those Reasons.

Cleo. Without doubt ; but what I mean, is, that the Reason of the Thing is as much the Motive of Action in the one, as it is in the other ; and I verily believe, that a Wild Woman, who had never seen, or not minded the Production of any young Animals, would have several Children before she would guess at the real Cause of them ; any more, than, if she had the Cholick, she would suspect that it proceeded from some delicious Fruit she had eaten ; especially if she had feasted upon it for several Months, without perceiving any Inconveniency from it. Children, all the World over, are brought forth with Pain, more or less, which seems to have no Affinity with Pleasure ; and an untaught Creature, however docil and attentive, would want several clear Experiments, before it would believe, that the one could produce or be the Cause of the other.

Hor. Most People marry in Hopes, and with a Design, of having Children.

Cleo. I doubt, not ; and believe, that there are as many, that would rather not have Children, or at least not so fast as often they come, as there are that wish for them, even in the State of Matrimony : But out of it, in the Amours of Thousands, that revel in Enjoyments, | Children are reckon'd to be the greatest [260] Calamity that can befal them ; and often, what criminal Love gave Birth to, without Thought, more criminal Pride destroys, with purpos'd and considerate Cruelty. But all this belongs to People in Society, that are knowing, and well acquainted with the natural Consequences of Things; what I urg'd, I spoke of a Savage.

Hor. Still the End of Love, between the different Sexes, in all Animals, is the Preservation of their Species.

Cleo. I have allow'd that already. But once more; the Savage is not prompted to Love, from that Consideration : He propagates, before he knows the Consequence of it; and I much question, whether the most civiliz'd Pair, in the most chaste of their Embraces, ever acted from the Care of their Species, as a real Principle. A rich Man may, with great Impatience, wish for a Son, to inherit his Name and his Estate; perhaps, he may marry from no other Motive, and for no other Purpose; but all the Satisfaction he seems to receive, from the flattering Prospect of an happy Posterity, can only arise from a pleasing Reflection on himself, as the Cause of those Descendants. How much soever this Man's Posterity might be thought to owe him for their Being, it is certain, that, the Motive he acted from, was to oblige [261] himself : Still here's a wishing for Posterity, | a Thought and Design of getting Children, which no wild Couple could have to boast of; yet they would be vain enough to look upon themselves, as the principal Cause of all their Offspring and Descendants; though they should live to see the fifth or sixth Generation.

Hor. I can find no Vanity in that, and I should think 'em so myself.

Cleo. Yet, as free Agents, it would be plain, that they had contributed nothing to the Existence of their Posterity.

Hor. Now surely, you have over-shot the Mark; nothing?

Cleo. No, nothing, even to that of their own Children, knowingly; if you'll allow, that Men have their Appetites from Nature. There is but one real Cause in the Universe, to produce that infinite Variety of stupendious Effects, and all the mighty Labours that are perform'd in Nature ; either within, or far beyond, the Reach of our Senses. Parents are the Efficients of their Offspring, with no more Truth or Propriety of Speech, than the Tools of an Artificer, that were made and contriv'd by himself, are the Cause of the most elaborate of his Works. The senseless Engine, that raises Water into the Copper, and the passive Mash-tub,[1] have between them, as great a Share in the Art and Action of Brewing, as the liveliest Male and Female ever had in the Production of an Animal.

| *Hor.* You make Stocks and Stones of us ; Is it not [262] in our choice, to act, or not to act?

Cleo. Yes, it is in my choice now, either to run my Head against the Wall, or to let it alone ; but, I hope, it does not puzzle you much to guess, which of the two I shall chuse.

Hor. But don't we move our Bodies as we list? and is not every Action determin'd by the Will?

Cleo. What signifies that, where there is a Passion that manifestly sways, and with a strict Hand governs that Will?

Hor. Still we act with Consciousness, and are intelligent Creatures.

Cleo. Not in the Affair I speak of ; where, willing or not willing, we are violently urg'd from within, and, in a manner, compell'd, not only to assist in, but likewise to long for, and, in spight of our Teeth, be highly pleased with, a Performance, that infinitely surpasses our Understanding. The Comparison I made is just, in every Part of it ; for the most loving, and, if you will, the most sagacious Couple, you can conceive, are as ignorant in the Mystery of Generation ; nay, must remain, after having had twenty Children,

---

[1] A vat in which malt is mashed.

together, as much uninform'd, and as little conscious of Nature's Transactions, and what has been wrought within them; as inanimate Utensils are of the most mystick and most ingenious Operations they have been employ'd in.

[263]　| *Hor.* I don't know any Man more expert in tracing human Pride, or more severe in humbling it, than yourself; but when the Subject comes in your Way, you don't know how to leave it. I wish you would, at once, go over to the Origin of Society; which, how to derive, or bring about at all, from the savage Family, as we left it, is past my Skill. It is impossible but those Children, when they grew up, would quarrel on innumerable Occasions: If Men had but three Appetites to gratify, that are the most obvious, they could never live together in Peace, without Government: For though they all paid a Deference to the Father, yet, if he was a Man void of all Prudence, that could give them no good Rules to walk by, I am persuaded that they would live in a perpetual State of War; and the more numerous his Offspring grew, the more the old Savage would be puzzled, between his Desire and Incapacity of Government. As they encreased in Numbers, they would be forced to extend their Limits, and the Spot they were born upon would not hold them long: No body would be willing to leave his native Vale, especially if it was a fruitful one. The more I think upon it, and the more I look into such Multitudes, the less I can conceive, which way they could ever be form'd into a Society.

[264]　| *Cleo.* The first thing that could make Man associate, would be common Danger, which unites the greatest Enemies: This Danger they would certainly be in, from wild Beasts, considering, that no uninhabited Country is without them, and the defenceless Condition, in which Men come into the World. This often must have been a cruel Article, to prevent the Increase of our Species.

Hor. The Supposition then, that this wild Man, with his Progeny, should for fifty Years live undisturbed, is not very probable ; and I need not trouble myself about our Savage's being embarrass'd with too numerous an Offspring.

Cleo. You say right ; there is no Probability, that a Man and his Progeny, all unarm'd, should so long escape the ravenous Hunger of Beasts of Prey, that are to live upon what Animals they can get ; that leave no Place unsearch'd, nor Pains untry'd, to come at Food, though with the Hazard of their Lives. The Reason why I made that Supposition, was to shew you, first, the Improbability that a wild, and altogether untaught Man, should have the Knowledge and Discretion, which Sir *William Temple* gives him ; [1] secondly, that Children, who convers'd with their own Species, though they were brought up by Savages, would be governable ; and consequently, that all such, when come to Maturity, would be fit for Society, how ignorant and unskillful soever their Parents might [265] have been.

Hor. I thank you for it ; for it has shewn me, that the very first Generation of the most brutish Savages, was sufficient to produce sociable Creatures ; but that to produce a Man fit to govern others, much more was required.

Cleo. I return to my Conjecture, concerning the first Motive, that would make Savages associate : It is not possible to know any thing, with Certainty, of Beginnings, where Men were destitute of Letters ; but I think, that the Nature of the thing makes it highly probable, that it must have been their common Danger from Beasts of Prey ; as well such sly ones, as lay in wait for their Children, and the defenceless Animals, Men made Use of for themselves ; as the more bold, that would openly attack grown Men and Women. What much confirms me in this Opinion, is,

[1] See *Fable* ii. 191–3.

the general Agreement of all the Relations we have,
from the most ancient Times, in different Countries :
For in the Infancy of all Nations, prophane History is
stuff'd with the Accounts of the Conflicts Men had
with wild Beasts. It took up the chief Labours of the
Heroes of remotest Antiquity, and their greatest
Prowess was shewn in killing of Dragons, and sub-
duing of other Monsters.

[266] | *Hor.* Do you lay any Stress upon Sphinxes,
Basilisks, flying Dragons, and Bulls that spit Fire?

Cleo. As much as I do on modern Witches. But
I believe, that all those Fictions had their Rise from
noxious Beasts, the Mischiefs they did, and other
Realities that struck Terrour into Man ; and, I believe,
that if no Man had ever been seen on a Horse's Back,
we should never have heard of Centaurs. The prodigious Force and Rage, that are apparent in some
savage Animals, and the astonishing Power, which
from the various Poysons of venemous Creatures, we
are sure must be hid in others ; the sudden and
unexpected Assaults of Serpents, the Variety of them,
the vast Bulks of Crocodiles ; the irregular and uncommon Shapes of some Fishes, and the Wings of
others, are all things that are capable of alarming Man's
Fear ; and it is incredible what Chimera's, that Passion
alone may produce in a terrify'd Mind : The Dangers
of the Day often haunt Men at Night with Addition
of Terror ; and from what they remember in their
Dreams, it is easy to forge Realities. If you will
consider likewise, that the natural Ignorance of Man,
and his hankering after Knowledge, will augment the
Credulity, which Hope and Fear first give Birth to ; the
Desire the Generality have of Applause, and the great
Esteem that is commonly ᵃ had for the *Merveilleux*,
[267] and the Wit-|nesses and Relaters of it : If, I say, you
will consider all these, you will easily discover ; how
many Creatures came to be talk'd of, describ'd, and
formally painted, that never had any Existence.

ᵃ comomnly *29*

Hor. I don't wonder at the Origin of monstrous Figures, or the Invention of any Fables whatever; but in the Reason you gave for the first Motive, that would make Men combine in one Interest, I find something very perplexing, which, I own, I never thought of before. When I reflect on the Condition of Man, as you have set it before me, naked and defenceless, and the Multitude of ravenous Animals, that thirst after his Blood, and are superior to him in Strength, and completely arm'd by Nature, it is inconceivable to me, how our Species should have subsisted.

Cleo. What you observe is well worthy our Attention.

Hor. It is astonishing. What filthy, abominable Beasts are Lions and Tygers!

Cleo. I think them to be very fine Creatures; there is nothing I admire more than a Lion.

Hor. We have strange Accounts of his Generosity and Gratitude; but do you believe them?

Cleo. I don't trouble my Head about them : What I admire, is his Fabrick, his Structure, and his Rage, so justly proportion'd to one | another. There are [268] Order, Symmetry, and superlative Wisdom to be observ'd in all the Works of Nature; but she has not a Machine, of which every Part more visibly answers the End, for which the whole was form'd.

Hor. The Destruction of other Animals.

Cleo. That's true; but how conspicuous is that End, without Mystery or Uncertainty! That Grapes were made for Wine, and Man for Society, are Truths not accomplish'd in every Individual : But there is a real Majesty stamp'd on every single Lion, at the Sight of which, the stoutest Animals submit and tremble. When we look upon, and examine his massy Talons, the Size of them, and the labour'd Firmness, with which they are fix'd in, and fasten'd to that prodigious Paw; his dreadful Teeth, the Strength of his

Jaws, and the Width of his Mouth equally terrible, the Use of them is obvious; but when we consider, moreover, the Make of his Limbs, the Toughness of his Flesh and Tendons, the Solidity of his Bones, beyond that of other Animals, and the whole Frame of him, together with his never-ceasing Anger, Speed and Agility; whilst in the Desart he ranges King of Beasts : When, I say, we consider all these Things, it is Stupidity, not to see the Design of Nature, and with what amazing Skill, the beautiful Creature is contrived, for offensive War and Conquest.[1]

[269] | *Hor.* You are a good Painter. But, after all, why would you judge of a Creature's Nature from what it was perverted to, rather than from its Original, the State it was first produced in? The Lion in Paradise was a gentle, loving Creature. Hear what *Milton* says of his Behaviour before *Adam* and *Eve, as they sate recline on the soft downy Bank, damask'd with Flowers :*

——— ——— *About them frisking play'd*
All Beasts of the Earth, since wild, and of all chace
In Wood or Wilderness, Forest or Den;
Sporting the Lion ramp'd, and in his Paw
Dandl'd the Kid; Bears, Tygres, Ounces, Pards,
Gambol'd before them.—— ——— ———[2]

What was it, the Lion fed upon; what Sustenance had all these Beasts of Prey, in Paradise?

Cleo. I don't know. No body, who believes the Bible, doubts, but that the whole State of Paradise, and the Intercourse [a] between God and the first Man, were as much preternatural, as the Creation out of Nothing; and therefore it cannot be suppos'd, that they should be accounted for by human Reason; and if they were, *Moses* would not be answerable for more than he advanced himself. The History which he has

[a] Intercouse 29

[1] Cf. *Fable* i. 179–80.   [2] *Paradise Lost* iv. 333–4 and 340–5.

given us of those Times | is extremely succinct, and [270] ought not to be charged with any thing, contain'd in the Glosses and Paraphrases, that have been made upon it by others.

Hor. *Milton* has said nothing of Paradise, but what he could justify from *Moses.*

Cleo. It is no where to be proved, from *Moses,* that the State of Innocence lasted so long, that Goats or any viviparous Animals could have bred, and brought forth young ones.

Hor. You mean, that there could have been no Kid. I should never have made that Cavil, in so fine a Poem. It was not in my Thoughts : What I aim'd at in repeating those Lines, was to shew you, how superfluous and impertinent a Lion must have been in Paradise ; and that those who pretend to find fault with the Works of Nature, might have censur'd her with Justice, for lavishing and throwing away so many Excellencies, upon a great Beast, to no Purpose. What a fine Variety of destructive Weapons, would they say, what prodigious Strength of Limbs and Sinews are here given to a Creature ! What to do with? To be quiet, and dandle a Kid. I own, that to me, this Province, the Employment assign'd to the Lion, seems to be as proper and well chosen, as if you'd make a Nurse of *Alexander the Great.*

Cleo. You might make as many Flights upon a Lion now, if you saw him asleep. No | body would think [271] that a Bull had Occasion for Horns, who had never seen him otherwise, than quietly grazing among a Parcel of Cows ; but, if one should see him attack'd by Dogs, by a Wolf, or a Rival of his own Species, he would soon find out, that his Horns were of great Use and Service to him. The Lion was not made to be always in Paradise.

Hor. There I would have you. If the Lion was contriv'd for Purposes, to be serv'd and executed out of Paradice, then it is manifest, from the very Creation, that the Fall of Man was determin'd and predestinated.

Cleo. Fore-known it was : Nothing could be hid from Omniscience : that is certain ; but that it was predestinated so as to have prejudiced, or any ways influenced the Free-Will of *Adam*, I utterly deny. But that Word, *predestinated*, has made so much Noise in the World, and the thing itself has been the Cause of so many fatal Quarrels, and is so inexplicable, that I am resolved never to engage in any Dispute concerning it.[1]

Hor. I can't make you ; but what you have extoll'd so much, must have cost the Lives of thousands of our Species ; and it is a Wonder to me how Men, when they were but few, could possibly defend themselves, before they had Fire Arms, or at least, Bows and Arrows ; for what Number of naked Men and Women, would be a Match for one Couple of Lions?

[272] | *Cleo.* Yet, here we are ; and none of those Animals are suffer'd to be wild, in any civiliz'd Nation ; our superior Understanding has got the Start of them.

Hor. My Reason tells me, it must be that ; but I can't help observing, that when human Understanding serves your Purpose to solve any thing, it is always ready and full grown ; but at other times, Knowledge and Reasoning are the Work of Time, and Men are not capable of thinking justly, 'till after many Generations. Pray, before Men had Arms, what could their

[1] Ch. 5 of Mandeville's *Free Thoughts* is devoted to a discussion of free-will and predestination. He records the great conflict that has raged between those who believed that God's omniscience must necessarily prevent the freedom of our will, since what He knows *must* come to pass, and those who held that, despite His omniscience, we are free, since, otherwise, if we are not free, God must be held responsible for the evil in the world. Then, attacking the question from the starting-point of the problem of evil, Mandeville attempts to demonstrate that neither hypothesis absolves God from responsibility for evil. He is, therefore, driven, as in the passage to which this is a note, to declare the matter unfit for finite intelligence and to appeal to revelation.

Understanding do against Lions, and what hindred wild Beasts from devouring Mankind, as soon as they were born?

Cleo. Providence.[1]

Hor. Daniel, indeed, was sav'd by Miracle; but what is that to the rest of Mankind? great Numbers, we know, have, at different times, been torn to Pieces by savage Beasts: What I want to know, is the Reason, that any of them escap'd, and the whole Species was not destroy'd by them; when Men had yet no Weapons to defend, nor strong Holds to shelter themselves from the Fury of those merciless Creatures.

Cleo. I have named it to you already, Providence.

Hor. But which Way can you prove this miraculous Assistance?

| *Cleo.* You still talk of Miracles, and I speak of [273] Providence, or the all-governing Wisdom of God.

Hor. If you can demonstrate to me, how that Wisdom interpos'd between our Species, and that of Lions, in the Beginning of the World, without Miracle, any more than it does at present, *Eris mihi magnus Apollo:*[2] For now, I am sure, a wild Lion would prey upon a naked Man, as soon, at least, as he would upon an Ox or an Horse.

Cleo. Won't you allow me, that all Properties, Instincts, and what we call the Nature of Things, animate or inanimate, are the Produce, the Effects of that Wisdom?

Hor. I never thought otherwise.

---

[1] Compare La Peyrère's argument: 'The Lord would have his people encreased to a full and sufficient number of inhabitants, which should be able to defend themselves from the beasts of *Canaan,* and secure the people.... And if God would not expose many hundred thousand Jews to the beasts of one Land, shall we think, that he would expose one single man and woman to the beasts of all Lands?' (*Theological Systeme,* ed. 1655, p. 134). —Cf. above, ii. 21, *n.* 2.

[2] Virgil, *Eclogues* iii. 104. This proverb is used by Mandeville in his *Treatise* (1730), p. 33, where he translates it, '*You shall be my Oracle*'.

Cleo. Then it will not be difficult to prove this to you. Lions are never brought forth wild, but in very hot Countries, as Bears are the Product of the cold. But the Generality of our Species, which loves moderate Warmth, are most delighted with the middle Regions. Men may, against their Wills, be inured to intense Cold, or by Use and Patience accustom themselves to excessive Heat ; but a mild Air, and Weather between both Extremes, being more agreeable to human Bodies, the greatest Part of Mankind would naturally settle in temperate Climates, and with the same Conveniency, as to every thing else, never chuse any [274] other. This would very much lessen the | Danger Men would be in from the fiercest and most irresistible wild Beasts.

Hor. But would Lions and Tygers in hot Countries, keep so close within their Bounds, and Bears in cold ones, as never to straggle or stray beyond them?

Cleo. I don't suppose they would ; and Men, as well as Cattle, have often been pick'd up by Lions, far from the Places where these were whelp'd. No wild Beasts are more fatal to our Species, than often we are to one another ; and Men pursued by their Enemies have fled into Climates and Countries, which they would never have chose. Avarice likewise and Curiosity, have, without Force or Necessity, often exposed Men to Dangers, which they might have avoided, if they had been satisfied with what Nature required ; and labour'd for Self-preservation in that simple Manner, which Creatures less vain and fantastical content themselves with. In all these Cases, I don't question, but Multitudes of our Species have suffer'd from Savage Beasts, and other noxious Animals ; and on their account only, I verily believe, it would have been impossible for any Number of Men, to have settled or subsisted in either very hot or very cold Countries, before the Invention of Bows and Arrows, or better Arms. But all this does nothing to overthrow my

Assertion : What I wanted to prove is, that all Creatures, chusing by Instinct that Degree of Heat or Cold | which is most natural to them, there would [275] be Room enough in the World for Man to multiply his Species, for many Ages, without running almost any Risque of being devour'd either by Lions or by Bears ; and that the most savage Man would find this out, without the help of his Reason. This I call the Work of Providence ; by which I mean the unalterable Wisdom of the Supreme Being, in the harmonious Disposition of the Universe ; the Fountain of that incomprehensible Chain of Causes, on which all Events have their undoubted Dependance.

Hor. You have made this out, better than I had expected ; but I am afraid, that what you alledged, as the first Motive toward Society, is come to nothing by it.

Cleo. Don't fear that ; there are other savage Beasts, against which Men could not guard themselves unarm'd, without joyning, and mutual Assistance : In temperate Climates, most uncultivated Countries abound with Wolves.

Hor. I have seen them in *Germany* ; they are of the Size of a large Mastiff ; but I thought their chief Prey had been Sheep.

Cleo. Any thing they can conquer is their Prey : They are desperate Creatures, and will fall upon Men, Cows, and Horses, as well as upon Sheep, when they are very hungry : They have Teeth like Mastiffs ; but besides them they have sharp Claws to tear with, | which Dogs have not. The stoutest Man is hardly [276] equal to them in Strength ; but what is worse, they often come in Troops, and whole Villages have been attack'd by them : They have five, six, and more Whelps at a Litter, and would soon over-run a Country, where they breed, if Men did not combine against, and make it their Business to destroy them. Wild Boars likewise, are terrible Creatures, that few large

Forests, and uninhabited Places, in temperate Climates, are free from.

Hor. Those Tusks of theirs are dreadful Weapons.

Cleo. And they are much superiour to Wolves in Bulk and Strength. History is full of the Mischief they have done in ancient Times, and of the Renown that valiant Men have gain'd by conquering them.

Hor. That's true; but those Heroes, that fought Monsters in former Days, were well arm'd; at least, the Generality of them; but what could a Number of naked Men, before they had any Arms at all, have, to oppose to the Teeth and Claws of ravenous Wolves, that came in Troops; and what Impression could the greatest Blow a Man can strike, make upon the thick bristly Hide of a wild Boar?

Cleo. As on the one hand, I have named every thing, that Man has to fear from wild Beasts; so, on [277] the other, we ought not to for-|get the Things that are in his Favour. In the first place, a wild Man inured to Hardship, would far exceed a tame one, in all Feats of Strength, Nimbleness, and Activity: In the second, his Anger would sooner and more usefully transport and assist him in his savage State, than it can do in Society; where, from his Infancy, he is so many ways taught, and forced, in his own Defence, to cramp and stifle with his Fears the noble Gift of Nature. In wild Creatures we see, that most of them, when their own Life, or that of their young ones, is at Stake, fight with great Obstinacy, and continue fighting to the last, and do what Mischief they can, whilst they have Breath, without regard to their being overmatch'd, or the Disadvantages they labour under. It is observ'd likewise, that the more untaught and inconsiderate Creatures are, the more entirely they are sway'd by the Passion that is uppermost: Natural Affection would make wild Men, and Women too, sacrifice their Lives, and die for their Children; but they would die fighting; and one Wolf would

not find it an easy Matter to carry off a Child from
his watchful Parents, if they were both resolute,
though they were naked. As to Man's being born
defenceless, it is not to be conceiv'd, that he should
long know the Strength of his Arms, without being
acquainted with the Articulation of his Fingers, or
at least, what is owing to it, his Faculty | of grasping [278]
and holding fast; and the most untaught Savage
would make Use of Clubs and Staves before he came
to Maturity. As the Danger Men are in from wild
Beasts would be of the highest Consequence, so it
would employ their utmost Care and Industry : They
would dig Holes, and invent other Stratagems, to
distress their Enemies, and destroy their young ones :
As soon as they found out Fire, they would make use
of that Element to guard themselves and annoy their
Foes : By the Help of it they would soon learn to
sharpen Wood, which presently would put 'em upon
making Spears and other Weapons that would cut.
When Men are angry enough with Creatures to strike
them, and these are running away, or flying from
them, they are apt to throw at what they cannot
reach : This, as soon as they had Spears, would
naturally lead them to the Invention of Darts and
Javelins. Here, perhaps, they might stop a while;
but the same Chain of Thinking would, in Time,
produce Bows and Arrows : The Elasticity of Sticks
and Boughs of Trees is very obvious; and to make
Strings of the Guts of Animals, I dare say, is more
ancient than the Use of Hemp. Experience teaches
us, that Men may have all these, and many more
Weapons, and be very expert in the Use of them,
before any manner of Government, except that of
Parents over their Children, is to be seen | among [279]
them : It is likewise very well known, that Savages
furnish'd with no better Arms, when they are strong
enough in Number, will venture to attack, and even
hunt after the fiercest wild Beasts, Lions and Tygers

not excepted. Another thing is to be consider'd, that likewise favours our Species, and relates to the Nature of the Creatures, of which in temperate Climates Man has Reason to stand in bodily fear of.

Hor. Wolves and wild Boars?

Cleo. Yes. That great Numbers of our Species have been devour'd by the first, is uncontested; but they most naturally go in quest of Sheep and Poultry; and, as long as they can get Carrion, or any thing to fill their Bellies with, they seldom hunt after Men, or other large Animals; which is the reason, that in the Summer our Species, as to personal Insults, have not much to fear from them. It is certain likewise, that Savage Swine will hunt after Men, and many of their Maws have been cramm'd with human Flesh: But they naturally feed on Acorns, Chesnuts, Beach-mast, and other Vegetables; and they are only carnivorous upon Occasion, and through Necessity, when they can get nothing else; in great Frosts, when the Country is bare, and every thing cover'd with Snow. It is evident then, that human Creatures are not in any great and immediate Danger from either of these Species of Beasts, but in hard Winters, which [280] | happen but seldom in temperate Climates. But as they are our perpetual Enemies, by spoiling and devouring every thing that may serve for the Sustenance of Man; it is highly necessary, that we should not only be always upon our guard against them, but likewise never cease to assist one another, in routing and destroying them.

Hor. I plainly see, that Mankind might subsist and survive to multiply, and get the Mastery over all other Creatures that should oppose them; and as this could never have been brought about, unless Men had assisted one another against Savage Beasts, it is possible, that the Necessity Men were in of joyning and uniting together, was the first Step toward Society. Thus far I am willing to allow you, to have proved your main

Point : But to ascribe all this to Providence, otherwise, than that nothing is done without the Divine
Permission, seems inconsistent with the Ideas we have
of a perfectly good, and merciful Being. It is possible,
that all poysonous Animals may have something in
them, that's beneficial to Men ; and I won't dispute
with you, whether the most venomous of all the
Serpents, which *Lucan* has made mention of,[1] did not
contain some Antidote, or other fine Medicine, still
undiscovered : But when I look upon the vast Variety
of ravenous and blood-thirsty Creatures, that are not
only superiour to us in Strength, but like-|wise visibly [281]
arm'd by Nature, as it were on purpose for our
Destruction ; when, I say, I look upon these, I can
find out no Use for them, nor what they could be
design'd for, unless it be to punish us : but I can
much less conceive, that the Divine Wisdom should
have made them the Means without which Men
could not have been civiliz'd. How many thousands
of our Species must have been devour'd in the Conflicts with them !

Cleo. Ten Troops of Wolves, with fifty in each,
would make a terrible Havock in a long Winter among
a Million of our Species with their Hands tied behind
them ; but among half that Number, one Pestilence
has been known to slaughter more, than so many
Wolves could have eaten in the same time ; notwithstanding the great Resistance that was made against it,
by approv'd of Medicines and able Physicians. It is
owing to the Principle of Pride we are born with, and
the high Value we all, for the Sake of one, have for
our Species, that Men imagine the whole Universe to
be principally made for their use ; and this Errour
makes them commit a thousand Extravagancies, and
have pitiful and most unworthy Notions of God and
his Works. It is not greater Cruelty, or more unnatural
in a Wolf to eat a piece of a Man, than it is in a Man

---

[1] In *Pharsalia* vi. 677 sqq. and ix. 700–838.

to eat part of a Lamb or a Chicken. What, or how many Purposes wild Beasts were made for, is not for [282] us to determine : But that | they were made, we know ; and that some of them must have been very calamitous to every Infant Nation, and Settlement of Men, is almost as certain : This you was fully persuaded of ; and thought moreover, that they must have been such an Obstacle to the very Subsistence of our Species, as was insurmountable : In answer to this difficulty, which you started, I shew'd you, from the different Instincts, and peculiar Tendencies of Animals, that in Nature a manifest Provision was made for our Species ; by which, notwithstanding the Rage and Power of the fiercest Beasts, we should make a shift, naked and defenceless, to escape their Fury, so as to be able to maintain ourselves and multiply our Kind, till by our Numbers, and Arms acquired by our own Industry, we could put to flight, or destroy all Savage Beasts without Exception, whatever Spot of the Globe we might have a mind to cultivate and settle on. The necessary Blessings we receive from the Sun, are obvious to a Child ; and it is demonstrable, that without it, none of the living Creatures that are now upon the Earth, could subsist. But if it were of no other Use, being eight [a] hundred thousand times bigger than the Earth at least, one thousandth part of it would do our Business as well, if it was but nearer to us in Proportion. From this Consideration alone, I am persuaded, that the Sun was made to enlighten [283] and cherish other Bodies, besides this Pla-|net of ours. Fire and Water were design'd for innumerable Purposes, and among the Uses that are made of them, some are immensly different from others. But whilst we receive the Benefit of these, and are only intent on ourselves, it is highly probable, that there are thousands of things, and perhaps our own Machines among them, that in the vast System of the Universe are now serving some very wise Ends, which we shall never know. Accord-

---

[a] eight] seven or eight *29 ; corrected as above 29 Errata, 30, 33.*

ing to that Plan of this Globe, I mean the Scheme of Government, in relation to the living Creatures that inhabit the Earth, the Destruction of Animals is as necessary as the Generation of them.

Hor. I have learn'd that from *the Fable of the Bees*;[1] and I believe what I have read there to be very true; that, if any one Species was to be exempt from Death, it would in time crush all the rest to pieces, tho' the first were Sheep, and the latter all Lions: But that the Supreme Being should have introduced Society at the Expence of so many Lives of our Species, I cannot believe, when it might have been done much better in a milder way.

Cleo. We are speaking of what probably was done, and not of what might have been done. There is no question, but the same Power that made Whales, might have made us seventy Feet high, and given us Strength in Proportion. But since the Plan of this | Globe requires, and you think it necessary your self, [284] that in every Species some should dye almost as fast as others are born, why would you take away any of the Means of dying?

Hor. Are there not Diseases enough, Physicians and Apothecaries, as well as Wars by Sea and Land, that may take off more than the Redundancy of our Species?

Cleo. They may, it is true; but in Fact, they are not always sufficient to do this: And in populous Nations we see, that War, wild Beasts, Hanging, Drowning, and an hundred Casualties together, with Sickness and all its Attendants, are hardly a Match for one invisible Faculty of ours, which is the Instinct Men have to preserve their Species. Every thing is easy to the Deity; but to speak after an human manner, it is evident, that in forming this Earth, and

[1] No such passage on the advantage of mortality is to be found in Part I of the *Fable* (unless *Fable* i. 250 be meant), nor have I found it in any of Mandeville's other works.—Montaigne has such a passage; cf. *Essais* (Bordeaux, 1906-20) iii. 346-7.

every thing that is in it, no less Wisdom or Sollicitude was required, in contriving the various Ways and Means, to get rid and destroy Animals, than seems to have been employ'd in producing them; and it is as demonstrable, that our Bodies were made on purpose not to last beyond such a Period, as it is, that some Houses are built with a Design not to stand longer than such a Term of Years. But it is Death itself to which our Aversion by Nature is universal; as to the manner of dying, Men differ in their Opinions; and I never heard of one yet that was generally liked of.

[285] | *Hor.* But no Body chuses a cruel one. What an unspeakable and infinitely excruciating Torment must it be, to be torn to pieces, and eat alive by a Savage Beast!

Cleo. Not greater, I can assure you, than are daily occasion'd by the Gout in the Stomach, and the Stone in the Bladder.

Hor. Which way can you give me this Assurance; how can you prove it?

Cleo. From our Fabrick itself, the Frame of human Bodies, that cannot admit of any Torment, infinitely excruciating. The Degrees of Pain, as well as of Pleasure, in this Life are limited, and exactly proportion'd to every one's Strength; whatever exceeds that, takes away the Senses; and whoever has once fainted away with the Extremity of any Torture, knows the full Extent of what here he can suffer, if he remembers what he felt. The real Mischief, which wild Beasts have done to our Species, and the Calamities they have brought upon it, are not to be compared to the cruel Usage, and the Multiplicity of mortal Injuries, which Men have receiv'd from one another. Set before your Eyes a robust Warriour, that having lost a Limb in Battle, is afterwards trampled upon by twenty Horses; and tell me, pray, whether you think, that lying thus helpless with most of his Ribs broke, and a fractur'd Skull, in the Agony of Death for several Hours, he suffers less, than if a Lion had dispatch'd him?

| *Hor.* They are both very bad. [286]

Cleo. In the choice of things we are more often directed by the Caprice of Fashions, and the Custom of the Age, than we are by solid Reason, or our own Understanding. There is no greater Comfort in dying of a Dropsy, and being eaten by Worms, than there is in being drown'd at Sea, and becoming the Prey of Fishes. But in our narrow way of thinking, there is something that subverts and corrupts our Judgment ; how else could Persons of known Elegancy in their Taste, prefer rotting and stinking in a loathsome Sepulchre, to their being burnt in the open Air to inoffensive Ashes?

Hor. I freely own, that I have an Aversion to every thing that is shocking and unnatural.

Cleo. What you call shocking, I don't know ; but nothing is more common to Nature, or more agreeable to her ordinary Course, than that Creatures should live upon one another : The whole System of animated Beings on the Earth seems to be built upon this ; and there is not one Species, that we know of, that has not another that feeds upon it, either alive or dead ; and most kind of Fish are forced to live upon Fish. That this in the last-mention'd, was not an Omission or Neglect, is evident from the large Provision Nature has made for it, far exceeding any thing she has done for other Animals.

| *Hor.* You mean the prodigious Quantity of Roe [287] they spawn.

Cleo.[a] Yes ; and that the Eggs, contain'd in them, receive not their Fecundity, till after they are excluded ; by which means the Female may be fill'd with as many of them as her Belly can hold, and the Eggs themselves may be more closely crowded together, than would be consistent with the Admission of any Substance from the Male : Without this, one Fish could not bring forth yearly such a prodigious Shoal.

---

[a] ' *Hor.*' *misprinted for* ' *Cleo.*', *and* ' *Cleo.*' *for* ' *Hor.*', *in this and the following four speeches 29, 33*

Hor. But might not the *aura seminalis* of the Male be subtile enough to penetrate the whole Cluster of Eggs, and influence every one of them, without taking up any room, as it does in Fowls and other oviparous Animals?

Cleo. The Ostrich excepted in the first place; in the second, there are no other oviparous Animals, in which the Eggs are so closely compacted together, as they are in Fish. But suppose that the prolifick Power should pervade the whole Mass of them ; if all the Eggs, which some of the Females are cramm'd with, were to be impregnated whilst they are within the Fish, it is impossible, but the *aura seminalis*, the prolifick Spirit of the Male, tho' it took up no room itself, would, as it does in all other Creatures, dilate, and more or less distend every Egg ; and the least Expansion of so many Individuals would swell the [288] whole Roe to a Bulk that would require | a much greater Space, than the Cavity that now contains them. Is not here a Contrivance beyond Imagination fine, to provide for the Continuance of a Species, tho' every Individual of it should be born with an Instinct to destroy it !

Hor. What you speak of, is only true at Sea, in a considerable part of *Europe* at least : For in fresh Water most kinds of Fish do not feed on their own Species, and yet they spawn in the same manner, and are as full of Roe as all the rest : Among them, the only great Destroyer with us, is the Pike.

Cleo. And he is a very ravenous one : We see in Ponds, that, where Pikes are suffer'd to be, no other Fish shall ever encrease in Number. But in Rivers, and all Waters near any Land, there are amphibious Fowls, and many sorts of them, that live mostly upon Fish : Of these Water-Fowls in many Places there are prodigious Quantities. Besides these, there are Otters, Beavers, and many other Creatures that live upon Fish. In Brooks and shallow Waters, the Hearn

and Bittern will have their Share : What is taken off
by them, perhaps, is but little ; but the young Fry,
and the Spawn that one pair of Swans are able to
consume in one Year, would very well serve to stock
a considerable River. So they are but eat, it is no
matter what eats them, either their own Species or
another : What I would prove, is, that Nature pro-
duces no extraor-|dinary Numbers of any Species, [289]
but she has contriv'd Means answerable to destroy
them. The Variety of Insects, in the several Parts of
the World, would be incredible to any one, that has
not examin'd into this matter ; and the different
Beauties to be observ'd in them is infinite : But neither
the Beauty nor the Variety of 'em are more surprizing,
than the Industry of Nature in the Multiplicity of
her Contrivances to kill them ; and if the Care and
Vigilance of all other Animals, in destroying them,
were to cease at once, in two Years time the greatest
part of the Earth which is ours now would be theirs,
and in many Countries Insects would be the only
Inhabitants.

Hor. I have heard that Whales live upon nothing
else ; That must make a fine Consumption.

Cleo. That is the general Opinion ; I suppose,
because they never find any Fish in them ; and because
there are vast Multitudes of Insects in those Seas,
hovering on the Surface of the Water. This Creature
likewise helps to corroborate my Assertion, that in the
Numbers produced of every Species, the greatest
Regard is had to the Consumption of them : This
prodigious Animal being too big to be swallow'd,
Nature in it has quite alter'd the OEconomy observed
in all other Fish ; for they are viviparous, engender
like other viviparous Animals, and have never above
two or three | young ones at a time. For the Continu- [290]
ance of every Species, among such an infinite Variety
of Creatures, as this Globe yields ; it was highly
necessary, that the Provision for their Destruction

should not be less ample, than that, which was made
for the Generation of them ; and therefore the Sollicitude of Nature in procuring Death, and the Consumption of Animals, is visibly superiour to the Care
she takes to feed and preserve them.

Hor. Prove that pray.

Cleo. Millions of her Creatures are starv'd every
Year, and doom'd to perish for want of Sustenance ;
but whenever any dye, there is always plenty of
Mouths to devour them. But then again, she gives
all she has : Nothing is so fine or elaborate, as that
she grudges it for Food ; nor is any thing more
extensive or impartial than her Bounty : She thinks
nothing too good for the meanest of her Broods, and
all Creatures are equally welcome to every thing they
can find to eat. How curious is the Workmanship in
the Structure of a common Fly ; how inimitable are
the Celerity of his Wings, and the Quickness of all his
Motions in hot Weather ! Should a *Pythagorean,* that
was likewise a good Master in Mechanicks, by the help
of a Microscope, pry into every minute part of this
changeable Creature, and duly consider the Elegancy
of its Machinery, would he not think it great pity,
that thousands of Millions of animated Beings, so
[291] | nicely wrought and admirably finish'd, should every
Day be devour'd by little Birds and Spiders, of which
we stand in so little need ? Nay, don't you think
yourself, that things would have been managed full
as well, if the quantity of Flies had been less, and there
had been no Spiders at all ?

Hor. I remember the Fable of the Acorn and the
Pumpkin [1] too well to answer you ; I don't trouble
my Head about it.

---

[1] For this fable see Mandeville's
*Æsop Dress'd ; or a Collection
of Fables Writ in Familiar Verse*
(n.d.), pp. 5–7. The fable (a para-
phrase of La Fontaine's *Le Gland*
et la Citrouille) tells of a lout who
ridicules the arrangement of the
universe because of the apparent
incongruity of a pumpkin growing
on so slender a stem when a huge

Cleo. Yet you found fault with the Means, which I supposed Providence had made use of to make Men associate ; I mean the common Danger they were in from wild Beasts : Tho' you own'd the Probability of its having been the first Motive of their uniting.

Hor. I cannot believe, that Providence should have no greater regard to our Species, than it has to Flies, and the Spawn of Fish ; or that Nature has ever sported with the Fate of human Creatures, as she does with the Lives of Insects, and been as wantonly lavish of the first, as she seems to be of the latter. I wonder how you can reconcile this to Religion ; you, that are such a Stickler for Christianity.

Cleo. Religion has nothing to do with it. But we are so full of our own Species, and the Excellency of it, that we have no Leisure seriously to consider the System of this Earth ; I mean the Plan on which the OEconomy of it is built, in relation to the living Creatures, that are in and upon it.

| *Hor.* I don't speak as to our Species, but in respect [292] to the Deity : Has Religion nothing to do with it, that you make God the Author of so much Cruelty and Malice?

Cleo. It is impossible, you should speak otherwise, than in relation to our Species, when you make use of those Expressions, which can only signify to us the Intentions things were done with, or the Sentiments human Creatures have of them ; and nothing can be call'd cruel, or malicious, in regard to him who did it, unless his Thoughts and Designs were such in doing it. All Actions in Nature, abstractly consider'd, are equally indifferent ; and whatever it may be to

oak is only called upon to support acorns. After this reflection, he seats himself beneath an oak, and an acorn, falling on his head, convinces him that the providence which refused to hang pumpkins on oaks was not so stupid after all :

THE World's vast Fabrick is so
    well
Contrived by its Creator's Skill;
There's nothing in't, but what is
    good
To him, by whom its understood....

individual Creatures, to die is not a greater Evil to this Earth, or the whole Universe, than it is to be born.

Hor. This is making the First Cause of Things not an Intelligent Being.

Cleo. Why so? Can you not conceive an Intelligent, and even a most Wise Being, that is not only exempt from, but likewise incapable of entertaining, any Malice or Cruelty?

Hor. Such a Being could not commit or order Things, that are malicious and cruel.

Cleo. Neither does God. But this will carry us into a Dispute about the Origin of Evil; and from thence we must inevitably fall on Free-Will and Predestination, which, as I have told you before, is an inexplicable Mystery, I will never meddle with. But I never said nor thought any thing irreverent to the [293] Deity : | On the contrary, the Idea I have of the Supreme Being, is as transcendently great, as my Capacity is able to form one, of what is incomprehensible ; and I could as soon believe, that he could cease to exist, as that he should be the Author of any real Evil. But I should be glad to hear the Method, after which you think Society might have been much better introduced : Pray, acquaint me with that milder way you spoke of.

Hor. You have thoroughly convinced me, that the natural Love, which it is pretended, we have for our Species, is not greater, than what many other Animals have for theirs : But if Nature had actually given us an Affection for one another, as sincere, and conspicuous, as that, which Parents are seen to have for their Children, whilst they are helpless, Men would have joyn'd together by Choice ; and nothing could have hindred them from associating, whether their Numbers had been great or small, and themselves either ignorant, or knowing.

Cleo. *O mentes hominum cæcas ! O Pectora cæca !* [1]

---

[1] Cf. Lucretius, *De Natura Rerum* ii. 14.

DIALOGUE. 253

Hor. You may exclaim as much as you please; I am persuaded, that this would have united Men in firmer Bonds of Friendship, than any common Danger from wild Beasts could have tied them with : But what Fault can you find with it, and what Mischief could have befaln us from mutual Affection?

| *Cleo.* It would have been inconsistent with the [294] Scheme, the Plan after which, it is evident, Providence has been pleas'd to order and dispose of things in the Universe. If such an Affection had been planted in Man by Instinct, there never could have been any fatal Quarrels among them, nor mortal Hatreds ; Men could never have been cruel to one another : In short, there could have been no Wars of any duration ; and no considerable Numbers of our Species could ever have been kill'd by one another's Malice.

Hor. You'd make a rare State-Physician, in prescribing War, Cruelty and Malice, for the Welfare and Maintenance of civil Society.

Cleo. Pray, don't misrepresent me : I have done no such thing : But if you believe the World is govern'd by Providence at all, you must believe likewise, that the Deity makes use of Means to bring about, perform, and execute his Will and Pleasure : As for Example, to have War kindled, there must be first Misunderstandings and Quarrels between the Subjects of different Nations, and Dissentions among the respective Princes, Rulers, or Governours of them : It is evident, that the Mind of Man is the general Mint, where the Means of this sort must be coin'd ; from whence I conclude, that if Providence had order'd Matters after that mild way, which you think would have been the best, very little of humane Blood could have been spilt, if any at all.

| *Hor.* Where would have been the Inconveniency [295] of that?

Cleo. You could not have had that Variety of living Creatures, there is now ; nay, there would not have been Room for Man himself, and his Sustenance : Our Species alone would have overstock'd the Earth, if there had been no Wars, and the common Course of Providence had not been more interrupted than it has been. Might I not justly say then, that this is quite contrary and destructive to the Scheme, on which it is plain this Earth was built? This is a Consideration which you will never give its due Weight. I have once already put you in mind of it, that you yourself have allow'd the Destruction of Animals to be as necessary as the Generation of them. There is as much Wisdom to be seen in the Contrivances, how Numbers of living Creatures might always be taken off and destroy'd, to make room for those that continually succeed them, as there is in making all the different sorts of them every one preserve their own Species. What do you think is the reason, that there is but one Way for us to come into the World?

Hor. Because that one is sufficient.

Cleo. Then from ᵃ a Parity of reason, we ought to think, that there are several Ways to go out of the World, because one would not have been sufficient. Now, if for the Support and Maintenance of that [296] variety of Crea-|tures which are here, that they should die, is a *postulatum* as necessary as it is, that they should be born ; and you cut off or obstruct the means of dying, and actually stop up one of the great Gates, through which we see Multitudes go to Death ; do you not oppose the Scheme, nay do you mar it less, than if you hinder'd Generation? If there never had been War, and no other means of dying, besides the ordinary ones, this Globe could not have born, or at least not maintain'd, the tenth part of the People that would have been in it. By War, I don't mean only such as one Nation has had against another, but civil as well as foreign Quarrels, general Massacres, private Murders, Poyson, Sword, and all hostile Force,

ᵃ for 33

by which Men, notwithstanding their Pretence of Love to their Species, have endeavour'd to take away one another's Lives throughout the World, from the time that *Cain* slew *Abel*, to this Day.

Hor. I don't believe, that a quarter of all these Mischiefs are upon Record ; but what may be known from History, would make a prodigious Number of Men ; much greater, I dare say, than ever was on this Earth at one time : But what would you infer from this? They would not have been immortal; and if they had not died in War, they must soon after have been slain by Diseases. When a Man of threescore is kill'd by a Bullet in the Field, it is odds, that he would not have lived | four Years longer, tho' he had stay'd at Home. [297]

Cleo. There are Soldiers of threescore perhaps in all Armies, but Men generally go to the War when they are young ; and when four or five thousand are lost in Battle, you'll find the greatest Number to have been under five and thirty : Consider now, that many Men do not marry till after that Age, who get ten or a dozen Children.

Hor. If all, that die by the Hands of another, were to get a dozen Children before they die ——

Cleo. There is no Occasion for that : I suppose nothing, that is either extravagant or improbable ; but that all such, as have been wilfully destroy'd by means of their Species, should have lived, and taken their Chance with the rest ; that every thing should have befaln them, that has befaln those that have not been kill'd that way ; and the same likewise to their Posterity ; and that all of them should have been subject to all the Casualties as well as Diseases, Doctors, Apothecaries, and other Accidents, that take away Man's Life, and shorten his Days ; War, and Violence from one another, only excepted.

Hor. But if the Earth had been too full of Inhabitants, might not Providence have sent Pestilences and Diseases oftener? More Children might have died when they were young, or more Women might have proved barren.

[298] | *Cleo.* I don't know whether your mild way would have been more generally pleasing ; but you entertain Notions of the Deity that are unworthy of him. Men might certainly have been born with the Instinct you speak of ; but if this had been the Creator's Pleasure, there must have been another OEconomy ; and things on Earth, from the beginning, would have been ordered in a manner quite different from what they are now. But to make a Scheme first, and afterwards to mend it, when it proves defective, is the Business of finite Wisdom : It belongs to human Prudence alone to mend Faults, to correct and redress what was done amiss before, and to alter the Measures which, Experience teaches Men, were ill concerted : But the Knowledge of God was consummate from Eternity. Infinite Wisdom is not liable to Errors or Mistakes ; therefore all his Works are universally good, and every thing is made exactly as he would have it : The firmness and stability of his Laws and Councils are everlasting, and therefore his Resolutions are as unalterable, as his Decrees are eternal. It is not a quarter of an Hour ago, that you named Wars among the necessary Means to carry off the Redundancy of our Species ; how come you now to think them useless? I can demonstrate to you, that Nature, in the Production of our Species, has amply provided against the Losses of our Sex, occasioned by Wars, by repairing them [299] visi-|bly, where they are sustained, in as palpable a manner, as she has provided for the great Destruction that is made of Fish, by their devouring one another.

Hor. How is that, pray?

Cleo. By sending more Males into the World than Females. You will easily allow me, that our Sex bears the Brunt of all the Toils and Hazards that are undergone by Sea and Land ; and that by this means a far

greater Number of Men must be destroy'd, than there
is of Women : Now if we see, as certainly we do, that
of the Infants yearly born, the Number of Males is
always considerably superior to that of the Females,
is it not manifest, that Nature has made a Provision
for great Multitudes, which, if they were not destroy'd,
would be not only superfluous, but of pernicious Consequence, in great Nations?

Hor. That Superiority in the Number of Males
born is wonderful indeed ; I remember the Account
that has been publish'd concerning it, as it was taken
from the Bills of Births and Burials in the City and
Suburbs.[1]

Cleo. For fourscore Years ;[2] in which the Number
of Females born was constantly much inferior to that
of the Males, sometimes by many Hundreds : And
that this Provision of Nature, to supply the Havock
that is made of Men by Wars and Navigation, is still
greater than could be imagin'd from that Difference
only, will soon appear, if we consider that ⦊ Women, [300]
in the first Place, are liable to all Diseases, within
a Trifle, that are incident to Men ; and that, in the
second, they are subject to many Disorders and
Calamities on account of their Sex, which great
Numbers die of, and which Men are wholly exempt
from.

Hor. This could not well be the Effect of Chance ;

[1] Mandeville is referring to
*Natural and Political Observations
. . . upon the Bills of Mortality,*
which is ascribed both to Sir
William Petty and Capt. John
Graunt. Chapter 8 of the *Observations* is devoted to develop-
ing the fact that, although,
because of their more hazardous
life, the mortality is higher
among males, yet, since their
birth-rate exceeds that of the
females ' by about a thirteenth

part ', the balance is preserved.
The author uses this fact as an
argument that Divine Providence
is against polygamy, since ' every
Woman may have an Husband '
without it.—The *Bills of Mortality* were mentioned by Mandeville in *Typhon* (1704), sign. [A3].

[2] In the matter of the pre-
ponderance of males, the *Bills*
really covered only the years
1628–62.

but it spoils the Consequence which you drew from my affectionate Scheme, in case there had been no Wars : For your Fear, that our Species would have encreased beyond all Bounds, was entirely built upon the Supposition, that those who have died in War should not have wanted Women, if they had lived ; which, from this Superiority in the Number of Males, it is evident, they should and must have wanted.

Cleo. What you observe is true ; but my chief Aim was to shew you, how disagreeable the Alteration, you required, would have been every way to the rest of the Scheme, by which it is manifest things are govern'd at present. For if the Provision had been made on the other side ; and Nature, in the Production of our Species, had continually taken Care to repair the Loss of Women, that die of Calamities not incident to Men, then certainly there would have been Women for all the Men, that have been destroy'd by their own Species, if they had lived ; and the Earth, without War, as I have said, would have been over-stocked ; [301] or if Nature had ever been | the same as she is now, that is, if more Males had been born than Females, and more Females had died of Diseases than Males, the World would constantly have had a great Superfluity of Men, if there never had been any Wars ; and this disproportion between their number and that of the Women, would have caused innumerable Mischiefs, that are now prevented by no other natural Causes, than the small Value Men set upon their Species, and their Dissentions with one another.

Hor. I can see no other mischief this would produce, than that the number of Males, which die without having ever tried Matrimony, would be greater than it is now ; and whether that would be a real Evil or not, is a very disputable Point.

Cleo. Don't you think, that this perpetual Scarcity of Women, and Superfluity of Men, would make great Uneasiness in all Societies, how well soever People might love one another ; and that the Value, the

Price of Women, would be so inhanced by it, that none but Men in tolerable good Circumstances would be able to purchase them? This alone would make us another World ; and Mankind could never have known that most necessary and now inexhaustible Spring, from which all Nations, where Slaves are not allow'd of, are constantly supply'd with willing Hands for all the Drudgery of hard and dirty Labour ; I mean the Children of the Poor, the great-|est and most exten- [302] sive of all temporal Blessings that accrue from Society, on which all the Comforts of Life, in the civilis'd State, have their unavoidable dependance.[1] There are many other things, from which it is plain, that such a real Love of Man for his Species would have been altogether inconsistent with the present Scheme ; the World must have been destitute of all that Industry, that is owing to Envy and Emulation ; no Society could have been easy with being a flourishing People, at the Expence of their Neighbours, or enduring to be counted a formidable Nation. All Men would have been Levellers, Government would have been un- necessary, and there could have been no great Bustle in the World. Look into the Men of greatest Renown, and the most celebrated Atchievements of Antiquity, and every thing that has been cried up, and admired in past Ages, by the fashionable part of Mankind : If the same Labours were to be perform'd over again, which Qualification, which help of Nature do you think, would be the most proper means to have them executed ; that Instinct of real Affection, you required, without Ambition or the Love of Glory ; or a stanch Principle of Pride and Selfishness, acting under Pre- tence to, and assuming the Resemblance of, that Affection? Consider, I beseech you, that no Men governed by this Instinct would require Services of any of their Species, which | they would not be ready [303] to perform for others ; and you will easily see, that its being universal would quite alter the Scene of Society

[1] Cf. *Fable* i. 287.

from what it is now. Such an Instinct might be very suitable to another Scheme different from this, in another World; where instead of Fickleness, and a restless desire after Changes and Novelty, there was observ'd an universal Steadiness continually preserv'd by a serene Spirit of Contentment, among other Creatures of different Appetites from ours, that had Frugality without Avarice, and Generosity without Pride; and whose Sollicitude after Happiness in a future State, was as active and apparent in Life, as our Pursuits are after the Enjoyments of this present. But as to the World we live in, examine into the various ways of earthly Greatness, and all the Engines that are made use of to attain to the Felicity of carnal Men, and you'll find, that the Instinct you speak of, must have destroy'd the Principles, and prevented the very Existence of that Pomp and Glory, to which human Societies have been, and are still raised by worldly Wisdom.

Hor. I give up my affectionate Scheme; you have convinced me, that there could not have been that Stir and Variety, nor, upon the whole, that Beauty in the World, which there have been, if all Men had been naturally Humble, Good, and Virtuous. I believe [304] | that Wars of all sorts, as well as Diseases, are natural Means to hinder Mankind from encreasing too fast; but that wild Beasts should likewise have been design'd to thin our Species, I cannot conceive; for they can only serve this End, when Men are but few, and their numbers should be encreas'd, instead of lessen'd; and afterwards, if they were made for that purpose, when Men are strong enough, they would not answer it.

Cleo. I never said, that wild Beasts were design'd to thin our Species. I have shew'd, that many things were made to serve a variety of different Purposes; that in the Scheme of this Earth, many things must have been consider'd, that Man has nothing to do with; and that it is ridiculous to think, that the

Universe was made for our sake. I have said likewise, that as all our Knowledge comes *à posteriori*, it is imprudent to reason otherwise than from Facts. That there are wild Beasts, and that there are savage Men, is certain; and that where there are but few of the latter, the first must always be very troublesome, and often fatal to them, is as certain; and when I reflect on the Passions, all Men are born with, and their Incapacity, whilst they are untaught; I can find no Cause or Motive, which is so likely to unite them together, and make them espouse the same Interest, as that common Danger they must always be in from | wild Beasts, in uncultivated Countries; whilst they [305] live in small Families, that all shift for themselves, without Government or Dependance upon one another : This first Step to Society, I believe to be an Effect, which that same Cause, the common Danger so often mentioned, will never fail to produce upon our Species in such Circumstances : What other, and how many Purposes wild Beasts might have been design'd for besides, I don't pretend to determine, as I have told you before.

Hor. But whatever other Purposes wild Beasts were design'd for, it still follows from your Opinion, that the uniting of Savages in common Defence, must have been one; which to me seems clashing with our Idea of the Divine Goodness.

Cleo. So will every thing seem to do, which we call Natural Evil; if you ascribe human Passions to the Deity, and measure infinite Wisdom by the Standard of our most shallow Capacity :[1] You have been at this twice already; I thought I had answer'd it. I would not make God the Author of Evil, any more than yourself; but I am likewise persuaded, that nothing could come by Chance, in respect to the supreme Being; and therefore, unless you imagine the World not to be govern'd by Providence, you must believe, that

---

[1] Cf. above, ii. 185, *n.* I.

Wars, and all the Calamities we can suffer from Man [306] or Beast, as well as Plagues and all other Dis-|eases, are under a wise Direction that is unfathomable. As there can be no Effect without a Cause, so nothing can be said to happen by Chance, but in respect to him who is ignorant of the Cause of it. I can make this evident to you, in an obvious and familiar Example. To a Man, who knows nothing of the Tennis-Court, the Skips and Rebounds of the Ball seem to be all fortuitous; as he is not able to guess at the several different Directions it will receive, before it comes to the Ground; so, as soon as it has hit the Place, to which it was plainly directed at first, it is Chance to him where it will fall : whereas the experienced Player, knowing perfectly well the Journey the Ball will make, goes directly to the Place, if he is not there already, where it will certainly come within his Reach. Nothing seems to be more the Effect of Chance than a Cast of the Dice : yet they obey the Laws of Gravity and Motion in general, as much as any thing else; and from the Impressions that are given them, it is impossible they should fall otherwise than they do : but the various Directions which they shall receive in the whole Course of the Throw being entirely unknown, and the Rapidity with which they change their Situation being such, that our slow Apprehension cannot trace them, what the Cast will be is a Mystery to human Understanding, at fair Play. But if the [307] same Variety of Directions was | given to two Cubes of ten Feet each, which a Pair of Dice receive as well from one another as the Box, the Caster's Fingers that cover it, and the Table they are flung upon, from the time they are taken up 'till they lye still, the same Effect would follow; and if the Quantity of Motion, the Force that is imparted to the Box and Dice was exactly known, and the Motion itself was so much retarded in the Performance, that what is done in three or four seconds, should take up an Hour's time, it would be easy to find out the Reason of every Throw, and Men might learn with Certainty to fore-tell which Side of the Cube would be uppermost. It is evident then, that the Words *fortuitous* and *casual*, have no other meaning, than what depends upon our want of Knowledge, Foresight and Penetration; the Reflection on which will shew us, by what an Infinity of Degrees all human Capacity falls short of that universal *intuitus*, with which the supreme Being beholds at once every thing without Exception, whether to us it be visible or invisible, past, present, or to come.

Hor. I yield : You have solved every Difficulty I have been able to raise; and I must confess, that your Supposition concerning the first Motive, that would make Savages associate, is neither clashing with good Sense, nor any Idea we ought to have of the Divine Attributes; but on the contrary, in answering my | Objections, you have demonstrated the Proba- [308] bility of your Conjecture, and rendred the Wisdom and Power of Providence, in the Scheme of this Earth, both as to the Contrivance and the Execution of it, more conspicuous and palpable to me, than any thing I ever heard or read, had done before.

Cleo. I am glad you are satisfied; tho' far from arrogating to my self so much Merit as your Civility would compliment me with.

Hor. It is very clear to me now; that as it is appointed for all Men to die, so it is necessary there should be Means to compass this End; that from the Number of those Means, or Causes of Death, it is impossible to exclude either the Malice of Men, or the Rage of wild Beasts, and all noxious Animals; and that, if they had been actually design'd by Nature, and contriv'd for that Purpose, we should have no more Reason justly to complain of them, than we have to find fault with Death itself, or that frightful Train of Diseases, which are daily and hourly the manifest occasion of it.

Cleo. They are all equally included in the Curse, which after the *Fall* was deservedly pronounc'd against the whole Earth; and if they be real Evils, they are to be look'd upon as the Consequence of Sin, and a condign Punishment, which the Transgression of our first Parents has drawn and entail'd upon all their [309] Posterity. I am fully persuaded, that | all the Nations in the World, and every Individual of our Species, civilis'd or savage, had their Origin from *Seth*,[1] *Cham*,[2] or *Japhet:* and as Experience has taught us, that the greatest Empires have their Periods, and the best govern'd States and Kingdoms may come to Ruin; so it is certain, that the politest People by being scatter'd and distress'd, may soon degenerate, and some of them by Accidents and Misfortunes, from knowing and well taught Ancestors, be reduced at last to Savages of the first and lowest Class.[3]

Hor. If what you are fully persuaded of, be true, the other is self-evident, from the Savages that are still subsisting.

Cleo. You once seem'd to insinuate, that all the Danger Men were in from wild Beasts, would entirely cease, as soon as they were civiliz'd, and lived in large and well-ordered Societies; but by this you may see, that our Species will never be wholly exempt from that Danger; because Mankind will always be liable to be reduced to Savages; for as this Calamity has actually befallen vast Multitudes that were the undoubted Descendants of *Noah*; so the greatest Prince upon Earth, that has Children, cannot be sure, that the same Disaster will never happen to any of his Posterity. Wild Beasts may be entirely extirpated in some Countries, that are duly cultivated; but they will multiply in others, that are wholly neglected; [310] and great Numbers of them range | now, and are

---

[1] Apparently a mistake for Shem.
[2] The Vulgate spelling, in common use in the eighteenth century, for Ham.
[3] Cf. above, ii. 197, *n.* 3.

Masters in many Places, where they had ᵃ been routed and kept out before. I shall always believe, that every Species of living Creatures in and upon this Globe, without Exception, continues to be, as it was at first, under the Care of that same Providence, that thought fit to produce it. You have had a great deal of Patience, but I would not tire it : This first Step towards Society, now we have master'd it, is a good Resting-place, and so we'll leave off for to-day.

Hor. With all my Heart : I have made you talk a great deal; but I long to hear the rest, as soon as you are at leisure.

Cleo. I am obliged to dine at *Windsor* to-morrow ; if you are not otherwise engaged, I can carry you, where the Honour of your Company will be highly esteem'd : My Coach shall be ready at Nine ; you know you are in my way.

Hor. A fine Opportunity indeed of three or four Hours Chat.

Cleo. I shall be all alone, without you.

Hor. I am your Man, and shall expect you.

Cleo. Adieu.

ᵃ have *33*

DIALOGUE

BETWEEN

Horatio and *Cleomenes.*

HORATIO.

OW we are off the Stones,[1] pray let us lose no time; I expect a great deal of Pleasure from what I am to hear further.

Cleo. The second Step to Society, is the Danger Men are in from one another : for which we are beholden to that stanch Principle of Pride and Ambition, that all Men are born with. Different Families may endeavour to live together, and be ready to join in common Danger ; but they are all of little use to one another, when there is no

---

[1] Evidently, off the London pavements and on the country roads that lead to Windsor. At the conclusion of the fifth dialogue, Cleomenes invites Horatio to drive there, and it is clear from pp. 338 and 355 that Mandeville had not forgotten this intention when he began the sixth dialogue.

common Enemy to oppose. If we consider, that Strength, Agility, and Courage would in such a State be the most valuable Qualifications, and that many Families could not live long | together, but some, [312] actuated by the Principle I named, would strive for Superiority : this must breed Quarrels, in which the most weak and fearful will, for their own Safety, always join with him, of whom they have the best Opinion.

Hor. This would naturally divide Multitudes into Bands and Companies, that would all have their different Leaders, and of which the strongest and most valiant would always swallow up the weakest and most fearful.

Cleo. What you say agrees exactly with the Accounts we have of the unciviliz'd Nations, that are still subsisting in the World ; and thus Men may live miserably many Ages.

Hor. The very first Generation, that was brought up under the Tuition of Parents, would be governable : and would not every succeeding Generation grow wiser than the foregoing?

Cleo. Without doubt they would encrease in Knowledge and Cunning : Time and Experience would have the same effect upon them as it has upon others ; and in the particular things, to which they apply'd themselves, they would become as expert and ingenious as the most civiliz'd Nations : But their unruly Passions, and the Discords occasioned by them, would never suffer them to be happy ; their mutual Contentions would be continually spoiling their Improvements, destroying their Inventions, and frustrating their Designs.

| *Hor.* But would not their Sufferings in time bring [313] them acquainted with the Causes of their Disagreement ; and would not that Knowledge put them upon making of Contracts, not to injure one another?

Cleo. Very probably they would ; but among such ill-bred and uncultivated People, no Man would keep a Contract longer than that Interest lasted, which made him submit to it.

Hor. But might not Religion, the Fear of an invisible Cause, be made serviceable to them, as to the keeping of their Contracts?

Cleo. It might, without dispute ; and would before many Generations passed away. But Religion could do no more among them, than it does among civilis'd Nations ; where the Divine Vengeance is seldom trusted to only, and Oaths themselves are thought to be of little Service, where there is no human Power to enforce the Obligation, and punish Perjury.

Hor. But don't you think, that the same Ambition that made a Man aspire to be a Leader, would make him likewise desirous of being obey'd in civil Matters, by the Numbers he led?

Cleo. I do ; and moreover that, notwithstanding this unsettled and precarious way Communities would live in, after three or four Generations human Nature would be look'd into, and begin to be understood : [314] Leaders would find out, that the more Strife | and Discord there was amongst the People they headed, the less use they could make of them : this would put them upon various ways of curbing Mankind ; they would forbid killing and striking one another ; the taking away by force the Wives, or Children of others in the same Community : they would invent Penalties, and very early find out, that no body ought to be a Judge in his own Cause ; and that old Men, generally speaking, knew more than young.

Hor. When once they have Prohibitions and Penalties, I should think all the Difficulty surmounted ; and I wonder why you said, that thus they might live miserably for many Ages.

Cleo. There is one thing of great moment, which has not been named yet ; and 'till that comes to pass, no considerable Numbers can ever be made happy : What signify the strongest Contracts, when we have nothing to shew for them ; and what Dependance can we have upon oral Tradition, in Matters that require Exactness ; especially whilst the Language that is spoken is yet very imperfect ? Verbal Reports are liable to a thousand Cavils and Disputes, that are prevented by Records, which every body knows to be unerring Witnesses ; and from the many Attempts that are made to wrest and distort the Sense of even written Laws, we may judge, how impracticable the Administration of Justice must be | among all Societies [315] that are destitute of them. Therefore the third and last Step to Society is the Invention of Letters. No Multitudes can live peaceably without Government ; no Government can subsist without Laws ; and no Laws can be effectual long, unless they are wrote down : The Consideration of this is alone sufficient to give us a great Insight into the Nature of Man.

Hor. I don't think so : The Reason why no Government can subsist without Laws is, because there are bad Men in all Multitudes ; but to take Patterns from them, when we would judge of human Nature, rather than from the good ones that follow the Dictates of their Reason, is an Injustice one would not be guilty of to brute Beasts ; and it would be very wrong in us, for a few vicious Horses, to condemn the whole Species as such, without taking notice of the many fine-spirited Creatures, that are naturally tame and gentle.

Cleo. At this rate I must repeat every thing that I have said Yesterday and the Day before : I thought you was convinced, that it was with Thought as it is with Speech ; and that, tho' Man was born with a Capacity beyond other Animals, to attain to both, yet, whilst he remain'd untaught, and never conversed with any of his Species, these Characteristicks were of little use to him. All Men uninstructed, whilst they are let alone, will follow the Impulse of their Nature, without regard to o-|thers ; and therefore [316] all of them are bad, that are not taught to be good :

so all Horses are ungovernable that are not well broken : for what we call vicious in them, is, when they bite or kick, endeavour to break their Halter, throw their Rider, and exert themselves with all their Strength to shake off the Yoke, and recover that Liberty which Nature prompts them to assert and desire. What you call Natural, is evidently Artificial, and belongs to Education : no fine-spirited Horse was ever tame or gentle, without Management. Some perhaps are not back'd, 'till they are four Years old, but then long before that time they are handled, spoke to, and dress'd ; they are fed by their Keepers, put under restraint, sometimes caress'd, and sometimes made to smart ; and nothing is omitted, whilst they are young, to inspire them with Awe and Veneration to our Species ; and make them not only submit to it, but likewise take a Pride in obeying the superior Genius of Man. But would you judge of the Nature of Horses in general, as to its Fitness to be govern'd, take the Foals of the best-bred Mares and finest Stallions, and turn an hundred of them loose, Fillys and Colts together, in a large Forest, till they are seven Years old, and then see how tractable they will be.

Hor. But this is never done.

Cleo. Whose Fault is that? It is not at the Request [317] of the Horses, that they are kept | from the Mares ; and that any of them are ever gentle or tame, is entirely owing to the Management of Man. Vice proceeds from the same Origin in Men, as it does in Horses ; the Desire of uncontroul'd Liberty, and Impatience of Restraint, are not more visible in the one, than they are in the other ; and a Man is then call'd vicious, when, breaking the Curb [a] of Precepts and Prohibitions, he wildly follows the unbridled Appetites of his untaught or ill-managed Nature. The Complaints against this Nature of ours, are every where the same : Man would have every thing he

[a] Curbs 30

likes, without considering, whether he has any Right to it or not; and he would do every thing he has a mind to do, without regard to the Consequence it would be of to others; at the same time that he dislikes every Body, that, acting from the same Principle, have in all their Behaviour not a special Regard to him.

Hor. That is, in short, Man naturally will not do, as he would be done by.

Cleo. That's true; and for this, there is another Reason in his Nature : All Men are partial in their Judgments, when they compare themselves to others; no two Equals think so well of each other, as both do of themselves; and where all Men have an equal Right to judge, there needs no greater Cause of Quarrel, than a Present amongst them with an Inscription of *detur digniori.* Man in his Anger | behaves [318] himself in the same manner as other Animals; disturbing, in the Pursuit of Self-preservation, those they are angry with; and all of them endeavour, according as the degree of their Passion is, either to destroy, or cause Pain and Displeasure to their Adversaries. That these Obstacles to Society are the Faults, or rather Properties of our Nature, we may know by this, that all Regulations and Prohibitions, that have been contriv'd for the temporal Happiness of Mankind, are made exactly to tally with them, and to obviate those Complaints, which I said were every where made against Mankind. The principal Laws of all Countries have the same Tendency; and there is not one, that does not point at some Frailty, Defect, or Unfitness for Society, that Men are naturally subject to; but all of them are plainly design'd as so many Remedies, to cure and disappoint that natural Instinct of Sovereignty, which teaches Man to look upon every thing as centring in himself, and prompts him to put in a Claim to every thing, he can lay his Hands on. This Tendency and Design to mend our Nature for the temporal Good of Society, is no where more visible, than in that compendious as well as complete Body of Laws, that was given by God himself.[1] The *Israelites*, whilst they were Slaves in *Ægypt*, were govern'd by the Laws of their Masters ; and as they were many [319] degrees remov'd from the lowest Sa-|vages, so they were yet far from being a civiliz'd Nation. It is reasonable to think, that, before they receiv'd the Law of God, they had Regulations and Agreements already establish'd, which the Ten Commandments did not abolish ; and that they must have had Notions of Right and Wrong, and Contracts among them against open Violence, and the Invasion of Property, is demonstrable.

Hor. How is that demonstrable?

Cleo. From the Decalogue itself : All wise Laws are adapted to the People that are to obey them. From the ninth Commandment, for Example, it is evident, that a Man's own Testimony was not sufficient to be believ'd in his own Affair, and that no Body was allow'd to be a Judge in his own Case.

Hor. It only forbids us to bear false Witness against our Neighbour.

Cleo. That's true ; and therefore the whole Tenor and Design of this Commandment presupposes, and must imply what I say. But the Prohibitions of Stealing, Adultery, and coveting any thing that belong'd to their Neighbours, are still more plainly intimating the same; and seem to be Additions and Amendments, to supply the Defects of some known Regulations and Contracts, that had been agreed upon before. If in this View we behold the three Commandments last hinted at, we shall find them to be strong Evidences, [320] not only of that Instinct of Sovereignty with-|in us, which at other times I have called a domineering Spirit, and a Principle of Selfishness ; but likewise of

[1] Pufendorf also deduced the nature of primitive man from the prohibitions of the Decalogue, but more crudely and with less freedom of mind than Mandeville; cf. Pufendorf's *Whole Duty of Man* (1698), author's pref., signn. a–a2[v].

the difficulty there is to destroy, eradicate and pull it out of the Heart of Man : For from the eighth Commandment it appears, that, tho' we debar ourselves from taking the Things of our Neighbour by Force, yet there is Danger that this Instinct will prompt us to get them unknown to him in a clandestine Manner, and deceive us with the Insinuations of an *oportet habere.* From the foregoing Precept, it is likewise manifest, that tho' we agree not to take away, and rob a Man of the Woman that is his own, it is yet to be fear'd, that if we like her, this innate Principle, that bids us gratify every Appetite, will advise us to make Use of her, as if she was our own ; tho' our Neighbour is at the Charge of maintaining her, and all the Children she brings forth. The last more especially is very ample in confirming my Assertion. It strikes directly at the Root of the Evil, and lays open the real Source of the Mischiefs that are apprehended in the seventh and the eighth Commandment : For without first actually trespassing against this, no Man is in Danger of breaking either of the former. This tenth Commandment moreover insinuates very plainly ; in the first place, that this Instinct of ours is of great Power, and a Frailty hardly to be cured ; in the Second, that there is nothing, which our Neighbour can | be possess'd of ; but, neglecting the Considera- [321] tion of Justice and Property, we may have a Desire after it ; for which Reason it absolutely forbids us to covet any thing that is *His :* The Divine Wisdom well knowing the Strength of this selfish Principle, which obliges us continually to assume every thing to ourselves ; and that, when once a Man heartily covets a thing, this Instinct, this Principle, will overrule and persuade him to leave no Stone unturn'd, to compass his Desires.

Hor. According to your way of expounding the Commandments, and making them tally so exactly with the Frailties of our Nature, it should follow from

the Ninth, that all Men are born with a strong Appetite
to forswear themselves ; which I never heard before.

Cleo. Nor I neither ; and I confess, that the Re-
buke there is, in this smart Turn of yours, is very
plausible ; but the Censure, how specious soever it
may appear, is unjust ; and you shall not find the
Consequence you hint at, if you will be pleas'd to
distinguish between the natural Appetites themselves,
and the various Crimes which they make us commit,
rather than not be obey'd : For tho' we are born
with no immediate Appetite to forswear ourselves, yet
we are born with more than one, that, if never check'd,
may in time oblige us to forswear ourselves, or do
worse, if it be possible, and they cannot be gratify'd
[322] without it ; and | the Commandment you mention,
plainly implies, that by Nature we are so unreasonably
attach'd to our Interest, on all Emergencies ; that it
is possible for a Man to be sway'd by it, not only to
the visible Detriment of others, as is manifest from
the Seventh and the Eighth, but even, tho' it should
be against his own Conscience : For no Body did ever
knowingly bear false Witness against his Neighbour,
but he did it for some End or other ; this End, whatever it is, I call his Interest. The Law which forbids
Murder, had already demonstrated to us, how immensely we undervalue every thing, when it comes
in Competition with ourselves ; for, tho' our greatest
Dread be Destruction, and we know no other Calamity,
equal to the Dissolution of our Being, yet such un-
equitable Judges this Instinct of Sovereignty is able
to make us, that rather than not have our Will, which
we count our Happiness, we chuse to inflict this
Calamity on others, and bring total Ruin on such, as
we think to be Obstacles to the Gratification of our
Appetites ; and this Men do, not only for Hindrances
that are present, or apprehended as to come, but likewise
for former Offences, and Things that are past redress.

Hor. By what you said last, you mean Revenge,
I suppose.

Cleo. I do so; and the Instinct of Sovereignty, which I assert to be in humane Nature, is in nothing so glaringly conspicuous as it is in | this Passion, which [323] no mere Man was ever born without, and which even the most Civiliz'd, as well as the most Learned, are seldom able to conquer: For whoever pretends to revenge himself, must claim a Right to a Judicature within, and an Authority to punish: Which, being destructive to the mutual Peace of all Multitudes, are for that Reason the first things, that in every civil Society are snatch'd away out of every Man's Hands, as dangerous Tools, and vested in the governing part, the Supreme Power only.

Hor. This Remark on Revenge has convinced me more, than any thing you have said yet, that there is some such thing as a Principle of Sovereignty in our Nature; but I cannot conceive yet, why the Vices of private, I mean particular, Persons should be thought to belong to the whole Species.

Cleo. Because every body is liable to fall into the Vices, that are peculiar to his Species; and it is with them, as it is with Distempers among Creatures of different Kinds: There are many Ailments that Horses are subject to, which are not incident to Cows. There is no Vice, but whoever commits it, had within him, before he was guilty of it, a Tendency towards it, a latent Cause that disposed him to it: Therefore all Lawgivers have two main Points to consider, at setting out; first, what things will procure Happiness to the Society under their Care; secondly, what Passions | and [324] Properties there are in Man's Nature, that may either promote or obstruct this Happiness. It is Prudence to watch your Fish-Ponds against the Insults of Hearns and Bitterns; but the same Precaution would be ridiculous against Turkies and Peacocks, or any other Creatures, that neither love Fish, nor are able to catch them.

Hor. What Frailty or Defect is it in our Nature that the two first Commandments have a Regard to, or as you call it tally with?

Cleo. Our natural Blindness and Ignorance of the true Deity : For tho' we all come into the World with an Instinct toward Religion, that manifests it self before we come to Maturity ; yet the Fear of an invisible Cause, or invisible Causes, which all Men are born with, is not more universal, than the Uncertainty which all untaught Men fluctuate in, as to the Nature and Properties of that Cause, or those Causes : There can be no greater Proof of this ——

Hor. I want none ; the History of all Ages is a sufficient Witness.

Cleo. Give me Leave : There can, I say, be no greater Proof of this, than the second Commandment, which palpably points at all the Absurdities and Abominations, which the ill-guided Fear of an invisible Cause had already made, and would still continue to make Men commit ; and in doing this, I can hardly think, that any thing but Divine Wisdom [325] | could in so few Words have comprehended the vast Extent and Sum total of human Extravagancies, as it is done in that Commandment : For there is nothing so high or remote in the Firmament, nor so low, or abject upon Earth ; but some Men have worship'd it, or made it one way or other the Object of their Superstition.

> Hor. —— *Crocodilon adorat*
> *Pars hæc : illa pavet saturam serpentibus Ibin.*
> *Effigies sacri nitet aurea Cercopitheci.*[1]

A holy Monkey ! I own it is a Reproach to our Species, that ever any part of it should have adored such a Creature as a God. But that is the Tip-top of Folly, that can be charged on Superstition.

Cleo. I don't think so ; a Monkey is still a living Creature, and consequently somewhat superiour to things inanimate.

Hor. I should have thought Men's Adoration of the Sun or Moon infinitely less absurd, than to have seen them fall down before so vile, so ridiculous an Animal.

---

[1] Juvenal, *Satires* xv. 2-4.

Cleo. Those who have adored the Sun and Moon never question'd, but they were intelligent as well as glorious Beings. But when I mentioned the Word *inanimate*, I was thinking on what the same Poet you quoted said, of the Veneration, Men paid to Leeks and | Onions, Deities they raised in their own Gardens. [326]

Porrum & cepe nefas violare, & frangere morsu :
O sanctas Genteis, quibus hæc nascuntur in hortis
Numina ! ——— ——— ———— [1]

But this is nothing to what has been done in *America*, fourteen hundred Years after the time of *Juvenal*. If the portentous Worship of the *Mexicans* had been known in his Days, he would not have thought it worth his while to take Notice of the *Ægyptians*. I have often admired at the uncommon Pains those poor People must have taken, to express the frightful and shocking as well as bizarre and unutterable Notions they entertain'd of the superlative Malice, and hellish implacable Nature of their *Vitzliputzli*, to whom they sacrific'd the Hearts of Men, cut out whilst they were alive.[2] The monstrous Figure and labour'd Deformity of that abominable Idol, are a lively Representation of the direful Ideas those Wretches framed to themselves of an invisible over-ruling Power ; and plainly shew us, how horrid and execrable they thought it to be, at the same time, that they paid it the highest Adoration[a] ; and at the Expence of human Blood endeavour'd, with Fear and Trembling, if not to

[a] Adoraaion 29

[1] Cf. Juvenal, *Satires* xv. 9–11.
[2] Huitzilopochtli was the hideous war-god and chief divinity of the Aztecs. Before his statue was a green stone of sacrifice, humped so that the priest could more easily carve out the heart of the human victim. Mandeville may have derived his information from de Solis's *History of the Conquest of Mexico* (trans. Townsend-Hooke, 1738, i. 398–400). In his *Free Thoughts* (ed. 1729, p. 270, *n.* a), Mandeville referred to a volume of the *Histoire des Ouvrages des Savans* (Sept. 1691 to June 1692) which contained a review of de Solis's book.—Vitzliputzli is again mentioned in Mandeville's *Origin of Honour*, p. 155.

[327] appease the Wrath | and Rage of it, at least to avert in some measure the manifold Mischiefs, they apprehended from it.

Hor. Nothing, I must own, can render declaiming against Idolatry more seasonable than a Reflection upon the second Commandment : But as what you have been saying, required no great Attention, I have been thinking of something else. Thinking on the Purport of the third Commandment furnishes me with an Objection, and I think a strong one, to what you have affirm'd about all Laws in general, and the Decalogue in particular. You know, I urged, that it was wrong to ascribe the Faults of bad Men to human Nature in general.

Cleo. I do ; and thought I had answered you.

Hor. Let me try only once more. Which of the two pray do you think, prophane swearing to proceed from, a Frailty in our Nature, or an ill Custom generally contracted by keeping of bad Company?

Cleo. Certainly the latter.

Hor. Then it is evident to me, that this Law is levell'd at the bad Men only, that are guilty of the Vice forbid in it ; and not any Frailty, belonging to human Nature in general.

Cleo. I believe, you mistake the Design of this Law ; and am of Opinion, that it has a much higher Aim than you seem to imagine. You remember my saying, [328] that Reverence to | Authority was necessary, to make human Creatures governable.

Hor. Very well ; and that Reverence was a Compound of Fear, Love and Esteem.

Cleo. Now let us take a View of what is done in the Decalogue : In the short Preamble to it, expressly made that the *Israelites* should know who it was that spoke to them, God manifests himself to those, whom he had chosen for his People by a most remarkable Instance of his own great Power, and their strong Obligation to him, in a Fact, that none of them could be ignorant of. There is a Plainness and Grandeur withal in this Sentence, than which nothing can be more truly sublime or majestick; and I defy the learned World, to shew me another as comprehensive, and of equal Weight and Dignity, that so fully executes its Purpose, and answers its Design, with the same Simplicity of Words. In that part of the second Commandment, which contains the Motives and Inducements, why Men should obey the Divine Laws, are set forth in the most emphatical manner; First, God's Wrath on those that hate him, and the Continuance of it on their Posterity; Secondly, the wide Extent of his Mercy to those, who love him and keep his Commandments. If we duely consider these Passages, we shall find, that Fear as well as Love, and the highest Esteem, are plainly and distinctly inculcated in them; and that the best Method is made use | of there, to [329] inspire Men with a deep Sense of the three Ingredients, that make up the Compound of Reverence. The Reason is plain : If People were to be govern'd by that Body of Laws, nothing was more necessary to enforce their Obedience to them, than their awful Regard and utmost Veneration to Him, at whose Command they were to keep them, and to whom they were accountable for the breaking of them.

Hor. What Answer is all this to my Objection?

Cleo. Have a Moment's Patience; I am coming to it. Mankind are naturally fickle, and delight in Change and Variety; they seldom retain long the same Impression of things they receiv'd at first, when they were new to them; and they are apt to undervalue, if not despise, the best, when they grow common. I am of Opinion, that the third Commandment points at this Frailty, this want of Steadiness in our Nature; the ill Consequences of which, in our Duty to the Creator, could not be better prevented than by a strict Observance of this Law, in never making use of his Name; but in the most solemn Manner on necessary Occasions, and in Matters of high Importance. As in the foregoing part of the Decalogue, Care had been already taken by the strongest Motives to create and attract Reverence, so nothing could be more wisely adapted [330] to strengthen, and make it everlasting, than | the Contents of this Law : For as too much Familiarity breeds Contempt, so our highest Regard due, to what is most Sacred, cannot be kept up better than by a quite contrary Practice.

Hor. I am answer'd.

Cleo. What Weight Reverence is thought to be of to procure Obedience, we may learn from the same Body of Laws in another Commandment. Children have no Opportunity of Learning their Duty, but from their Parents, and those who act by their Authority or in their Stead : Therefore it was requisite, that Men should not only stand in great Dread of the Law of God, but likewise have great Reverence for those, who first inculcated it, and communicated to them, that this was the Law of God.

Hor. But you said, that the Reverence of Children to Parents was a natural Consequence of what the [a] first experienc'd from the latter.

Cleo. You think there was no Occasion for this Law, if Man would do what is commanded in it, of his own Accord : But I desire, you would consider, that tho' the Reverence of Children to Parents is a natural Consequence, partly of the Benefits and Chastisements they receive from them, and partly of the great Opinion they form of the superiour Capacity they observe in them ; Experience teaches us, that this [331] Reverence may be over-|ruled by stronger Passions ; and therefore, it being of the highest Moment to all Government, and Sociableness itself, God thought fit to fortify and strengthen it in us, by a particular Command of his own ; and moreover to encourage it, by the Promise of a Reward for the keeping of it. It is our Parents, that first cure us of our natural Wildness, and break in us the Spirit of Independancy, we are all born with : It is to them we owe the first Rudiments of our Submission ; and to the Honour and Deference,

[a] they 30

which Children pay to Parents, all Societies are oblig'd for the Principle of human Obedience. The Instinct of Sovereignty in our Nature, and the Waywardness of Infants, which is the Consequence of it, discover themselves with the least glimmering of our Understanding, and before : Children that have been most neglected, and the least taught, are always the most stubborn and obstinate; and none are more unruly, and fonder of following their own Will, than those that are least capable of governing themselves.

Hor. Then this Commandment you think not obligatory, when we come to years of Maturity.

Cleo. Far from it : for though the Benefit politically intended by this Law, be chiefly receiv'd by us, whilst we are under Age and the Tuition of Parents; yet for that very reason ought the Duty, commanded in it, never | to cease. We are fond of imitating our [332] Superiors from our Cradle, and whilst this Honour and Reverence to Parents continue to be paid by their Children, when they are grown Men and Women, and act for themselves, the Example is of singular use to all Minors, in teaching them their Duty, and not to refuse what they see others, that are older and wiser, comply with by Choice : For by this means, as their Understanding encreases, this Duty by degrees becomes a Fashion, which at last their Pride will not suffer them to neglect.

Hor. What you said last is certainly the reason, that among fashionable People, even the most vicious and wicked do outward Homage, and pay Respect to Parents, at least before the World; tho' they act against and in their Hearts hate them.

Cleo. Here is another Instance to convince us, that good Manners are not inconsistent with Wickedness; and that Men may be strict Observers of Decorums, and take Pains to seem well-bred, and at the same time have no Regard to the Laws of God, and live in Contempt of Religion : and therefore to procure an outward Compliance with this fifth Commandment, no Lecture can be of such force, nor any Instruction so edifying to Youth, among the modish sort of People, as the Sight of a strong and vigorous, as well as polite and well dress'd Man, in a dispute giving way and submitting to a decrepit Parent.

[333] | *Hor.* But do you imagine that all the Divine Laws, even those that seem only to relate to God himself, his Power and Glory, and our Obedience to his Will, abstract from any Consideration of our Neighbour, had likewise a regard to the Good of Society, and the temporal Happiness of his People?

Cleo. There is no doubt of that ; witness the keeping of the Sabbath.

Hor. We have seen that very handsomely proved in one of the *Spectators.*[1]

Cleo. But the Usefulness of it in human Affairs, is of far greater Moment, than that which the Author of that Paper chiefly takes notice of. Of all the Difficulties, that Mankind have labour'd under in completing Society, nothing has been more puzling or perplexing than the Division of Time. Our annual Course round the Sun, not answering exactly any number of compleat Days or Hours, has been the occasion of immense Study and Labour ; and nothing has more rack'd the Brain of Man, than the adjusting the Year, to prevent the Confusion of Seasons : but even when the Year was divided into Lunar Months, the Computation of Time must have been impracticable among the common People : To remember twenty nine, or thirty Days, where Feasts are irregular, and all other Days shew alike, must have been a great Burden to the Memory, and caused a continual Con-[334] fusion among the ignorant ; whereas a short Pe-|riod soon returning is easily remembred, and one fix'd Day in seven, so remarkably distinguish'd from the rest, must rub up the Memory of the most un-thinking.

Hor. I believe that the Sabbath is a considerable Help in the Computation of Time, and of greater use

[1] *Spectator* no. 112, for Monday, 9 July 1711, by Addison.

DIALOGUE. 283

in human Affairs, than can be easily imagin'd by those, who never knew the Want of it.

Cleo. But what is most remarkable in this fourth Commandment, is God's revealing himself to his People, and acquainting an infant Nation with a Truth, which the rest of the World remain'd ignorant [a] of for many Ages. Men were soon made sensible of the Sun's Power, observed every Meteor in the Sky, and suspected the Influence of the Moon and other Stars: but it was a long time, and Man was far advanced in sublime Notions, before the Light of Nature could raise mortal Thought to the Contemplation of an infinite Being, that is the Author of the whole.

Hor. You have descanted on this sufficiently, when you spoke of *Moses :* Pray let us proceed to the further Establishment of Society. I am satisfied that the third Step towards it is the Invention of Letters ; that without them no Laws can be long effectual, and that the principal Laws of all Countries are Remedies against human Frailties ; I mean, that they are design'd as Antidotes, to prevent the ill Consequences of some Properties, insepa-[rable from our Nature; [335] which yet in themselves, without Management or Restraint, are obstructive and pernicious to Society : I am persuaded likewise, that these Frailties are palpably pointed at in the Decalogue ; that it was wrote with great Wisdom, and that there is not one Commandment in it, that has not a regard to the temporal Good of Society, as well as Matters of higher moment.

Cleo. These are the Things, indeed, that I have endeavor'd to prove ; and now all the great Difficulties and chief Obstructions, that can hinder a Multitude from being form'd into a Body Politick, are removed : When once Men come to be govern'd by written Laws, all the rest comes on a-pace. Now Property, and Safety of Life and Limb, may be secured : This naturally will forward the Love of

[a] ingnorant 29

Peace, and make it spread. No number of Men, when
once they enjoy Quiet, and no Man needs to fear his
Neighbour, will be long without learning to divide
and subdivide their Labour.

Hor. I don't understand you.

Cleo. Man, as I have hinted before, naturally loves
to imitate what he sees others do, which is the reason
that savage People all do the same thing : This hinders
them from meliorating their Condition, though they
are always wishing for it : But if one will wholly apply
himself to the making of Bows and Arrows, whilst
[336] another provides Food, a | third builds Huts, a fourth
makes Garments, and a fifth Utensils, they not only
become useful to one another, but the Callings and
Employments themselves will in the same Number of
Years receive much greater Improvements, than if all
had been promiscuously follow'd by every one of the
Five.

Hor. I believe you are perfectly right there ; and
the truth of what you say is in nothing so conspicuous,
as it is in Watch-making, which is come to a higher
degree of Perfection, than it would have been arrived
at yet, if the whole had always remain'd the Employment of one Person ; and I am persuaded, that even
the Plenty we have of Clocks and Watches, as well as
the Exactness and Beauty they may be made of, are
chiefly owing to the Division that has been made of
that Art into many Branches.

Cleo. The use of Letters must likewise very much
improve Speech it self, which before that time cannot
but be very barren and precarious.

Hor. I am glad to hear you mention Speech again :
I would not interrupt you, when you named it once
before :[1] Pray what Language did your wild Couple
speak, when first they met?

Cleo. From what I have said already it is evident,
that they could have had none at all ; at least, that
is [a] my Opinion.

[a] is] it is *29–30*   [1] Cf. *Fable* ii. 190–1.

| *Hor.* Then wild People must have an Instinct to [337] understand one another, which they lose when they are civiliz'd.

Cleo. I am persuaded, that Nature has made all Animals of the same kind, in their mutual Commerce, intelligible to one another, as far as is requisite for the Preservation of themselves and their Species : And as to my wild Couple, as you call them, I believe there would be a very good Understanding, before many Sounds past between them. It is not without some Difficulty, that a Man born in Society can form an Idea of such Savages, and their Condition ; and unless he has used himself to abstract thinking, he can hardly represent to himself such a State of Simplicity, in which Man can have so few Desires, and no Appetites roving beyond the immediate Call of untaught Nature : To me it seems very plain, that such a Couple would not only be destitute of Language, but likewise never find out or imagine, that they stood in need of any ; or that the want of it was any real Inconvenience to them.

Hor. Why do you think so?

Cleo. Because it is impossible, that any Creature should know the Want of what it can have no Idea of : I believe moreover, that if Savages, after they are grown Men and Women, should hear others speak, be made acquainted with the Usefulness of Speech, | and [338] consequently become sensible of the want of it in themselves, their Inclination to learn it would be as inconsiderable as their Capacity ; and if they should attempt it, they would find it an immense labour, a thing not to be surmounted ; because the Suppleness and Flexibility in the Organs of Speech, that Children are endued with, and which I have often hinted at, would be lost in them ; and they might learn to play masterly upon the Violin, or any other the most difficult musical Instrument, before they could make any tolerable Proficiency in speaking.

Hor. Brutes make several distinct Sounds to express different Passions by : As for Example ; Anguish, and great Danger, Dogs of all sorts express with another Noise than they do Rage and Anger; and the whole Species express Grief by howling.

Cleo. This is no Argument to make us believe, that Nature has endued Man with Speech : There are innumerable other Privileges and Instincts which some Brutes enjoy, and Men are destitute of : Chickens run about as soon as they are hatch'd ; and most Quadrupedes can walk without help, as soon as they are brought forth. If ever Language came by Instinct, the People that spoke it, must have known every individual Word in it; and a Man in the wild State of Nature would have no occasion for a thousandth part of the most barren Language that ever had [339] a | Name. When a Man's Knowledge is confin'd within a narrow Compass, and he has nothing to obey, but the simple Dictates of Nature, the Want of Speech is easily supply'd by dumb Signs; and it is more natural to untaught Men to express themselves by Gestures, than by Sounds ; but we are all born with a Capacity of making ourselves understood, beyond other Animals, without Speech : To express Grief, Joy, Love, Wonder and Fear, there are certain Tokens, that are common to the whole Species. Who doubts that the crying of Children was given them by Nature, to call Assistance and raise Pity, which latter it does so unaccountably beyond any other Sound?

Hor. In Mothers and Nurses, you mean.

Cleo. I mean in the generality of human Creatures. Will you allow me, that warlike Musick generally rouses and supports the Spirits, and keeps them from sinking?

Hor. I believe I must.

Cleo. Then I'll engage, that the crying (I mean the *Vagitus*) of helpless Infants will stir up Compassion in the generality of our Species, that are within the hearing of it, with much greater Certainty than Drums and Trumpets will dissipate and chase away Fear, in those they are applied to. Weeping, laughing, smiling, frowning, sighing, exclaiming, we spoke of before. How universal, as well as copious, is the Language of the Eyes, by | the help of which the remotest Nations [340] understand one another at first Sight, taught or untaught, in the weightiest temporal Concern that belongs to the Species? and in that Language our wild Couple would at their first meeting intelligibly say more to one another without guile, than any civiliz'd Pair would dare to name without blushing.

Hor. A Man without doubt may be as impudent with his Eyes, as he can be with his Tongue.

Cleo. All such Looks therefore, and several Motions, that are natural, are carefully avoided among polite People, upon no other Account, than that they are too significant : It is for the same reason that stretching ourselves before others, whilst we are yawning, is an absolute Breach of good Manners ; especially in mix'd Company of both Sexes. As it is indecent to display any of these Tokens, so it is unfashionable to take Notice of, or seem to understand, them : This Disuse and Neglect of them is the Cause, that whenever they happen to be made either through Ignorance or wilful Rudeness, many of them are lost and really not understood, by the *beau monde* ; that would be very plain to Savages without Language, who could have no other Means of conversing than by Signs and Motions.

Hor. But if the old Stock would never either be able or willing to acquire Speech, it is impossible they could teach it their Chil-|dren : Then which way [341] could any Language ever come into the World from two Savages?

Cleo. By slow degrees, as all other Arts and Sciences have done, and length of time ; Agriculture, Physick, Astronomy, Architecture, Painting, *&c.* From what we see in Children that are backward with their Tongues, we have reason to think, that a wild Pair would make themselves intelligible to each other by Signs and Gestures, before they would attempt it by Sounds : But when they lived together for many

Years, it is very probable, that for the Things they
were most conversant with they would find out
Sounds, to stir up in each other the Idea's of such
Things, when they were out of sight; these Sounds
they would communicate to their young ones; and
the longer they lived together the greater Variety of
Sounds they would invent, as well for Actions as the
Things themselves : They would find that the Volu-
bility of Tongue, and Flexibility of Voice, were much
greater in their young ones, than they could remember
it ever to have been in themselves : It is impossible,
but some of these young ones would, either by Accident
or Design, make use of this superior Aptitude of the
Organs at one time or other; which every Generation would still improve upon; and this must have
been the Origin of all Languages, and Speech it self,
that were not taught by Inspiration.[1]   I believe more-
[342] over, that after Language (I | mean such as is of

---

[1] In these pages, in his insis-
tence on the non-divine origin
of language and its halting and
undirected evolution, Mandeville
is a pioneer. Most of his contemporaries—he conciliates them
in the last clause of the sentence
to which this is a note—thought
either that language had been
given ready-made to man by
God or, at least, was the immediate result of a specific aptitude
infused by God into Adam. The
exceptions, who, like Richard
Simon (*Histoire Critique du Vieux
Testament,* Amsterdam, 1685,
pp. 84 sqq.), thought language a
product of human invention,
were forced by their acceptance
of biblical chronology and their
belief in Adam to suppose the
self-conscious invention and comparatively rapid elaboration of
language rather than the slow
evolution postulated by modern
scholars.   Thus Locke entirely
missed the evolutionary aspect of
the matter, considering words as
arbitrarily invented (*Essay* iii. ii.
1). And Leibniz (*Nouveaux Essais*
iii. i–ii), although recognizing the
fact of language-development,
lacked Mandeville's feeling for
the tentativeness, accidents, and
difficulties of its original appearance, and the great slowness of
its growth.   The Greeks, too,
neglected the fact of prehistoric
evolution recognized by Mandeville, debating instead (as in
Plato's *Cratylus*) whether words
were φύσει or θέσει—the inevitable reflection of their respective
objects, or arbitrarily established
by convention or the gods.   The
anticipations in Lucretius v.
1026–30, Diodorus Siculus i. i,
and Vitruvius ii. (33) i are re-
latively slight.

human Invention) was come to a great degree of Perfection, and even when People had distinct Words for every Action in Life, as well as every Thing they meddled or convers'd with, Signs and Gestures still continued to be made for a great while, to accompany Speech; because both are intended for the same Purpose.

Hor. The Design of Speech is to make our Thoughts known to others.

Cleo. I don't think so.

Hor. What! Don't Men speak to be understood?

Cleo. In one Sense they do; but there is a double Meaning in those Words, which I believe you did not intend: If by Man's *speaking to be understood* you mean, that when Men speak, they desire that the Purport of the Sounds they utter should be known and apprehended by others, I answer in the Affirmative: But if you mean by it, that Men speak, in order that their Thoughts may be known, and their Sentiments laid open and seen through by others, which likewise may be meant by *speaking to be understood,* I answer in the Negative. The first Sign or Sound that ever Man made, born of a Woman, was made in Behalf, and intended for the use of him who made it; and I am of Opinion, that the first Design of Speech was to persuade others, either to give Credit to what the speaking Person would have them | believe; or else [343] to act or suffer such Things, as he would compel them to act or suffer, if they were entirely in his Power.

Hor. Speech is likewise made use of to teach, advise, and inform others for their Benefit, as well as to persuade them in our own Behalf.

Cleo. And so by the help of it Men may accuse themselves and own their Crimes; but no Body would have invented Speech for those purposes; I speak of the Design, the first Motive and Intention that put Man upon speaking. We see in Children that the first things they endeavour to express with Words are their

Wants and their Will ; and their Speech is but a Confirmation of what they ask'd, deny'd, or affirm'd, by Signs before.

Hor. But why do you imagine that People would continue to make use of Signs and Gestures, after they could sufficiently express themselves in Words?

Cleo. Because Signs confirm Words, as much as Words do Signs ; and we see, even in polite People, that when they are very eager they can hardly forbear making use of both. When an Infant, in broken imperfect Gibberish, calls for a Cake or a Play-thing, and at the same time points at and reaches after it, this double Endeavour makes a stronger Impression upon us, than if the Child had either spoke its Wants in plain Words, without making any Signs, or else [344] look'd at and reach'd | after the thing wanted, without attempting to speak. Speech and Action assist and corroborate one another, and Experience teaches us that they move us much more, and are more persuasive jointly than separately ; *vis unita fortior* ; and when an Infant makes use of both, he acts from the same Principle, that an Orator does, when he joins proper Gestures to an elaborate Declamation.

Hor. From what you have said, it should seem that Action is not only more natural, but likewise more ancient than Speech it self, which before I should have thought a Paradox.

Cleo. Yet it is true ; and you shall always find, that the most forward, volatile, and fiery Tempers make more use of Gestures, when they speak, than others that are more patient and sedate.

Hor. It is a very diverting Scene to see how this is overdone among the *French*, and still more among the *Portuguese :* I have often been amazed to see, what Distortions of Face and Body, as well as other strange Gesticulations with Hands and Feet, some of them will make in their ordinary Discourses : But nothing was more offensive to me, when I was abroad, than

the Loudness and Violence which most Foreigners
speak with, even among Persons of Quality, when
a Dispute arises, or any thing is to be debated : Before
I was used to it, it put me always upon my Guard ;
for I | did not question but they were angry ; and [345]
I often recollected what had been said, in order to
consider, whether it was not something I ought to
have resented.

Cleo. The natural Ambition and strong Desire Men
have to triumph over, as well as persuade others, are
the occasion of all this. Heightning and lowring the
Voice, at proper Seasons, is a bewitching Engine to
captivate mean Understandings ; and Loudness is an
Assistant to Speech, as well as Action is : Uncorrect-
ness, false Grammar, and even want of Sense, are often
happily drown'd in Noise and great Bustle ; and many
an Argument has been convincing, that had all its
Force from the Vehemence it was made with : The
Weakness of the Language it self may be palliatively
cured by strength of Elocution.

Hor. I am glad that speaking low is the Fashion
among well-bred People in *England* ; for Bawling and
Impetuosity I cannot endure.

Cleo. Yet this latter is more natural ; and no Man
ever gave in to the contrary Practice, the Fashion
you like, that was not taught it, either by Precept or
Example : And if Men do not accustom themselves to
it, whilst they are young, it is very difficult to comply
with it afterwards : But it is the most lovely, as well
as most rational Piece of good Manners, that human
Invention has to boast of in the Art of Flattery ; for
when a Man | addresses himself to me in a calm manner, [346]
without making Gestures, or other Motions with Head
or Body, and continues his Discourse in the same sub-
missive Strain and Composure of Voice, without exalt-
ing or depressing it, he, in the first place, displays his
own Modesty and Humility in an agreeable manner ;
and, in the second, makes me a great Compliment, in

T 2

the Opinion which he seems to have of me; for by
such a Behaviour he gives me the Pleasure to imagine,
that he thinks me not influenc'd by my Passions, but
altogether sway'd by my Reason : He seems to lay
his Stress on my Judgment, and therefore to desire,
that I should weigh and consider what he says, without
being ruffled or disturbed : No Man would do this
unless he trusted entirely to my good Sense, and the
Rectitude of my Understanding.

Hor. I have always admired this unaffected manner
of speaking, tho' I never examined so deeply into the
Meaning of it.

Cleo. I can't help thinking, but that, next to the
Laconick and manly Spirit, that runs through the
Nation, we are very much beholden for the Strength
and Beauty of our Language to this Tranquility in
Discourse, which for many Years has been in *England,*
more than any where else, a Custom peculiar to the
beau monde, who, in all Countries, are the undoubted
Refiners of Language.

[347] | *Hor.* I thought that it was the Preachers, Play-
wrights, Orators, and fine Writers that refin'd upon
Language.

Cleo. They make the best of what is ready coin'd
to their Hands; but the true and only Mint of Words
and Phrases is the Court; and the polite Part of every
Nation are in Possession of the *Jus & norma loquendi.*[1]
All technick Words indeed, and Terms of Art, belong
to the respective Artists and Dealers, that primarily
and literally make use of them in their Business; but
whatever is borrow'd from them for metaphorical Use,
or from other Languages, living or dead, must first
have the Stamp of the Court, and the Approbation of
the *beau monde,* before it can pass for current; and
whatever is not used among them, or comes abroad
without their Sanction, is either vulgar, pedantick, or
obsolete. Orators therefore, Historians, and all whole-

---

[1] Horace, *Ars Poetica* 72.

sale Dealers in Words, are confin'd to those, that have been already well receiv'd, and from that Treasure they may pick and chuse what is most for their purpose ; but they are not allow'd to make new ones of their own, any more than Bankers are suffer'd to coin.

Hor. All this while I cannot comprehend what Advantage or Disadvantage speaking loud or low can be of to the Language it self ; and if what I am saying now was set down, it must be a real Conjurer that, half a Year hence, | should be able to tell [348] by the Writing, whether it had been bawl'd out or whisper'd.

Cleo. I am of Opinion that when People of Skill and Address accustom themselves to speak in the manner aforesaid, it must in time have an Influence upon the Language, and render it strong and expressive.

Hor. But your Reason?

Cleo. When a Man has only his Words to trust to, and the Hearer is not to be affected by the Delivery of them otherwise, than if he was to read them himself, it will infallibly put Men upon studying not only for nervous Thoughts and Perspicuity, but likewise for Words of great Energy, for Purity of Diction, Compactness of Style, and Fullness as well as Elegancy of Expressions.

Hor. This seems to be far fetch'd, and yet I don't know but there may be something in it.

Cleo. I am sure you will think so, when you consider that all Men, that do speak, are equally desirous and endeavouring to persuade and gain the Point they labour for, whether they speak loud or low, with Gestures or without.

Hor. Speech, you say, was invented to persuade ; I am afraid you lay too much Stress upon that : It certainly is made use of likewise for many other Purposes.

Cleo. I don't deny that.

| *Hor.* When People scold, call Names, and pelt one [349]

another with Scurrilities, what Design is that done with? If it be to persuade others, to have a worse Opinion of themselves, than they are supposed to entertain, I believe it is seldom done with Success.

Cleo. Calling Names is shewing others, and shewing them with Pleasure and Ostentation, the vile and wretched Opinion we have of them ; and Persons that make use of opprobrious Language are often endeavouring to make those, whom they give it to, believe that they think worse of them than they really do.

Hor. Worse than they do ! Whence does that ever appear?

Cleo. From the Behaviour and the common Practice of those that scold and call Names. They rip up and exaggerate not only the Faults and Imperfections of their Adversary himself, but likewise every thing that is ridiculous or contemptible in his Friends or Relations : They will fly to, and reflect upon every thing, which he is but in the least concern'd in, if any thing can possibly be said of it that is reproachful ; the Occupation he follows, the Party he sides with, or the Country he is of. They repeat with Joy the Calamities and Misfortunes that have befal'n him or his Family : They see the Justice of Providence in them, and they are sure, they are Punishments he has [350] deserv'd. Whatever Crime he has been sus-|pected of, they charge him with, as if it had been proved upon him. They call in every thing to their Assistance ; bare Surmises, loose Reports, and known Calumnies ; and often upbraid him with what they themselves at other times have own'd not to believe.

Hor. But how comes the Practice of scolding and calling Names to be so common among the Vulgar all the World over ? There must be a Pleasure in it, tho' I cannot conceive it : I ask to be inform'd ; what Satisfaction or other Benefit is it, that Men receive or expect from it ? What View is it done with ?

Cleo. The real Cause and inward Motive Men act

from, when they use ill Language, or call Names in earnest, is, in the first place, to give vent to their Anger, which it is troublesome to stifle and conceal. Secondly, to vex and afflict their Enemies, with greater hopes of Impunity, than they could reasonably entertain, if they did them any more substantial Mischief, which the Law would revenge : But this never comes to be a Custom, nor is thought of, before Language is arrived to great Perfection, and Society is carried to some degree of Politeness.

Hor. That's merry enough, to assert that Scurrility is the effect of Politeness.

Cleo. You shall call it what you please, but in its original it is a plain Shift to avoid fighting, and the ill Consequences of it ; for no Body ever call'd another Rogue and Rascal, | but he would have struck him, if [351] it had been in his own Power, and himself had not been with-held by the Fear of something or other : Therefore where People call Names, without doing further Injury, it is a sign not only that they have wholesome Laws amongst them against open Force and Violence, but likewise that they obey and stand in awe of them ; and a Man begins to be a tolerable Subject, and is nigh half civiliz'd, that in his Passion will take up and content himself with this paultry Equivalent ; which never was done without great Self-denial at first : For otherwise the obvious, ready, and unstudy'd manner of venting and expressing Anger, which Nature teaches, is the same in human Creatures that it is in other Animals, and is done by fighting ; as we may observe in Infants of two or three Months old, that never yet saw any Body out of Humour : For even at that Age they'll scratch, fling, and strike with their Heads as well as Arms and Legs, when any thing raises their Anger, which is easily and at most times unaccountably provok'd ; often by Hunger, Pain, and other inward Ailments. That they do this by Instinct, something implanted in the Frame, the Mechanism of the Body, before any Marks of Wit or Reason are to be seen in them, I am fully persuaded; as I am likewise, that Nature teaches them the manner of fighting peculiar to their Species; and Children strike with their Arms [352] as naturally | as Horses kick, Dogs bite, and Bulls push with their Horns. I beg your Pardon for this Digression.

Hor. It was natural enough, but if it had been less so, you would not have slipt the Opportunity of having a Fling at human Nature, which you never spare.

Cleo. We have not a more dangerous Enemy than our own inborn Pride: I shall ever attack and endeavour to mortify it, when it is in my Power: For the more we are persuaded that the greatest Excellencies the best Men have to boast of, are acquired, the greater Stress it will teach us to lay upon Education; and the more truly sollicitous it will render us about it: And the absolute Necessity of good and early Instructions, can be no way more clearly demonstrated, than by exposing the Deformity as well as the Weakness of our untaught Nature.

Hor. Let us return to Speech: If the chief Design of it is to persuade, the *French* have got the start of us a great way; theirs is really a charming Language.

Cleo. So it is without doubt to a *Frenchman.*

Hor. And every Body else, I should think, that understands it, and has any Taste: Don't you think it to be very engaging?

Cleo. Yes, to one that loves his Belly; for it is very copious in the Art of Cookery, and every thing that belongs to eating and drinking.[1]

[353] | *Hor.* But without Banter, don't you think that the *French* Tongue is more proper, more fit to persuade in, than ours?

Cleo. To coax and wheedle in, I believe it may.

Hor. I can't conceive what Nicety it is you aim at, in that Distinction.

Cleo. The Word you named includes no Idea of

---

[1] According to Spingarn (*Critical Essays of the Seventeenth* *Century,* Oxford, 1908, ii. 343, *n.* 30) this criticism was common

Reproach or Disparagement; the greatest Capacities may, without Discredit to them, yield to Persuasion, as well as the least; but those, who can be gain'd by coaxing and wheedling, are commonly supposed to be Persons of mean Parts and weak Understandings.

Hor. But pray come to the Point; which of the two do you take to be the finest Language?

Cleo. That is hard to determine: Nothing is more difficult, than to compare the Beauties of two Languages together, because what is very much esteem'd in the one, is often not relish'd at all in the other: In this Point the *Pulchrum & Honestum* varies, and is different every where, as the Genius of the People differs. I don't set up for a Judge, but what I have commonly observed in the two Languages, is this: All favourite Expressions in *French* are such, as either sooth or tickle; and nothing is more admired in *English*, than what pierces or strikes.

Hor. Do you take yourself to be entirely impartial now?

| *Cleo.* I think so; but if I am not, I don't know [354] how to be sorry for it: There are some things, in which it is the Interest of the Society that Men should be biass'd; and I don't think it amiss, that Men should be inclined to love their own Language, from the same Principle, that they love their Country. The *French* call us Barbarous, and we say, they are Fawning: I won't believe the first, let them believe what they please. Do you remember the six Lines in the *Cid*, which *Corneille* is said to have had a Present of six thousand Livres for?

Hor. Very well.

Mon Pere est mort, Elvire, & la premiere Espée
Dont [a] *s'est armé Rodrigue a sa trame coupée.*
Pleurès, pleurès mes yeux, & fondes vous en eau,
La moitié de ma vie a mis l'autre au tombeau;
Et m'oblige à venger, apres ce coup funeste,
Celle [b] *que je n'ay plus sur celle qui me reste.* [1]

[a] *D'on 29*   [b] *Cell 29, 30*
[1] *Le Cid* iii. iii (ll. 797–802).

Cleo. The same Thought express'd in our Language, to all the Advantage it has in the *French*, would be hiss'd by an *English* Audience.[1]

Hor. That's no Compliment to the Taste of your Country.

[355] | *Cleo.* I don't know that : Men may have no bad Taste, and yet not be so ready at conceiving, which way *one half of one's Life can put the other into the Grave :* To me, I own it is puzling, and it has too much the Air of a Riddle, to be seen in heroick Poetry.

Hor. Can you find no Delicacy at all in the Thought ?

Cleo. Yes ; but it is too fine spun, it is the Delicacy of a Cobweb ; there is no Strength in it.

Hor. I have always admired these Lines ; but now you have made me out of Conceit with them, me-thinks I spy another Fault that's much greater.

Cleo. What is that ?

Hor. The Author makes his Heroine say a thing, which was false in Fact : *One half*, says Chimene, *of my Life has put the other into the Grave, and obliges me to revenge,* &c. Which is the Nominative of the Verb *obliges ?*

Cleo. One half of my Life.

Hor. Here lies the Fault ; it is this, which I think

---

[1] With this discussion of French poetry compare the *Virgin Unmask'd* (1724), pp. 157–60 : ' . . . it is very diffi-cult to judge of Poetry in two Languages, for two Reasons ; the first is, that there is not one in ten Thousand that ever attains to that Perfection in another Language, as to understand the Beauties of it, as well as he does those of his own. The second is, because the Rules of Poetry in two Countries, according to the several Humours of Nations, are sometimes as different as the Languages themselves, so that the Faults of the one, are often Beauties in the other ; and it is next to an Impossibility, that People should like, even to Fond-ness, what they have been us'd to, and at the same time be as much pleas'd with what runs quite con-trary to it ' (*Virgin Unmask'd,* p. 158).

Concerning Mandeville's inter-est in French poetry, it should be remembered that he prepared English versions of La Fontaine and of Scarron (see above, i. xxxi).

is not true; For the *one half of her Life*, here mention'd, is plainly that half which was left; it is *Rodrigues* her Lover : Which way did he oblige her to seek for Revenge ?

Cleo. By what he had done, killing her Father.

Hor. No, *Cleomenes*, this Excuse is insufficient. *Chimene's* Calamity sprung from the *Dilemma* she was in between her Love and | her Duty ; when the latter [356] was inexorable, and violently pressing her, to sollicit the Punishment, and employ with Zeal all her Interest and Eloquence, to obtain the Death of him, whom the first had made dearer to her than her own Life ; and therefore it was the half that was gone, that was put in the Grave, her dead Father, and not *Rodrigues* which *obliged* her to sue for Justice : Had the *Obligation* she lay under come from this quarter, it might soon have been cancell'd, and herself releas'd without crying out her Eyes.

Cleo. I beg Pardon for differing from you, but I believe the Poet is in the right.

Hor. Pray, consider which it was, that made *Chimene* prosecute *Rodrigues*, Love, or Honour.

Cleo. I do ; but still I can't help thinking, but that her Lover, by having kill'd her Father, obliged *Chimene* to prosecute him ; in the same manner as a Man, who will give no Satisfaction to his Creditors, obliges them to arrest him ; or as we would say to a Coxcomb who is offending us with his Discourse, *If you go on thus, Sir, you'll oblige me to treat you ill :* Tho' all this while the Debtor might be as little desirous of being arrested, and the Coxcomb of being ill treated, as *Rodrigues* was of being prosecuted.

Hor. I believe you are in the right, and I beg *Corneille's* Pardon. But now I desire you would tell me, what you have further to say | of Society : What [357] other Advantages do Multitudes receive from the Invention of Letters, besides the Improvements it makes in their Laws and Language?

Cleo. It is an Incouragement to all other Inventions
in general; by preserving the Knowledge of every
useful Improvement that is made. When Laws begin
to be well known, and the Execution of them is
facilitated by general Approbation, Multitudes may
be kept in tolerable Concord among themselves : It
is then that it appears, and not before, how much the
Superiority of Man's Understanding beyond other
Animals, contributes to his Sociableness, which is only
retarded by it in his Savage State.

Hor. How so, pray? I don't understand you.

Cleo. The Superiority of Understanding, in the first
place, makes Man sooner sensible of Grief and Joy,
and capable of entertaining either, with greater difference as to the Degrees, than they are felt in other
Creatures. Secondly, it renders him more industrious
to please himself, that is, it furnishes Self-love with
a greater Variety of Shifts to exert itself on all Emergencies, than is made use of by Animals of less Capacity.
Superiority of Understanding likewise gives us a Foresight, and inspires us with Hopes, of which other
Creatures have little, and that only of things im-
[358] mediately before them. All these things are | so
many Tools, Arguments, by which Self-love reasons
us into Content, and renders us patient under many
Afflictions, for the sake of supplying those Wants that
are most pressing : This is of infinite use to a Man,
who finds himself born in a Body Politick, and it must
make him fond of Society : Whereas the same Endow-
ment before that time, the same Superiority of
Understanding in the State of Nature, can only serve
to render Man incurably averse to Society, and more
obstinately tenacious of his Savage Liberty, than any
other Creature would be, that is equally necessitous.

Hor. I don't know how to refute you : There is
a Justness of Thought in what you say, which I am
forc'd to assent to ; and yet it seems strange : How
come you by this Insight into the Heart of Man, and

which way is that Skill of unravelling humane Nature to be obtain'd?

Cleo. By diligently observing what Excellencies and Qualifications are really acquired, in a well-accomplish'd Man; and having done this impartially, we may be sure that the Remainder of him is Nature. It is for want of duly separating and keeping asunder these two things, that Men have utter'd such Absurdities on this Subject; alledging as the Causes of Man's Fitness for Society, such Qualifications as no Man ever was endued with, that was not educated in a Society, a civil Establish-|ment, of several hundred Years [359] standing. But the Flatterers of our Species keep this carefully from our View : Instead of separating what is acquired from what is natural, and distinguishing between them, they take Pains to unite and confound them together.

Hor. Why do they? I don't see the Compliment ; since the acquired, as well as natural Parts, belong to the same Person ; and the one is not more inseparable from him than the other.

Cleo. Nothing is so near to a Man, nor so really and entirely his own, as what he has from Nature; and when that dear Self, for the sake of which he values or despises, loves or hates every thing else, comes to be stript and abstracted from all Foreign Acquisitions, humane Nature makes a poor Figure; it shews a Nakedness, or at least an Undress, which no Man cares to be seen in. There is nothing we can be possess'd of, that is worth having, which we do not endeavour, closely to annex, and make an Ornament of to ourselves ; even Wealth and Power, and all the Gifts of Fortune, that are plainly adventitious, and altogether remote from our Persons ; whilst they are our Right and Property, we don't love to be consider'd without them. We see likewise that Men, who are come to be great in the World from despicable Beginnings, don't love to hear of their Origin.

[360] | *Hor.* That is no general Rule.

Cleo. I believe it is, tho' there may be Exceptions
from it ; and these are not without Reasons. When
a Man is proud of his Parts, and wants to be esteem'd
for his Diligence, Penetration, Quickness and Assiduity,
he'll make perhaps an ingenuous Confession, even to
the exposing of his Parents ; and in order to set off
the Merit that rais'd him, be speaking himself of his
original Meanness. But this is commonly done before
Inferiours, whose Envy will be lessen'd by it, and who
will applaud his Candor and Humility in owning this
Blemish : But not a Word of this before his Betters,
who value themselves upon their Families ; and such
Men could heartily wish that their Parentage was
unknown, whenever they are with those that are their
Equals in Quality, tho' superior to them in Birth ; by
whom they know, that they are hated for their
Advancement, and despis'd for the Lowness of their
Extraction. But I have a shorter way of proving my
Assertion. Pray, is it good Manners to tell a Man,
that he is meanly born, or to hint at his Descent, when
it is known to be Vulgar?

Hor. No : I don't say it is.

Cleo. That decides it, by shewing the general
Opinion about it. Noble Ancestors, and every thing
else that is honourable and esteem'd, and can be
drawn within our Sphere, are an Advantage to our
[361] Persons, and we all | desire, they should be look'd
upon as our own.

Hor. Ovid did not think so, when he said, *Nam
genus & proavos & quæ non fecimus ipsi, vix ea nostra
voco.*[1]

Cleo. A pretty piece of Modesty in a Speech, where
a Man takes Pains to prove that *Jupiter* was his Great
Grandfather. What signifies a Theory, which a Man
destroys by his Practice? Did you ever know a Person
of Quality pleas'd with being call'd a Bastard, tho' he

---

[1] Ovid, *Metamorphoses* xiii. 140–1.

owed his Being, as well as his Greatness, chiefly to his Mother's Impudicity.

Hor. By things acquired, I thought you meant Learning and Virtue ; how come you to talk of Birth and Descent?

Cleo. By shewing you, that Men are unwilling to have any thing that is honourable separated from themselves, tho' it is remote from, and has nothing to do with their Persons : I would convince you of the little Probability there is, that we should be pleased with being consider'd, abstract from what really belongs to us ; and Qualifications, that in the Opinion of the best and wisest are the only things, for which we ought to be valued. When Men are well-accomplish'd, they are ashamed of the lowest Steps, from which they rose to that Perfection ; and the more civiliz'd they are, the more they think it injurious, to have their Nature seen, without the Improvements that have been made upon it. The | most correct [362] Authors would blush to see every thing publish'd, which in the composing of their Works they blotted out, and stifled ; and which yet it is certain they once conceiv'd : For this Reason they are justly compared to Architects, that remove the Scaffolding before they shew their Buildings. All Ornaments bespeak the Value we have for the Things adorn'd. Don't you think, that the first red or white that ever was laid upon a Face, and the first false Hair that was wore, were put on with great Secrecy, and with a Design to deceive?

Hor. In *France* Painting is now look'd upon as Part of a Woman's Dress ; they make no Mystery of it.

Cleo. So it is with all the Impositions of this nature, when they come to be so gross that they can be hid no longer ; as Men's Perukes all over *Europe :* But if these things could be conceal'd, and were not known, the Tawny Coquette would heartily wish, that the ridiculous Dawbing she plaisters herself with, might pass for Complexion ; and the bald-pated Beau would be as glad, to have his full-botom'd Wig look'd upon as a natural head of Hair.   No body puts in artificial Teeth, but to hide the Loss of his own.

Hor. But is not a Man's Knowledge a real Part of himself?

Cleo. Yes, and so is his Politeness ; but neither of [363] them belong to his Nature, any | more than his Gold Watch or his Diamond Ring ; and even from these he endeavours to draw a Value and Respect to his Person. The most admired among the fashionable People that delight in outward Vanity, and know how to dress well, would be highly displeas'd if their Clothes, and Skill in putting them on, should be look'd upon otherwise than as Part of themselves ; nay, it is this Part of them only, which whilst they are unknown, can procure them Access to the highest Companies, the Courts of Princes ; where it is manifest, that both Sexes are either admitted or refused, by no other Judgment than what is form'd of them from their Dress, without the least Regard to their Goodness, or their Understanding.

Hor. I believe I apprehend you. It is our Fondness of that Self, which we hardly know what it consists in, that could first make us think of embellishing our Persons ; and when we have taken Pains in correcting, polishing, and beautifying Nature, the same Self-love makes us unwilling to have the Ornaments seen separately from the Thing adorned.

Cleo. The Reason is obvious. It is that Self we are in love with, before it is adorn'd as well as after, and every thing which is confess'd to be acquired, seems to point at our original Nakedness, and to upbraid us with our natural Wants ; I would say, the Meanness [364] and Deficiency of our Nature. | That no Bravery is so useful in War, as that which is artificial, is undeniable; yet the Soldier that by Art and Discipline has manifestly been trick'd and wheedled into Courage, after he has behaved himself in two or three Battles with Intrepidity, will never endure to hear, that he has not natural Valour;[1] tho' all his Acquaintance, as well as himself, remember the time, that he was an arrant Coward.

Hor. But since the Love, Affection, and Benevolence, we naturally have for our Species, is not greater than other Creatures have for theirs, how comes it, that Man gives more ample Demonstrations of this Love on thousand Occasions, than any other Animal?

Cleo. Because no other Animal has the same Capacity or Opportunity to do it. But you may ask the same of his Hatred : The greater Knowledge and the more Wealth and Power a Man has, the more capable he is of rendring others sensible of the Passion he is affected with, as well when he hates as when he loves them. The more a Man remains unciviliz'd, and the less he is remov'd from the State of Nature, the less his Love is to be depended upon.

Hor. There is more Honesty and less Deceit among plain, untaught People, than there is among those that are more artful ; and therefore I should have look'd for true Love and unfeign'd Affection, among those that live | in a natural Simplicity, rather than any where else. [365]

Cleo. You speak of Sincerity ; but the Love which I said was less to be depended upon in untaught than in civilis'd People, I supposed to be real and sincere in both. Artful People may dissemble Love, and pretend to Friendship, where they have none ; but they are influenc'd by their Passions, and natural Appetites, as well as Savages, though they gratify them in another manner : Well-bred People behave themselves in the Choice of Diet and the taking of their Repastes, very differently from Savages ; so they do in their Amours ; but Hunger and Lust are the same in both. An artful Man, nay, the greatest Hypocrite, whatever his Behaviour is abroad, may love his Wife and Children

---

[1] Cf. *Fable* i. 207–9.

at his Heart, and the sincerest Man can do no more. My Business is to demonstrate to you, that the good Qualities Men compliment our Nature and the whole Species with, are the Result of Art and Education. The Reason why Love is little to be depended upon in those that are uncivilis'd, is because the Passions in them are more fleeting and inconstant; they oftener jostle out and succeed one another, than they are and do in well-bred People, Persons that are well educated, have learn'd to study their Ease, and the Comforts of Life; to tye themselves up to Rules and Decorums for their own Advantage, and often to [366] submit to small | Inconveniencies to avoid greater. Among the lowest Vulgar, and those of the meanest Education of all, you seldom see a lasting Harmony : You shall have a Man and his Wife, that have a real Affection for one another, be full of Love one Hour, and disagree the next, for a Trifle ; and the Lives of many are made miserable from no other Faults in themselves, than their Want of Manners and Discretion. Without Design they will often talk imprudently, 'till they raise one another's Anger ; which neither of them being able to stifle, she scolds at him ; he beats her ; she bursts out into Tears ; this moves him, he is sorry ; both repent, and are Friends again ; and with all the Sincerity imaginable resolve never to quarrel for the future, as long as they live : All this will pass between them in less than half a Day, and will perhaps be repeated once a Month, or oftner, as Provocations offer, or either of them is more or less prone to Anger. Affection never remain'd long uninterrupted between two Persons, without Art; and the best Friends, if they are always together, will fall out, unless great Discretion be used on both Sides.

Hor. I have always been of your Opinion, that the more Men were civilis'd the happier they were ; but since Nations can never be made polite, but by length of Time, and Mankind must have been always miserable

before they had written Laws, how come Poets | and [367]
others to launch out so much in praise of the Golden
Age, in which they pretend there was so much Peace,
Love, and Sincerity?

Cleo. For the same reason, that Heralds compliment
obscure Men of unknown Extraction with illustrious
Pedigrees : As there is no Mortal of high descent,
but who values himself upon his Family, so extolling
the Virtue and Happiness of their Ancestors, can never
fail pleasing every Member of a Society : But what
Stress would you lay upon the Fictions of Poets?

Hor. You reason very clearly, and with great Freedom, against all heathen Superstition, and never suffer
yourself ᵃ to be imposed upon by any Fraud from that
Quarter ; but when you meet with any thing belonging to the *Jewish* or Christian Religion, you are as
credulous as any of the Vulgar.

Cleo. I am sorry you should think so.

Hor. What I say is fact. A Man that contentedly
swallows every thing that is said of *Noah* and his Ark,
ought not to laugh at the Story of *Deucalion* and
*Pyrrha.*¹

Cleo. Is it as credible, that human Creatures should
spring from Stones, because an old Man and his Wife
threw them over their Heads ; as that a Man and
his Family, with a great Number of Birds and Beasts,
should be preserv'd in a large Ship, made convenient
for that Purpose?

| *Hor.* But you are partial : What odds is there [368]
between a Stone and a Lump of Earth, for either of
them to become a human Creature? I can as easily
conceive how a Stone should be turn'd into a Man or
a Woman, as how a Man or a Woman should be turn'd
into a Stone ; and I think it not more strange, that
a Woman should be chang'd into a Tree, as was

ᵃ youself 29

¹ See Pseudo-Lucian, *De Syria Dea* 12 and Ovid, *Metamorphoses* i.
240–415.

Daphne, or into Marble as *Niobe*,[1] than that she should be transform'd into a Pillar of Salt, as the Wife of *Lot* was. Pray suffer me to catechize you a little.

Cleo. You'll hear me afterwards, I hope.

Hor. Yes, yes. Do you believe *Hesiod*?

Cleo. No.

Hor. Ovid's Metamorphosis?

Cleo. No.

Hor. But you believe the Story of *Adam* and *Eve*, and Paradise.

Cleo. Yes.

Hor. That they were produced at once, I mean at their full Growth; he from a Lump of Earth, and she from one of his Ribbs?

Cleo. Yes.

Hor. And that as soon as they were made, they could speak, reason, and were endued with Knowledge?

Cleo. Yes.

Hor. In short, you believe the Innocence, the Delight, and all the Wonders of Paradise, that are related by one Man; at the same time that you will [369] not believe what has been told | us by many, of the Uprightness, the Concord, and the Happiness of a Golden Age.

Cleo. That's very true.

Hor. Now give me leave to shew you, how un-accountable, as well as partial, you are in this. In the first Place, the Things naturally impossible, which you believe, are contrary to your own Doctrine, the Opinion you have laid down, and which I believe to. be true : For you have proved, that no Man would ever be able to speak, unless he was taught it; that Reasoning and Thinking come upon us by slow Degrees; and that we can know nothing that has not from without been conveyed to the Brain, and communicated to us through the Organs of the Senses. Secondly, in what you reject as fabulous, there is no

[1] See Ovid, *Metamorphoses* i. 452–567 and vi. 146–312.

manner of Improbability. We know from History, and daily Experience teaches us, that almost all the Wars and private Quarrels, that have at any time disturbed Mankind, have had their Rise from the Differences about Superiority, and the *meum & tuum :* Therefore before Cunning, Covetousness, and Deceit crept into the World, before Titles of Honour, and the Distinction between Servant and Master were known : Why might not moderate Numbers of People have lived together in Peace and Amity, when they enjoy'd every thing in common; and have been content with the Product of the Earth in a fertile Soil and a happy Climate? Why can't you believe this?

| *Cleo.* Because it is inconsistent with the Nature [370] of human Creatures, that any Number of them should ever live together in tolerable Concord, without Laws or Government, let the Soil, the Climate, and their Plenty be whatever the most luxuriant Imagination shall be pleas'd to fancy them. But *Adam* was altogether the Workmanship of God ; a præternatural Production : His Speech and Knowledge, his Goodness and Innocence were as miraculous, as every other Part of his Frame.

Hor. Indeed, *Cleomenes*, this is insufferable ; when we are talking Philosophy you foist in Miracles : Why may not I do the same, and say that the People of the Golden Age were made happy by Miracle?

Cleo. It is more probable, that one Miracle should at a stated time have produced a Male and Female, from whom all the rest of Mankind are descended in a natural Way ; than that by a continued Series of Miracles several Generations of People should have all been made to live and act contrary to their Nature ; for this must follow from the Account we have of the Golden and Silver Ages.[1] In *Moses*, the first natural Man, the first that was born of a Woman, by envying

---

[1] Cf. Ovid, *Metamorphoses* i. 89-124.

and slaying his Brother, gives an ample Evidence of the domineering Spirit, and the Principle of Sovereignty, which I have asserted to belong to our Nature.

[371] | *Hor.* You will not be counted credulous, and yet you believe all those Stories, which even some of our Divines have call'd ridiculous, if literally understood. But I don't insist upon the Golden Age, if you'll give up Paradise : A Man of Sense, and a Philosopher, should believe neither.

Cleo. Yet you have told me that you believ'd the Old and New Testament.

Hor. I never said, that I believ'd every thing that is in them in a litteral Sense. But why should you believe Miracles at all?

Cleo. Because I can't help it : and I promise never to mention the Name to you again, if you can shew me the bare Possibility, that Man could have ever been produced, brought into the World, without Miracle. Do you believe there ever was a Man, who had made himself?

Hor. No : That's a plain Contradiction.

Cleo. Then it is manifest the first Man must have been made by something ; and what I say of Man, I may say of all Matter and Motion in general. The Doctrine of *Epicurus*, that every thing is deriv'd from the Concourse and fortuitous Jumble of Atoms, is monstrous and extravagant beyond all other Follies.

Hor. Yet there is no mathematical Demonstration against it.

Cleo. Nor is there one to prove, that the Sun is not in Love with the Moon, if one had a Mind to advance [372] it : and yet I think it a | greater Reproach to human Understanding, to believe either, than it is to believe the most childish Stories that are told of Fairies and Hobgoblins.

Hor. But there is an Axiom very little inferior to

a mathematical Demonstration, *ex nihilo nihil fit,* that is directly clashing with and contradicts the Creation out of Nothing. Do you understand, how Something can come from Nothing?

Cleo. I do not, I confess, any more than I can comprehend Eternity, or the Deity itself : but when I cannot comprehend what my Reason assures me must necessarily exist, there is no Axiom or Demonstration clearer to me, than that the Fault lies in my want of Capacity, the Shallowness of my Understanding. From the little we know of the Sun and Stars, their Magnitudes, Distances, and Motion ; and what we are more nearly acquainted with, the gross, visible Parts in the Structure of Animals, and their Oeconomy, it is demonstrable, that they are the Effects of an intelligent Cause, and the Contrivance of a Being infinite in Wisdom as well as Power.

Hor. But let Wisdom be as superlative, and Power as extensive as it is possible for them to be, still it is impossible to conceive, how they should exert themselves, unless they had something to act upon.

Cleo. This is not the only thing which, tho' it be true, we are not able to conceive : | How came the [373] first Man to exist? and yet here we are. Heat and Moisture are the plain Effects from manifest Causes, and tho' they bear a great Sway, even in the mineral as well as the animal and vegetable World ; yet they cannot produce a Sprig of Grass, without a previous Seed.

Hor. As we our selves, and every thing we see, are the undoubted Parts of some one Whole, some are of Opinion, that this all,[a] the τὸ πᾶν, the Universe, was from all Eternity.

Cleo. This is not more satisfactory or comprehensible, than the System of *Epicurus,* who derives every thing from wild Chance, and an undesign'd Struggle

[a] all,] all *29-33*

of senseless Atoms. When we behold things, which our Reason tells us could not have been produced without Wisdom and Power, in a degree far beyond our Comprehension, can any thing be more contrary to, or clashing with that same Reason, than that the things, in which that high Wisdom and great Power are visibly display'd, should be coeval with the Wisdom and Power themselves, that contriv'd and wrought them? Yet this Doctrine, which is *Spinosism* in Epitome, after having been neglected many Years, begins to prevail again, and the Atoms lose ground : for of Atheism, as well as Superstition, there are different Kinds, that have their Periods and Returns, after they have been long exploded.

[374]　| *Hor.* What makes you couple together two things so diametrically opposite?

Cleo. There is greater Affinity between them than you imagine : They are of the same Origin.

Hor. What, Atheism and Superstition !

Cleo. Yes, indeed ; they both have their Rise from the same Cause, the same Defect in the Mind of Man, our want of Capacity in discerning Truth, and natural Ignorance of the Divine Essence. Men, that from their most early Youth have not been imbued with the Principles of the true Religion, and have not afterwards continued to be strictly educated in the same, are all in great Danger of falling either into the one or the other, according to the Difference there is in the Temperament and Complexion they are of, the Circumstances they are in, and the Company they converse with. Weak Minds, and those that are brought up in Ignorance, and a low Condition, such as are much exposed to Fortune, Men of slavish Principles, the Covetous and Mean-spirited, are all naturally inclin'd to, and easily susceptible of Superstition ; and there is no Absurdity so gross, nor Contradiction so plain, which the Dregs of the People, most Gamesters, and nineteen Women in twenty, may not be

taught to Believe, concerning invisible Causes. Therefore Multitudes are never tainted with Irreligion;
and, the less civiliz'd Nations are, the more bound-
| less is their Credulity. On the contrary, Men of [375]
Parts and Spirit, of Thought and Reflection, the
Assertors of Liberty, such as meddle with Mathematicks and natural Philosophy, most inquisitive Men,
the disinterested, that live in Ease and Plenty; if
their Youth has been neglected, and they are not well
grounded in the Principles of the true Religion, are
prone to Infidelity; especially such amongst them,
whose Pride and Sufficiency are greater than ordinary;
and if Persons of this sort fall into Hands of Unbelievers,
they run great Hazard of becoming *Atheists* or *Scepticks.*

Hor. The Method of Education you recommend,
in pinning Men down to an Opinion, may be very
good to make Bigots, and raise a strong Party to the
Priests; but to have good Subjects, and moral Men,
nothing is better than to inspire Youth with the Love
of Virtue, and strongly to imbue them with Sentiments of Justice and Probity, and the true Notions of
Honour and Politeness. These are the true *Specificks*
to cure Man's Nature, and destroy in him the Savage
Principles of Sovereignty and Selfishness, that infest
and are so mischievous to it. As to religious Matters,
prepossessing the Mind, and forcing Youth into a
Belief, is more partial and unfair, than it is to leave
them unbiass'd, and unprejudiced till they come to
Maturity, and are fit to judge, as well as chuse for
themselves.

| *Cleo.* It is this fair and impartial Management you [376]
speak in praise of, that will ever promote and encrease
Unbelief; and nothing has contributed more to the
growth of Deism in this Kingdom, than the Remisness
of Education in Sacred Matters, which for some time
has been in Fashion among the better sort.

Hor. The Publick Welfare ought to be our principal
Care; and I am well assured, that it is not Bigotry to

a Sect or Persuasion; but common Honesty, Uprightness in all Dealings, and Benevolence to one another, which the Society stands most in need of.

Cleo.[a] I don't speak up for Bigotry; and where the Christian Religion is thoroughly taught, as it should be, it is impossible, that Honesty, Uprightness, or Benevolence should ever be forgot; and no Appearances of those Virtues are to be trusted to, unless they proceed from that Motive; for without the Belief of another World, a Man is under no Obligation for his Sincerity in this: His very Oath is no Tye upon him.

Hor. What is it upon an Hypocrite, that dares to be perjured?

Cleo. No Man's Oath is ever taken, if it is known that once he has been forsworn; nor can I ever be deceiv'd by an Hypocrite, when he tells me that he is one; and I shall never believe a Man to be an Atheist, unless he owns it himself.

[377] | *Hor.* I don't believe there are real Atheists in the World.

Cleo. I won't quarrel about Words; but our Modern Deism is no greater Security than Atheism: For a Man's acknowledging the Being of a God, even an intelligent first Cause, is of no use, either to himself or others, if he denies a Providence and a Future State.

Hor. After all, I don't think, that Virtue has any more Relation to Credulity, than it has to Want of Faith.

Cleo. Yet it would and ought to have, if we were consistent with ourselves; and if Men were sway'd in their Actions by the Principles they side with, and the Opinion they profess themselves to be of, all Atheists would be Devils, and superstitious Men Saints: But this is not true; there are Atheists of good Morals, and great Villains superstitious: Nay, I don't believe, there is any Wickedness that the worst Atheist can

[a] *Hor. 29, 33*

commit, but superstitious Men may be guilty of it; Impiety not excepted; for nothing is more common amongst Rakes and Gamesters, than to hear Men blaspheme, that believe in Spirits, and are afraid of the Devil. I have no greater Opinion of Superstition, than I have of Atheism; what I aim'd at, was to prevent and guard against both; and I am persuaded, that there is no other Antidote, to be obtain'd by human Means, so powerful and infallible against the Poyson of either, as what I have mention'd. As to the | Truth of our Descent from *Adam,* I would not be [378] a Believer, and cease to be a rational Creature : what I have to say for it, is this. We are convinc'd, that human Understanding is limited; and by the help of very little Reflection, we may be as certain, that the Narrowness of its bounds, its being so limited, is the very thing, the sole Cause, which palpably hinders us from diving into our Origin by dint of Penetration : the Consequence is, that to come at the Truth of this Origin, which is of very great Concern to us, something is to be believ'd : But what or whom to believe is the Question. If I cannot demonstrate to you, that *Moses* was divinely inspired, you'll be forc'd to confess, that there never was any thing more extraordinary in the World, than that in a most superstitious Age one Man brought up among the grossest Idolaters, that had the vilest and most abominable Notions of the Godhead, should, without Help as we know of, find out the most hidden and most important Truths by his natural Capacity only; for, besides the deep Insight he had in human Nature, as appears from the Decalogue, it is manifest, that he was acquainted with the Creation out of nothing, the Unity and immense Greatness of that invisible Power, that has made the Universe; and that he taught this to the *Israëlites,* fifteen Centuries before any other Nation upon Earth was so far enlighten'd : It is undeniable moreover, that the | History of *Moses,* concerning the Beginning of [379] the World and Mankind, is the most ancient and least improbable of any that are extant ; that others, who have wrote after him on the same Subject, appear most of them to be imperfect Copiers of him ; and that the Relations, which seem not to have been borrow'd from *Moses*, as the Accounts we have of *Sommona-codom*,[1] *Confucius*,[2] and others, are less rational, and fifty times more extravagant, and incredible, than any thing contain'd in the *Pentateuch*. As to the things reveal'd, the Plan itself, abstract from Faith and Religion ; when we have weigh'd every System, that has been advanced, we shall find ; that, since we must have had a Beginning, nothing is more rational or more agreeable to good Sense, than to derive our Origin from an incomprehensible creative Power, that was the first Mover and Author of all things.

Hor. I never heard any Body entertain higher Notions, or more noble Sentiments of the Deity, than at different times I have heard from you ; pray, when you read *Moses*, don't you meet with several Things in the Oeconomy of Paradise, and the Conversation between God and *Adam*, that seem to be low, unworthy, and altogether inconsistent with the sublime Ideas, you are used to form of the Supreme Being?

Cleo. I freely own, not only that I have thought so, [380] but likewise that I have long | stumbled at it : But when I consider, on the one hand, that the more human Knowledge encreases, the more consummate and unerring the Divine Wisdom appears to be, in every thing we can have any Insight into ; and on the other, that the things hitherto detected, either

---

[1] There is an article on Sommonacodom, the Siamese demigod, in Bayle's *Dictionary*. As his story closely parallels that of Christ, Mandeville may have mentioned him disingenuously (cf. above, ii. 21, *n.* 2).

[2] The *Shu*, or History, of Confucius begins with historic times and contains none of the account of the Creation credited to him by Mandeville. However, the Chinese have an elaborate myth of the Creation, for which see John Ross, *Origin of the Chinese People*, ch. 1.

by Chance or Industry, are very inconsiderable, both in Number and Value, if compared to the vast Multitude of weightier Matters, that are left behind, and remain still undiscover'd : When, I say, I consider these things, I can't help thinking, that there may be very wise Reasons for what we find Fault with, that are, and perhaps ever will be, unknown to Men as long as the World endures.

Hor. But why should we remain labouring under Difficulties, we can easily solve, and not say with Dr. *Burnet* and several others, that those things are Allegories, and to be understood in a figurative Sense?[1]

Cleo. I have nothing against it ; and shall always applaud the Ingenuity and good Offices of Men, who endeavour to reconcile Religious Mysteries to human Reason and Probability ; but I insist upon it, that no Body can disprove any thing that is said in the *Pentateuch* in the most literal Sense ; and I defy the Wit of Man to frame or contrive a Story, the best concerted Fable they can invent, how Man came into the World, which I shall not find as much Fault with,

[1] Thomas Burnet's *The Theory of the Earth : Containing an Account of the Original of the Earth*, a translation from the earlier-published Latin original, *Telluris Theoria Sacra*, appeared in 1684. This work attempted to give a scientific geological account of the beginnings of the earth which should not conflict with the biblical account. Burnet found it necessary, in defence of this theory, to publish, in 1692, his *Archæologiæ Philosophicæ : sive Doctrina Antiqua de Rerum Originibus*, in which, to save his theory, he interpreted the first chapter of Genesis allegorically (cf. *Archæologiæ*, ed. 1692, pp. 283-4—bk. 2, ch. 7). The book made a public scandal.

The allegorical interpretation of Scripture dates back to the Fathers. The 'several others ', however, mentioned by Mandeville may well have included Anthony Collins, as witness his *Discourse of the Grounds and Reasons of the Christian Religion*, 1724, Spinoza (see his letter to Oldenburg of 7 Feb. 1676), Charles Blount (*Miscellaneous Works*, ed. 1695, p. 68, in *Oracles of Reason*), and Thomas Woolston, whose six discourses on the 'Miracles of our Saviour ', published in 1727, 1728, and 1729, procured him a term of imprisonment.

and be able to make as strong Objections to, as the
[381] Enemies of | Religion have found with, and rais'd
against the Account of *Moses :* If I may be allow'd
to take the same Liberty with their known Forgery,
which they take with the Bible, before they have
brought one Argument against the Veracity of it.

Hor. It may be so. But as first I was the Occasion
of this long Digression, by mentioning the Golden
Age ; so now, I desire we may return to our Subject.
What Time, how many Ages, do you think, it would
require to have a well-civiliz'd Nation from such
a Savage Pair as yours?

Cleo. That's very uncertain ; and I believe it
impossible, to determine any thing about it. From
what has been said, it is manifest, that the Family
descending from such a Stock, would be crumbled to
pieces, re-united, and dispers'd again several times,
before the whole or any part of it could be advanced
to any degree of Politeness. The best Forms of
Government are subject to Revolutions, and a great
many things must concur, to keep a Society of Men
together, till they become a civiliz'd Nation.

Hor. Is not a vast deal owing, in the raising of
a Nation, to the difference there is in the Spirit and
Genius of People?

Cleo. Nothing, but what depends upon Climates,
which is soon over-ballanc'd by skilful Government.
Courage and Cowardice, in all Bodies of Men, depend
[382] entirely upon Exer-|cise and Discipline. Arts and
Sciences seldom come before Riches, and both flow in
faster or slower, according to the Capacity of the
Governours, the Situation of the People, and the
Opportunities they have of Improvements ; but the
first is the Chief : To preserve Peace and Tranquility among Multitudes of different Views, and
make them all labour for one Interest, is a great Task ;
and nothing in human Affairs requires greater Knowledge, than the Art of Governing.

Hor. According to your System, it should be little more, than guarding against human Nature.

Cleo. But it is a great while, before that Nature can be rightly understood ; and it is the Work of Ages to find out the true Use of the Passions, and to raise a Politician, that can make every Frailty of the Members add Strength to the whole Body, and by dextrous Management turn *private Vices into publick Benefits.*[1]

Hor. It must be a great Advantage to an Age, when many extraordinary Persons are born in it.

Cleo. It is not Genius, so much as Experience, that helps Men to good Laws : *Solon, Lycurgus, Socrates* and *Plato* all travell'd for their Knowledge,[2] which they communicated to others. The wisest Laws of human Invention are generally owing to the Evasions of bad Men, whose Cunning had eluded the | Force [383] of former Ordinances, that had been made with less Caution.

Hor. I fancy that the Invention of Iron, and working the Oar into a Metal, must contribute very much to the completing of Society ; because Men can have no Tools nor Agriculture without it.

Cleo. Iron is certainly very useful ; but Shells and Flints, and hardning of Wood by Fire, are Substitutes, that Men make a Shift with ; if they can but have Peace, live in Quiet, and enjoy the Fruits of their Labour. Could you ever have believ'd, that a Man without Hands could have shaved himself, wrote good Characters, and made use of a Needle and Thread with his Feet? Yet this we have seen. It is said by some Men of Reputation, that the *Americans* in *Mexico* and *Peru* have all the Signs of an infant World ; because when the *Europeans* first came among them,

---

[1] Cf. *Fable* i. 369.
[2] Cf. Saavedra Fajardo's *Royal Politician* (1700) ii. 122 : ' Twas Travel made *Plato, Lycurgus,* *Solon,* and *Pythagoras,* such prudent Lawgivers and Philosophers.' Cf. above, i. 194, *n.* 3.

they wanted a great many things, that seem to be of easy Invention. But considering, that they had no Body to borrow from, and no Iron at all, it is amasing which way they could arrive at the Perfection we found them in. First, it is impossible to know, how long Multitudes may have been troublesome to one another, before the Invention of Letters came among them, and they had any written Laws. Secondly, from the many Chasms in History we know by Experience, that the Accounts of Transactions and Times in which Letters [a] [384] are known, | may be entirely lost. Wars and human Discord may destroy the most civiliz'd Nations, only by dispersing them; and general Devastations spare Arts and Sciences no more than they do Cities and Palaces. That all Men are born with a strong Desire, and no Capacity at all to govern, has occasion'd an Infinity of Good and Evil. Invasions and Persecutions, by mixing and scattering our Species, have made strange Alterations in the World. Sometimes large Empires are divided into several Parts, and produce new Kingdoms and Principalities; at others, great Conquerors in few Years bring different Nations under one Dominion. From the Decay of the *Roman* Empire alone we may learn, that Arts and Sciences are more perishable, much sooner lost, than Buildings or Inscriptions; and that a Deluge of Ignorance may overspread Countries, without their ceasing to be inhabited.

Hor. But what is it at last, that raises opulent Cities and powerful Nations from the smallest Beginnings?

Cleo. Providence.

Hor. But Providence makes use of Means that are visible; I want to know the Engines it is perform'd with.

Cleo. All the Ground Work, that is required to aggrandise Nations, you have seen in *the Fable of the Bees.* All sound Politicks, and the whole Art of

[a] Lettes 29

governing, are entirely built upon the Knowledge of human Nature. The | great Business in general of [385] a Politician is to promote, and, if he can, reward all good and useful Actions on the one hand ; and on the other, to punish, or at least discourage, every thing that is destructive or hurtful to Society. To name Particulars would be an endless Task. Anger, Lust, and Pride may be the Causes of innumerable Mischiefs, that are all carefully to be guarded against : But setting them aside, the Regulations only, that are required to defeat and prevent all the Machinations and Contrivances, that Avarice and Envy may put Man ª upon, to the Detriment of his Neighbour, are almost infinite. Would you be convinc'd of these Truths, do but employ yourself for a Month or two, in surveying and minutely examining into every Art and Science, every Trade, Handicraft and Occupation, that are profess'd and follow'd in such a City as *London* ; and all the Laws, Prohibitions, Ordinances and Restrictions, that have been found absolutely necessary, to hinder both private Men and Bodies corporate, in so many different Stations, first from interfering with the Publick Peace and Welfare ; secondly, from openly wronging and secretly over-reaching, or any other way injuring, one another : If you will give yourself this Trouble, you will find the Number of Clauses and Proviso's, to govern a large flourishing City well, to be prodigious beyond Imagination ; and yet every one of them tending to the same | Purpose, the curbing, restrain- [386] ing and disappointing the inordinate Passions, and hurtful Frailties of Man. You will find moreover, which is still more to be admired, the greater part of the Articles, in this vast Multitude of Regulations, when well understood, to be the Result of consummate Wisdom.

Hor. How could these things exist, if there had not been Men of very bright Parts and uncommon Talents ?

Cleo. Among the things I hint at, there are very

ª Man] a Man *33*

few, that are the Work of one Man, or of one Generation ; the greatest part of them are the Product, the joynt Labour of several Ages. Remember, what in our third Conversation I told you, concerning the Arts of Ship-building and Politeness.[1] The Wisdom I speak of, is not the Offspring of a fine Understanding, or intense Thinking, but of sound and deliberate Judgment, acquired from a long Experience in Business, and a Multiplicity of Observations. By this sort of Wisdom, and Length of Time, it may be brought about, that there shall be no greater Difficulty in governing a large City, than (pardon the Lowness of the Simile) there is in weaving of Stockings.

Hor.[a] Very low indeed.

Cleo. Yet I know nothing to which the Laws and establish'd Oeconomy of a well-order'd City may be more justly compared, than the Knitting-frame. The [387] Machine, at | first View, is intricate and unintelligible ; yet the Effects of it are exact and beautiful ; and in what is produced by it, there is a surprizing Regularity : But the Beauty and Exactness in the Manufacture are principally, if not altogether, owing to the Happiness of the Invention, the Contrivance of the Engine. For the greatest Artist at it can furnish us with no better Work, than may be made by almost any Scoundrel after half a Year's Practice.

Hor. Tho' your Comparison be low, I must own, that it very well illustrates your Meaning.

Cleo. Whilst you spoke, I have thought of another, which is better. It is common now, to have Clocks, that are made to play several Tunes with great Exactness : The Study and Labour, as well as Trouble of Disappointments, which, in doing and undoing, such a Contrivance must necessarily have cost from the Beginning to the End, are not to be thought of without Astonishment : There is something analogous to this in the Government of a flourishing City, that has

---

[a] *Hor.*] *Hor, 29*   [1] Cf. *Fable* ii. 141 sqq.

lasted uninterrupted for several Ages : There is no Part of the wholesome Regulations, belonging to it, even the most trifling and minute, about which great Pains and Consideration have not been employ'd, as well as Length of Time ; and if you will look into the History and Antiquity of any such City, you will find that the Changes, Repeals, Additions and A-|mend- [388] ments, that have been made in and to the Laws and Ordinances by which it is ruled, are in Number prodigious : But that when once they are brought to as much Perfection, as Art and human Wisdom can carry them, the whole Machine may be made to play of itself, with as little Skill, as is required to wind up a Clock ; and the Government of a large City, once put into good Order, the Magistrates only following their Noses, will continue to go right for a great while, tho' there was not a wise Man in it : Provided that the Care of Providence was to watch over it in the same manner as it did before.

Hor. But supposing the Government of a large City, when it is once establish'd, to be very easy, it is not so with whole States and Kingdoms : Is it not a great Blessing to a Nation, to have all Places of Honour and great Trust fill'd with Men of Parts and Application, of Probity and Virtue?

Cleo. Yes ; and of Learning, Moderation, Frugality, Candour and Affability : Look out for such as fast as you can : But in the mean time the Places can't stand open, the Offices must be served by such as you can get.

Hor. You seem to insinuate, that there is a great Scarcity of good Men in the Nation.

Cleo. I don't speak of our Nation in particular, but of all States and Kingdoms in general. What I would say, is, that it is the Interest of every Nation to have their Home | Government, and every Branch of the [389] Civil Administration, so wisely contriv'd, that every Man of midling Capacity and Reputation may be fit for any of the highest Posts.

Hor. That's absolutely impossible, at least in such a Nation as ours : For what would you do for Judges and Chancellours?

Cleo. The Study of the Law is very crabbed and very tedious ; but the Profession of it is as gainful, and has great Honours annex'd to it : The Consequence of this is, that few come to be eminent in it, but Men of tolerable Parts and great Application. And whoever is a good Lawyer, and not noted for Dishonesty, is always fit to be a Judge, as soon as he is old and grave enough. To be a Lord Chancellour indeed, requires higher Talents ; and he ought not only to be a good Lawyer and an honest Man, but likewise a Person of general Knowledge, and great Penetration. But this is but one Man ; and considering, what I have said of the Law, and the Power which Ambition and the Love of Gain have upon Mankind, it is morally impossible, that, in the common Course of Things among the Practicioners in *Chancery*, there should not at all times be one or other fit for the Seals.

Hor. Must not every Nation have Men that are fit for Publick Negotiations, and Persons of great Capacity to serve for Envoys, Ambassadors and Pleni-[390] potentiaries? must they not | have others at Home, that are likewise able to treat with Foreign Ministers?

Cleo. That every Nation must have such People, is certain ; but I wonder, that the Company you have kept both at Home and Abroad, have not convinced you, that the things you speak of require no such extraordinary Qualifications. Among the People of Quality, that are bred up in Courts of Princes, all midling Capacities must be Persons of Address and a becoming Boldness, which are the most useful Talents in all Conferences and Negotiations.

Hor. In a Nation so involved in Debts of different kinds, and loaded with such a Variety of Taxes, as ours is, to be thoroughly acquainted with all the Funds, and the Appropriations of them, must be a Science not to be attain'd to without good natural Parts and great Application ; and therefore the chief Management of the Treasury must be a Post of the highest Trust, as well as endless Difficulty.

Cleo. I don't think so : Most Branches of the Publick Administration are in reality less difficult to those, that are in them, than they seem to be to those that are out of them, and are Strangers to them. If a Jack and the Weights of it were out of Sight, a sensible Man, unacquainted with that Matter, would be very much puzled, if he was to account | for the regular [391] turning of two or three Spits well loaded, for Hours together ; and it is ten to one, but he would have a greater Opinion of the Cook or the Scullion, than either of them deserved. In all Business that belongs [a] to the *Exchequer*, the Constitution does nine parts in ten ; and has taken effectual Care, that the happy Person, whom the King shall be pleas'd to favour with the Superintendency of it, should never be greatly tired or perplex'd with his Office ; and likewise that the Trust, the Confidence, that must be reposed in him, should be very near as moderate as his Trouble. By dividing the Employments in a great Office, and subdividing them into many parts, every Man's Business may be made so plain and certain, that, when he is a little used to it, it is hardly possible for him to make Mistakes : And again, by careful Limitations of every Man's Power, and judicious Cheques upon every Body's Trust, every Officer's Fidelity may be placed in so clear a Light, that, the Moment he forfeits it, he must be detected. It is by these Arts that the weightiest Affairs, and a vast Multiplicity of them, may be managed with Safety as well as Dispatch, by ordinary Men, whose highest Good is Wealth and Pleasure ; and that the utmost Regularity may be observed in a great Office, and every part of it ; at the same time, that the whole Oeconomy of it seems

[a] belong *29, 30*

to be intricate and perplex'd to the last degree, not [392] only to Strang-|ers, but the greatest part of the very Officers that are employ'd in it.

Hor. The Oeconomy of our *Exchequer*, I own, is an admirable Contrivance to prevent Frauds and Encroachments of all kinds ; but in the Office, which is at the Head of it, and gives Motion to it, there is greater Latitude.

Cleo. Why so ? A Lord Treasurer, or if his Office be executed by Commissioners, the Chancellour of the *Exchequer*, are no more lawless, and have no greater Power with Impunity to embezle Money, than the meanest Clerk that is employ'd under them.

Hor. Is not the King's Warrant their Discharge ?

Cleo. Yes ; for Sums, which the King has a Right to dispose of, or the Payment of Money for Uses directed by Parliament ; not otherwise ; and if the King, who can do no Wrong, should be imposed upon, and his Warrant be obtain'd for Money at Random, whether it is appropriated or not, contrary to, or without a direct Order of the Legislature, the Treasurer obeys at his Peril.

Hor. But there are other Posts, or at least there is one still of higher Moment, and that requires a much greater, and more general Capacity than any yet named.

Cleo. Pardon me : As the Lord Chancellour's is the highest Office in Dignity, so the Execution of it actually demands greater, and more uncommon Abilities than any other whatever.

[393] | *Hor.* What say you to the Prime Minister, who governs all, and acts immediately under the King ?

Cleo. There is no such Officer belonging to our Constitution ; ¹ for by this, the whole Administration is, for very wise Reasons, divided into several Branches.

¹ Not until 2 Dec. 1905 was the office of Prime Minister legally recognized, although from the early eighteenth century there had been, for all practical purposes, as Horatio remarks, such

Hor. But who must give Orders and Instructions to Admirals, Generals, Governours, and all our Ministers in Foreign Courts? who is to take Care of the King's Interest throughout the Kingdom, and of his Safety?

Cleo. The King and his Council, without which, Royal Authority is not suppos'd to act, superintend, and govern all; and whatever the Monarch has not a Mind immediately to take care of himself, falls in course to that part of the Administration it belongs to, in which every Body has plain Laws to walk by. As to the King's Interest, it is the same with that of the Nation; his Guards are to take Care of his Person; and there is no Business of what nature soever, that can happen in or to the Nation, which is not within the Province, and under the Inspection of some one or other of the great Officers of the Crown, that are all known, dignify'd, and distinguish'd by their respective Titles; and amongst them, I can assure you, there is no such Name as Prime Minister.

Hor. But why will you prevaricate with me after this manner? You know yourself, | and all the World [394] knows and sees, that there is such a Minister; and it is easily proved, that there always have been such Ministers: And in the Situation we are, I don't believe a King could do without. When there are

a minister, Sir Robert Walpole being known as the earliest. There is an ulterior motive behind Mandeville's tribute to the abilities of Lord Chancellors. Lord Macclesfield, Mandeville's friend and patron, had been Chancellor. The ulterior motive becomes more clear when it is realized that the two offices of Prime Minister and Lord Treasurer—with which the Chancellorship is favourably compared—were both held by Macclesfield's particular enemy,

Robert Walpole. It was Walpole who had instituted the investigation that caused Macclesfield in May 1725 to be removed from the bench for corruption, and fined £30,000. And, after the death of George I, who had promised to repay the fine, and who had actually repaid Macclesfield £1,000, it was Walpole who, as Chancellor of the Exchequer, refused to reimburse Macclesfield any further.

a great many disaffected People in the Kingdom, and
Parliament-men are to be chosen, Elections must be
look'd after with great Care, and a thousand things
are to be done, that are necessary, to disappoint the
sinister ends of Malecontents, and keep out the
Pretender; things of which the Management often
requires great Penetration, and uncommon Talents, as
well as Secrecy and Dispatch.

Cleo. How sincerely soever you may seem to speak
in Defence of these Things, *Horatio*, I am sure, from
your Principles, that you are not in earnest. I am
not to judge of the Exigency of our Affairs : But as
I would not pry into the Conduct, or scan the Actions
of Princes, and their Ministers, so I pretend to justify
or defend no Wisdom, but that of the Constitution
itself.

Hor. I don't desire you should : Only tell me,
whether you don't think, that a Man, who has and
can carry this vast Burden upon his Shoulders, and all
Europe's Business in his Breast, must be a Person of
a prodigious Genius, as well as general Knowledge,
and other great Abilities.

Cleo. That a Man, invested with so much real
[395] Power, and an Authority so extensive, as | such
Ministers generally have, must make a great Figure,
and be considerable above all other Subjects, is
most certain : But it is my Opinion, that there are
always fifty Men in the Kingdom, that, if employ'd,
would be fit for this Post, and after a little Practice
shine in it, to one, who is equally qualify'd to be
a Lord High Chancellor of *Great Britain.* A Prime
Minister has a vast, an unspeakable Advantage, barely
by being so, and by every Body's knowing him to be,
and treating him as, such : A Man, who, in every
Office and every Branch of it throughout the Administration, has the Power, as well as the Liberty, to ask
and see whom and what he pleases, has more Knowledge within his Reach, and can speak of every thing

with greater Exactness, than any other Man, that is much better vers'd in Affairs, and has ten times greater Capacity. It is hardly possible, that an active Man of tolerable Education, that is not destitute of a Spirit nor of Vanity, should fail of appearing to be wise, vigilant, and expert, who has the Opportunity, whenever he thinks fit, to make use of all the Cunning and Experience, as well as Diligence and Labour, of every Officer in the civil Administration ; and if he has but Money enough, and will employ Men to keep up a strict Correspondence in every Part of the Kingdom, he can remain ignorant of nothing ; and there is hardly any Affair or Transaction, Civil or Military, Fo-|reign or Domestick, which he will not be able [396] greatly to influence, when he has a Mind, either to promote or obstruct it.

Hor. There seems to be a great deal in what you say, I must confess ; but I begin to suspect, that what often inclines me to be of your Opinion, is your Dexterity in placing Things in the Light, you would have them seen in, and the great Skill you have in depreciating what is valuable, and detracting from Merit.

Cleo. I protest, that I speak from my Heart.

Hor. When I reflect on what I have beheld with my own Eyes, and what I still see every Day of the Transactions, between Statesmen and Politicians, I am very well assured, you are in the wrong : When I consider all the Stratagems, and the Force, as well as *Finesse*, that are made use of, to supplant and undo Prime Ministers ; the Wit and Cunning, Industry and Address, that are employ'd to misrepresent all their Actions ; the Calumnies and false Reports that are spread of them, the Ballads and Lampoons that are publish'd ; the set Speeches and study'd Invectives that are made against them ; when I consider, I say, and reflect on these Things, and every thing else that is said and done, either to ridicule or to render them odious, I am convinced; that to defeat so much Art and Strength, and disappoint so [397] much Malice and | Envy, as prime Ministers are generally attack'd with, require extraordinary Talents : No Man of only common Prudence and Fortitude could maintain himself in that Post for a Twelvemonth, much less for many Years together, tho' he understood the World very well, and had all the Virtue, Faithfulness, and Integrity in it; therefore there must be some Fallacy in your Assertion.

Cleo. Either I have been deficient in explaining myself, or else I have had the Misfortune to be misunderstood. When I insinuated, that Men might be prime Ministers without extraordinary Endowments, I spoke only in regard to the Business itself, that Province, which if there was no such Minister, the King and Council would have the trouble of managing.

Hor. To direct and manage the whole Machine of Government, he must be a consummate Statesman in the first place.

Cleo. You have too sublime a Notion of that Post. To be a consummate Statesman, is the highest Qualification human Nature is capable of possessing : To deserve that Name, a Man must be well versed in ancient and modern History, and thoroughly acquainted with all the Courts of *Europe* ; that he may know not only the publick Interest in every Nation, but likewise the private Views, as well as Inclinations, Virtues and Vices of Princes and Ministers : Of every Country [398] in | Christendom and the Borders of it, he ought to know the Product and Geography ; the principal Cities and Fortresses ; and of these, the Trade and Manufactures ; their Situation, natural Advantages, Strength and Number of Inhabitants ; he must have read Men as well as Books, and perfectly well understand human Nature, and the use of the Passions : He must moreover be a great Master in concealing the Sentiments of his Heart, have an entire Command over his Features, and be well skill'd in all the Wiles and Stratagems to draw out Secrets from others. A Man, of whom all this, or the greatest Part of it, may not be said with truth, and that he has had great Experience in publick Affairs, cannot be call'd a consummate Statesman ; but he may be fit to be a prime Minister, tho' he had not a hundredth Part of those Qualifications. As the King's Favour creates prime Ministers, and makes their Station the Post of the greatest Power as well as Profit ; so the same Favour is the only Bottom, which those that are in it have to stand upon : The Consequence is, that the most ambitious Men in all Monarchies are ever contending for this Post, as the highest Prize, of which the Enjoyment is easy, and all the Difficulty in obtaining and preserving it. We see accordingly, that the Accomplishments I spoke of to make a Statesman are neglected, and others aim'd at and study'd, that are more useful and more easily | acquired. The Capacities you observe [399] in prime Ministers, are of another Nature, and consist in being finish'd Courtiers, and thoroughly understanding the Art of pleasing and cajoling with Address. To procure a Prince what he wants, when it is known, and to be diligent in entertaining him with the Pleasures he calls for, are ordinary Services : Asking is no better than Complaining ; therefore being forced to ask, is to have Cause of Complaint, and to see a Prince submit to the Slavery of it, argues great Rusticity in his Courtiers ; a polite Minister penetrates into his Master's Wishes, and furnishes him with what he delights in, without giving him the trouble to name it. Every common Flatterer can praise and extol promiscuously every thing that is said or done ; and find Wisdom and Prudence in the most indifferent Actions ; but it belongs to the skilful Courtier to set fine Glosses upon manifest Imperfections, and make every Failing, every Frailty of his Prince, have the real Appearance of the Virtues that

are the nearest, or to speak more justly, the least
opposite to them. By the Observance of these necessary Duties it is, that the Favour of Princes may be
long preserv'd as well as obtain'd. Whoever can make
himself agreeable at a Court, will seldom fail of being
thought necessary; and when a Favourite has once
established himself in the good Opinion of his Master,
[400] it is easy for | him to make his own Family, engross
the King's Ear, and keep every body from him, but
his own Creatures : Nor is it more difficult, in length
of time, to turn out of the Administration every body
that was not of his own bringing in, and constantly
be tripping up the Heels of those, who attempt to
raise themselves by any other Interest or Assistance.
A prime Minister has by his Place great Advantages
over all that oppose him; one of them is, that no
body, without Exception, ever fill'd that Post, but
who had many Enemies, whether he was a Plunderer
or a Patriot : Which being well known, many things
that are laid to a prime Minister's Charge, are not
credited among the impartial and more discreet Part
of Mankind, even when they are true. As to the
defeating and disappointing all the Envy and Malice
they are generally attack'd with; if the Favourite
was to do all that himself, it would certainly, as you
say, require extraordinary Talents, and a great Capacity,
as well as continual Vigilance and Application; but
this is the Province of their Creatures, a Task divided
into a great Number of Parts; and every body that
has the least Dependance upon, or has any thing to
hope from the Minister, makes it his Business and his
Study, as it is his Interest, on the one hand, to cry
up their Patron, magnify his Virtues and Abilities,
and justify his Conduct; on the other, to exclaim
[401] against his Ad-|versaries, blacken their Reputation,
and play at them every Engine, and the same ª Stratagems that are made use of to supplant the Minister.

ª some 29

Hor. Then every well-polish'd Courtier is fit to be a prime Minister, without Learning, or Languages, Skill in Politicks, or any other Qualification besides.

Cleo. No other than what are often and easily met with : It is necessary, that he should be a Man, at least, of plain common Sense, and not remarkable for any gross Frailties or Imperfections ; and of such there is no Scarcity almost in any Nation : He ought to be a Man of tolerable Health and Constitution, and one who delights in Vanity, that he may relish, as well as be able to bear, the gaudy Crouds that honour his Levées ; the constant Addresses, Bows, and Cringes of Solicitors ; and the rest of the Homage that is perpetually paid him. The Accomplishment he stands most in need of, is to be bold and resolute, so as not to be easily shock'd or ruffled ; if he be thus qualify'd, has a good Memory, and is moreover able to attend a Multiplicity of Business, if not with a continual Presence of Mind, at least seemingly without Hurry or Perplexity, his Capacity can never fail of being extoll'd to the Skies.

Hor. You say nothing of his Virtue nor his Honesty ; there is a vast Trust put in a prime Minister : If he should be covetous and | have no Probity, nor Love [402] for his Country, he might make strange Havock with the Publick Treasure.

Cleo. There is no Man that has any Pride, but he has some Value for his Reputation ; and common Prudence is sufficient to hinder a Man of very indifferent Principles from stealing, where he would be in great Danger of being detected, and has no manner of Security that he shall not be punish'd for it.

Hor. But great Confidence is reposed in him where he cannot be traced ; as in the Money for Secret Services, of which, for Reasons of State, it may be often improper even to mention, much more to scrutinize into the Particulars ; and in Negotiations with other Courts, should he be only sway'd by Selfishness and private Views, without regard to Virtue or the Publick, is it not in his Power to betray his Country, sell the Nation, and do all manner of Mischief?

Cleo. Not amongst us, where Parliaments are every Year sitting. In Foreign Affairs nothing of moment can be transacted, but what all the World must know; and should any thing be done or attempted, that would be palpably ruinous to the Kingdom, and in the Opinion of Natives and Foreigners, grosly and manifestly clashing with our Interest, it would raise a general Clamour, and throw the Minister into Dangers, which no Man of the least Prudence, who [403] intends | to stay in his Country, would ever run into. As to the Money for Secret Services, and perhaps other Sums, which Ministers have the Disposal of, and where they have great Latitudes, I don't question, but they have Opportunities of embezling the Nation's Treasure: But to do this without being discover'd, it must be done sparingly, and with great Discretion: The malicious Overlookers that envy them their Places, and watch all their Motions, are a great Awe upon them: The Animosities between those Antagonists, and the Quarrels between Parties, are a considerable Part of the Nation's Security.

Hor. But would it not be a greater Security to have Men of Honour, of Sense and Knowledge, of Application and Frugality, preferr'd to publick Employments?

Cleo. Yes, without doubt.

Hor. What Confidence can we have in the Justice or Integrity of Men; that, on the one hand, shew themselves on all Occasions mercenary and greedy after Riches; and on the other, make it evident, by their manner of living, that no Wealth or Estate could ever suffice to support their Expences, or satisfy their Desires? Besides, would it not be a great Encouragement to Virtue and Merit, if from the Posts of Honour and Profit all were to be debarr'd and excluded, that

either wanted Capacity, or were Enemies to Business ;
all the selfish, ambitious, vain, and voluptuous?

| *Cleo.* No body disputes it with you ; and if Virtue, [404]
Religion, and future Happiness were sought after by
the Generality of Mankind, with the same Sollicitude,
as sensual Pleasure, Politeness, and worldly Glory are,
it would certainly be best, that none but Men of good
Lives, and known Ability, should have any Place in
the Government whatever : But to expect that this
ever should happen, or to live in hopes of it in a large,
opulent and flourishing Kingdom, is to betray great
Ignorance in human Affairs ; and whoever reckons
a general Temperance, Frugality, and Disinterestedness among the national Blessings, and at the same
time sollicites Heaven for Ease and Plenty, and the
Encrease of Trade, seems to me, little to understand
what he is about. The best of all then not being to
be had, let us look out for the next best, and we shall
find, that of all possible Means to secure and per-
petuate to Nations their Establishment, and whatever
they value, there is no better Method than with wise
Laws to guard and entrench their Constitution, and
contrive such Forms of Administration, that the
Common-Weal can receive no great Detriment from
the Want of Knowledge or Probity of Ministers, if
any of them should prove less able or honest, than they
could wish them. The Publick Administration must
always go forward ; it is a Ship that can never lie at
Anchor : The most knowing, the most virtuous, | and [405]
the least self-interested Ministers are the best ; but
in the mean time there must be Ministers. Swearing
and Drunkenness are crying Sins among Seafaring
Men, and I should think it a very desirable Blessing
to the Nation, if it was possible to reform them :
But all this while we must have Sailors ; and if none
were to be admitted on board of any of his Majesty's
Ships, that had sworn above a thousand Oaths, or had
been drunk above ten times in their Lives, I am

persuaded that the Sea Service would suffer very much by the well-meaning Regulation.

Hor. Why don't you speak more openly, and say that there is no Virtue or Probity in the World? for all the drift of your Discourse is tending to prove that.

Cleo. I have amply declared my self upon this Subject already in a former Conversation; and I wonder you will lay again to my Charge what I once absolutely denied: I never thought that there were no virtuous or religious Men; what I differ in with the Flatterers of our Species, is about the Numbers, which they contend for; and I am persuaded that you your self, in reality, don't believe that there are so many virtuous Men as you imagine you do.

Hor. How come you to know my Thoughts better than I do my self?

Cleo. You know I have tried you upon this Head [406] already, when I ludicrously extoll'd and | set a fine Gloss on the Merit of several Callings and Professions in the Society, from the lowest Stations of Life to the highest: It then plainly appear'd, that, tho' you have a very high Opinion of Mankind in general, when we come to Particulars, you was as severe, and every whit as censorious, as my self. I must observe one thing to you, which is worth Consideration. Most, if not all, People are desirous of being thought impartial; yet nothing is more difficult than to preserve our Judgment unbiass'd, when we are influenc'd either by our Love or our Hatred; and how just and equitable soever People are, we see that their Friends are seldom so good, or their Enemies so bad, as they represent them, when they are angry with the one, or highly pleas'd with the other. For my Part, I don't think that, generally speaking, Prime Ministers are much worse than their Adversaries, who, for their own Interest, defame them, and, at the same time, move Heaven and Earth to be in their Places. Let us look

out for two Persons of Eminence, in any Court of
Europe, that are equal in Merit and Capacity, and as
well match'd in Virtues and Vices, but of contrary
Parties ; and whenever we meet with two such, one
in Favour, and the other neglected, we shall always
find, that whoever is uppermost, and in great Employ,
has the Applause of his Party ; and, if things go
tollerably well, his Friends will attribute every good
| Success to his Conduct, and derive all his Actions [407]
from laudable Motives : The opposite Side can discover
no Virtues in him ; they will not allow him to act
from any Principles but his Passions ; and, if any
thing be done amiss, are very sure that it would not
have happen'd if their Patron had been in the same
Post. This is the Way of the World. How immensely
do often People of the same Kingdom differ in the
Opinion they have of their Chiefs and Commanders,
even when they are successful to Admiration ! We
have been Witnesses our selves, that one Part of the
Nation has ascrib'd the Victories of a General,
entirely to his consummate Knowledge in Martial
Affairs, and superlative Capacity in Action ; and
maintain'd, that it was impossible for a Man to bear
all the Toils and Fatigues he underwent with Alacrity,
or to court the Dangers he voluntarily expos'd himself to, if he had not been supported, as well as animated, by the true Spirit of Heroism, and a most
generous Love for his Country : These, you know,
were the Sentiments of one Part of the Nation, whilst
the other attributed all his Successes to the Bravery
of his Troops, and the extraordinary Care that was
taken at Home to supply his Army ; and insisted upon
it, that, from the whole Course of his Life, it was
demonstrable, that he had never been buoy'd up
or actuated by any other | Principles than excess [408]
of Ambition, and an insatiable greediness after
Riches.

Hor. I don't know but I may have said so my self.

But, after all, the Duke of *Marlborough* was a very great Man, an extraordinary Genius.

Cleo. Indeed was he, and I am glad to hear you own it at last.

> *Virtutem incolumem odimus,*
> *Sublatam ex oculis quærimus invidi.*[1]

Hor. A propos. I wish you would bid them stop for two or three Minutes : Some of the Horses perhaps may stale the while.

Cleo. No Excuses, pray. You command here. Besides, we have Time enough. —— Do you want to go out?

Hor. No; but I want to set down something, now I think of it, which I have heard you repeat several times. I have often had a mind to ask you for it, and it always went out of my Head again. It is the Epitaph which your Friend made upon the Duke.[a]

Cleo. Of *Marlborough?*[2] with all my Heart. Have you Paper?

Hor. I'll write it upon the Back of this Letter ; and, as it happens, I mended my Pencil this Morning. How does it begin?

Cleo. Qui Belli, aut Pacis virtutibus astra petebant.
[409] | *Hor.* Well.

Cleo.   Finxerunt homines Sæcula prisca Deos.

Hor. I have it. But tell me a whole Distich at a time ; the Sense is clearer.

Cleo. Quæ Martem sine patre tulit, sine matre Miner-
> *vam,*
> *Illustres Mendax Græcia jactet Avos.*

Hor. That is really a happy Thought. Courage and Conduct : just the two Qualifications he excelled in. What's the next?

---

[a] Duke.] Duke *29-33*

[1] Horace, *Odes* III. xxiv. 31-2.

[2] The Duke of Marlborough died 16 June 1722.

Cleo. Anglia quem genuit jacet hâc, Homo, conditus
  Urnâ,
Antiqui qualem non habuere Deum.

Hor. —— I thank you. They may go on now.
I have seen several things since first I heard this
Epitaph of you, that are manifestly borrow'd from it.
Was it never publish'd?

Cleo. I believe not. The first time I saw it was the
Day the Duke was buried, and ever since it has been
handed about in Manuscript; but I never met with it
in Print yet.

Hor. It is worth all his *Fable of the Bees*, in my
Opinion.

Cleo. If you like it so well, I can shew you a Translation of it, lately done by a Gentleman of *Oxford*, if
I have not lost it. It only takes in the first and last
Distich, which in-|deed contain the main Thought : [410]
The second does not carry it on, and is rather a Digression.

Hor. But it demonstrates the Truth of the first, in
a very convincing manner; and that *Mars* had no
Father, and *Minerva* no Mother, is the most fortunate
thing a Man could wish for, who wanted to prove
that the Account we have of them is fabulous.

Cleo. Oh, here it is. I don't know whether you can
read it : I copied it in haste.

Hor. Very well.

The grateful Ages past a God declar'd,
Who wisely council'd, or who bravely war'd :
Hence Greece *her* Mars *and* Pallas *deify'd;*
Made him the Hero's, her the Patriot's Guide.
Ancients, within this Urn a Mortal lies;
Shew me his Peer among your Deities.

It is very good.

Cleo. Very lively; and what is aim'd at in the
Latin, is rather more clearly express'd in the *English.*

Hor. You know I am fond of no *English* Verse but *Milton*'s.[1] But don't let this hinder our Conversation.

Cleo. I was speaking of the Partiality of Mankind in general, and putting you in mind how differently Men judg'd of Actions, according as they liked or disliked the Persons that perform'd them.

[411] | *Hor.* But before that you was arguing against the Necessity, which I think there is, for Men of great Accomplishments and extraordinary Qualifications in the Administration of Publick Affairs. Had you any thing to add?

Cleo. No; at least I don't remember that I had.

Hor. I don't believe you have an ill Design in advancing these Notions; but supposing them to be true, I can't comprehend that divulging them can have any other Effect than the Increase of Sloth and Ignorance; for if Men may fill the highest Places in the Government without Learning or Capacity, Genius or Knowledge, there's an End of all the Labour of the Brain, and the Fatigue of hard Study.

Cleo. I have made no such general Assertion; but that an artful Man may make a considerable Figure in the highest Post of the Administration, and other great Employments, without extraordinary Talents, is certain: As to consummate Statesmen, I don't believe there ever were three Persons upon Earth, at the same time, that deserv'd that Name. There is not a quarter of the Wisdom, solid Knowledge, or intrinsick Worth, in the World, that Men talk of, and compliment one another with; and of Virtue or Religion there is not an hundredth Part in Reality of what there is in Appearance.

[412] | *Hor.* I allow that those who set out from no better

---

[1] Mandeville is here possibly hitting at his adversary John Dennis, who considered Milton the greatest of poets. In his *Letter to Dion* (p. 46), Mandeville speaks of Dennis as ‘a noted Critick who seems to hate all Books that sell, and no other’.—See below, ii. 407–9, for an account of Dennis's attack on Mandeville.

Motives, than Avarice and Ambition, aim at no other
Ends but Wealth and Honour ; which, if they can
but get any ways they are satisfied ; but Men, who
act from Principles of Virtue and a publick Spirit, take
Pains with Alacrity to attain the Accomplishments
that will make them capable of serving their Country :
And if Virtue be so scarce, how come there to be Men
of Skill in their Professions? for that there are Men of
Learning, and Men of Capacity, is most certain.

Cleo. The Foundation of all Accomplishments must
be laid in our Youth, before we are able or allow'd to
chuse for ourselves, or to judge, which is the most
profitable way of employing our Time. It is to good
Discipline, and the prudent Care of Parents and
Masters, that Men are beholden for the greatest Part
of their Improvements ; and few Parents are so bad
as not to wish their Offspring might be well accomplish'd : The same natural Affection, that makes Men
take Pains to leave their Children rich, renders them
sollicitous about their Education. Besides, it is unfashionable, and consequently a Disgrace, to neglect
them. The chief Design of Parents in bringing up
their Children to a Calling or Profession, is to procure
them a Livelihood. What promotes and encourages
Arts and Sciences, is the Reward, Money and Honour ;
and thousands of | Perfections are attain'd to, that [413]
would have had no Existence, if Men had been less
proud or less covetous. Ambition, Avarice, and often
Necessity, are great Spurs to Industry and Application ;
and often rouse Men from Sloth and Indolence, when
they are grown up, whom no Persuasions, or Chastise-
ment of Fathers or Tutors, made any Impression upon
in their Youth. Whilst Professions are lucrative, and
have great Dignities belonging to them, there will
always be Men that excell in them. In a large polite
Nation therefore all sorts of Learning will ever abound,
whilst the People flourish. Rich Parents, and such as
can afford it, seldom fail bringing up their Children

to Literature : From this inexhaustible Spring it is,
that we always draw much larger Supplies than we
stand in need of, for all the Callings and Professions
where the Knowledge of the learned Languages is
required. Of those that are brought up to Letters,
some neglect them, and throw by their Books, as soon
as they are their own Masters ; others grow fonder of
Study, as they increase in Years ; but the greatest
Part will always retain a Value for what has cost them
Pains to acquire. Among the Wealthy, there will be
always Lovers of Knowledge, as well as idle People :
Every Science will have its Admirers, as Men differ in
their Tastes and Pleasures ; and there is no Part of
Learning but some Body or other will look into it,
[414] and labour at it, from | no better Principles, than
some Men are Fox-hunters, and others take delight
in Angling. Look upon the mighty Labours of
Antiquaries, Botanists, and the Vertuoso's in Butter-
flies, Cockle-shells, and other odd Productions of
Nature ; and mind the magnificent Terms they all
make use of in their respective Provinces, and the
pompous Names they often give, to what others, who
have no Taste that way, would not think worth any
Mortal's Notice. Curiosity is often as bewitching to
the Rich, as Lucre is to the Poor ; and what Interest
does in some, Vanity does in others ; and great
Wonders are often produced from a happy Mixture
of both. Is it not amazing, that a temperate Man
should be at the Expence of four or five Thousand
a Year, or, which is much the same thing, be contented
to lose the Interest of above a hundred thousand
Pounds, to have the Reputation of being the Possessor
and Owner of Rarities and Knicknacks in a very great
abundance, at the same time that he loves Money, and
continues slaving for it in his old Age? It is the
Hopes either of Gain or Reputation, of large Revenues
and great Dignities, that promote Learning ; and when
we say that any Calling, Art or Science, is not encou-

raged, we mean no more by it, than that the Masters or Professors of it are not sufficiently rewarded for their Pains, either with Honour or Profit. The most Holy Functions are no Exception to what I say; and | few Ministers of the Gospel are so disinterested as [415] to have a less regard to the Honours and Emoluments, that are or ought to be annex'd to their Employment, than they have to the Service and Benefit they should be of to others; and among those of them, that study hard and take uncommon Pains, it is not easily proved that many are excited to their extraordinary Labour by a publick Spirit, or Solicitude for the Spiritual Wellfare of the Laity: On the contrary, it is visible, in the greatest Part of them, that they are animated by the Love of Glory and the Hopes of Preferment; neither is it uncommon to see the most useful [a] Parts of Learning neglected for the most trifling, when, from the latter, Men have Reason to hope that they shall have greater Opportunities of shewing their Parts, than offer themselves from the former. Ostentation and Envy have made more Authors than Virtue and Benevolence. Men of known Capacity and Erudition are often labouring hard to eclipse and ruin one another's Glory. What Principle must we say two Adversaries act from, both Men of unquestionable good Sense and extensive Knowledge, when all the Skill and Prudence they are Masters of are not able to stifle, in their study'd Performances, and hide from the World the Rancour of their Minds, the Spleen and Animosity they both write with against one another?

| *Hor.*[b] I don't say that such act from Principles of [416] Virtue.

Cleo. Yet you know an Instance of this in two grave Divines,[1] Men of Fame and great Merit, of

---

[a] ufeful 29   [b] *Hor.*] *Hor,* 29

[1] Richard Bentley and John Le Clerc. Le Clerc, in 1709, published an edition of the frag- ments of Menander and Philemon, a task for which his limited knowledge of Greek, and especially of

whom each would think himself very much injured, should his Virtue be call'd in question.

Hor. When Men have an Opportunity, under pretence of Zeal for Religion, or the Publick Good, to vent their Passion, they take great Liberties. What was the Quarrel?

Cleo. De lanâ caprinâ.¹

Hor. A Trifle. I can't guess yet.

Cleo. About the Metre of the Comick Poets among the Ancients.

Hor. I know what you mean now; the manner of scanding and chanting those Verses.

Cleo. Can you think of any thing belonging to Literature, of less Importance, or more useless?

Hor. Not readily.

Cleo. Yet the great Contest between them, you see, is which of them understands it best, and has known it the longest. This Instance, I think, hints to us, how highly improbable it is, tho' Men should act from no better Principles than Envy, Avarice and Ambition, that, when Learning is once establish'd, any Part of it, even the most unprofitable, should ever be neglected in such a large, opulent Nation as ours is; where there [417] are so many Places of | Honour, and great Revenues to be disposed of among Scholars.

Hor. But since Men are fit to serve in most Places

Greek prosody, unfitted him. In criticism of this, Bentley wrote his *Emendationes in Menandri et Philemonis Reliquias, ex Nupera Editione Joannis Clerici*, and chose to send it for publication to Le Clerc's Dutch enemy, Peter Burman. The book appeared in 1710 under Bentley's famous pseudonym of *Philaleutherus Lipsiensis*, with a preface by Burman, triumphing over his injured enemy. The book made a sensation. Other scholars soon joined the fray. At this juncture, Le Clerc received anonymously some notes by a scholar whom time has shown to have been John Cornelius de Pauw, and the harassed Le Clerc published these and some notes by Salvini as a defence against Bentley. The tone of this production was anything but civil. (See Monk's *Life of Richard Bentley*, ed. 1833, i. 266–80.)

¹ Cf. Horace, *Epistles* i. xviii. 15.

with so little Capacity, as you insinuate, why should they give themselves that unnecessary trouble of studying hard, and acquiring more Learning, than there is occasion for?

Cleo. I thought, I had answer'd that already; a great many, because they take Delight in Study and Knowledge.

Hor. But there are Men that labour at it with so much Application, as to impair their Healths, and actually to kill themselves with the Fatigue of it.

Cleo. Not so many, as there are, that injure their Healths, and actually kill themselves with hard drinking, which is the most unreasonable Pleasure of the two, and a much greater Fatigue. But I don't deny that there are Men, who take Pains to qualify themselves in order to serve their Country; what I insist upon, is, that the Number of those, who do the same thing to serve themselves with little regard to their Country, is infinitely greater. Mr. *Hutcheson*, who wrote the *Inquiry into the Original of our Ideas of Beauty and Virtue*, seems to be very expert at weighing and measuring the Quantities of Affection, Benevolence, &c.[1] I wish that curious Metaphysician would

[1] Francis Hutcheson was Mandeville's most persistent opponent. He first attacked the *Fable* 14 and 24 Nov. 1724, in the *London Journal*, in a communication announcing and anticipating his *Inquiry into the Original of Our Ideas of Beauty and Virtue* (1725), in which, as Hutcheson put it, 'the Principles of . . . Shaftsbury are . . . defended against . . . the Fable of the Bees'. In 1726 Hutcheson again took up the cudgels in three letters to the *Dublin Journal* for 5, 12, and 19 Feb. These letters formed the latter half of a book issued first in 1750, posthumously, called

Reflections upon Laughter, and Remarks upon the Fable of the Bees.

Hutcheson was one of the most famous of Shaftesbury's disciples. Like Shaftesbury (see above, i. lxxiii–lxxv), he showed certain superficial resemblances to Mandeville. With Mandeville, he argued that our knowledge comes *a posteriori*, through sensation and perception; and, also like Mandeville, he was a pioneer of the English utilitarian movement. Unlike Mandeville, however, he held that sensation and perception were sufficient foundation for absolute truth;

give himself the Trouble, at his Leisure, to weigh [418] two things | separately : First, the real Love Men have for their Country, abstracted from Selfishness. Secondly, the Ambition they have, of being thought to act from that Love, tho' they feel none. I wish, I say, that this ingenious Gentleman would once weigh these two asunder ; and afterwards, having taken in impartially all he could find of either, in this or any other Nation, shew us in his demonstrative way, what Proportion the Quantities bore to each other. —— *Quisque sibi commissus est,* says *Seneca* ;[1] and certainly, it is not the Care of others, but the Care of itself, which Nature has trusted and charged every individual Creature with. When Men exert them-

the universal harmony of nature being arranged to this end. And, also unlike Mandeville, he maintained that we were endowed with a 'moral sense' capable of leading us inevitably to correct moral judgements without invoking the utilitarian test. This moral sense he held to be of divine origin, a part of the eternal harmony, thus being in opposition to Mandeville, who is throughout an opponent of the 'Divine Original' of virtue. Hutcheson's utilitarianism, too, was, in a way, only skin deep : the hedonistic test was to him merely an *index* of correct action; he refused to make this test also the *sanction* of its virtue. And being thus convinced that divine ordinance and practical utility are always at one, he could, when the latter seemed to shock his moral sensibilities, ignore it and adopt the common and convenient dialectic artifice of saying that what here seemed useful was not *truly* so, because it violated the divine ordinance. Thus, he tended to consider as lacking in virtuousness such actions, however advantageous, as proceeded from selfish motives. Mandeville, therefore, who attempted the proof that the most useful actions are consistently prompted by selfishness, was here again galling Hutcheson's philosophic kibe.

It was in demonstrating the existence of the moral sense and the intricacy of the 'divine harmony' as embodied in man that Hutcheson indulged in the 'weighing and measuring the Quantities' of the emotions to which Mandeville ironically alludes. This weighing Hutcheson did by actual mathematical formulae. Thus, he expressed ' *Benevolence* ' as ' $B = \dfrac{M - I}{A}$ ' or ' $B = \dfrac{M + I}{A}$ ' (*Inquiry*, p. 170).

[1] Cf. Seneca, *Epist.* cxxi. 18 (bk. 20, ep. 4, § 18).

selves in an extraordinary manner, they generally do it to be the better for it themselves; to excel, to be talk'd of, and to be preferr'd to others, that follow the same Business, or court the same Favours.

Hor. Do you think it more probable, that Men of Parts and Learning should be preferr'd, than others of less Capacity?

Cleo. Cæteris paribus, I do.

Hor. Then you must allow, that there is Virtue at least in those, who have the Disposal of Places.

Cleo. I don't say there is not; but there is likewise Glory, and real Honour accruing to Patrons, for advancing Men of Merit; and if a Person, who has a good Living in his Gift, bestows it upon a very able Man, every Body | applauds him, and every Parishioner [419] is counted to be particularly obliged to him. A vain Man does not love to have his Choice disapprov'd of, and exclaim'd against by all the World, any more than a virtuous Man; and the Love of Applause, which is innate to our Species, would alone be sufficient to make the Generality of Men, and even the greatest part of the most vicious, always chuse the most worthy, out of any Number of Candidates; if they knew the Truth, and no stronger Motive arising from Consanguinity, Friendship, Interest, or something else, was to interfere with the Principle I named.

Hor. But, methinks, according to your System, those should be soonest preferr'd, that can best coax and flatter.

Cleo. Among the Learned there are Persons of Art and Address, that can mind their Studies without neglecting the World : These are the Men, that know how to ingratiate themselves with Persons of Quality; employing to the best advantage all their Parts and Industry for that Purpose. Do but look into the Lives and the Deportment of such eminent Men, as we have been speaking of, and you will soon discover the End and Advantages they seem to propose to themselves

from their hard Study and severe Lucubrations. When
you see Men in Holy Orders, without Call or Necessity,
hovering about the Courts of Princes; when you see
[420] them continually addressing and scrap-|ing Acquaint-
ance with the Favorites; when you hear them exclaim
against the Luxury of the Age, and complain of the
Necessity they are under, of complying with it; and
at the same time you see, that they are forward, nay
eager and take pains with Satisfaction, in their way of
Living, to imitate the *Beau Monde*, as far as it is in
their Power : That no sooner they are in Possession
of one Preferment, but they are ready, and actually
solliciting for another, more gainful and more reput-
able; and that on all Emergencies, Wealth, Power,
Honour and Superiority are the things they grasp at,
and take delight in; when, I say, you see these things,
this Concurrence of Evidences, is it any longer difficult
to guess at, or rather is there room to doubt of, the
Principles they act from, or the Tendency of their
Labours?

Hor. I have little to say to Priests, and do not look
for Virtue from that Quarter.

Cleo. Yet you'll find as much of it among Divines,
as you will among any other Class of Men; but every
where less in Reality, than there is in Appearance.
No Body would be thought insincere, or to pre-
varicate; but there are few Men, tho' they are so
honest as to own what they would have, that will
acquaint us with the true Reason, why they would
have it : Therefore the Disagreement between the
Words and Actions of Men is at no time more conspicuous, than when we would learn from them their
[421] Sentiments con-|cerning the real Worth of Things.
Virtue is without doubt the most valuable Treasure,
which Man can be possess'd of; it has every Body's
good Word; but where is the Country in which it
is heartily embraced, *præmia si tollas?*[1]   Money, on

---

[1] Juvenal, *Satires* x. 142.

the other hand, is deservedly call'd the Root of all Evil : There has not been a Moralist nor a Satyrist of Note, that has not had a Fling at it ; yet what Pains are taken, and what Hazards are run to acquire it, under various Pretences of designing to do good with it ! As for my part, I verily believe, that as an accessary Cause, it has done more Mischief in the World than any one thing besides : Yet it is impossible to name another, that is so absolutely necessary to the Order, Oeconomy, and the very Existence of the Civil Society ; for as this is entirely built upon the Variety of our Wants, so the whole Superstructure is made up of the reciprocal Services, which Men do to each other. How to get these Services perform'd by others, when we have Occasion for them, is the grand and almost constant Sollicitude in Life of every individual Person. To expect, that others should serve us for nothing, is unreasonable ; therefore all Commerce, that Men can have together, must be a continual bartering of one thing for another. The Seller, who transfers the Property of a Thing, has his own Interest as much at Heart as the Buyer, who purchases that Property ; and, if you | want or like a thing, the [422] Owner of it, whatever Stock or Provision he may have of the same, or how greatly soever you may stand in need of it, will never part with it, but for a Consideration, which he likes better, than he does the thing you want. Which way shall I persuade a Man to serve me, when the Service, I can repay him in, is such as he does not want or care for? No Body, who is at Peace, and has no Contention with any of the Society, will do any thing for a Lawyer ; and a Physician can purchase nothing of a Man, whose whole Family is in perfect Health. Money obviates and takes away all those Difficulties, by being an acceptable Reward for all the Services Men can do to one another.

Hor. But all Men valuing themselves above their

Worth, every Body will over-rate his Labour. Would not this follow from your System?

Cleo. It certainly would, and does. But what is to be admired is, that the larger the Numbers are in a Society, the more extensive they have rendred the Variety of their Desires, and the more operose the Gratification of them is become among them by Custom; the less mischievous is the Consequence of that Evil, where they have the use of Money : Whereas, without it, the smaller the Number was of a Society, and the more strictly the Members of it, in supplying their Wants, would confine themselves to those only [423] that | were necessary for their Subsistance, the more easy it would be for them to agree about the reciprocal Services I spoke of. But to procure all the Comforts of Life, and what is call'd temporal Happiness, in a large polite Nation, would be every whit as practicable without Speech, as it would be without Money, or an Equivalent to be used instead of it. Where this is not wanting, and due Care is taken of it by the Legislature, it will always be the Standard, which the Worth of every Thing will be weigh'd by. There are great Blessings that arise from Necessity; and that every Body is obliged to eat and drink, is the Cement of civil Society. Let Men set what high Value they please upon themselves, that Labour, which most People are capable of doing, will ever be the cheapest. Nothing can be dear, of which there is great Plenty, how beneficial soever it may be to Man; and Scarcity inhances the Price of Things much oftener than the Usefulness of them. Hence it is evident why those Arts and Sciences will always be the most lucrative that cannot be attain'd to, but in great length of Time, by tedious Study and close Application; or else require a particular Genius, not often to be met with. It is likewise evident, to whose Lot, in all Societies, the hard and dirty Labour, which no Body would meddle with, if he could help it, will ever fall : But you have seen enough of this in the *Fable of the Bees.*

| *Hor.* I have so, and one remarkable Saying I have [424] read there on this Subject, which I shall never forget. *The Poor*, says the Author, *have nothing to stir them up to labour, but their Wants, which it is Wisdom to relieve, but Folly to cure.*[1]

Cleo. I believe the Maxim to be just, and that it is not less calculated for the real Advantage of the Poor, than it appears to be for the Benefit of the Rich. For, among the labouring People, those will ever be the least wretched as to themselves, as well as most useful to the Publick, that being meanly born and bred, submit to the Station they are in with Chearfulness ; and contented, that their Children should succeed them in the same low Condition, inure them from their Infancy to Labour and Submission, as well as the cheapest Diet and Apparel ; when, on the contrary, that sort of them will always be the least serviceable to others, and themselves the most unhappy, who, dissatisfy'd with their Labour, are always grumbling and repining at the meanness of their Condition ; and, under Pretence of having a great Regard for the Welfare of their Children, recommend the Education of them to the Charity of others ; and you shall always find, that of this latter Class of Poor, the greatest Part are idle, sottish People, that, leading dissolute Lives themselves, are neglectful of their Families, and only want, as far as it is in their Power, to shake off the | Burden of providing for their Brats [425] from their own Shoulders.

Hor. I am no Advocate for Charity-Schools ; yet I think it is barbarous, that the Children of the labouring Poor should be for ever pinn'd down, they, and all their Posterity, to that slavish Condition ; and that those who are meanly born, what Parts or Genius

[1] *Fable* i. 194 and 248.

soever they might be of, should be hinder'd and
debarr'd from raising themselves higher.

Cleo. So should I think it barbarous, if what you
speak of was done any where, or proposed to be done.
But there is no Degree of Men in Christendom that
are pinn'd down, they and their Posterity, to Slavery
for ever. Among the very lowest sort, there are
fortunate Men in every Country; and we daily see
Persons that, without Education or Friends, by their
own Industry and Application, raise themselves from
nothing to Mediocrity, and sometimes above it, if
once they come rightly to love Money and take
Delight in saving it : And this happens more often
to People of common and mean Capacities, than it
does to those of brighter Parts. But there is a prodigious Difference between debarring the Children
of the Poor from ever rising higher in the World, and
refusing to force Education upon Thousands of them
promiscuously, when they should be more usefully employ'd. As some of the Rich must come to be Poor, so
[426] some of the Poor will come to | be Rich in the common
Course of Things. But that universal Benevolence,
that should every where industriously lift up the
indigent Labourer from his Meanness, would not be
less injurious to the whole Kingdom than a tyrannical
Power, that should, without a Cause, cast down the
Wealthy from their Ease and Affluence. Let us suppose, that the hard and dirty Labour throughout the
Nation requires three Millions of Hands, and that
every Branch of it is perform'd by the Children of
the Poor, Illiterate, and such as had little or no Education themselves; it is evident, that if a tenth Part of
these Children, by Force and Design, were to be
exempt from the lowest Drudgery, either there must
be so much Work left undone, as would demand three
hundred thousand People; or the Defect, occasion'd
by the Numbers taken off, must be supply'd by the
Children of others, that had been better bred.

Hor. So that what is done at first out of Charity to some, may, at long Run, prove to be Cruelty to others.

Cleo. And will, depend upon it. In the Compound of all Nations, the different Degrees of Men ought to bear a certain Proportion to each other, as to Numbers, in order to render the whole a well-proportion'd Mixture. And as this due Proportion is the Result and natural Consequence of the difference there is in the Qualifications of Men, and the | Vicissitudes that [427] happen among them, so it is never better attained to, or preserv'd, than when no body meddles with it.[1] Hence we may learn, how the short-sighted Wisdom, of perhaps well-meaning People, may rob us of a Felicity, that would flow spontaneously from the Nature of every large Society, if none were to divert or interrupt the Stream.

Hor. I don't care to enter into these abstruse Matters ; what have you further to say in Praise of Money?

Cleo. I have no design to speak either for, or against it ; but be it good or bad, the Power and Dominion of it are both of vast extent, and the Influence of it upon Mankind has never been stronger or more general in any Empire, State or Kingdom, than in the most knowing and politest Ages, when they were in their greatest Grandeur and Prosperity ; and when Arts and Sciences were the most flourishing in them : Therefore the Invention of Money seems to me to be a thing more skilfully adapted to the whole Bent of our Nature, than any other of human Contrivance. There is no greater remedy against Sloth or Stubbornness ; and with Astonishment I have beheld the Readiness and Alacrity with which it often makes the proudest Men pay Homage to their Inferiors : It purchases all Services and cancels all Debts ; nay, it does more, for when a Person is employ'd in his Occupation, and he who sets him to work, a good

[1] Cf. *Fable* i. 299.

[428] Pay-|Master, how laborious, how difficult, or irksome soever the Service be, the Obligation is always reckoned to lie upon him who performs it.

Hor. Don't you think, that many eminent Men in the learned Professions would dissent from you in this?

Cleo. I know very well, that none ought to do it, if ever they courted Business or hunted after Employment.

Hor. All you have said is true, among mercenary People; but upon noble Minds that despise Lucre, Honour has a far greater Efficacy than Money.

Cleo. The highest Titles, and the most illustrious Births are no Security against Covetousness; and Persons of the first Quality, that are actually generous and munificent, are often as greedy after Gain, when it is worth their while, as the most sordid Mechanicks are for Trifles : The Year Twenty has taught us, how difficult it is to find out those noble Minds that despise Lucre, when there is a Prospect of getting vastly.[1] Besides, nothing is more universally charming than Money; it suits with every Station; the high, the low, the wealthy, and the poor : whereas Honour has little influence on the mean, slaving People, and rarely affects any of the vulgar; but if it does, Money will almost every where purchase Honour; nay, Riches of themselves are an honour to [429] all those, who know how | to use them fashionably. Honour on the contrary wants Riches for its support; without them it is a dead Weight that oppresses its Owner; and Titles of Honour, joyn'd to a necessitous Condition, are a greater Burden together, than the same degree of Poverty is alone : for the higher a Man's Quality is, the more considerable are his Wants in Life; but the more Money he has, the better he is able to supply the greatest Extravagancy of them. Lucre is the best Restorative in the World, in a literal

---

[1] See above, i. 276, *n.* 1.

Sense, and works upon the Spirits mechanically; for it is not only a Spur, that excites Men to labour, and makes them in love with it; but it likewise gives Relief in Weariness, and actually supports Men in all Fatigues and Difficulties. A Labourer of any sort, who is paid in proportion to his Diligence, can do more work than another, who is paid by the Day or the Week, and has standing Wages.

Hor. Don't you think then, that there are Men in laborious Offices, who for a fix'd Salary discharge their Duties with Diligence and Assiduity?

Cleo. Yes, many; but there is no Place or Employment, in which there are required or expected, that continual Attendance and uncommon Severity of Application, that some Men harrass and punish themselves with by Choice, when every fresh Trouble meets with a new Recompence; and you never saw | Men [430] so entirely devote themselves to their Calling, and pursue Business with that Eagerness, Dispatch and Perseverance in any Office or Preferment, in which the yearly Income is certain and unalterable, as they often do in those Professions, where the Reward continually accompanies the Labour, and the Fee immediately, either precedes the Service they do to others, as it is with the Lawyers, or follows it, as it is with the Physicians.--- I am sure you have hinted at this in our first Conversation yourself.

Hor. Here's the Castle before us.

Cleo. Which I suppose you are not sorry for.

Hor. Indeed I am, and would have been glad to have heard you speak of Kings and other Sovereigns, with the same Candor as well as Freedom, with which you have treated Prime Ministers and their envious Adversaries. When I see a Man entirely impartial, I shall always do him that Justice, as to think, that, if he is not in the right in what he says, at least he aims at Truth. The more I examine your Sentiments, by what I see in the World, the more I am obliged to

z 2

come into them ; and all this Morning I have said nothing in Opposition to you, but to be better inform'd, and to give you an Opportunity to explain yourself more amply. I am your Convert, and shall henceforth look upon the *Fable of the Bees* very [431] differently from what I did ; for tho' in | the *Characteristicks* the Language and the Diction are better, the System of Man's Sociableness is more lovely and more plausible, and Things are set off with more Art and Learning ; yet in the other there is certainly more Truth, and Nature is more faithfully copied in it, almost every where.

Cleo. I wish you would read them both once more, and, after that, I believe you'll say that you never saw two Authors who seem to have wrote with more different Views. My Friend, the Author of the *Fable*, to engage and keep his Readers in good Humour, seems to be very merry, and to do something else, whilst he detects the Corruption of our Nature ; and, having shewn Man to himself in various Lights, he points indirectly at the Necessity, not only of Revelation and Believing, but likewise of the Practice of Christianity, manifestly to be seen in Men's Lives.

Hor. I have not observ'd that : Which way has he done it indirectly?

Cleo. By exposing, on the one hand, the Vanity of the World, and the most polite Enjoyments of it ; and, on the other, the Insufficiency of Human Reason and Heathen Virtue to procure real Felicity ; for I cannot see what other Meaning a Man could have by doing this in a Christian Country, and among People, that all pretend to seek after Happiness.

[432] | *Hor.* And what say you of Lord *Shaftsbury*[a]?

Cleo. First, I agree with you, that he was a Man of Erudition, and a very polite Writer ; he has display'd a copious Imagination, and a fine Turn of thinking, in courtly Language and nervous Expres-

[a] *Shatsbury 29*

sions : But as, on the one hand, it must be confess'd, that his Sentiments on Liberty and Humanity are noble and sublime, and that there is nothing trite or vulgar in the *Characteristicks*; so, on the other, it cannot be denied, that the Ideas he had form'd of the Goodness and Excellency of our Nature, were as romantick and chimerical as they are beautiful and amiable; that he labour'd hard to unite two Contraries that can never be reconcil'd together, Innocence of Manners and worldly Greatness; that to compass this End he favour'd Deism, and, under Pretence of lashing Priestcraft and Superstition, attack'd the Bible it self; and lastly, that by ridiculing many Passages of Holy Writ, he seems to have endeavour'd to sap the Foundation of all reveal'd Religion, with Design of establishing Heathen Virtue on the Ruins of Christianity.

F I N I S.

I N D E X.ᵃ ¹

N.B. *The Roman Figures refer to the Preface.*

A.

A Belard, page 101.

Absurd, nothing is thought so that we have been used to, 159. *Absurdities* in sacred matters not incompatible with Politeness and worldly Wisdom, 243, 244. 249.

Acclamations made at Church, 163.

Active, stirring Man. The difference between such a one, and an easy indolent Man in the same Circumstances, from 108 to 120.

Accomplishments. The Foundation of them is laid in our Youth, 412.

Adam. All Men are his Descendants, 220. was not predestinated to fall, 271. A miraculous Production, 370.

Administration (the civil) how it ought to be contriv'd, 389. What Men it requires, *ibid.* 390. most Branches of it seem to be more difficult than they are, *ibid.* Is wisely divided in several Branches, 393. Is a Ship that never lies at Anchor, 404.

Affections of the Mind mechanically influence the Body, 175.

Affectionate Scheme, 293. would have been inconsistent with the present Plan, 294. When it might take place, 303.

Age (the golden) fabulous, 367. Inconsistent with human Nature, 370.

Alexander Severus, his absurd Worship, 243.

| *Americans.* The disadvantage they labour'd under, 383. may be [434] very ancient, *ibid.* 384.

Ananas (the) or Pine-apple excels all other Fruit, 218. To whom we owe the Production and Culture of it in *England,* 219.

ᵃ *This is the original index. Except that corrections are added in square brackets, references are left as in 29 (see marginal pagination of the present edition).*

¹ That Mandeville made this index himself is indicated by the humour of the entries under *Hutcheson* and *Proposal.* Cf. above, i. 371, *n.* 1.

[436]

The I N D E X. 363

| *Creatures.* How some came to be talk'd of that never had any Exis- [438]
tence, 266, 267.
Creatures (living) compared to an Engine that raises Water by Fire,
181. The Production of their Numbers in every Species proportion'd to the Consumption of them, 289. This is very conspicuous
in Whales, *ibid.*
Cruelty. Not greater in a Wolf that eats a Man than it is in a Man
who eats a Chicken, 281.

D.

Danger (the) from wild Beasts the first Inducement to make Savages
associate, 264, 265. The Effects of it upon Man's Fear, *ibid.* 266.
Objections to this Conjecture, 267. 271. 275. 280, 281. 283. 304, 305.
This Danger is what our Species will never be entirely exempt from
upon Earth, 309.
Death (it is) and not the manner of Dying to which our Aversion is
universal, 284, 285.
Debate (a) about Pride, and what sort of People are most affected with
it, 48, 49, 50. About Money to Servants, 56, 57. About the
Principles a fine Gentleman may act from, 61, 62, 63. About which
it is that enclines Men most to be Religious, Fear or Gratitude, from
237 to 247. About the first Step to Society, from 264 to 309.
Deism (modern) what has encreas'd it in this Kingdom, 376. no
greater Tie than Atheism, 377.
Deity (Notions worthy of the) 207. 233. 250. 293. 298. 305. The
same, unworthy, 249. 250. 297, 298.
Dialogues. The Reputation that has been gain'd by writing them, vii.
Why they are in Disrepute, *ibid.*
Dice spoke of to illustrate what Chance is, 306.
Discourse (a) on the social Virtues according to the System of Lord
Shaftsbury, from 17 to 43. on Duelling, natural and artificial
Courage, from 72 to 97. on the different Effects the same Passions
have on Men of different Tempers, from 108 to 113. on Pride and
the various Effects and Symptoms of it, from 123 to 131. on the
Origin of Politeness, from 132 to 154. on Compliments, Tokens
of Respect, Laughing, *&c.* from 157 to 176. on the Faculty of
Thinking, from 178 to 192. on the Sociableness of Man, from 195
to 223. on the | first Motive that could make Savages associate, [439]
from 264 to 311. on the second Step to Society, and the Necessity
of written Laws, from 311 to 335. on Language, from 336 to 357.
on diverse Subjects relating to our Nature, and the Origin of Things,
from 357 to 381. on Government, Capacities, and the Motives to
Study, on Ministers, Partiality and the Power of Money, *to the End.*
Docility depends upon the Pliableness of the Parts, 201. Lost if
neglected in Youth, 211. The superior Docility in Man in a great
measure owing to his remaining young longer than other Creatures,
213.

ᵃ Usefuluess 29　　　　　ᵇ 28 29

[a] Oratos 29

ª Philosopher's *30, 33*

Claims every thing he is concern'd in, 238. 257. Is more inquisitive into the Cause of Evil, than he is into that of Good, 238. Is born with a Desire of Superiority, 254. 311. Has been more mischievous to his Species, than wild Beasts have, 285. What gives us an Insight into the Nature of Man, 315. | Is not naturally inclined to do as [446] he would be done by, 317. Whether he is born with an Inclination to forswear himself, 321. Thinks nothing so much his own as what he has from Nature, 359. The higher his Quality is, the more necessitous he is, 199. Why he can give more ample Demonstrations of his Love than other Creatures, 364. Could not have existed without a Miracle, 371. 378, 379.

Man of War, 149.

Manners (the Doctrine of good) has many Lessons against the outward Appearances of Pride, but none against the Passion itself, 49. What good Manners consists in, 104. Their Beginning in Society, 154. Have nothing to do with Virtue or Religion, 155.

Marlborough (the Duke of) opposite Opinions concerning him, 407, 408. Was an extraordinary Genius, *ibid.* A *Latin* Epitaph upon him, 409. The same in *English*, 410.

Mathematicks of no Use in the curative Part of Physick, 174.

Memory. The total Loss of it makes an Idiot, 192.

Men of very good Sense may be ignorant of their own Frailties, 65, 66. All Men are partial Judges of themselves, 107. All bad that are not taught to be good, 316.

Mexicans. Their Idolatry, 326.

Milton quoted, 269.

Minister (the Prime.) No such Officer belonging to our Constitution, 393. Has Opportunities of knowing more than any other Man, 395. The Stratagems plaid against him, 396. Needs not to be a consummate Statesman, 397. What Capacities he ought to be of, 309 [399]. 401. Prime Ministers not often worse than their Antagonists, 406.

Miracles. What they are, 231. Our Origin inexplicable without them, 371. 378, 379.

Mobs not more wicked than the *Beau Monde*, 42. In them Pride is often the Cause of Cruelty, 131.

Money to Servants. A short Debate about it, 56, 57.

Money is the Root of all Evil, 421. The Necessity of it in a large Nation, *ibid.* 422. Will always be the Standard of Worth upon Earth, 423. The Invention of it adapted to human Nature beyond all others, 427. | Nothing is so universally charming as it, 428. [447] Works mechanically on the Spirits, 429, 430.

Montain. A Saying of his, 136.

Moreri censured, 244.

Moses vindicated, 220, 221. 248, 249, 250. 269, 270. 368. 378, 379, 380.

ᵃ soon *33*　　　ᵇ Speeies *29*　　　ᶜ Narure *29*

Right and Wrong. The Notions of it acquired, 251, 252. 254.

Roman Catholicks are no Subjects to be relied upon, but in the Dominions of his Holiness, 92.

Rome (the Court of) the greatest Academy of refin'd Politicks, 34. Has little Regard for Religion or Piety, 35.

Rule (a) to know what is natural, from what is acquired, 358.

S.

Sabbath. (the) The Usefulness of it in worldly Affairs, 333, 334.

Savages of the first Class are not to be made sociable when grown up, 137. It would require many Ages to make a polite Nation from Savages, 137, 138. The Descendants of civilis'd Men may degenerate into Savages, 220. 309. There are Savages in many Parts of the World, 224. Savages do all the same Things, 335. Those of the first Class could have no Language, 336. nor imagine they wanted it, 337. Are incapable of learning any when full grown, 338.

Savage (a) of the first Class of Wildness, would take every thing to be his own, 223. Be incapable of governing his Off-spring, 225. 227. Would create Reverence in his Child, 226. Would want Conduct, 228. Could only worship an invisible Cause out of Fear, 234. Could have no Notions of Right and Wrong, 252. Propagates his Species by Instinct, 258. Contributes nothing to the Existence of his Children as a voluntary Agent, 261. The Children of his bringing-up would be all fit for Society, 264.

Scheme (the) of Deformity. The System of the *Fable of the Bees* so call'd by *Horatio*, 2. 5.

Scheme (the) or Plan of this Globe, requires the Destruction, as well as the Generation of Animals, 283. Mutual Affection in our Species would have been destructive to it, 296 &c.

| *Scolding*, and calling Names, bespeak some degree of Politeness, 350. [452] The Practice of it could not have been introduced without Self-denial at first, 351.

Security of the Nation. What a great Part of it consists in, 403.

Self-liking different from Self-love, 134. Given by Nature for Self-preservation, *ibid.* The Effect it has upon Creatures, 135. 141. Is the Cause of Pride, 136. What Creatures don't shew it, *ibid.* What Benefit Creatures receive from *Self-liking,* 139. Is the Cause of many Evils, *ibid.* Encomiums upon it, 141, 142. Suicide impracticable whilst *Self-liking* lasts, *ibid.*

Selfishness (the) of human Nature, visible in the Ten Commandments, 318, 320.

Self-love the Cause of Suicide, 142. Hates to see what is Acquired separated from what is Natural, 359, 360, 361.

Services (reciprocal) are what Society consists in, 421. Are impracticable without Money, 422, 423.

Shaftsbury (the Lord) Remarks upon him. For jesting with Reveal'd

[453]

F I N I S. [b]

[a] the *om.* 33   [b] *Page of advertisements of books follows in 30*

APPENDIXES

Mandeville's Family

Description of the Editions

Criticisms of the *Fable*

References to Mandeville's Work

b. = Born   bp. = Ba

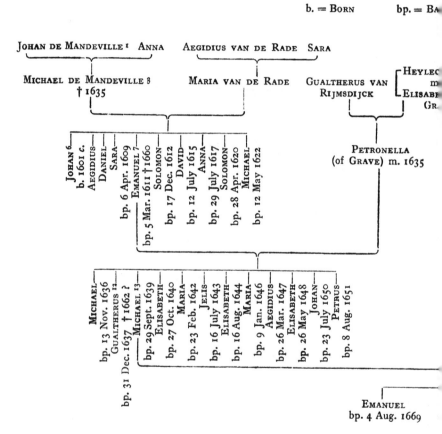

) MANDEVILLE

= Married   † = Died

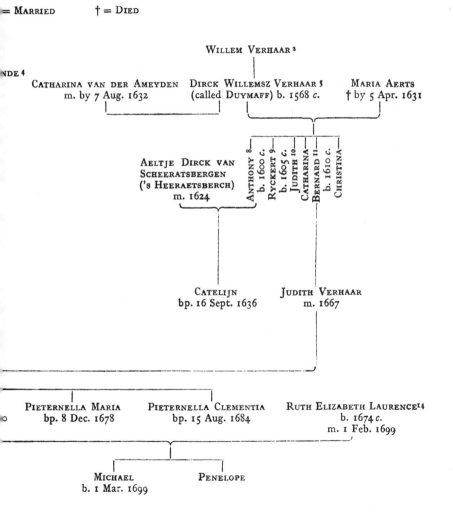

WILLEM VERHAAR²

NDE⁴

CATHARINA VAN DER AMEYDEN   DIRCK WILLEMSZ VERHAAR⁵   MARIA AERTS
m. by 7 Aug. 1632   (called DUYMAFF) b. 1568 c.   † by 5 Apr. 1631

AELTJE DIRCK VAN SCHEERATSBERGEN ('s HEERAETSBERCH) m. 1624

ANTHONY 8 — b. 1600 c. — RYCKERT 9 — b. 1605 c. — JUDITH 10 — CATHARINA — BERNARD 11 — b. 1610 c. — CHRISTINA

CATELIJN bp. 16 Sept. 1636   JUDITH VERHAAR m. 1667

PIETERNELLA MARIA bp. 8 Dec. 1678   PIETERNELLA CLEMENTIA bp. 15 Aug. 1684   RUTH ELIZABETH LAURENCE¹⁴ b. 1674 c. m. 1 Feb. 1699

MICHAEL b. 1 Mar. 1699   PENELOPE

See overleaf for notes.

MANDEVILLE'S FAMILY

NOTES TO THE GENEALOGY

 LL information in the following notes not otherwise accounted for relative to Rotterdam and Schieland has been furnished me by Dr. E. Wiersum, the Archivist of Rotterdam ; the facts concerning Nijmegen, Grave, and Beeck, by Dr. M. Daniëls, the Archivist of Nijmegen.

¹ The names of Mandeville's great-great-grandparents are not on record. The custom of the day, however, of naming eldest sons after the father's father, eldest daughters after the mother's mother, second sons after the mother's father, and second daughters after the father's mother makes the names I have here inferred a fair deduction, especially since this custom seems to have been followed by the de Mandevilles.

² His name is indicated by the suffix ' sz ' (son of) to his son's middle name.

³ In the records neither of Nijmegen nor of the other cities associated with the family is there record of Michael's birth. Perhaps he emigrated to Holland from France, whence their name shows the family to have come. He was appointed *ordinaris medicus* of the city and Rector of the Latin School in 1601. In 1607 the Magistrates requested him to resign the Rectorship and devote himself entirely to his prosperous medical practice. He and seven of his children were made citizens of Nijmegen in 1617. From 1618 till his death he was an alderman and member of the town council. He belonged to the Reformed Church. He died, apparently, in 1635, for on 11 Nov. 1635 his son Emanuel was appointed his successor. According to the *Nieuw Nederlandsch Biografisch Woordenboek* (ed. Molhuysen and Blok), he played an heroic part in the plague which raged at the time of his death.

⁴ She was the widow of Jan van Meckern. That not she, but Gualtherus' second wife was the mother of Petronella is deducible from the name of Petronella's eldest daughter (see above, *n.* 1).

⁵ Captain and Commander Verhaar was 50 years old in 1618. His naval career was a long one. His ship was sunk in battle Mar. 1604. In Apr. 1631 he commanded the warships in the upper and lower Meuse. He was still in service 30 Nov. 1641.

⁶ Johan was entered as a student of theology at the University of Leyden 3 Mar. 1623, aged 22 (*Album Studiosorum Academiae Lugduno Batavae*, ed. 1875, column 166). In 1624 he was permitted to lecture on Hebrew at the Hoogeschool des Kwartiers van Veluwe at Harderwijk (Bouman, *Geschiedenis van de Voormalige Geldersche Hoogeschool*, Utrecht, 1844, i. 114).

⁷ Emanuel was married at Grave, the banns having been first published at Nijmegen 22 Nov. 1635. He succeeded his father as *ordinaris medicus* 11 Nov. 1635. In 1656 the Magistrates appointed him Professor of Medicine at the Illustris Tetrarchiae Noviomagensis Universitas. He seems to have died in 1660, for his son Gualtherus succeeded him 24 Oct. 1660.

⁸ Captain Anthony Verhaar was of age by 12 Apr. 1628. He was betrothed 23 June 1624 to Aeltje, widow of Anthony Dircksz. In 1630 he helped to overcome the Antwerp flood.

⁹ Captain Ryckert Verhaar was of age by 12 Apr. 1628. About 1630 he was in service in the East Indies.

¹⁰ Judith married Anthony Dircksz Schick and Anthony Brassem.

¹¹ Captain Bernard Verhaar was not yet of age by 12 Apr. 1628. He was in the service of the Rotterdam Admiralty 30 July 1628. He was still in service Oct. 1654, and still living 6 Sept. 1668, when, with Petronella van Rijmsdijck, he was named in the will of his son-in-law, Michael de Mandeville, as a chief legatee. In 1689 his grandson called him ‘ Reipublicae Schoonhoviensis Consuli ’ (Mandeville, *Disputatio Philosophica*, dedication).

¹² Gualtherus was registered at Leyden as a student of medicine 30 Sept. 1656 (*Album Studiosorum Academiae Lugduno Batavae*, column 452). On 23 Dec. 1657 the Nijmegen Magistrates promised that he should succeed to his father's professorship when the latter died. Gualtherus was made *ordinaris medicus* and public lecturer on medicine 24 Oct. 1660. The next year the city of Nijmegen sent him to Paris to study (Y. H. Rogge, ‘ De Academie te Nijmegen ’, in *Oud-Holland* for 1900, p. 169). By 10 June 1663 he was dead (according to his mother's petition for a year of grace).

¹³ Michael was registered as a student of law at Leyden 5 Oct. 1665

(*Album Studiosorum Academiae*, column 525), but did not continue in this course of work, for he was made 'pestdoctor' at Nijmegen 3 Aug. 1666. He was married at Beeck after the banns had been published 14 July 1667 at Nijmegen. By 6 Sept. 1668 he had removed to Rotterdam, for he and his wife made a will there then before Notary A. Hoogendijk. His son Bernard stated that Michael was a leading physician at both Rotterdam and Amsterdam for over 30 years (*Treatise of the Hypochondriack . . . Passions*, ed. 1711, pp. xii and 40). This declaration is borne out by the fact that Michael was Lieutenant of the Rotterdam militia 1673–5 and 1686–91, Regent of the Hospital 1679–87, and was made *Schepen* of Schieland 8 June 1681, 30 May 1684, and 30 May 1685.

14 See above, i. xx.

I note here some probable relations of Mandeville whose kinship I am unable to ascertain.

A Bernard de Mandeville of Nijmegen was godfather of the first Michael de Mandeville's youngest son.

A Jacobus de Magneville is recorded as having attended Leyden University 10 Aug. 1607, aged 15, as 'studiosus Litterarum' (*Album Studiosorum Academiae Lugduno Batavae*, column 88). He is again recorded (as Jacobus de Magnoville) 18 June 1611 (*Album*, column 102).

Johan van Rijmsdijck, burgomaster [of Grave ; see *De Navorscher* for 1885, xxxv. 189], was godfather to three of the first Emanuel de Mandeville's children.

Prof. Dr. L. Knappert of the University of Leyden informs me of one Emmanuel de Mandeville, who was born at Middelburg in 1609. He married Elisabeth Beth (born in Amsterdam 1608) 9 Jan. 1635 and Maria Kinseland (born 1619) 16 Sept. 1645.

Dr. Knappert also tells me of a brother of the above—one Robert, who was born at Middelburg in 1617. He married Sara Trodenburch (born 1622). A daughter, Oratia, was baptized at Amsterdam 4 Apr. 1655.

Samuel de Mandeville, born at Nijmegen, was registered as 20 years old and a student of medicine at Leyden 16 Nov. 1627 (*Album Studiosorum Academiae Lugduno Batavae*, column 206).

Dr. Wiersum informs me of a Nathaniel Mandeville, who died July 1651, and of one Willem Mandeville, who was broker to the English Court about 1650.

Dr. Knappert writes me of a Julius de Mandeville who married Susanna Verdael. Their daughters Petronella and Maria Elisabeth were baptized at Hulst 9 Apr. 1688 and 3 Sept. 1690. Julius was buried at Hulst 26 Feb. 1692. His wife was buried 3 Apr. 1694.

Maria Verhaar, of Cuyck, gave Michael de Mandeville—Bernard's father—power of attorney 28 Dec. 1689 (protocol of Notary Hans Smits of Rotterdam, inventory no. 728, instrument no. 181).

One Emmanuel de Mandeville, merchant, 20 years old, married Anna Robijn 20 Mar. 1703 at Amsterdam, according to the Amsterdam archives.

De Navorscher contains further information about the Rijmsdijcks, the van de Rades, and the Verhaars.

DESCRIPTION OF

THE EDITIONS

ERE are listed the full title-pages of all the accessible editions of the *Fable of the Bees,* together with descriptions of the editions. In reproducing titles, I have indicated always whether the type is roman or italic, upper case or lower case, but, beyond this, no attempt has been made to differentiate type. All capitals, no matter what size, have been transliterated into small capitals, except that in words where an initial capital is followed by smaller capitals or lower case I have used a full capital for the initial letter. Long ' s ' has been modernized. The German type used in the translations of 1761 and 1818 has been transliterated into roman. In the collations, although I have in general indicated all departures from normal folding, I have not noted the number of leaves in the last folding, since this is here sufficiently indicated by the pagination. Concerning the misprints in pagination which I have recorded, it should be remembered that any of these might have been corrected in the press in copies not seen by me. Where, in the collations, both the page-numbers delimiting a part of a book are enclosed within one pair of brackets (e.g., pp. [340–8]), none of the pages in the group are numbered in the original; where page-numbers are individually enclosed in brackets (e.g., pp. [1]–[24] or pp. [15]–27), the intervening pages of the group are numbered in the original.

The Grumbling Hive

1. THE Grumbling Hive. . . . 1705.
See the reproduction opposite (reducéd from 127 × 180·5 mm.).
    Collation : 4to. Title, p. [i] ; blank, p. [ii] ; *Grumbling Hive,* pp. 1–26. Signatures omitted on A sheet.
Copies in the Bodleian and in my possession.

THE

Grumbling Hive:

OR,

KNAVES

TURN'D

HONEST.

LONDON:

Printed for *Sam. Ballard*, at the *Blue-Ball*, in *Little-Britain* :
And Sold by *A. Baldwin*, in *Warwick-Lane.* 1705.

2. THE / Grumbling Hive : / OR, / KNAVES / Turn'd HONEST. [1705.]
Collation : 4to (half-sheet).   *Grumbling Hive,* pp. 1 (A)–4.
This has no title-page.   The above title heads the four double-columned pages of the pamphlet.   At the end is stated, 'Printed in the Year, 1705.' This is the pirated edition (see *Fable* i. 4).   Copy in the British Museum.

3. THE / GRUMBLING HIVE, / OR, / KNAVES TURN'D HONEST. / BOSTON [MASS.] : / PRINTED FOR THE PEOPLE. / 1811.
Collation : Format uncertain, signatures irregular (A2 on p. 5, B on p. 13, C on p. 17).   Title, p. [1] ; blank, p. [2] ; *Grumbling Hive,* pp. 3–18(C^v).
Copy in the Library of Congress.

The Fable of the Bees.   Part I

I. THE FABLE OF THE BEES. . . . 1714.
See the reproduction opposite.
Collation : 12mo.   Title, p. [i] ; blank, p. [ii] ; preface, pp. [iii(A2)–xiv] ; table of contents, pp. [xv–xxiii] ; *Errata,* p. [xxiv] ; *Grumbling Hive,* pp. 1(B)–20 ; introduction, pp. [21–2] ; *Enquiry into the Origin of Moral Virtue,* pp. 23(†)–41 ; *Remarks,* pp. 42–228.   Signature I3 misprinted 'I2'.

The table of contents, which was not printed in any edition after the second, reads as follows :

THE CONTENTS.¹

¹ The page references are given as originally printed in the 1714 editions.   To find the corresponding pages in the present edition see below, ii. 392.

THE
FABLE
OF THE
BEES:
OR,
Private Vices,
Publick Benefits.

LONDON:

Printed for J. RORERTS, near the *Oxford Arms* in *Warwick Lane,* 1714.

[THE CONTENTS.]

[THE CONTENTS.]

For further information concerning this edition see the description below of the 1723 edition.

B b 2

2. THE FABLE OF THE BEES. . . . 1714.

See the reproduction opposite.

Collation : 12mo ; identical with that of the preceding edition, of which it is a page-for-page reprint. In this edition signature B3 is misprinted 'B5' and I 3, 'I 2'.

That the edition here considered is the later of the two 1714 ones is shown by the fact that a misprint (p. 36, l. 12) noted in the *Errata* has been corrected in the text.

3. THE FABLE OF THE BEES. . . . 1723.

See the reproduction opposite p. 393.

Collation : 8vo (signatures A and Ee, four leaves). Title, p. [i] ; blank, p. [ii] ; preface, pp. [iii(A2)–viii] ; *Grumbling Hive,* pp. [1](B)–[24](C4ᵛ) ; introduction, pp. [25–6] ; *Enquiry into the Origin of Moral Virtue,* pp. [27]–44 ; *Remarks,* pp. [45]–284 ; *Essay on Charity,* pp. [285]–370(Bbᵛ) ; *Search into the Nature of Society,* pp. [371](Bb2)–428(Ff2ᵛ) ; index, pp. [429(Ff2)–439] ; *Errata,* p. [439]. Signature Ff3 is misprinted 'Ff2'.

The variants show that Mandeville, in preparing this edition, used the first, not the second, edition of 1714 as a nucleus.

The following columns describe this edition by paralleling its structure with that of the edition of 1714, with the purpose of showing at what date the various parts of the *Fable* were first published.[1]

1714	1723 [2]
Preface.	Preface. [A footnote is added on p.[iii], and a final sentence, to bring the work up to date.]
Table of Contents. [3]	[Omitted.]
The Grumbling Hive : pp. 1–20.	*The Grumbling Hive :* pp. 1–24.
Introduction : pp. 21–2	Introduction : pp. 25–6.
Enquiry into the Origin of Moral Virtue: pp. 23–41.	*Enquiry into the Origin of Moral Virtue:* pp. 27–44. [Brief addition, p. 41.]
Remark A : pp. 42–6.	Remark A : pp. 45–9.
Remark B : pp. 46–9.	Remark B : pp. 49–52.
Remark C : pp. 49–55.	Remark C : pp. 52–74. [New matter added, p. 57 to end of Remark.]
Remark D : pp. 55–6.	Remark D : pp. 74–5.
Remark E : pp. 56–61.	Remark E : pp. 76–80.
Remark F : pp. 61–2.	Remark F : pp. 80–1.
Remark G : pp. 62–3.	Remark G : pp. 82–92. [All except first paragraph is new.]
Remark H : pp. 63–70.	Remark H : pp. 93–9.
Remark I : pp. 70–4.	Remark I : pp. 100–3.
Remark K : pp. 74–9.	Remark K : pp. 103–8.
Remark L : pp. 79–97.	Remark L : pp. 108–25. [New paragraph added, p. 114.]
Remark M : pp. 98–113.	Remark M : pp. 125–39.
. . . . . .	Remark N : pp. 139–56. [New.]
Remark N : pp. 113–40.	Remark O : pp. 156–81. [Slight additions, pp. 176 and 179.]
Remark O : pp. 141–58.	Remark P : pp. 181–97.
Remark P : pp. 158–79.	Remark Q : pp. 197–216. [Addition, p. 212.]

[1] Slight verbal changes are not noted. For such verbal changes see the variant readings of the present edition.

[2] Except for the preface and index the pagination of this edition is practi-cally identical with that of 1732, and references to it may therefore be located in my edition by means of the marginal page-numbers.

[3] See above, ii. 389–91.

THE
FABLE
OF THE
BEES:
OR,
Private Vices
Publick Benefits.

CONTAINING,

Several Difcourfes, to demonftrate,
That Human Frailties, *during the de-*
generacy of MANKIND, may be turn'd
to the Advantage of the CIVIL
SÒCIETY, and made to fupply
the Place of *Moral Virtues.*

Lux e Tenebris.

LONDON:

Printed for J. ROBERTS, near the Oxford Arms in Warwick Lane, 1714.

THE
FABLE
OF THE
BEES:

OR,

Private Vices, Publick Benefits.

The SECOND EDITION,
Enlarged with many ADDITIONS.

AS ALSO
An ESSAY on CHARITY and
CHARITY-SCHOOLS.

And a Search into
The NATURE of SOCIETY.

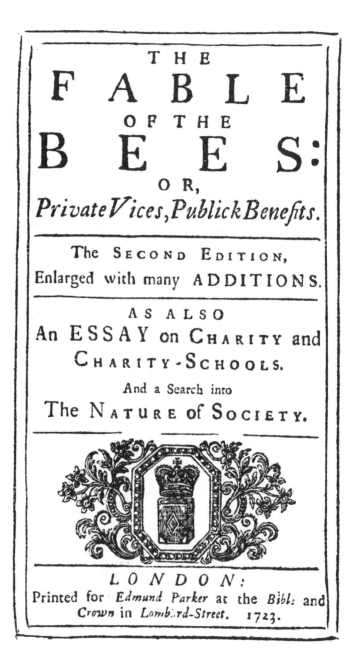

LONDON:
Printed for *Edmund Parker* at the *Bibl:* and
Crown in *Lombard-Street.* 1723.

1714	1723
Remark Q : pp. 179–212.	Remark R : pp. 216–47.
Remark R : pp. 213–15.	Remark S : pp. 247–9.
. . . . . .	Remark T : pp. 249–66. [New.]
Remark S : pp. 215–24.	Remark V : pp. 267–75.
Remark T : pp. 224–7.	Remark X : pp. 276–8.
Remark V : pp. 227–8.	Remark Y : pp. 278–84. [All but first paragraph is new.]
. . . .	*An Essay on Charity.* [New.]
. . . .	*A Search into the Nature of Society.* [New.]
. . . .	Index. [New.]

4. THE / FABLE / OF THE / BEES : / OR, / *Private Vices, Publick Benefits.* / With an ESSAY on / CHARITY *and* CHARITY-SCHOOLS. / AND / *A Search into the Nature of Society.* / The THIRD EDITION. / To which is added / A VINDICATION of the BOOK / from the Aspersions contain'd in a Presentment / of the Grand-Jury of *Middlesex,* and / an abusive Letter to Lord *C.* / *LONDON:* / Printed for J. TONSON, at *Shakespear's-Head,* / over-against *Katharine-Street* in the *Strand.* / M DCC XXIV.

Collation : 8vo. Title, p. [i]; blank, p. [ii] ; preface, pp. [iii](A2)–xvi] ; *Grumbling Hive,* pp. [1](B)–[24](C4ᵛ) ; *Enquiry into the Origin of Moral Virtue,* pp. [27]–44 ; *Remarks,* pp. [45]–284 ; *Essay on Charity,* pp. [285]–370(Bbᵛ) ; *Search into the Nature of Society,* pp. [371](Bb2)–428 ; index, pp. [429–40(Ff4ᵛ)] ; half-title, p. [441] ; blank, p. [442] ; *Vindication,* pp. [443]–477 ; *Errata,* p. 477. Signature Ff3 misprinted ' F3 ' ; p. 74 misnumbered ' 82 ', p. 75, ' 83 ', and p. 139, ' 193 '.
The chief distinction between this edition and the preceding is the addition of the *Vindication* and the enlargement by two pages of the preface.

5. THE / FABLE / OF THE / BEES : / OR, / *Private Vices, Publick Benefits.* / With an ESSAY on / CHARITY *and* CHARITY-SCHOOLS. / AND / *A Search into the Nature of Society.* / The FOURTH EDITION. / To which is added, / A VINDICATION of the BOOK / from the Aspersions contain'd in a Presentment / of the Grand-Jury of *Middlesex,* and / an abusive Letter to Lord *C.* / *LONDON:* / Printed for J. TONSON, at *Shakespear's-Head,* / over-against *Katharine-Street* in the *Strand.* / MDCCXXV.

Collation : 8vo ; identical with that of the preceding edition except that the list of errata is omitted, that, instead of the misprints noted in the collation of the 1724 edition, this edition has p. 400 misnumbered ' 352 ', and that the *Essay on Charity* collates pp. [285](2)–370(Bbᵛ).

6. THE / FABLE / OF THE / BEES : / OR, / *Private Vices, Publick Benefits.* / With an ESSAY on / CHARITY *and* CHARITY-SCHOOLS. / AND / *A Search into the Nature of Society.* / The FIFTH EDITION. / To which is added, / A VINDICATION of the BOOK / from the Aspersions contain'd in a Present-/ment of the Grand-Jury of *Middlesex,* / and an abusive Letter to Lord *C.*/ *LONDON:* / Printed for J. TONSON, at *Shakespear's Head,* / over-against *Katherine-Street* in the *Strand../* MDCCXXVIII.

Collation : 8vo ; identical with that of the preceding edition, from which the variants show it to have been printed, except that, instead of the misprints noted in the collation of the 1725 edition, this edition has p. 21 misnumbered ' 12 ', p. 80,

' 58 ', and p. 447, ' 347 ', and that the collation of the *Essay on Charity* is the same as in the edition of 1724.

7. THE / FABLE / OF THE / BEES : / OR, / *Private Vices, Publick Benefits.* / With an ESSAY on / Charity *and* Charity-Schools. / AND / *A Search into the Nature of Society.* / The SIXTH EDITION. / To which is added, / A VINDICATION of the BOOK / from the Aspersions contain'd in a Present-/ment of the Grand-Jury of *Middlesex,* and / an abusive Letter to Lord *C.* / *LONDON,* / Printed : And Sold by J. TONSON, at *Shake-/spear's-Head,* over-against *Katherine-Street* in / the *Strand.* / M DCC XXIX.

Collation : 12mo (sheet A in sixes). Title, p. [i]; blank, p. [ii]; preface, pp. [iii(A2)–xi]; advertisement, p. [xii]; *Grumbling Hive,* pp. [1](B)–12; introduction, pp. [13–14]; *Enquiry into the Origin of Moral Virtue,* pp. [15]–27(C2); *Remarks,* pp. [28] (C2ᵛ)–201(K5); *Essay on Charity,* pp. [202](K5ᵛ)–267(N2); *Search into the Nature of Society,* pp. 267(N2)–311; index, pp. [311–23]; *Vindication,* pp. [324]–348. P. 51 is misnumbered ' 31 '.

8. THE FABLE OF THE BEES. . . . SIXTH EDITION. . . . 1732.
See the reproduction above, i. 1.
Collation : 8vo; identical with that of the edition of 1728, from which the variants show it to have been printed, except that, instead of the misprints noted in the collation of the 1728 edition, this edition has p. 106 misnumbered ' 107 ', p. 107, ' 106 ', and p. 333, ' 332 '.

The Vindication

The Vindication, which now forms the last section of the first part of the *Fable,* is a compound of three articles, each originally issued separately. The Presentment of the Grand Jury was printed in the *Evening Post* 11 July 1723 ; the abusive Letter to Lord C. appeared 27 July in the *London Journal* ; Mandeville's letter of defence against these attacks came out in the same paper 10 Aug. These three documents, unified by a few connecting sentences, were published by Mandeville that year as a six-penny pamphlet in octavo (see above, i. 14, *n.* 2). I have found no copy of this pamphlet either separately or bound with the 1723 edition.

The Fable of the Bees. Part II

1. THE FABLE OF THE BEES. PART II. . . . 1729.
See the reproduction above, ii. 1.
Collation : 8vo (title-page and preface signed in fours, A, a–c; d, one leaf). Title, p. [i]; blank, p. [ii]; preface, pp. [i](A2)–xxxi(d); *Errata,* p. [xxxii](dᵛ); dialogues, pp. [1](B)–432; index, pp. [433(Ff)–456]. P. 4 is misnumbered ' 2 '.
In some copies of this edition sheet O has been reset, and some minor variants (indicated in my footnotes) have resulted. Evidently, there was a shortage of the original sheet O, either because of accident to both formes (unlikely), failure to print enough of sheet O originally, or accident to the printed sheets. Which of the two sheet O's is the first printing ? A clue to the answer is to be found in the ' figures ' (numbers placed usually on the verso of some leaf in a sheet to indicate the division of labour among the presses ; see R. W. Chapman, ' Print-

ing with Figures', in the *Library* for 1922, 4th ser., iii. 175–6). One sheet O is without 'figures'; the other is 'figured' in both formes—' 7 ' on sign. O^v (inner forme) and ' 1 ' on sign. O4^v (outer forme). Let us inspect the rest of the book to see what bearing this matter of 'figures' has. In the body of the book we find four sheets with no 'figures', two sheets (H and X) with two 'figures', and the rest with one 'figure'. (The preface—signed in half-sheets—has one 'figure'—in the first half-sheet; the index shows no 'figures'.) In the case of the two sheets 'figured' twice, the two 'figures' are identical for each sheet (two ' 5's' in H ; two ' 2's' in X). The presence of double 'figures', therefore, is evidently the result of accidental duplication : only one press was used for both formes of sheets H and X. The 'figured' sheet O, consequently, is the only sheet of which the two formes were given to different presses. Examination of other books from the Roberts establishment confirms the presumption that giving one sheet to two presses was an exceptional performance. The 'figured' sheet O, accordingly, seems to have been printed under unusual circumstances—circumstances such as might have been due to a sudden shortage of the original printing of sheet O. Such shortage, indeed, with the resultant need for hasty duplication of the sheet, would be a very natural cause of dividing the sheet between two presses.

There is still another reason why the 'figured' sheet is the later. Inspection of books of the period shows that the same volume often contained both 'figured' and 'unfigured' sheets. It is very possible that several sheets were assigned to the same press, each batch of sheets assigned to one press being 'figured' once. There was no need to 'figure' each sheet, since the press from which it issued could be identified by the one 'figured' sheet in the group. On the other hand, for a sheet printed separately a 'figure' would be more necessary. Thus it would be not unnatural for the first printing of sheet O to be without 'figures', but abnormal for the second—and separate—printing to be without them. I have, therefore, assumed the 'unfigured' sheet O to be the original one, and have adopted it for my basic text.

In some exemplars of this edition, the ornamental initial which introduces the sixth dialogue differs.

2. THE | FABLE | OF THE | BEES, | PART II. | By the AUTHOR of the First. | *Opinionum enim Commenta delet dies*; *Naturæ ju-|dicia confirmat.* Cicero de Nat. Deor. Lib. 2. | [Ornament] | *LONDON,* | Printed : And Sold by J. ROBERTS in | *Warwick-Lane.* M DCC XXX.

Collation : 12mo. Title, p. [i] ; blank, p. [ii] ; preface, pp. [i](A2)–xx (‡) ; dialogues, pp. [1]–315(P) ; index, pp. 315(P)–[341] ; advertisement of ' BOOKS *Printed by and for* Samuel Fairbrother *in* Skinner-Row', p. [342]. There are two versions of the two leaves forming the Q gathering, which were apparently set in duplicate.

This book is printed from the same style type and has the same decorations as the 1729 edition of Part I.

3. THE | FABLE | OF THE | BEES. | PART II. | By the AUTHOR of the First. | *Opinionum enim Commenta delet dies*; *Naturæ ju-|dicia confirmat.* | Cicero de Nat. Deor. Lib. 2. | The SECOND EDITION. | *LONDON,* | Printed : and Sold by J. ROBERTS in | *Warwick-Lane.* M DCC XXXIII.

Collation : 8vo (title-page and preface signed in fours, A, a–c). Title, p. [i] ; blank, p. [ii] ; preface, pp. [i](A2)–xxx ; dialogues, pp. [1](B)–432 ; index, pp. [433(Ff)–456]. P. 423 misnumbered ' 223 '.

This edition was printed, the variants show, from that of 1729.

The Fable of the Bees. Parts I and II

The Fable of the Bees. . . . A New Edition. Printed for J. Tonson. [1734.]

8vo. 2 vol. Price, 12*s.*
I have cited this edition, of which I can trace no exemplar, from a notice in the *London Magazine* for Dec. 1733, p. 647. That the book is dated 1734 is probable, first, because of the practice of dating ahead works published at the close of a year, and, secondly, because 1734 was the date placed on the 'faked' title-page of the 1755 edition (see discussion below of second issue of 1755 edition).

[Vol. 1] THE / FABLE / OF THE / BEES : / OR ; / Private Vices, Public Benefits. / With, An ESSAY on / CHARITY and CHARITY-SCHOOLS ; / AND, / A SEARCH into the Nature of SOCIETY. / The ninth EDITION : / To WHICH IS ADDED, / A VINDICATION of the BOOK from the / Aspersions contained in a Presentment of the / Grand Jury of *Middlesex*, and an abusive Let-/ter to the Lord *C.* / *EDINBURGH:* / Printed for W. GRAY and W. PETER. / Sold at their shop in the *Parliament Close.* / MDCCLV.

[Vol. 2] THE / FABLE / OF THE / BEES. / PART II. / By the AUTHOR of the First. / *Opinionum enim commenta delet dies ; naturæ | judicia confirmat.* / CICERO de Nat. Deor. Lib. II. / *EDINBURGH:* / Printed for W. GRAY and W. PETER. / MDCCLV.

Collation: 12mo. Vol. 1: title, p. [i] ; blank, p. [ii] ; pref., pp. [iii](A 2)–ix ; blank, p. [x] ; *Grumbling Hive*, pp. [i]–13 ; introduction, p. [14] ; *Enquiry into the Origin of Moral Virtue*, pp. [15](B)–28 ; *Remarks*, pp. [29]–220 ; *Essay on Charity*, pp. 221–91 ; *Search into the Nature of Society*, pp. 292–339 ; index, pp. [340–8] ; half-title, p. [349] ; *Vindication*, pp. [350]–74. P. 51 misnumbered '5'. Vol. 2: title, p. [i] ; blank, p. [ii] ; preface, pp. [i](a2)–xxii ; dialogues, pp. [1]–345 ; index, pp. [346–72]. P. 306 misnumbered '303'. The leaf with pp. 1 and 2 is not included in the regular signatures and has been inserted between sheets a and B.

Dr. A. E. Case sends me the following explanation of this last irregularity : For some reason, the extra leaf carrying pp. 1 and 2 was printed as the last leaf of a half-sheet the first five leaves of which carried the end of the index. Chain-lines verify this in some copies ; in others they do not, of course, if wholesale binding was being done, there is no reason why the single leaf and the last five leaves in each book should always be mates. In order to save time the printer set up this single leaf and the last five leaves twice, and printed with full sheets, cutting them afterwards. There are, therefore, two versions of the extra leaf and last five leaves.

One of the pair of final half-sheets was signed 'R' in error for 'S'. Because of the apparent duplication of R sheets, therefore, in some copies of vol. 2 the last half-sheet is omitted. In one copy, to cover this up, 'FINIS' has been added with a hand-stamp at the close of the real R sheet.

[Vol. 1] THE / FABLE / OF THE / BEES : / OR, Private Vices, Public Benefits. / With, An ESSAY on / CHARITY and CHARITY-SCHOOLS ; / AND, / A SEARCH into the Nature of SOCIETY. / IN TWO VOLUMES. / By BERNARD MANDEVILLE, M.D. / VOLUME the FIRST. / LONDON : / Printed for J. TONSON in the Strand. / M DCC XXXIV.

[Vol. 2] THE / FABLE / OF THE / BEES. / VOLUME the SECOND. / By the AUTHOR of the First. / *Opinionum enim commenta delet dies ;*

naturæ | judicia confirmat | CICERO de Nat. Deor. Lib. II. | LONDON : | Printed for J. TONSON in the Strand. | M DCC XXXIV.

Collation : 12mo. Identical with that of the preceding edition, of which this is merely a reissue with new title-page.

The reason for issuing this edition with a title-page announcing a false publisher and a date twenty-one years earlier than the real date may perhaps have been to avoid possible trouble over copyright in London sales made by the publishers or the bookseller to whom they may have sold the sheets. This supposition would lead us to infer that the 'faked' title-page was intended to imitate the genuine two-volume edition of Tonson.

THE | FABLE | OF THE | BEES : | OR, | Private Vices, Public Benefits. | IN TWO VOLUMES. | WITH | An ESSAY on Charity and Charity-Schools : | AND | A SEARCH into the Nature of SOCIETY. | To which is added, | A VINDICATION of the BOOK from the Aspersions | contained in a Presentment of the Grand Jury of | Middlesex, and an abusive Letter to the Lord C—. | Opinionum enim commenta delet dies ; naturae judicia confirmat. | *Cic. de nat. Deor. Lib.* II. | VOLUME FIRST. | EDINBURGH : | Printed for J. WOOD, and sold by the Booksellers in Great | Britain and Ireland. | MDCCLXXII.

The title-page of the second volume is identical, except for the substitution of ' VOLUME SECOND ' for ' VOLUME FIRST '.

Collation : 12mo (signed in sixes). Vol. 1 : title, p. [i] ; blank, p. [ii] ; preface, pp. [iii](A2)–viii; *Grumbling Hive,* pp. [9]–19 ; introduction, p. [20] ; *Enquiry into the Origin of Moral Virtue,* pp. [21]–31 ; *Remarks,* pp. 32–186(Q3ᵛ) ; *Essay on Charity,* pp. 187–244(X2ᵛ) ; *Search into the Nature of Society,* pp. 245(X3)–284 ; index, pp. [285–92](Bb2ᵛ) ; half-title, p. [293](Bb3) ; *Vindication,* pp. 294(Bb3ᵛ)–316(Dd2ᵛ). Vol. 2 : title, p. [i] ; blank, p. [ii] ; preface, pp. [iii](A2)–xxii ; dialogues, pp. [23]–298 ; index, pp. [299–315](Dd2).

THE | FABLE OF THE BEES ; | OR, | *Private Vices, Public Benefits.* | WITH AN ESSAY ON | CHARITY AND CHARITY SCHOOLS, | AND | A SEARCH INTO THE NATURE OF SOCIETY. | ALSO, | *A* VINDICATION *of the* BOOK *from the Aspersions contained in a Presentment | of the* GRAND JURY *of Middlesex, and an Abusive Letter to* LORD C—. | LONDON : | PRINTED FOR C. BATHURST, C. NOURSE, T. CARNAN, F. NEWBERY, | R. CATER, R. BROTHERTON, W. JOHNSTONE, P. VALLIANT, | N. CONANT, T. DAVIES, L. DAVIES, A. MILLAR, | R. TONSON, G. KEITH, W. OWEN, | AND L. HAWIS. | 1795.

Collation : 8vo (sign. a, four leaves, b, two leaves). Half-title, p. [—]; blank, p. [—]; title, p. [i] ; blank, p. [ii]; table of contents, p. [iii](a2) ; blank, p. [iv] (a2ᵛ) ; preface, pp. [v]–ix(b) ; blank, p. [x](bᵛ) ; half-title, p. [xi] ; blank, p. [xii] ; *Grumbling Hive,* pp. [1](B)–11 ; introduction, p. [12] ; *Inquiry into the Origin of Moral Virtue,* pp. [13]–22(C3ᵛ) ; *Remarks,* pp. [23](C4)–153 ; blank, p. [154] ; *Essay on Charity,* pp. [155]–203; blank, p. [204] ; *Search into the Nature of Society,* pp. [205]–238(6ᵛ); *Vindication,* pp. [239]–258(S3ᵛ) ; half-title, p. [259] ; blank, p. [260] ; preface, pp. [261](S3)–278(T3ᵛ) ; dialogues, pp. [279](T4)–519 ; blank, p. [520] ; index, pp. [521]–534. P. 287 misnumbered ' 187 '.

THE | FABLE OF THE BEES ; | OR, | *Private Vices, Public Benefits.* | WITH AN ESSAY ON | CHARITY AND CHARITY SCHOOLS, | AND | A SEARCH INTO THE NATURE OF SOCIETY. | ALSO, | *A* VINDICATION *of the* BOOK *from the Aspersions contained in a Presentment | of the* GRAND JURY *of*

Middlesex, and an Abusive Letter to LORD C—. | LONDON : | PRINTED
FOR ALLEN & WEST, NO. 15. PATER NOSTER ROW, | AND FOR J. MUNDELL
& CO. EDINBURGH. | 1795

Collation : 8vo ; identical with that of the preceding edition, being merely
another issue with altered title-page. In the copy seen by me there was no
preliminary half-title.

THE | FABLE OF THE BEES ; | OR, | *PRIVATE VICES PUBLIC BENEFITS :* |
WITH AN ESSAY ON | CHARITY AND CHARITY SCHOOLS, | AND A SEARCH INTO|
THE NATURE OF SOCIETY : | ALSO, | *A VINDICATION OF THE BOOK
FROM THE ASPERSIONS CONTAINED | IN A PRESENTMENT OF THE
GRAND JURY OF MIDDLESEX, | AND AN ABUSIVE LETTER TO
LORD C—.* | LONDON : | PUBLISHED BY T. OSTELL, AVE-MARIA LANE,
LONDON, AND | MUNDELL AND SON, EDINBURGH. | 1806.

8vo. *Collation :* identical with that of the 1795 edition, of which this is
merely a reissue with new title-page. The verso of the title-page states,
' *Edinburgh, printed by Mundell and Son.*'

Translations—French

LA FABLE | DES | ABEILLES, | OU | LES FRIPONS | DEVENUS | HONNÈTES
GENS. | AVEC | LE COMMENTAIRE, | *Où l'on prouve que les Vices des
Particuliers | tendent à l'avantage du Public.* | *TRADUIT DE L'ANGLOIS* |
Sur la Sixième Edition. | TOME PREMIER. | A LONDRES,[1] | *AUX DEPENS
DE LA COMPAGNIE.* | MDCCXL.

Volume 3 inserts on its title-page, after ' TOME TROISIEME', the regulation motto
from Cicero to Part II, omitting ' *enim* '. Volume 4 has instead a quotation
from Seneca : ' *Pars sanitatis, velle sanari, fuit.* / ANN. SENEC. Hypol. Act. I.'
Collation : 8vo. Vol. 1 : title, p. [—] ; blank, p. [—] ; *Avertissement des
Libraires*, pp. [I](*)-VIII(*4ᵛ) ; preface, pp. [IX](*5)-XXII(**3ᵛ) ; *Errata*, p. XXII
(**3ᵛ) ; blank, pp. [XXIII-XXIV] ; La *Ruche Murmurante*, pp. [I](A)-26(B5ᵛ) ;
introduction, pp. [27]-28 ; *Remarks*, pp. [29]-333. Sign. **, four leaves. Vol.
2 : title, p. [—] ; blank, p. [—] ; *Recherches sur l'Origine de la Vertu Morale*,
pp. [I](A)-23(B4) ; *Essai sur la Charité*, pp. 24 (B4ᵛ)-138(I5ᵛ) ; *Recherches sur
la Nature de la Socie'te'*, pp. 139-216(O4ᵛ) ; half-title of *De'fense*, p. [217](O5) ;
blank, p. [218] (O5ᵛ) ; *De'fense*, pp. 219-67. Vol. 3 : title, p. [—] ; blank, p.
[—] ; preface to Part II, pp. [I](*)-XLVIII ; dialogues 1-4, pp. 1(A)-282(Tᵛ).
S gathering, four leaves. Vol. 4 : title, p. [—] ; blank, p. [—] ; dialogues 5-6,
pp. [I](A)-270.

LA FABLE | DES | ABEILLES. | OU | LES FRIPONS | DEVENUS | HONNESTES
GENS. | AVEC | LE COMMENTAIRE, | *Où l'on prouve que les vices des
Particuliers | tendent á l'avantage du Public.* | *TRADUIT DE L'ANGLOIS* |
Sur la Sixiéme Edition. | TOME PREMIER. | *Opinionum commenta
delet dies, naturæ judicia | confirmat.* CICERO de Nat. Deor. Lib. II.
| A LONDRES, | Chez JEAN NOURSE. | M.DCC.L.

[1] Dunkel's *Historisch-critische Nach-*
richten von verstorbenen Gelehrten
(1753-7), i. 102, states : ' Der franzö-
sischen Druck ist zweifelsohne in
Holland veranstaltet worden, obgleich
London auf dem Titel steht.'

Collation : 12mo, signed alternately in eights and fours, the groups of eight showing the watermark in the upper outer margin of the seventh and eighth leaves, the groups of four having a different watermark similarly placed on the third and fourth leaves ; the chain-lines being horizontal.[1] Vol. 1 : half-title, p. [—] ; blank, p. [—] ; title, p. [i] ; blank, p. [ii] ; *Avertissement des Libraires*, pp. iii(*)–xiv ; preface, pp. xv–xxxiij ; blank, p. [xxxiv] ; *La Ruche Murmurante*, pp. [1](A)–34 ; introduction, pp. 35–6 ; *Remarks*, pp. 37–396. P. 354 misnumbered ' 4 '. Vol. 2 : half-title, p. [—] ; blank, p. [—] ; title, p. [—] ; blank, p. [—] ; *Recherches sur l'Origine de la Vertu Morale*, pp. [1](A)–27(Cij) ; *Essai sur la Charité*, pp. 28(Cij^v)–167 ; *Recherches sur la Nature de la Socié'te'*, pp. 168–261 ; blank, p. [262] ; half-title of *De'fense*, p. [263] ; blank, p. [264] ; *De'fense*, pp. 265(Z)–321 ; index, pp. 322–62(Ff^v) ; *Errata*, p. 362(Ff^v). P. 278 misnumbered ' 778 '. Vol. 3 : half-title, p. [—] ; blank, p. [—] ; title, p. [i] ; blank, p. [ii] ; preface to Part II, pp. [iii](aij)–lxvj(f^v) ; dialogues 1–4, pp. [1](A)–339. Sign. f, one leaf. P. 334 misnumbered ' 134 ' ; p. 336, ' 356 '. Vol. 4 : half-title, p. [—] ; blank, p. [—] ; title, p. [—] ; blank, p. [—] ; dialogues 5–6, pp. [1](A)–322 ; index, pp. 323–61(Hh) ; *Errata*, p. [362](Hh^v). Signature Ddiiij misprinted ' Ddiij '.

La Fable des Abeilles. 1760.

See above, i. xxxvii, *n.* 2.

Translations—German

Anti=Shaftsbury / oder die / Entlarvte Eitelkeit / der / Selbstliebe und Ruhmsucht. / In philosophischen Gesprächen, / nach dem Engländischen. / [Ornament] / Frankfurt am Mayn, / bey Johann Gottlieb Gorbe, 1761.[2]

Collation : 8vo (sign. a, seven leaves, unless plate part of sheet ; b, three leaves). Plate, p. [—^v] ; title, p. [i]; blank, p. [ii] ; preface, pp. [iii](a2)–xviii(b2^v)]; table of contents, p. [xix] ; blank, p. [xx] ; dialogues, pp. [1](A)–472 ; *Einige Verbesserungen dieses Werkes*, p. [473].[3]
This book is a translation of *Part II* only. A preface by the translator is substituted for Mandeville's.

Bernhard von Mandeville's Fabel von den Bienen. 1817.

See above, i. xxxvii, *n.* 6.

Bernhard von Mandeville's / Fabel von den Bienen. / Aus dem Englischen übersetzt / und / mit einer Einleitung / und / einem

[1] The printer set up the book in 12mo ; then cut off the last third of each sheet, having given this part a separate signature. The original sheets had a double watermark. That the groups signed in fours were cut from the same sheet as the preceding groups of eight is proved by the fact that the watermark which usually appears in the group of eight sometimes appears in the gathering signed in fours, and vice versa. This could not have happened if different sheets had been used for the two gatherings. I am indebted to Mr. Arundell Esdaile for this explanation.

[2] Heinsius (*Allgemeines Bücher-Lexikon*, ed. 1812, iv. 97) and Kayser (*Vollständiges Bücher-Lexicon*, ed. 1834, i. 82) give Gebhard as publisher (possibly incorrectly for Gorbe), and Kayser also records a copy published by Hermann of Frankfort. The price was 1 reichsthaler, 4 groschen.
[3] The title-page of this edition is from a photograph ; the description was sent me by two independent scholars, whose accounts agree, and is checked by over a hundred rotographs. Some minor irregularities may, of course, have been overlooked.

400 *Description of the Editions.*

neuen Commentar / versehen, / von / Dr. S. Ascher. / Leipzig, 1818. / Bei Achenwall und Comp.

Collation : 8vo. Title, p. [1]; blank, p. [ii]; preface [Ascher's], pp. [iii(*2)-XIV; table of contents, pp. XV-XVI; half-title (*Einleitung, oder Apologie des gesellschaftlichen Lebens*), p. [1](A); motto, p. [2](A^v); introduction [Ascher's], pp. [3](A2)-66(E^v); half-title (*Die Bienen*), p. [67](E2); *Grumbling Hive*, pp. [68](E2^v)-99(G2) (English text on verso, German translation on recto throughout); blank, p. [100](G2^v); half-title (*Anmerkungen. Oder Beiträge zur Apologie des gesellschaftlichen Lebens*), p. [101]; blank, p. [102]; *Remarks*, pp. [103]-246.

MANDEVILLES / BIENENFABEL / HERAUSGEGEBEN VON / OTTO BOBERTAG / [Device] / 1 · 9 · 1· 4 / MÜNCHEN BEI GEORG MÜLLER [Half-title : BIBLIOTHEK DER PHILOSOPHEN / GELEITET VON FRITZ MAUTHNER / FÜNFZEHNTER BAND].

Collation : 8vo (sign. II, seven leaves). Half-title, p. [I]; blank, p. [II]; title, p. [III]; blank, p. [IV]; *Einleitung des Herausgebers*, pp. V-XXX; half-title, p. [1]; blank, p. [2]; *Vorwort*, pp. 3(1*)-10; *Der Unzufriedene Bienenstock*, pp. 11-23; blank, p. [24]; *Einleitung*, pp. 25-6; *Untersuchung über den Ursprung der Sittlichkeit*, pp. 27-41; blank, p. [42]; *Anmerkungen*, pp. 43-244 (16*^v), half-title, p. [245]; blank, p. [246]; *Abhandlung über Barmherzigkeit*, pp. 247-88; half-title, p. [289]; blank, p. [290]; *Untersuchung über das Wesen der Gesellschaft*, pp. 291(19*)-337(22); blank, p. [338] (22^v); half-title, p. [339]; blank, p. [340]; selection from Berkeley's *Alciphron*, pp. 341-46; half-title, p. [347]; blank, p. [348]; *Brief an Dion*, pp. 349-98; *Register*, pp. 399-400; *Inhaltsverzeichnis*, pp. [401]; blank, p. [402]; printer's notice that 150 copies were printed on '*holländisch Büttenpapier*', p. [403].

In this translation, Part II is omitted. Part I is given complete except for the excision of about a third of the *Essay on Charity*, the omission of Mandeville's *Vindication*, and the condensation of his index. The edition includes a translation of Mandeville's *Letter to Dion*, slightly condensed, and of §§ 4 and 5 from the second dialogue of Berkeley's *Alciphron*.

CRITICISMS OF THE
FABLE

HIS section—a supplement to chapter 5 of my introduction—analyses significant aspects of the arguments of some representative critics of Mandeville.
Paul Sakmann's *Bernard de Mandeville und die
Bienenfabel-Controverse* (Freiburg, Leipsic, and
Tübingen, 1897) contains additional outlines of the
arguments of Mandeville's opponents and may serve as a further
supplement. I have taken the opportunity offered here for incidental
explanation of Mandeville's positions.

William Law's Remarks upon a Late Book, Entituled, the Fable of the Bees.[1] 1724[2]

This is the ablest of all the replies to Mandeville, and in some ways
to be ranked, as literature, with the *Fable*. It is a masterpiece of
controversial writing. Law was the opposite of a relativist ; Mandeville's pyrrhonism, which made ethics a matter of taste and custom,
and goodness an affair of the passions, was abhorrent to him. To Law,
ethical truths were as immutable and definite as mathematical ones.

. . . moral Virtue . . . is *Truth* and *Reason*, consider'd in relation to
Actions ; and the difference between one Action and another, is as
immutable and eternal, as the difference between one Line and another,
and can no more be destroy'd.

[1] References apply to the editions of 1724, 1725, and 1726.
[2] Advertised in the *Whitehall Evening Post* for Thurs., 16 Jan., to Sat., 18 Jan. 1724, as ' On Monday next will be publish'd ', and in the *Post-Boy* for Sat., 18 Jan., to Tues., 21 Jan., as ' This Day is publish'd '.

As *things* are different by their own proper Natures, independant of our Wills, so *Actions* have their own peculiar Qualities from themselves, and not from our Thoughts about them. In these immutable Qualities of Actions, is founded, the fitness and reasonableness of them, which we can no more alter, than we can change the Proportions or Relations of Lines and Figures (p. 23).

Here, Sir, is the Noble and Divine Origin of moral Virtue, it is founded in the immutable Relations of Things, in the Perfections and Attributes of God, and not in the *Pride* of Man, or the Craft of cunning Politicians (p. 26).

This was Law's ultimatum, the declaration of inalienable difference from Mandeville, the rejection by an absolutist of anything smacking of relativity in ethics. Virtue is of divine, not human origin ; its criteria are fixed and simple, not subject to the differences and mutability of purely human decisions. With this as his basis and bias, Law now attacked Mandeville in more detail. And first, animated by the desire to have his rules of eternal validity, he attacked the account which Mandeville had given of the origin of virtue. He took literally the allegory in which Mandeville described the foisting of virtue upon people through the playing of politicians upon their pride: '... the Moral Virtues are the Political Offspring which Flattery begot upon Pride' (*Fable* i. 51). He had, of course, no trouble in demonstrating that virtue is no such deliberate invention, nor arbitrary imposition from without.

Were not the first Principles and Reasons of Morality connatural to us, and essential to our Minds, there would have been nothing for the moral Philosophers to have improv'd upon (pp. 19–20).

However, Mandeville would have been the first to admit that his allegory was not to be taken literally and that the growth of morality was a gradual one.[1] 'Of course,' he would have answered, 'there were *always* in men the germs of morality, for they were always the slaves of pride.'[2]

On scriptural grounds[3] also, Law attacked Mandeville's account of the origin of morality, arguing that the rules of virtue are direct revelations from God.

He then left this phase of Mandeville's thought for the kindred

[1] On this point, see above, i. lxiv–lxvi.
[2] This is precisely what he does say

in his *Origin of Honour*, p. 40.
[3] See above, ii. 197, *n.* 3, where Law's arguments are cited.

matter of Mandeville's anti-rationalistic reduction of all human conduct to the interplay of passions.

That we are rational Beings, [Law maintained (p. 28)] is as plain, as that we have Bodies, and bodily Senses. As there is no Man so refin'd and elevated, but gives frequent Proof, that He is subject also to Instincts and Passions; so there is no one so addicted to an Animal Life, as to shew no Signs of an higher Principle within him.

And (pp. 4–5),

If Man had nothing but *Instincts* and *Passions*, he could not *dispute* about them ; for to *dispute* is no more an *Instinct*, or *Passion*, than it is a *Leg*, or an *Arm*.

Law here, however, was not quite facing Mandeville's main point. The important thing to Mandeville was not that man lacks reason, but that this reason, for all its powers of logic, cannot transcend the sub-rational desires, of which, according to Mandeville, it is merely the able servant.

Law turned now from Mandeville's empiricism to Mandeville's contrary assertion that all the passions and their doings which he had shown so useful to humanity are nevertheless wicked. This is the matter on which Law concentrated the greatest dialectical effort, and yet the paradox is that the position he here attacked was the development of a rigorism which he shared with Mandeville. It was one of Law's most cherished doctrines that goodness was 'being virtuous upon Principle, and thro' a *Love of Goodness*' (p. 32) because of one's duty to God. In the *Serious Call* Law's rigorism was so extreme that he would not allow that a good man might ever act directly from a desire for pleasure. Yet Law could not abide the paradox which Mandeville drew from this rigorism—that under it virtue was impracticable and happiness wicked. Our conduct, argued Law, is not rendered evil by the fact that our passions play their part in it :

An Action is virtuous, because it is an Obedience to Reason, and the Laws of God ; and does not cease to be so, because the Body is either form'd by Use, or created by Disposition, easy and ready for the Performance of it (p. 37).

Nor need our constant desire for happiness bar us from virtue. On the contrary,

. . . Happiness is the only reasonable *End* of every Being. . . . he who thro' long habits of Goodness, has made the Practice of Virtue to have less of Self-denial in it, is the most virtuous Man (p. 33).

To believe otherwise would be to deny that God, who does right in accord with his nature and desire, is good (p. 33). Thus, by this attempted truce, Law tried to hold off the embarrassing consequences Mandeville had inferred from the rigoristic code. It should be noted, however, that fundamentally Law was not deserting the creed of his *Serious Call*: happiness to him could never be the direct incentive to good conduct unless, perhaps, when a man was so perfected that he derived his happiness from obeying the impersonal dictates of duty; no other type of happiness could ever be a legitimate direct end of action, though it might be a secondary motive or concomitant.

It may seem at first that, in his vindication of natural motives, Law was making a telling point against Mandeville's ethics. He was, however, really once more agreeing with it. Mandeville would have had no objection to admitting that a man so exercised in doing good from a mere rational desire of being virtuous as to take pleasure in it was the best man. Law and Mandeville were in absolute harmony as to their ideal. *But* Mandeville devoted the greater part of his work to a demonstration that this ideal is never realized. God may do good in this manner, but mere man, never. It was specifically with regard to the impossibility of realizing the ideal which he and Law both professed that Mandeville told his brilliant parable of small beer (*Fable* i. 235–8). Man as he really is, in contradistinction to man as the moralists tell us he should be, never does act as the moralists would have him.

If it be urg'd [said Mandeville (i. 134)], that if there are not, it is possible there might be such [virtuous] People; I answer that it is as possible that Cats, instead of killing Rats and Mice, should feed them, and go about the House to suckle and nurse their young ones; or that a Kite should call the Hens to their Meat, as the Cock does, and sit brooding over their Chickens instead of devouring 'em; but if they should all do so, they would cease to be Cats and Kites; it is inconsistent with their Natures, and the Species of Creatures which now we mean, when we name Cats and Kites, would be extinct as soon as that could come to pass.

The disagreement, then, between Law and Mandeville was not in their formal creeds, but in their belief as to the practicability of these creeds.

And this kind of disagreement in agreement ran throughout all their thought. The immutable criteria of right and wrong to which Law clung, Mandeville ridiculed. He admitted that virtue was action in accordance with them, but believed that the search for them was a 'Wild-Goose-Chace'. It was the object of the *Fable* to demonstrate the inevitable absence of what the William Laws deemed necessary.

Small wonder, then, that Law was so excited by Mandeville. It was no consolation to have Mandeville admit, between roars of laughter, that the world was a wicked place, since he allowed of no escape from it. Such agreement was worse than none at all. To Law, the evil in the world was not something to be calmly accepted; it was the spur to find something higher to hold to. Law's despair of this world was a force which drove him to a belief in immutable moral criteria free from worldly taint, by cleaving to which he could escape the evil of the world. It made him cling closer to a belief in the existence of a divine perfection which would supply what the world lacked, and in whose shelter the world might be defied.

In other words, the recognition of preponderant evil demands the complementary recognition that there is a way of escaping that evil. A man with Law's views of the world *had* to find such salvation. But Mandeville denied all possibility of escape. Consequently, the more Mandeville insisted on the wickedness of the world, the more horrible to Law it was. It was as if Mandeville had kept shouting gleefully, ' Yes, we are all drowning; we are strangling in a sea of iniquity, but nobody will throw us a rope, and we couldn't catch it if some one did '.

The real crux of the matter is that Mandeville and Law were speaking from the most opposite temperaments. Under their superficial agreement, their whole feeling towards the world was different. Law really felt the distrust of the world which Mandeville only announced; Mandeville did not feel it at all. Wicked or not, the world was a good place to him. Leslie Stephen half summed this matter up when he stated as Mandeville's motto, ' You are all Yahoos . . ., and I am a Yahoo; and so—let us eat, drink, and be merry '.[1] This statement would be complete with the qualification that Mandeville did not really *feel* that men are Yahoos ; he simply recognized facts which caused people of another temperament to call men that.

[1] Stephen, *Essays on Freethinking and Plainspeaking* (N.Y., 1908), p. 280. Also in Stephen's *History of English Thought in the Eighteenth Century* (1902) ii. 34.

But, to Law, the facts which Mandeville recognized with such equanimity, and the existence of anything besides which Mandeville denied, did mean that man was really a Yahoo. These facts were, therefore, insupportable to Law, and he refused to believe that they are the whole story. He thought he saw a higher truth behind them. It was, therefore, against Mandeville's vision, or, rather, against the basal attitude towards the world which allowed Mandeville to be satisfied with this vision, and not against his formal creed, that Law really rebelled.

Richard Fiddes's General Treatise of Morality. 1724[1]

Fiddes was representative of that large class of clergymen who, though orthodox, were thoroughly permeated by the philosophy of the period which had made the deists. His natural bent was not to a religion derived from revelation, but to one arrived at by the human reason. He acknowledged revelation, to be sure, but rather as a short cut to truth than as a necessity (pp. 272-4, 449 sqq.). Since his stress on the other-worldly element in religion was comparatively so faint, he was not so outraged by Mandeville as Law was. In fact, he was one of the most civil of Mandeville's contemporary opponents. He found himself forced to admit the truth of almost every fact that Mandeville insisted upon (pp. xix and lxxx), but he contrived to wriggle out of Mandeville's conclusions. Fiddes allowed that Mandeville's reduction of human actions, whether apparently virtuous or not, to selfish passion had foundation, but he argued that, nevertheless, people *might* act in accord with the desired ideal of virtue. To show this, Fiddes first protested against the bias which, he urged, led Mandeville, where a motive was hidden, always to posit a selfish one :

> *Now where several Motives may be reasonably assigned for any Action, it is more human, more just, and equitable, to ascribe it to the best Motives* . . . (p. xx).

In the next place, Fiddes pleaded what might be called the argument from divinity : God would not, he maintained, make demands upon

---

[1] Advertised as 'This Day is publish'd', in the *London Journal* for 29 Feb. 1724. Only the preface deals specifically with Mandeville. That Mandeville had read Fiddes's book is shown by the *Letter to Dion* (1732), p. 46.

us for virtuous conduct which we could not fulfil (pp. xcii–xcv and cv–cviii).

Fiddes was clear-sighted enough to recognize that the paradoxical consequences Mandeville deduced as to the necessity of vice depended on his unqualified ascetic rigorism ; and Fiddes attacked this rigorism. There is no reason, he urged, why an action should be vitiated because a man takes pleasure in it (p. xxii) ; nor are all natural passions necessarily bad (pp. xxvi–xxvii). To distinguish between good and evil passions, and in general to oppose Mandeville, Fiddes invoked a modified utilitarianism (pp. lx–lxiii, xcv–xcviii, cii). In this way he attempted to evade Mandeville's inferences as to the equal depravity of all conduct naturally possible to men. But Fiddes's utilitarianism was, after all, for practical purposes only : utility to him was the *index* of virtue ; the basal ethical *sanction* of conduct was that it was ' *Obedience to the supreme Legislator* ' (p. xcix). Indeed, for all his practical utilitarianism, Fiddes was so far a rigorist as to hold it unlawful ' *to commit a Sin, though he might, thereby, save the Commonwealth* ' (*ibid.*). Thus Fiddes exemplified, in a less startling manner, the combination of the empirical and rigoristic attitudes which Mandeville himself embodied.

John Dennis's Vice and Luxury Publick Mischiefs. 1724 [1]

John Dennis was one of those who imagine that making a syllogism is the same as stating a truth. The world was a table of classifications to him, in which A was always A and never shaded into B. ' And how is it possible for any Man to conceive a *Ciceronian Jack-pudding* ? ' he asked in one of his critical works.[2] ' Never was any Buffoon eloquent, or wise, or witty, or virtuous. All the good and ill Qualities of a Buffoon are summ'd up in one Word, and that is a Buffoon.' The remark is typical. Dennis thought of importance only that phase of things which could be formulated ; it was the generalization and not the concrete instance that interested him. He was an extreme rationalist. In his criticism of poetry,

---

[1] Advertised as ' This Day will be deliver'd to the Subscribers', in the *Post-Boy* for 7–9 Apr. 1724.
[2] See *On the Genius and Writings of Shakespeare*, in *Eighteenth Century Essays on Shakespeare*, ed. Gregory Smith, p. 33.

this took the form of a great stress on the importance to a poet of a thorough knowledge of the 'rules'; in his attack on Mandeville, it appeared in his statement that

Thought is certainly the only Source of every human Action, as thinking rightly is the only Source of every thing that is rightly done.[1]

One may imagine the feelings with which he regarded Mandeville, who maintained that men never act reasonably from their principles, but that reason is the most utter tool of their passions, and who intensified the anti-rationalism of this statement by a complete denial that those nice generalizations and principles of which Dennis was so fond could ever be of more than the merest pragmatic value. Indeed, along with Law, Dennis was by nature the most contrasted of all types to Mandeville. Just as the mystic Law abhorred Mandeville's happy-go-lucky empiricism because it opposed a religious escape from this world of contrarieties and evanescence, so Dennis must have hated it because it equally opposed an escape from such a world through the reason.

Dennis, however, did not know that this was a main reason for his fighting Mandeville. He arranged his attack on the most elaborate syllogistic lines. His heavy artillery was the following logical sequence : The original social contract is the basis of the English government ; it is only the explicit oath which the sovereign takes to observe the good of his country, and the implicit one of the people to obey him, which make English civilization possible. Now, the keeping of these oaths depends on the sanctity which oaths in general have for people. This sanctity, like all other good (p. 48), is dependent upon their religion. Anything, therefore, which disturbs this religion shakes the reliability of these oaths, and therefore all English civilization. But Mandeville threatens this religion. Ergo, the *Fable of the Bees* has shaken the foundations of the Kingdom (pp. ix sqq.).[2]

Most of the time Dennis did not comprehend the matters he was attempting to refute. He understood Mandeville's statement that private vices are public benefits as if Mandeville were using his terms with the ordinary connotations. But, of course, what Mandeville meant by private vice was not something practically disadvantageous to the individual, but something wrong according to rigoristic morality.

---

[1] *Vice and Luxury Publick Mischiefs,* p. xxvi.
[2] Cf. the reasoning in the present-ment of the Grand Jury quoted in *Fable* i. 384.

Dennis especially attacked Mandeville's defence of luxury as a public benefit. This he did partly under a misconception as to what Mandeville meant by luxury—correlative to his error as to what Mandeville implied by vice—but largely, also, because of a real difference of attitude. Dennis believed in a Spartan state. He ransacked history to furnish examples of nations undone by the refinements of civilization, predicted the ruin of England, and pointed to the originating national debt as one of the luxury-engendered instruments of this impending calamity (e. g., pp. 25–8, 51 sqq.).

Only for a moment did Dennis have a glimpse of the fact that Mandeville's paradox depended on his initial rigoristic definition. This transient insight was in the matter of Mandeville's denominating as luxury everything not essential to the barest needs of life. And as Dennis attempted to distinguish between luxurious and legitimate excess, it is interesting to note that he was impelled to grasp for an instant at a utilitarian criterion (pp. 52–4).

George Bluet's Enquiry. . . . In which the Pleas Offered by the Author of the Fable of the Bees . . . are considered. 1725 [1]

This is by far the most painstaking of the answers to Mandeville.

Although I do not intend in this section to consider matters of practical policy, it is worth recording that Bluet's book contains able criticism of Mandeville's economic theories and of certain other practical aspects of his teaching.

A great part of Bluet's attack was based, like that of almost all the controversialists, on a too literal interpretation of Mandeville. But, being one of the very ablest of these contenders, he made a more effective use of his misinterpretation. How foolish, he argued, were the politicians, who, according to Mandeville, brought virtue into being, if vice is for the good of the community. And, likewise, how stupid of our present magistrates to discourage wickedness, since this

---

[1] Concerning my reasons for assigning this anonymous book to George Bluet (known also as George Blewitt and Thomas Bluett), see my article 'The Writings of Bernard Mandeville', in the *Journal of English and Germanic Philology* for 1921, xx. 461, *n*. 61. For various references in the present edition to Bluet's book see the index to commentary.

evil is our only salvation (p. 22). In this way, Bluet seized upon Mandeville's statement that the laws should be enforced, and that vices should be punished when they become prejudicial to the state, to accuse him of inconsistency. Why punish such actions? he asked, since the more vicious the acts, the greater the good to be expected from them.

The answer is that, when Mandeville spoke of virtue, he meant *so-called* virtue, which was to him simply a rearrangement of vicious passions; so that he could advocate the usefulness of *such* virtue without denying the need of vice, since such virtue *is* vice. And when he advocated the suppression of vices inimical to society he was in opposition only to the theory that *all* vice is desirable, which he had never seriously maintained. Mandeville's position was that some vice may by dexterous management be made useful, and that this fraction of vice so used is indispensable as the world is constituted.

Bluet, however, also had sight of more real issues in the *Fable*. He attacked the rigorism by which Mandeville could, after showing the necessity and practical benefit of the passions, call them evil, thus being able to make the paradox that vices are virtues. He refused to accept Mandeville's rigoristic definition of virtue and vice, on which, he saw, the *Fable* was built (*Enquiry*, p. 25). To the rigoristic demand for a complete perfection in morals, from which Mandeville inferred that our so-called good qualities are ethically futile because they have always some alloy of imperfection (*Fable* i. 56 and 254), Bluet answered (p. 111),

... Piety to Parents is not the less a Virtue, because it may chance that a Highwayman has relieved his Parents in Distress; nor (to put it yet stronger) would be the less a Virtue in itself, though it should chance that a Man robb'd for this very Purpose. For if all his other Qualities were answerable to this Regard to his Parents, he would not have robb'd, but have acted in all Things like a good Man.

The passions in general, said Bluet, are not intrinsically evil, and their necessity to conduct is, therefore, no insuperable barrier to virtue (pp. 73–4). Indeed 'the Pleasure of doing an Action' is not only a legitimate stimulus; it 'is the only Motive human Nature can act upon' (p. 85). But how know whether a passion or an action is good or bad? Mandeville's rigoristic code condemned all natural conduct equally. To make the necessary distinctions, Bluet, like Law and Fiddes, had recourse to a utilitarian touchstone (pp. 36–8). This utilitarianism he elsewhere in his book (p. 115) crystallized into the form known as 'theological' utilitarianism, in which the rewards or penalties of the future life enter into the calculation of benefits.

But Bluet also saw that the rigorism which he condemned in Mandeville was only on the surface. Bluet realized that Mandeville's real sentiments were that the passions whose management makes a state great and happy are justly to be encouraged and sympathized with; that his rejection of them was merely verbal and superficial, and that he would much regret it if the world were run according to rigoristic morality.

'Tis only to disguise his main Design [said Bluet (pp. 13–14)], that he employs his ingenious Raillery in ridiculing *Fools,* who *only strive*

> *To make a great an honest Hive,*

that is, for endeavouring at what is *impossible* to obtain. His real Sentiments appear, when he calls *the grumbling Hive* Rogues and Fools, for having by their impertinent Prayers procur'd *in Fact* such a State and Condition [of ascetic virtue], and consequently such Ruin and Poverty. The *Knaves* are actually *turned honest,* a Curse which the great and good Gods sent them in their Vengeance as the greatest they could inflict. . . .

And again (p. 92),

He does not . . . blame his *grumbling Hive* for taking *improper Methods* to root out Vice, but for rooting it out *at all.* . . . What a fine consistent System of *Ethicks* is this !

In this demonstration of Mandeville's inconsistencies, however, Bluet was objecting to a dualism of which he also was a victim. As Mandeville superimposed a rigoristic system on an attitude which Bluet rightly felt to be anti-rigoristic, so Bluet assailed Mandeville's rigorism while, all the time, Bluet cherished the basal rigoristic principle : '. . . nothing can make a Man honest or virtuous but a Regard to some religious or moral Principles' (*Enquiry,* p. 139)— precisely the rigoristic position from which Mandeville was arguing when he asserted that our so-called virtues were really vices, because not based only on this regard to principle. Thus the author of the *Enquiry* is still another illustration of the mingling of contradictory criteria which the *Fable* itself embodies.

Berkeley and Hervey. 1732.

Hervey's *Some Remarks on the Minute Philosopher* was an attack upon Berkeley's *Alciphron: or, the Minute Philosopher,* which was an attack on the *Fable of the Bees*; yet both attacks agreed in one detail, a point which was one of the most telling of all the criticisms passed upon Mandeville's book. Hervey put it thus (pp. 45–7) :

> I would have said, that his [Mandeville's] endeavouring to show, that People do Actions they have reason to be proud of, from Motives, which if nicely scrutinized, they would have reason to be ashamed of, will never contribute to the multiplying such Actions. . . .
>
> If it could be proved, that *Herostratus*, who fired the Temple of *Ephesus*, and *Decius*, who threw himself, for the sake of his Country, into the Gulph that open'd in *Rome*, acted both from the same Motive, and were equally influenced by the Vanity of being mentioned in History, and perpetuating their Names to Posterity . . . ; if this, I say, could be demonstrated, I would be glad to ask the Author of the *Fable of the Bees*, whether he thinks it would promote and encourage that Virtue call'd *the Love of one's Country,* to shew that the most renown'd Patriot in Antiquity, and the most infamous *Incendiary*, were in the same Way of Thinking, and actuated by the same Passion ?

Berkeley stated this same objection as to the practical dangers of Mandeville's theory of human nature, whether true or not, when he said ironically, in answer to it,

> It should seem then that Plato's fearing lest youth might be corrupted by those fables which represented the gods vicious was an effect of his weakness and ignorance.[1]

And it must be added that Mandeville himself admitted the value of deceiving men into goodness.[2]

This argument is a crucial one ; it embodies an essential difference between ' tough-minded ' thinkers such as Mandeville, and ' tender-minded ' ones like Berkeley. The latter combine an exalted ideal of virtue and humanity with a distrust of actual virtuousness and people. As a result there arises a dual tendency—first, always to subordinate the demands of the actual which they distrust to the ideal that they wor-

[1] See Berkeley, *Works*, ed. Fraser, 1901, ii. 75.   [2] See, for example, his *Origin of Honour,* p. 86.

ship, which makes them rigorists in morality ; and, secondly, for their own comfort to persuade themselves into believing that their ideal is to be found actually embodied, and is, indeed, the natural thing to expect. It may seem a self-contradiction that a distrust of actual humanity should be bound up with the belief that this distrusted humanity embodies the ideal in comparison with which it is contemned, but it is, none the less, a fact. It is a manifestation of the general tendency to believe that what is desired either actually exists or can be brought to pass. On this account, therefore, Berkeley could at once deny that men were so far from the ideal as Mandeville asserted them to be, and, at the same time, in the argument quoted above, betray his complete want of confidence in this humanity by maintaining that they were so untrustworthy that they would be unable to withstand the deleterious effects of Mandeville's disillusionizing doctrines. The matter comes, finally, to this paradox, that the Berkeleys not only resented the denial by Mandeville of their superlative conception of man, but felt such distrust of this supposedly exalted creature that they feared for the practical ill effects which would follow men's conviction that they were not divine, but the creatures of selfish passions.

Mandeville realized the nature of the gulf between himself and Berkeley. In his reply to the Bishop's book, he wrote (*Letter to Dion*, p. 48),

You, Sir, think it for the Good of Society, that human Nature should be extoll'd as much as possible : I think, the real Meanness and Deformity of it to be more instructive.

The fact is that the cynical Mandeville, who spent his life telling how bad people were, really felt enormously more confidence in them than the uncynical Berkeley ; and this is why he was able to call them so many bad names and still be happy. ' Use every man according to his deserts, and who should 'scape whipping ? ' asked Hamlet. And because he had Berkeley's and not Mandeville's temperament, he was rendered miserable by this. But Mandeville said, ' Treat every one as he deserves, and who shall escape hanging ? ' and continued on perfectly good terms with everybody. He did not believe that men need, in order to be tolerable, to live up to the ideal deserts that Hamlet and Berkeley insisted upon. That is why he refused to flatter them into morality, and why he analysed motives in the way which Hervey thought so dangerous. Mandeville had no such fear of people as to feel the necessity of deceiving either himself or them as to their real nature. Indeed, one might say that he abused mankind as we whimsically give bad names to good friends.

Adam Smith and John Brown. 1759 and 1751

Adam Smith's brilliant criticism is summed up in this culminating paragraph:

It is the great fallacy of Dr. Mandeville's book to represent every passion as wholly vicious which is so in any degree and in any direction. It is thus that he treats every thing as vanity which has any reference either to what are or to what ought to be the sentiments of others: and it is by means of this sophistry that he establishes his favourite conclusion, that private vices are public benefits. If the love of magnificence, a taste for the elegant arts and improvements of human life, for whatever is agreeable in dress, furniture, or equipage, for architecture, statuary, painting and music, is to be regarded as luxury, sensuality and ostentation, even in those whose situation allows, without any inconveniency, the indulgence of those passions, it is certain that luxury, sensuality and ostentation are public benefits: since, without the qualities upon which he thinks proper to bestow such opprobrious names, the arts of refinement could never find encouragement, and must languish for want of employment. Some popular ascetic doctrines which had been current before his time, and which placed virtue in the entire extirpation and annihilation of all our passions, were the real foundation of this licentious system. It was easy for Dr. Mandeville to prove, first, that this entire conquest never actually took place among men; and, secondly, that, if it was to take place, universally, it would be pernicious to society, by putting an end to all industry and commerce, and in a manner to the whole business of human life. By the first of these propositions he seemed to prove that there was no real virtue, and that what pretended to be such was a meer cheat and imposition upon mankind; and by the second, that private vices were public benefits, since without them no society could prosper or flourish.[1]

Notice here that Adam Smith did not fall into the vulgar error of thinking that Mandeville was confounding the *practical* effects of vice, and calling all vice equally beneficial to society, but that he attacked Mandeville for making all actions equally reprehensible from a *moral* standpoint. Briefly, he condemned Mandeville's moral nihilism, the

[1] Smith, *Theory of Moral Sentiments* (1759), pp. 485-6.

absence of any criterion to distinguish between moral good and evil except the impracticable and repulsive one of identifying virtue with complete self-denial.

A similar indictment of Mandeville was drawn up by John Brown in his *Essays on the Characteristics.* He, also, recognized that Mandeville took advantage of an ethical system which,

contending for the permanent *Reality* of Virtue, and, not content to fix it on its proper Basis, attempts to establish certain *absolute* and *immutable* Forms of Beauty [or virtue], without Regard to any *further End.* . . . [Mandeville], intent on destroying the permanent Reality of Virtue and Vice, and perceiving how Weak a Basis the noble Writer [Shaftesbury] had laid for their Establishment, after proving *this* to be imaginary, as wisely as honestly infers, there is no real one in Nature (*Essays*, ed. 1751, p. 145).

This, according to Brown, was the cause of the absence of definite criteria in Mandeville; this is the reason why Mandeville maintained that in morals there is no greater certainty than in the matter of whether fashionable society will prefer broad-brimmed or narrow-brimmed hats (see *Fable* i. 327-8).

But Brown went further; he tried to supply the deficiency which he and Smith found in Mandeville by offering utility as the missing test of moral truth. He set up ' the great End of public Happiness . . . as the *one, uniform* Circumstance that constitutes the *Rectitude* of human Actions ' (pp. 140-1). By this means he thought to restore to ethics that certainty of which Mandeville attempted to rob it, without setting up the rigoristic creed which drove Mandeville into this theft.

There are visible in this controversy, roughly speaking, two main kinds of criticism. The first is that of men like Law and Berkeley, who may be termed the religious-minded. What they objected to primarily in Mandeville was his refusal to recognize the existence of anything above human experience. They rebelled at the manner in which he made morality an affair of the passions and denied the existence of any absolute standards of right and wrong. The fact that Mandeville formally admitted the necessity for action in accord with such standards did not reconcile these critics to him. It simply enraged them the more, since Mandeville admitted their creed only in order to show its impracticability. As a result, they usually, in their anguish, threw logic to the winds, and criticized him for the most inconsistent reasons. The same men would attack not only his basal empiricism, but his acceptance of the rigoristic ethics in which they themselves believed. Appalled at the result of his adoption of their own code, they turned upon it to rend themselves. They complained because he *called* human nature bad; but they really objected because he *felt* such utter reliance upon it. They felt what he said and said what he felt. The paradoxes in Mandeville's book were at least equalled by those in the minds of his readers.

On the other hand were critics like Adam Smith and John Brown. These men were not roused to anger by Mandeville's empiricism, for they largely shared it. Still, as it happens, they objected to his teachings for reasons which superficially resemble the objections of men like Law. They condemned the rigorism which caused Mandeville to identify self-gratification with vice, and his failure to offer practical criteria according to which to determine moral values. Mandeville had simply said—although he did not really feel this—that all things were equally vicious. Smith and Brown, however, objected to Mandeville's asceticism for a very different reason from that of the other type of critic. Law and Bluet, for instance, combated Mandeville's asceticism because they felt that he did not really believe it; but Smith and Brown objected because they thought that he did. The latter wished a scheme of morals in which man should be the measure of all things, and his happiness the end of conduct. In this respect they were in harmony with what is really basic in Mandeville's thought. They were simply refining away that part of Mandeville which is out of keeping with his own true trend. It may be said, then, that the more they refuted Mandeville, the more they agreed with him.

The attack of such critics as Smith and Brown upon Mandeville's pyrrhonism, or denial of final criteria, was, also, like their attack on his asceticism, only in superficial agreement with the similar attack of thinkers like Law. Both types of critics agreed in demanding some standard of moral values. But, whereas Fiddes and Law would have set up a code of divine origin whose ultimate sanction was not utilitarian, the other critics wished a standard which should be quite relative to human needs. Brown, for instance, offered definitely a utilitarian scheme of ethics. But, in this, as in their attack on Mandeville's formal asceticism, thinkers of Smith's type were bringing out what is latent in Mandeville, and attacked him because they did not realize that, under his superficial difference, he was really at one with them, Mandeville, as is noted above (i. lviii–lxi), being at bottom as utilitarian as John Brown. Here too, then, the effect of this class of critics was not so much a refutation of Mandeville's teachings as a development of them.

A LIST

CHRONOLOGICALLY ARRANGED

of references to

MANDEVILLE'S WORK

THIS is not intended to be a complete list. Only such references have been recorded as from contemporaneousness, representativeness, astuteness, or the importance of their author are of some interest. Purely biographical references are not noted. Although later editions are often referred to, works are listed under the date of the earliest edition to include the indicated reference to Mandeville. Certain works are placed, proper indication being made, not under date of first publication, but under date of composition. Capitalization in titles has been standardized. Dates of editions have uniformly been expressed in arabic numerals.

[1716] COWPER, MARY, COUNTESS. Diary of Mary Countess Cowper, Lady of the Bedchamber to the Princess of Wales 1714–1720. 1864.
'*Mr. Horneck,* who wrote *The High German Doctor.* . . . told me that Sir *Richard Steele* had no Hand in writing the *Town Talk,* which was attributed to him; that it was one Dr. *Mandeville* and an Apothecary of his Acquaintance that wrote that Paper; and that some Passages were wrote on purpose to make believe it was Sir *R. Steele*' (see under date of 1 Feb. 1716). There seem no grounds for this assertion.

[1722] MEMOIRES HISTORIQUES ET CRITIQUES. Amsterdam. 1722. [Periodical]
See pp. 45–54 (July) for fair-minded review of *Pensées Libres*: '. . . il raisonne clairement et solidement, mais il faut avoüer aussi, qu'il n'est pas toûjours heureux dans les applications qu'il fait. . . . Son premier chapitre, où il traitte de la religion en général, est magnifiquement bien conçu. . . . Rien de plus grand, rien de plus vrai que ce qu'il en pense' (p. 46). '. . . de politesse, de précision et de vivacité [of the style]. . . . Ces sortes de vivacité . . . ne font jamais honneur à un Autheur Chretien' (p. 54).

References to Mandeville's Work. 419

EVENING POST. [Periodical]   [1723]
The issue of 11 July contained the Grand Jury's presentment of the *Fable*;
see *Fable* i. 383–6.

FORTGESETZTE SAMMLUNG VON ALTEN UND NEUEN THEOLOGISCHEN SACHEN. Leipsic. 1723. [Periodical]
[Also known as *Unschuldige Nachrichten*.]
See pp. 751–3 for review of French version of *Free Thoughts*.

LONDON JOURNAL. 27 July 1723. [Periodical]
The 'abusive' letter to Lord *C.* against Mandeville, signed Theophilus Philo-
Britannus. It is reprinted in *Fable* i. 386–401.

MAENDELYKE UITTREKSELS, of Boekzael der Geleerde Werelt. Amsterdam. 1723. [Periodical]
See xvi. 688–714, xvii. 71–96 and 152–72 for reviews of the French and
Dutch translations of the *Free Thoughts*.

NEUER ZEITUNGEN VON GELEHRTEN SACHEN. Leipsic. 1723. [Periodical]
See pp. 252–3 for complimentary notice of the French translation of the *Free
Thoughts*.

PASQUIN. 13 May 1723. [Periodical]
Contains the earliest reference which I know to the *Fable*.

'I am obliged to a Book, intitled, *The Fable of the Bees, or private Vices
publick Benefits*, for another good Argument in Defence of my Clients in this
particular, which is contained in this following Paradox, (*viz.*) *That if every
Body paid his Debts* honestly, *a great many honest Men would be ruined*: For,
as it is learnedly argued in the aforesaid Book, that we are indebted to particular, *private* Vices for the flourishing Condition and Welfare of the *Publick*;
and as, if *Luxury* ceased, great part of our *Commerce* would cease with it;
and if the *Reformation of Manners* should so far prevail as to abolish *Fornica-
tion*, Multitudes of *Surgeons* would be ruined; so, if every Body should grow
honest and *pay his Debts* willingly, what would become of the long *Robe* and
Westminster-hall?'

BARNES, W. G. Charity and Charity Schools Defended. A Sermon [1724]
Preach'd at St. Martin's Palace, in Norwich, on March 6. 1723
[1724]. By the Appointment of the Right Reverend Father in God,
Thomas Late Lord Bishop of that Diocese: and since at St. Mary's
in White-Chapel. 1727.
This sermon attacks 'Cato's' 'Letter' on charity-schools, and the *Fable* as being
representative of the arguments against these schools.

COLERUS.
A review of Mandeville's *Free Thoughts*, in the *Auserlesene Theologische
Bibliothec* i. 515. [This attack is cited from Lilienthal's *Theologische Bibliothec*
(1741), pp. 327–8. The *Neuer Zeitungen von Gelehrten Sachen* for 1724 refers
to parts 5 and 6 of the *Auserlesene Theologische Bibliothec* for a consideration
of the French translation of the *Free Thoughts*. Walch's *Bibliotheca Theologica*
(1757–65) i. 762, *n.*, mentions a review of the *Free Thoughts* in the
Auserlesene Theologische Bibliothec i. 379 and 489. I have been unable to
secure this work to check up these references.]

2522·2   D d

DENNIS, John. Vice and Luxury Publick Mischiefs : or, Remarks on a Book intituled, the Fable of the Bees. 1724.
See above, ii. 407-9.

FIDDES, Richard. A General Treatise of Morality, Form'd upon the Principles of Natural Reason Only. With a Preface in Answer to Two Essays lately Published in the Fable of the Bees. 1724.
See above, ii. 406-7.

[HAYWOOD, Eliza.] The Tea-Table. [Periodical]
See no. 25, for 15 May 1724: '. . . I have a very high Opinion of this Author's Parts. . . . I am very far from endeavouring to refute what he therein [in the *Fable*] advances, I am too sensible that is not so easily done. I would only intreat the Author to consider . . . whether the propagating such Opinions as these, can possibly be of any Benefit . . . but whether, on the contrary, they are not likely to do a great deal of Mischief, which I . . . believe the Author was very far from intending ' (p. [2]).

[HUTCHESON, Francis.] A letter, signed Philanthropos, ' To the Author of the *London Journal* ', published in two parts in that paper on 14 and 21 Nov. 1724.
This letter announces and anticipates the *Inquiry into the Original of our Ideas of Beauty and Virtue,* noticed below under year 1725.

LAW, William. Remarks upon a Late Book, entituled, the Fable of the Bees. . . . In a Letter to the Author. To which is added, a Post-script, containing an Observation or Two upon Mr. Bayle. 1724.
See above, ii. 401-6.

LÖSCHER, V. Nötige Reflexiones über das im Jahr 1722 zum Vorschein gebrachte Buch Pensées libres sur la religion etc. oder freye Gedanken von der Religion, nebst wohlgemeinter Warnung vor dergleichen Büchern abgefasst von Valentin Ernst Löschern D. Oberkonsistoriali und Superintendenten zu Dressden. 1724.
[Cited from Sakmann, *Bernard de Mandeville,* p. 214.]

NEUER ZEITUNGEN VON GELEHRTEN SACHEN. Leipsic. 1724. [Periodical]
See pp. 840-1, 982-3, and 1060 for notice of French translation of *Free Thoughts.*

[THOMASIUS, Christian.] Vernünfftige und christliche aber nicht scheinheilige Thomasische Gedancken und Erinnerungen über allerhand gemischte philosophische und juristische Händel. Andrer Theil. Halle. 1724.
See pp. 686 and 688-90. This is more a review of Löscher's *Nötige Reflexiones* than of the *Free Thoughts.*

THE WEEKLY JOURNAL or SATURDAY'S-POST [MIST'S]. [Periodical]
See issue of 8 Aug. 1724, for attack : ' . . . a Composition of Dulness and Wickedness, as even this extraordinary Age has not produced before.'

[WILSON], THOMAS, Bishop of Sodor and Man. The True Christian Method of Educating the Children both of the Poor and Rich, Recommended more especially to the Masters and Mistresses of the Charity-Schools, in a Sermon Preach'd in the Parish-Church of St. Sepulchre, May 28, 1724. 1724.
See pp. 11–12.

BIBLIOTHEQUE ANGLOISE, ou Histoire Litteraire de la Grande [1725] Bretagne, par Armand de la Chapelle. Amsterdam. [Periodical]
See xiii. 97–125 (review of the *Fable*) and 197–225 (review of Bluet's *Enquiry*). 'Assurément le dessein ne sauroit être plus mauvais' (xiii. 99). 'Le luxe, comme on le sait, est un de ces vices qui paroissent les moins odieux, parce qu'il est un des plus sociables, et c'est apparemment pour cette raison que l'auteur de la *Fable* l'a choisi, comme par préférence sur tous les autres, pour en tirer sa conclusion générale' (xiii. 206).

[BLUET, GEORGE.] An Enquiry whether a General Practice of Virtue tends to the Wealth or Poverty, Benefit or Disadvantage of a People ? In which the Pleas . . . of the Fable of the Bees . . . are considered. 1725.
See above, ii. 410–12.

FORTGESETZTE SAMMLUNG VON ALTEN UND NEUEN THEOLOGISCHEN SACHEN. Leipsic. 1725. [Periodical] [Also known as *Unschuldige Nachrichten.*]
See pp. 516–20 for review of V. E. Löscher's '*Nöthige Reflexions über die Pensées libres*', Wittenberg, 1724. 'Diese gottlosen *Pensées* . . .' (p. 516).

HENDLEY, WILLIAM. A Defence of the Charity-Schools. Wherein the Many False, Scandalous and Malicious Objections of those Advocates for Ignorance and Irreligion, the Author of the Fable of the Bees, and Cato's Letter in the British Journal, June 15. 1723. are fully and distinctly answer'd ; and the Usefulness and Excellency of Such Schools clearly set forth. To which is added by Way of Appendix, the Presentment of the Grand Jury of the British Journal, at their Meeting at Westminster, July 3. 1723. 1725.
See above, i. 14, *n.* 1.

[HUTCHESON, FRANCIS.] An Inquiry into the Original of our Ideas of Beauty and Virtue ; in Two Treatises. In which the Principles of . . . Shaftesbury are . . . defended against . . . the Fable of the Bees. 1725.
Announced as 'On Monday next will be publish'd', in the *Post-Boy* for 25–27 Feb. 172⅘. See above, ii. 420, under HUTCHESON, and ii. 345, *n.* 1.

NEUER ZEITUNGEN VON GELEHRTEN SACHEN. Leipsic. [Periodical]
See pp. 838–43 for review of *Fable*, and pp. 847–50 for a notice of Bluet's *Enquiry* cited from the *Bibliothèque Angloise* of this same year.

[1726] ALOGIST, Isaac (pseudonym). Three Letters to the *Dublin Journal*, published therein on 10 and 17 Sept. and 22 Oct. 1726. They were reprinted in *A Collection of Letters and Essays . . . Publish'd in the Dublin Journal*, ed. Arbuckle, ii. 181–200 and 239–50.

'All the Papers subscribed *Isaac Alogist*', says Arbuckle (ii. 429), 'came to me from a Gentleman, who will not so much as permit me to enquire after him, far less to publish his Name.'

FORTGESETZTE SAMMLUNG VON ALTEN UND NEUEN THEOLOGISCHEN SACHEN. Leipsic. 1726. [Periodical] [Also known as *Unschuldige Nachrichten*.]

See pp. 841–3 for derogatory review of the German version of the *Free Thoughts*.

[HUTCHESON, Francis.] Three Letters to the *Dublin Journal*, published therein on 5, 12, and 19 Feb. 1726. These three letters make up the last half of Hutcheson's *Reflections upon Laughter, and Remarks upon the Fable of the Bees*, 1750. They were reprinted in *A Collection of Letters and Essays on Several Subjects, lately Publish'd in the Dublin Journal*, ed. Arbuckle, also known as *Hibernicus' Letters* (1729) i. 370–407.

JOURNAL DES SÇAVANS, . . . Augmenté de Divers Articles qui ne se trouvent point dans l'Edition de Paris. Amsterdam. 1726. [Periodical]

See lxxviii. 465–73 for a review—unfavourable to Mandeville—of Bluet's answer to Mandeville.

NEUER ZEITUNGEN VON GELEHRTEN SACHEN. Leipsic. 1726. [Periodical]

See p. 510 for an excerpt from the review in the *Journal des Sçavans* of Bluet's reply.

REIMARUS, H. S. Programma quo Fabulam de Apibus examinat simulque ad Orationes IV. de Religionis et Probitatis in Republica Commodis ex Legato Peterseniano a Qvatuor Alumnis Classis Primae ad D.V. Sept. hor. IX matut. habendas Literarum Patronos O. O. Observanter invitat. M. Hermannus Samuel Reimarus. Lcy. Wism. Rect. Wismariae. Typis Zanderianis. [1726.]

[Cited from Sakmann, *Bernard de Mandeville*, p. 212.]

THOROLD, John. A Short Examination of the Notions Advanc'd in a (Late) Book, intituled, the Fable of the Bees or Private Vices, Publick Benefits. 1726.

THE TRUE MEANING OF THE FABLE OF THE BEES ; in a Letter to the Author of a Book entitled an Enquiry whether a General Practice of Virtue . . . ? Shewing that he has manifestly mistaken the True Meaning of the Fable of the Bees. 1726.

Concerning the mistaken attribution of this work to Mandeville, see my 'Writings of Bernard Mandeville', in the *Journal of English and Germanic Philology* for 1921, xx. 463–4.

[ARBUCKLE, James.] A Collection of Letters and Essays on Several [1727] Subjects, lately Publish'd in the Dublin Journal. 2 vol. Dublin. 1729.

See ii. 429. First published in the *Dublin Journal* for 25 March 1727.

MOSHEIM, Joh. Lor. Heilige Reden über wichtige Wahrheiten der Lehren Jesu Christi. Zweyter Theil. Hamburg. 1727.

[This title is cited from the *Neuer Zeitungen von Gelehrten Sachen* (1727), p. 796, which mentions it as dealing with the *Fable.* Vogt's *Catalogus Historico-Criticus Librorum Rariorum* (1747), p. 276, also mentions Mosheim's book in this connexion.]

NEUER ZEITUNGEN VON GELEHRTEN SACHEN. Leipsic. 1727. [Periodical]

See pp. 796-7 for attribution of the *Fable* to Jakob Masse.

CHANDLER, Sam. Doing Good Recommended from the Example of [1728] Christ. A Sermon Preach'd for the Benefit of the Charity-School in Gravel-Lane, Southwark, January 172⅞. To which is added, an Answer to an Essay on Charity-Schools, by the Author of the Fable of the Bees. 1728.

Summarized in Sakmann, *Bernard de Mandeville,* p. 200. The exact date of the sermon was 1 Jan. ; see Isaac Watts, *Works* (1812) vi. 9, *n.*

DAILY JOURNAL. [Periodical]

The issue of 11 March contained the advertisement of Innes's book mentioned in *Fable* ii. 23-4.

[GIBSON, Edmund.] The Bishop of London's Pastoral Letter to the People of his Diocese. . . . Occasion'd by Some Late Writings in Favour of Infidelity. 1728.

See p. 2.

GRAND JURY'S PRESENTMENT.

This second presentment of the *Fable* is reprinted in *Remarks upon Two Late Presentments* (1729), pp. 3-6 (cf. above, i. 13, *n.* 1).

INNES, Alexander. ΑΡΕΤΗ-ΛΟΓΙΑ or, an Enquiry into the Original of Moral Virtue. 1728.

See *Fable* ii. 24-8 and below, ii. 426, under CAMPBELL.

THE LONDON EVENING POST. [Periodical]

The issues of 9 March and 16-19 March (p. 4) contained the advertisement of Innes's book mentioned in *Fable* ii. 23-4.

THE PRESENT STATE OF THE REPUBLICK OF LETTERS. 1728. [Periodical]

See ii. 462 (December) for notice and description (in the tone of an advertise-ment) of Part II of the *Fable.*

WATTS, Isaac. An Essay towards the Encouragement of Charity Schools, particularly those . . . supported by Protestant Dissenters. 1728.

This is an elaboration of a sermon preached in Nov. 1727 against the *Fable* and other attacks on charity-schools.

WHITEHALL EVENING POST. [Periodical]
The issue of 21-3 March (p. 4) contained the advertisement of Innes's book mentioned in *Fable* ii. 23-4.

[1729] BIBLIOTHEQUE RAISONNÉE des Ouvrages des Savans de l'Europe. Amsterdam. 1729. [Periodical]
See viii. 402-45 for review of both parts of the *Fable*: 'Les endroits où il prétend accorder la Raison & la Revelation sont ceux qui nous paroissent les plus foibles du second Volume ; les raisonnemens qu'il fait sur ce sujet sont si extraordinaires que s'ils avoient le moindre sens on seroit tenté d'y en chercher encore un autre ' (viii. 445).

BYROM, JOHN. The Private Journals and Literary Remains. . . . Edited by Richard Parkinson. (Chetham Society, vol. 32, 34, 40, 44.) 1824-7.
Cf. above, i. xxviii, *n.* 1.

THE LONDON JOURNAL. 7 and 14 June 1729. [Periodical]
Both these issues contain several columns attacking the *Fable*.

NEUER ZEITUNGEN VON GELEHRTEN SACHEN. Leipsic. 1729. [Periodical]
See p. 98 for notice of Innes's reply.

[1731] THE GENTLEMAN'S MAGAZINE : or, Monthly Intelligencer for the Year 1731. [Periodical]
See p. 118.

READ'S WEEKLY JOURNAL, OR BRITISH-GAZETTEER. 27 March 1731. [Periodical]
Contains attack on *Fable*.

REIMMANN, JACOB FRIEDRICH. Catalogus Bibliothecæ Theologicæ, Systematico-Criticus, in quo, Libri Theologici, in Bibliotheca Reimanniana Extantes, Editi & Inediti, in Certas Classes Digesti, qua fieri potuit Solertia, enumerantur. Hildesheim. 1731.
See pp. 1066-7 for notice of *Free Thoughts*.

[1732] BERKELEY, GEORGE. Alciphron : or, the Minute Philosopher. In Seven Dialogues. Containing an Apology for the Christian Religion, against those who are called Free-Thinkers. 2 vol. 1732.
See above, ii. 412-14.

BIBLIOTHEQUE RAISONNÉE des Ouvrages des Savans de l'Europe. Amsterdam. 1732. [Periodical]
See viii. 227 for notice of the *Origin of Honour*, and ix. 232 for notice of the *Letter to Dion*.

THE CHARACTER OF THE TIMES DELINEATED. . . . Design'd for the Use of those who . . . are convinc'd, by Sad Experience, that Private Vices are Publick and Real Mischiefs. 1732.
A general jeremiad rather than an attack on Mandeville.
> *And, if* GOD-MAN Vice *to abolish* came,
> *Who* Vice *commends,* MAN-DEVIL *be his Name* (p. 10).

CLARKE, Dr. A. A letter to Mrs. Clayton from Winchester, dated 22 April 1732, in which Dr. Clarke gives his opinion and a one-page summary of the *Origin of Honour* [in Sundon, *Memoirs* (1848) ii. 110–11].

Cf. above, i. xxvii, *n.*

THE CRAFTSMAN. By Caleb D'Anvers, of Gray's-Inn, Esq. Vol. IX. 1737. [Periodical]

This contains letters (pp. 1–6 and 154–6) against the *Fable*, addressed to Caleb D'Anvers, in the issues for 29 Jan. and 24 June 1732. One of the letters is mentioned in Mandeville's *Letter to Dion*, p. 6.

THE GENTLEMAN'S MAGAZINE : or, Monthly Intelligencer. 1732. [Periodical]

See ii. 687 for citation of an attack on the *Fable* in *Read's Weekly Journal* for 1 April.

[HERVEY, John, Lord.] Some Remarks on the Minute Philosopher. In a Letter from a Country Clergyman to his Friend in London. 1732.

See above, ii. 412.

INDEX EXPURGATORIUS.

The French version of the *Free Thoughts* was damned by decree of 21 Jan. 1732 (*Index Librorum Prohibitorum* . . . *Pii Sexti*, ed. 1806, p. 112).

JOURNAL HISTORIQUE DE LA REPUBLIQUE DES LETTRES. Leyden. 1732. [Periodical]

See i. 420 for brief review of *Letter to Dion*.

MOYNE, Abraham le. Preservatif contre l'Incredulité & le Libertinage en Trois Lettres Pastorales de Monseigneur l'Eveque de Londres. The Hague. 1732. [Title cited from Freytag, *Analecta Litteraria* (1750), p. 330. Reusch's *Index der verbotenen Bücher* (ed. 1883–5, ii. 865, *n.* 2) also mentions this translation.]

Only the first pastoral letter refers specifically to the *Fable*. For notice of the pastoral letters here translated, see in this bibliography under Edmund Gibson in the year 1728.

NOVA ACTA ERUDITORUM. Leipsic. 1732. [Periodical]

See pp. 212–23 in the May issue for mention of Innes's reply to Mandeville: the ΑΡΕΤΗ-ΛΟΓΙΑ.

POPE, Alexander. Moral Essays.

Courthope, in the Elwin and Courthope edition of Pope, thinks the following lines inspired by Mandeville: iii. 13–14 and 25–6.

See below, Elwin and Courthope, under year 1871.

THE PRESENT STATE OF THE REPUBLICK OF LETTERS 1732. [Periodical]

See ix. 32–6 (January) and ix. 93–105 (February) for two reviews of the *Origin of Honour*; and ix. 142–63 (February) for a review of Berkeley's answer to Mandeville.

'We cannot say that every thing in this Piece is new, the Author of a Book intitled: *Les pensées sur les Cometes* . . . has very justly shewn us, in that ingenious Performance, how much Men in their manner of living deviate from their Principles . . .' (p. 32).

'This book . . . is written in an agreeable, correct, and masterly Stile, as all the other Writings of this Author . . .' (p. 93).

SWIFT, JONATHAN [?]. A True and Faithful Narrative of what passed in London, during the General Consternation. See *Prose Works*, ed. Temple Scott, iv. 283. Cf. above, ii. 24, *n.*

[1733] BIBLIOTHEQUE BRITANNIQUE, ou Histoire des Ouvrages des Savans de la Grande-Bretagne. 1733. [Periodical]
See i. 1–36 and ii. 1–16 for a careful description of *The Origin of Honour.* A brief obituary of Mandeville is contained in i. 244–5.

[BRAMSTON, JAMES.] The Man of Taste. Occasion'd by an Epistle of Mr. Pope's on that Subject. By the Author of the Art of Politics. 1733.
The author writes ironically :
> T'improve in Morals *Mandevil* I read,
> And *Tyndal*'s Scruples are my settled Creed (p. 9).

CAMPBELL, ARCHIBALD. An Enquiry into the Original of Moral Virtue wherein it is shewn, (against the Author of the Fable of the Bees, &c.) that Virtue is founded in the Nature of Things, is Unalterable, and Eternal, and the Great Means of Private and Publick Happiness. Edinburgh. 1733.
See above, ii. 25, *n.* 1. Campbell has substituted his own preface for Innes's and enlarged the book.

THE COMEDIAN, or Philosophic Enquirer. Numb. IX, and Last. 1733. [Periodical]
See pp. 30–1. '. . . *Fable of the Bees* . . . discovers a great Knowledge of human Nature . . . has several Strokes of true Humour in it . . ., but the Philosophy thereof is ill grounded . . . and the Diction is very inaccurate and vulgar' (p. 30).

JOURNAL HISTORIQUE DE LA REPUBLIQUE DES LETTRES. Leyden. 1733. [Periodical]
See ii. 422–3 for a letter from London protesting against the leniency towards Mandeville of the *Journal Historique* (see above under the year 1732). '[The *Fable*] . . . annéantit toute Différence réelle entre le Vice & la Vertu. . . .'

JOURNAL LITTERAIRE. The Hague. 1733. [Periodical]
See xx. 207–8 for brief account of Berkeley's *Alciphron* and the *Letter to Dion.*

POPE, ALEXANDER. Essay on Man.
Elwin, in his edition of Pope, thinks the following lines derived from Mandeville : ii. 129–30, ii. 157–8, ii. 193–4, and iv. 220. Note, also that Pope's original manuscript had (instead of the present line ii. 240) 'And public good extracts from private vice'.
See below, under ELWIN and COURTHOPE, ii. 445.

[1734] HALLER, ALBRECHT VON. Ueber den Ursprung des Uebels.
> Und dieses ist die Welt, worüber Weise klagen,
> Die man zum Kerker macht, worin sich Thoren plagen !
> Wo mancher Mandewil des guten Merkmal misst,
> Die Thaten Bosheit würkt und fühlen leiden ist (i. 71–4).

JOURNAL LITTERAIRE. The Hague. 1734. [Periodical]
See xxi. 223 for review of Archibald Campbell's reply to Mandeville (see above under year 1733) and xxii. 72 for a review of Berkeley's *Alciphron*—a review favourable to Berkeley, but not hostile to Mandeville.

LEIPZIGE GELEHRTE ZEITUNGEN. 1734. [Periodical]
See p. 61 for notice of Campbell's reply to Mandeville. [Cited from Trinius's *Freydenker-Lexicon*, p. 347.]

MERCURE DE FRANCE. Paris. 1734. [Periodical]
See p. 1401 for brief notice of the *Origin of Honour*.

NIEDERSÄCHS. NACHR. VON GELEHRTEN SACHEN. 1734. [Periodical]
See p. 320. [Cited from the *Fortsetzung ... zu ... Jöchers allgemeinem Gelehrten-Lexiko* iv. 553.]

A VINDICATION OF THE REVEREND D—— B——Y, from the Scandalous Imputation of being Author of ... Alciphron. 1734.
'Especially seeing he [Berkeley] thought fit to borrow from that Quiver his best Weapons against the *Fable of the Bees* ...; as may be evident to any who will be at the Pains to compare it with the three Papers published among *Hibernicus's Letters*, written by ... *Hutcheson*...' (p. 22).

NOVELLE DELLA REPUBLICA DELLE LETTERE. Venice. [1735] 1735. [Periodical]
See pp. 357-8 for a review of Berkeley's *Alciphron*. '... la famosa *Favola delle Api* ...' (p. 357).

UFFENBACH, ZACHAR. CONRADUS AB. Bibliotheca Uffenbachiana, seu Catalogus Librorum. 4 vol. Frankfort. 1735.
See i. 248 for inclusion of *Fable*, edition of 1725, under 'Appendix. Exhibens Libros Vulgo Prohibitos, Sive Suspectæ Fidei et Argumenti Paradoxi atque Profani Scripta.'

BERKELEY, GEORGE. A Discourse Addressed to Magistrates and [1736] Men in Authority.
'We esteem it a horrible thing ... with him who wrote the *Fable of the Bees*, to maintain that "moral virtues are the political offspring which flattery begot upon pride"' (*Works*, ed. Fraser, 1901, iv. 499).

DU CHÂTELET-LOMONT, GABRIELLE ÉMILIE. A letter to Algarotti, dated 20 May 1736.
'Je traduis *The fable of the bees* de Mandeville; c'est un livre qui mérite que vous le lisiez si vous ne le connaissez pas. Il est amusant et instructif' (*Lettres*, ed. Asse, 1882, p. 90).

VOLTAIRE, F. A. DE. Le Mondain.
For the indebtedness of this to the *Fable*, see Morize, *L'Apologie du Luxe au XVIIIe Siècle et "Le Mondain" de Voltaire* (1909).

[COVENTRY, HENRY.] Philemon to Hydaspes; Relating a Second [1737] Conversation with Hortensius upon the Subject of False Religion. 1737.
See pp. 96-7, *n.*: 'This false Notion of confounding Superfluities and Vices, is what runs thro' that whole Piece; otherwise, (as all that Author's Pieces are) very ingeniously written.'

428 *References to Mandeville's Work.*

Coventry is identified as author by a reference in *Bibliotheca Parriana* (1827), pp. 85–6, in the *Gentleman's Magazine* for 1779, xlix. 413, *n.*, and by Horace Walpole, *Letters* (ed. Cunningham) i. 7.

GELEHRTE ZEIT. 1737.
[Cited from Lilienthal's *Theologische Bibliothec* (1741), p. 326, which refers to p. 697 of the above journal as noticing the *Free Thoughts*.]

VOLTAIRE, F. A. DE. Défense du Mondain ou l'Apologie du Luxe.
According to Morize (*L'Apologie du Luxe au XVIIIe Siècle*, pp. 162 and 166), lines 11 and 12 are derived from the *Fable*.

[1738] BIRCH, THOMAS. A General Dictionary, Historical and Critical : in which a . . . Translation of that of . . . Bayle . . . is included. 10 vol. 1734–41.
See the article on Mandeville, contributed by Birch. The articles on Mandeville in Chaufepié's *Nouveau Dictionnaire Historique et Critique* (1753) and in the *Supplement to Biographia Britannica* are derived from the *General Dictionary*.

REPUBL. DER GELEERDEN. 1738. [Periodical]
See article 2 in the issue for September and October for consideration of the *Free Thoughts*. [Cited from Trinius's *Freydenker-Lexicon*, p. 345.]

VOGT, JOHANN. Catalogus Historico-Criticus Librorum Rariorum. Hamburg. 1738.
See p. 251.

VOLTAIRE, F. A. DE. Observations sur MM. Jean Lass, Melon et Dutot sur le Commerce, le Luxe, les Monnaies, et les Impots. 1738.
Compare xxii. 363 (*Œuvres Complètes*, ed. Moland, 1877–85) with *Fable* i. 123 and i. 170 for derivation by Voltaire.

WARBURTON, WILLIAM. The Divine Legation of Moses Demonstrated.
See *Works* (1811) i. 281–6 : '. . . the low buffoonery and impure rhetoric of this wordy declaimer' (i. 281). Cf. above, i. cxxviii, *n.* 5. Warburton also has references to Mandeville in his edition of Pope [1751]; see Pope, *Works*, ed. Elwin and Courthope, ii. 493–4 and iv. 159, *n.* 4.

[1740] BIBLIOTHEQUE FRANÇOISE, ou Histoire Litteraire de la France. Amsterdam. 1740. [Periodical]
See xxxii. 315–19. 'Les digressions de Mr. Mandeville sont ennuyeuses, les plaisanteries sont froides, les peintures des mœurs sont sans noblesse & sans finesse. . . . a . . . merité le froid accueil qu'on lui a fait en France' (xxxii. 319).

BIBLIOTHEQUE RAISONNÉE des Ouvrages des Savans de l'Europe. Amsterdam. 1740. [Periodical]
See xxiv. 240 for notice of the French version of the *Fable*.

FORTGESETZTE SAMMLUNG VON ALTEN UND NEUEN THEOLOGISCHEN SACHEN. Leipsic. 1740. [Periodical]
See pp. 482–3 for notice of *Fable*. 'Die höchst ärgerliche Engelländische Schrifft des Mondeville . . .' (p. 482).

GÖTTINGISCHE ZEITUNGEN von gelehrten Sachen auf das Jahr MDCCXL. Göttingen. 1740. [Periodical]

See pp. 67–8 for notice of the French version of the *Fable*, ' auf Kosten der holländischen Buchhändlergesellschaft . . . gedrucket ' (p. 67).

MEMOIRES pour l'Histoire des Sciences & des Beaux Arts [Mémoires de Trévoux]. Trévoux. 1740. [Periodical]

See pp. 941–81, 1596–1636, and 2103–47 for serial review of the *Fable*. '. . . la Traduction est reçue bien plus paisiblement en France . . .' [than the original in England] (p. 981).

[STOLLE, GOTTLIEB.] Kurtze Nachricht von den Büchern und deren Urhebern in der Stollischen Bibliothec. Der neundte Theil. Jena. 1740.

See pp. 52–67 for review of the *Free Thoughts* in the form of excerpts.

LILIENTHAL, MICHAEL. Theologische Bibliothec, das ist : rich- [1741] tiges Verzeichniss, zulängliche Beschreibung, und bescheidene Beurtheilung der dahin gehörigen vornehmsten Schriften welche in M. Michael Lilienthals . . . Bücher-Vorrath befindlich sind. Königsberg. 1741.

See pp. 326–30 for review of *Free Thoughts* and pp. 330–2 for review of *Fable*. There is a statement (p. 326) that some people judged the *Free Thoughts* to be by B. Masle.

CASTEL, CHARLES IRENÉE, Abbé de St. Pierre. Contre l'Opinion de Mandeville. Que Toutes les Passions sont des Vices Injustes & que les Passions, même Injustes sont plus Utiles que Nuizibles à l'Augmantation du Bonheur de la Societié. [In *Ouvrajes de Morale et de Politique* (Rotterdam, 1741) xvi. 143–56.]

This is a somewhat altered version of the article of similar title in vol. 15 of the same date—pp. 197–212.

[BROWN, JOHN.] Honour a Poem. Inscribed to . . . Lord Viscount [1743] Lonsdale. 1743.

> Th' envenom'd Stream that flows from *Toland*'s Quill,
> And the rank Dregs of *Hobbes* and *Mandeville*.
> Detested Names ! yet sentenc'd ne'er to die ;
> Snatch'd from Oblivion's Grave by Infamy ! (ll. 176–9).

NOTIZIE LETTERARIE OLTRAMONTANE [*Giornale de' Letterati*]. Rome. 1743.

' Il fu Dottor Mandeville va più lungi [than Morgan and Chubb]. Arriva insino a combattere questa Religione, che gli altri ne' loro scritti rispettano ' (ii [2]. 321–2). Then follows a short and accurate summary of the *Fable* and the *Origin of Honour*.

POPE, ALEXANDER. The Dunciad Variorum. With the Prolegomena of Scriblerus.

See ii. 414 (*Works*, ed. Elwin and Courthope, iv. 159): '. . . Morgan and Mandevil could prate no more. . . .' This line first appeared in 1743.

FORTGESETZTE SAMMLUNG VON ALTEN UND NEUEN [1745] THEOLOGISCHEN SACHEN. Leipsic. 1745. [Periodical]

See pp. 950–6.

430 *References to Mandeville's Work.*

INDEX EXPURGATORIUS. The French version of the *Fable* was placed on the *Index* by decree of 22 May 1745 (*Index Librorum Prohibitorum . . . Pii Sexti*, ed. 1806, p. 112).

[1746] DUNKEL, JOHANN GOTTLOB WILHELM. Diatriba Philosophica, qua Sententia, Auctoris Fabulae de Apibus refutatur. Berlin. 1747.

According to the *Fortsetzung . . . zu . . . Jöchers allgemeinem Gelehrten-Lexiko*, iv. 554, Jacob Elsner published an answer to the *Fable* at Berlin in 1747. This work was, I conjecture, the one referred to by Dunkel, in his *Historisch-critische Nachrichten* (1753–7) i. 102–3, who states : 'Im Jahre 1746 habe ich selbst, auf Veranlassung des sel. D. Jacob Elsners in Berlin, eine absonderliche Diatribam philosophicam . . . ausgearbeitet, und die Handschrift davon um 1747, weil er solche zum Druck zu befördern sich erbot, an ihn nach Berlin übersendet : ob er aber solches Manuscript an einen andern Ort verschickt, oder unter seinen geschriebenen Sachen nach seinem Tode hinterlassen habe, kann ich nicht wissen.'

LEWIS, EDWARD. Private Vices the Occasion of Publick Calamities. . . . An Essay. 1747.

Noticed in *London Magazine* for Nov. 1746. Only the title and a phrase on p. 11 seem to refer to Mandeville.

LUC, JACQUES-FRANÇOIS DE. Lettre Critique sur la " Fable des Abeilles " de M. Mandeville. Geneva. 1746.

[Cited from Quérard, *La France Littéraire* (1830) ii. 464.]

[1747] [VAUVENARGUES, LUC DE CLAPIERS, MARQUIS DE.] Introduction a la Connoissance de l'Esprit Humain. Paris. 1747.

Several passages may refer to Mandeville—for example this passage from the third book, 'Du bien et du mal moral' : ' On demande si la plûpart des vices ne concourent pas au bien public, comme les plus pures vertus. Qui feroit fleurir le commerce sans la vanité, l'avarice, &c.?' En un sens cela est très-vrai ; mais il faut m'accorder aussi, que le bien produit par le vice est toujours mêlé de grands maux' (p. 103).

[1748] FEUERLEIN, D. and P. Specimen Concordiae Fidei et Rationis in Vindiciis Religionis Christianae adversus Petrum Baelium, Fingentem, Rempublicam, quae Tota e Veris Christianis est composita, conseruare se non posse. Göttingen. 1748.

[Cited from Dunkel, *Historisch-critische Nachrichten* (1753–7) i. 102.]

HOLBERG, LUDVIG. Epistler. Udgivne . . . af Chr. Bruun. 5 vol. Copenhagen. 1865–75.

See i. 92–9 (letter 21). ' Den LACEDÆMONISKE Lovgiver LYCURGUS haver ved sin Stiftelse viset, at et Land uden saadanne Laster, om hvis Nødvendighed MANDEVILLE prædiker, ikke alleene kand beskytte sig mod andre, men og blive anseelig' (i. 95).

[MONTESQUIEU, BARON DE LA BRÈDE ET DE.] De l'Esprit des Loix. Geneva. 1748.

See book 7, ch. 1 : ' Plus il y a d'hommes ensemble, plus ils sont vains & sentent naître en eux l'envie de se signaler par de petites choses.' A footnote to this reads : ' Dans une grande Ville, dit l'Auteur de la *Fable des Abeilles*, tome I, p. 133, on s'y habille au dessus de sa qualité, pour être estimé plus qu'on n'est par la multitude. C'est un plaisir pour un esprit foible, presqu'aussi grand que celui de l'accomplissement de ses desirs.'

[BAUMGARTEN, Siegm. Jac.] Nachrichten von einer Hallischen [1749] Bibliothek. Halle. 1748–52.

See iii. 133, *n.*, for bibliographical notice of the *Fable*.

BURGMANN, Dr. According to Dunkel's *Historisch-critische Nachrichten* (1753–7) i. 102, he delivered an address against the *Fable* at Rostock in 1749. Dunkel is uncertain whether the address was printed.

FIELDING, Henry. Tom Jones.

Sakmann (*Bernard de Mandeville*, p. 207) believes bk. 6, ch. 1 directed against Mandeville. A comparison with *Amelia*, bk. 3, ch. 5, where the same criticism is offered, and, here, specifically coupled with Mandeville, indicates Sakmann to be correct. Although Fielding thus attacks Mandeville, he shows kinship to him in some of his economic beliefs. See his *Causes of the Increase of Robbers*, § 1, fourth and fifth paragraphs from the end.

HOLBERG, Ludvig. Epistler. Udgivne . . . af Chr. Bruun. 5 vol. Copenhagen. 1865–75.

See iii. 86–90 (letter 209) for further development, in answer to objections, of letter 21 (see above under year 1748).

JAKOBI, J. F. Betrachtungen über die weisen Absichten Gottes bei den Dingen, die wir in der menschlichen Gesellschaft und der Offenbarung antreffen. 4 vol. Hanover. 1749.

See vol. 3, remark 13, §§ 57–103. [Cited from Sakmann, *Bernard de Mandeville*, pp. 213–14.]

SKELTON, Philip. Deism Revealed or the Attack on Christianity candidly Reviewed in its Real Merits as they stand in the Celebrated Writings of . . . Mandeville.

See *Complete Works*, ed. Lynam, 1824, iv. 508–9.

FREYTAG, Frider Gotthilf. Analecta Litteraria de Libris [1750] Rarioribus. Leipsic. 1750.

See pp. 329–30.

HUTCHESON, Francis. Reflections upon Laughter, and Remarks upon the Fable of the Bees. Carefully Corrected. Glasgow. 1750.

Although first issued as a book in 1750, this appeared in 1725 and 1726 in the form of letters to the *Dublin Journal*. See above, under Hutcheson in year 1726.

'Private vices public benefits, may signify any one of these five distinct propositions: viz. "Private vices are themselves public benefits": or, "private vices naturally tend, as the direct and necessary means, to produce public happiness": or, "private vices by dextrous management of governors may be made to tend to public happiness": or, "private vices natively and necessarily flow from public happiness": or, lastly, "private vices will probably flow from public prosperity through the present corruption of men"' (p. 41).

MERCURE DE FRANCE. Paris. 1750. [Periodical]

See pp. 124–6 (Oct.) for review of second edition of *La Fable des Abeilles*. 'Comme le Livre que nous annonçons n'est pas nouveau, nous n'en combattons pas les principes; nous dirons seulement que les longueurs, les répetitions, les obscurités, les épisodes qu'on y trouve, ne doivent pas empêcher les gens d'esprit de lire & peut-être d'examiner un ouvrage lumineux & profond, qui intéresse la Politique, la Philosophie & la Religion' (p. 126).

WESLEY, JOHN. A Letter, written 1750, cited in Abbey's *English Church and its Bishops* (1887) i. 32.
' Some (I hope but a few) do cordially believe that "private vices are public benefits ". I myself heard this in Cork when I was there last.'

[1751] BROWN, JOHN. Essays on the Characteristics. 1751.
See the second essay for able criticism. Cf. above, ii. 415–16.

C * * *, M. Lettres Critiques sur Divers Écrits de Nos Jours, Contraires à la Religion & aux Mœurs. 2 vol. London. 1751.
See letter 9.

FIELDING, HENRY. Amelia.
See bk. 3, ch. 5, *Works*, ed. Browne, 1903, viii. 273–4.

THE GENTLEMAN'S MAGAZINE, AND HISTORICAL CHRONICLE. 1751. [Periodical]
See xxi. 251–2 and 298, in a very favourable review of John Brown's *Essays on the Characteristics.*

[1752] [BAUMGARTEN, SIEGM. JAC.] Nachrichten von einer Hallischen Bibliothek. Halle. 1748–52.
viii. 50–1 deals with *Free Thoughts* ; viii. 56–61, with *Origin of Honour* ; viii. 61–4 and iii. 133, *n.*, with the *Fable.*

FIELDING, HENRY. The Covent-Garden Journal by Sir Alexander Drawcansir Knt. Censor of Great Britain. Edited by Gerard Edward Jensen. 2 vol. New Haven. 1915.
See i. 258–63 for a letter, signed Iago, probably by Fielding, in which Mandeville's doctrines are ironically treated.

HUME, DAVID. The Philosophical Works. . . . Edited by T. H. Green and T. H. Grose. 4 vol. 1874–5.
See i. 308–9, in the essay *Of Refinement in the Arts* (originally termed *Of Luxury*). Although this seems to be his only specific reference to Mandeville, Hume's thought is often close to Mandeville's.

[1753] DUNKEL, JOHANN GOTTLOB WILHELM. Historisch-critische Nachrichten von verstorbenen Gelehrten und deren Schriften. 3 vol. Dessau and Cöthen. 1753–7.
See i. 101–3. '. . . ungeheure Meinungen . . .' (i. 103).

M[ASCH], A. G. M. Beschlus der Abhandlung von der Religion der Heiden u. der Christen. Des zweiten Hauptstücks zweiter und dritter Abschnit. Halle. 1753.
See the appendix, pp. 101–6.

MEMORIE PER SERVIRE ALL' ISTORIA LETTERARIA. Venice. 1753. [Periodical]
'. . . Autore . . . quello . . . tanto noto, quanto empio della *fable des abeilles* ' (ii (July). 18).

ROUSSEAU, J. J. Narcisse, ou l'Amant de lui-même, Preface.
'Les premiers philosophes se firent une grande réputation en enseignant aux hommes la pratique de leurs devoirs et les principes de la vertu. Mais bientôt ces préceptes étant devenus communs, il fallut se distinguer en frayant des routes contraires. Telle est l'origine des systèmes absurdes des Leucippe, des Diogène, des Pyrrhon, des Protagore, des Lucrèce. Les Hobbes, les Mandeville, et mille autres, ont affecté de se distinguer de même parmi nous. . .' (*Œuvres*, ed. Paris, 1822-5, xi. 259-60).

BAUMGARTEN, Siegm. Jac. Siegm. Jac. Baumgartens Nachrichten [1755] von merkwürdigen Büchern. Achter Band so das 43ste bis 48ste Stück enthält. Halle. 1755.
See viii. 445-7.

DIDEROT, Denis. Œuvres Complètes de Diderot . . . Étude sur Diderot . . . par J. Assézat. 20 vol. Paris. 1875-7.
See iv. 102-3. This has sometimes been attributed to Rousseau, because Rousseau inserted it in his *Discours sur l'Inegalité des Conditions parmi les Hommes*. According to Assézat (iv. 100-1) it is by Diderot.
'Mandeville a bien senti qu'avec toute leur morale les hommes n'eussent jamais été que des monstres, si la nature ne leur eût donné la pitié à l'appui de la raison : mais il n'a pas vu que de cette seule qualité découlent toutes les vertus sociales qu'il veut disputer aux hommes.'

LE JOURNAL BRITANNIQUE. The Hague. 1755. [Periodical]
See xvii. 393-417 for review of Hutcheson's *System of Moral Philosophy*. 'Ce pernicieux essai [the *Fable*] fut attaqué par divers Auteurs ; mais par aucun plus fortement que par Mr. Hutcheson' (xvii. 402). M. Maty edited this paper.

[SMITH, Adam.] A Letter to the Authors of the Edinburgh Review. [Published in no. 1, pp. 63-79 of that journal, 1755.]
See pp. 73-5. '. . . the second volume of the Fable of the Bees has given occasion to the system of Mr. Rousseau . . .' (p. 73).

WESLEY, John. The Journal of the Rev. John Wesley . . . Edited [1756] by Nehemiah Curnock. 8 vol. [1909-16.]
See iv. 157. 'I looked over a celebrated book, The Fable of the Bees. Till now I imagined there had never appeared in the world such a book as the works of Machiavel. But de Mandeville goes far beyond it. . . . Surely Voltaire would hardly have said so much [for wickedness] ; and even Mr. Sandeman could not have said more' [entry for 14 April 1756].

[BROWN, John.] An Estimate of the Manners and Principles of the [1757] Times. 2 vol. 1758.
'Or what can come forth from such Scenes of unprincipled Licentiousness, but Pick-pockets, Prostitutes, Thieves, Highwaymen, and Murderers ! These are your Triumphs, O Bolingbroke, Tindal, Mandeville, Morgan, Hume !' (ii. 86).

[SANDEMAN, R.] Letters on Theron and Aspasio. . . . The Fourth Edition. 2 vol. 1768.
See i. 393-6. Intelligent criticism.

WALCH, Io. George. Bibliotheca Theologica Selecta Litterariis Adnotationibus Instructa. 4 vol. Jena. 1757-65.
See i. 761-2.

[1759] MONTAGU, EDWARD W., JUN. Reflections on the Rise and Fall of Ancient Republicks. Adapted to the Present State of Great Britain. 1759.

'That in such times these evils [luxury and blind partisanship] will gain a fresh accession of strength from their very effects ; because corruption will occasion a greater circulation of the publick money ; and the dissipations of luxury, by promoting trade [a footnote here states, " Fable of the bees "], will gild over private vices with the plausible appearance of publick benefits ' (p. 145).

[MORÉRI'S] LE GRAND DICTIONNAIRE HISTORIQUE. 10 vol. Paris. 1759.

See the article on Mandeville.

SMITH, ADAM. The Theory of Moral Sentiments. 1759.

See above, ii. 414–16. '. . . the lively and humorous, tho' coarse and rustic eloquence of Dr. Mandeville ' (p. 474).

SORBONNE'S (THE) CONDEMNATION OF HELVÉTIUS. [In Archives Nationales MM 257, ff. 514–561, under title of ' Determinatio Sacræ Facultatis Parisiensis super libro cui titulus *De L'esprit* '.]

The Sorbonne points out writers such as Montesquieu, Hume, and Hobbes, from whom it considers Helvétius to have drawn, and names Mandeville as a chief source. The Sorbonne cites various specific passages in the *Fable* as the inspiration of the chapters ' De l'Âme ' and ' De la Morale ' ; cf. ff. 513, 518, and 524–5.

TRINIUS, JOHANN ANTON. Freydenker-Lexicon. Leipsic and Bernburg. 1759.

See pp. 343–9.

[1761] FREYSTEIN, JUST GERMAN VON. See his preface to his translation of Part II of the *Fable*.

Freystein compares Mandeville to Shaftesbury and, drawing material from Mandeville's own preface to Part II, sympathetically outlines Mandeville's position.

[1762] LUC, JACQUES FRANÇOIS DE. Observations sur les Savans Incredules, et sur quelques-uns de leurs Ecrits. Geneva. 1762.

See pp. 302–35 for destructive criticism. ' Quoique l'expèrience n'ait que trop dèmontrè qu'il est des hommes assez pervers pour faire de bonnes actions par de mauvais principes, il n'est pas moins injuste d'en infèrer que toutes les actions vertueuses tirent leur origine de quelque principe vicieux : Car quoique les vertus des plus saints Personnages tiennent toujours par quelqu'-endroit à la corruption de nôtre Nature, elles ne prouvent pas moins cette vèritè rèvèlèe : DIEU *crèa l'homme à son Image* ' (p. 311).

MALLET, DAVID. Tyburn: to the Marine Society. [In *Poems on Several Occasions* (1762), pp. 25–43.]

See p. 35 [Tyburn-tree is speaking] :

FIRST, that there is much good in ill,
My great apostle MANDEVILLE
Has made most clear. Read, if you please,
His *moral* FABLE of the BEES.

References to Mandeville's Work. 435

ROUSSEAU, J. J. Émile.

See *La "Profession de Foi du Vicaire Savoyard" de Jean-Jacques Rousseau Edition Critique . . . par Pierre-Maurice Masson* (1914), where M. Masson declares (pp. 253 and 259) Rousseau indebted to Mandeville in some matters.

[DU LAURENS, H.-J.] L'Arretin. 2 vol. Rome. 1763. [Certain [1763] editions are entitled *L'Arretin Moderne*.]

Du Laurens derives from Mandeville, especially in the chapter headed 'L'Utilite' des vices' (ii. 18–35), in which the *Fable* is specifically cited.

MABLY, GABRIEL BONNOT DE. Le Droit Public de l'Europe. [1764] . . . Troisième Édition. 3 vol. Geneva. 1764.

See ii. 448–9 : '. . . si votre sublime politique croit avec l'Auteur de *la Fable des Abeilles*, qu'il faut choyer nos vices . . . ; pour faire fleurir le commerce, n'en hâtez pas la ruine.'

DIDEROT, DENIS. Salon de 1765. [1765]

See *Œuvres*, ed. Assézat, x. 299 : '. . . vous autres défenseurs de la *Fable des Abeilles*. . . . Au diable les sophistes. . . .'

HERDER, J. G. VON. Haben wir noch jetzt das Publikum und Vaterland der Alten ?

See *Sämmtliche Werke*, ed. Suphan, i. 24–5 : '. . . ein Mandeville, der uns blos in Bienen verwandelt . . .' (i. 24).

CHAUDON, L. M., et al. Nouveau Dictionnaire Historique. . . . [1766] Quatriéme Édition. 6 vol. Caen. 1779.

See the disapproving article on Mandeville, an expanded version of that in the earlier editions.

[HALL-STEVENSON, JOHN.] Makarony Fables; with the New [1767] Fable of the Bees. In two Cantos. Addressed to the Society. By Cosmo, Mythogelastick Professor, and F. M. S. . . . The Second Edition. 1768.

> I Never yet beheld that Man,
> (With all the temper that you please)
> That started fair, and fairly ran
> Through the old fable of the bees :
> Because the verse the author chose,
> If verse, like ours, be verse indeed,
> Was made to introduce the prose,
> But never meant to take the lead . . . (p. 33).
> 'Tis Anti-Mandivally true,
> True as the Gospel, or St. Paul,
> The private vices of a few,
> Will be the ruin of us all (p. 58).

VOLTAIRE, F. A. DE. Le Marseillois et le Lion. [1768]

This (*Œuvres Complètes*, ed. Moland, 1877–85, x. 140–8) is a versification of the encounter between a merchant and a lion described by Mandeville in *Fable* i. 176–80. Voltaire states this in his 'Avertissement' to the poem.

VOLTAIRE, F. A. DE. Questions sur l'Encyclopédie, Première [1770] Partie.

See the article *Abeilles* (*Œuvres Complètes*, ed. Moland, 1877–85, xvii. 29–30).

2522.2 E e

[1771] VOLTAIRE, F. A. DE. Questions sur l'Encyclopédie, Cinquième Partie.

'Je crois que Mandeville . . . est le premier qui ait voulu prouver que l'envie est une fort bonne chose' (*Œuvres Complètes*, ed. Moland, 1877–85, xviii. 557). This is in the article 'Envie'.

[1774] BENTHAM, JEREMY. Commonplace Book.

'The paradoxes of Hobbes and Mandeville . . . contained many original and bold truths, mixed with an alloy of falsehood, which succeeding writers, profiting by that share of light which these had cast upon the subject, have been enabled to separate' (*Works*, ed. Bowring, 1843, x. 73).

MACMAHON, THOMAS O'BRIEN. An Essay on the Depravity and Corruption of Human Nature. Wherein the Opinion of La Bruiere, Rochefoucault, Esprit, Senault, Hobbes, Mandeville, Helvetius, &c. on that Subject, are supported on Principles entirely New, against Mr. D. Hume, Lord Shaftesbury, Mr. Sterne, Mr. Brown, and other Apologists for Mankind. 1774.

[1775] [WARREN, MRS. MERCY OTIS.] The Group; as lately Acted, and to be re-acted the Wonder of All Superior Intelligences, nigh Head-Quarters at Amboyne. Boston. 1775.

The following stage direction introduces Act II (p. 7): 'The scene changes to a large dining room. . . . In one corner of the room is discovered a small cabinet of books, for the use of the studious and contemplative ; containing Hobbs's Leviathan, Sipthrop's Sermons ; Hutchinson's History, Fable of the Bees, Philalethes on Philanthrop, with an appendix by Massachusettensis, Hoyle on Whist, Lives of the Stewarts, Statutes of Henry the eighth,—and William the Conqueror, Wedderburn's speeches, and Acts of Parliament, for 1774.'

[1776] HOLBACH, PAUL, BARON D'. La Morale Universelle, ou les Devoirs de l'Homme. 3 vol. Paris. 1820.

See i. xxi–xxiii. '. . . les vices des particuliers influent toujours d'une façon plus ou moins fâcheuse sur le bien-être des nations' (i. xxii).

[1778] ELOY, N. F. J. Dictionnaire Historique de la Médecine Ancienne et Moderne. 4 vol. Mons. 1778.

'Mais pour ne laisser aucun doute sur la perversité de son cœur & de son esprit, *De Mandeville* publia ensuite ses pensées sur la Religion. . . . Ces pensées firent grand bruit . . . & souleverent les personnes judicieuses contre leur Auteur, à cause de son irréligion & de ses impiétés' (iii. 148).

JOHNSON, SAMUEL. Boswell's *Life*, under date of 1778, records a brilliant criticism by Johnson of the *Fable*.

Johnson says, in part, 'The fallacy of that book is, that Mandeville defines neither vices nor benefits. He reckons among vices everything that gives pleasure. He takes the narrowest system of morality, monastick morality, which holds pleasure itself to be a vice . . . and he reckons wealth as a publick benefit, which is by no means always true' (ed. Hill, iii. 291–2). Cf. above, i. cxix, *n.* 4, and i. cxxxviii, *n.* 2.

[1780] BENTHAM, JEREMY. Introduction to Principles of Morals and Legislation.

See § 13, *n.* (*Works*, ed. Bowring, 1843, i. 49, *n.*). This essay was first published 1789, although printed 1780.

[PLUQUET, L'Abbé.] Traité Philosophique et Politique sur le Luxe. [1785] 2 vol. Paris. 1786.

Mandeville is referred to throughout, often by name. ' Ainsi, au moins selon mes connoissances, ce n'est que depuis Mandeville, que l'on a recherché et discuté philosophiquement et politiquement la nature du luxe, pour en prouver, ou pour en combattre l'utilité ' (i. 16). Pluquet completed this book in 1785 (see *Traité* ii. 501).

FLÖGEL, Carl Friedrich. Geschichte der komischen Litteratur. [1786] 4 vol. Liegnitz and Leipsic. 1784-7.

See iii. 588-9.

HAWKINS, Sir John. The Life of Samuel Johnson, LL.D. [1787] 1787.

See above, i. xxii–xxiii. '. . . Johnson would often commend [Mandeville's *Treatise*] . . .' (p. 263, *n.*). '. . . the poison of Mandeville had affected many' (p. 264).

[TYLER, Royall.] The Contrast, a Comedy; in Five Acts: Written by a Citizen of the United States. Philadelphia. 1790. [First acted in New York City, 16 April 1787.]

' It must be so, Montague! and it is not all the tribe of Mandevilles shall convince me, that a nation, to become great, must first become dissipated. Luxury is surely the bane of a nation' (III. ii). [See A. H. Quinn's *Representative American Plays*, p. 67.]

KANT, Immanuel. Kritik der praktischen Vernunft. [In *Kant's* [1788] *gesammelte Schriften* (Berlin, 1900-) v. 40.]

See above, i. cxvii.

GIBBON, Edward. The Autobiographies. . . . Edited by John [1789] Murray. 1896.

'. . . the Fable of the Bees . . . that licentious treatise . . .' (p. 389). [This citation comes from the last paragraph of the sketch the date of which Murray gives as 1788-9 (p. 353, *n.* *). In the first sentence of the sketch, Gibbon, who was born 8 May 1737, dated the fragment by stating that he was in his fifty-second year.]

BOSWELL, James. Boswell's Life of Johnson. . . . Edited by George [1791] Birkbeck Hill. 6 vol. Oxford. 1887.

See the index for references to Mandeville. Note especially Johnson's critique, iii. 291-3.

[D'ISRAELI, Isaac.] Curiosities of Literature. 1791.

' The " prating Mandeville ", pert, frothy, and empty, in his Misanthropic Compositions, compared Addison, after having passed an evening in his company, to " a silent Parson in a tye-wig ". It is no shame for an *Addison* to receive the censures of a *Mandeville* . . .' (p. 157).

GODWIN, William. An Enquiry concerning Political Justice. [1793] 2 vol. 1793.

See ii. 815: ' It has been affirmed " that private vices are public benefits ". But this principle, thus coarsely stated by one of its original advocates [a footnote states, " Mandeville "], was remodelled by his more elegant successors.'

[1795] CHAMFORT, S. R. NICHOLAS. Œuvres . . . Précédées d'une Étude . . . par Arsène Houssaye. Paris. 1857.

See p. 278, in *Maximes et Pensées.*

[1796] GODWIN, WILLIAM. Enquiry concerning Political Justice, and its Influence on Morals and Happiness. 2 vol. 1796.

'The great champion of this doctrine [that the benefits of civilization are inseparable from its evils] is Mandeville. It is not, however, easy to determine whether he is seriously, or only ironically, the defender of the present system of society. His principal work [Fable of the Bees] is highly worthy of the attention of every man who would learn profoundly to philosophise upon human affairs. No author has displayed in stronger terms the deformity of existing abuses, or proved more satisfactorily how inseparably the parts are connected together. Hume [Essays; Part II, Essay II.] has endeavoured to communicate to the Mandevilian system his own lustre and brilliancy of colouring. But it has unfortunately happened, that what he adds in beauty he has subtracted from profoundness' (ii. 484-5, *n.*). The first edition of 1793 (see above) is without this note, but possesses another reference. Between editions Godwin had apparently either read or re-read Mandeville.

[1797] THE NEW-YORK WEEKLY MAGAZINE: OR, MISCELLA-NEOUS REPOSITORY. 1797. [Periodical]

See the issue for 24 May (ii. 372); some lines from the *Grumbling Hive* are used as a motto.

[1800] PARR, SAMUEL. The Works of Samuel Parr . . . with Memoirs . . . by John Johnstone. 8 vol. 1828.

See ii. 362 and 458-60, in *A Spital Sermon*, and the notes thereon.

STEWART, DUGALD. Lectures on Political Economy.

See *Collected Works*, ed. Hamilton, 1854-60, viii. 311 and 323. Cf. above, i. cxxxv.

[1802] HERDER, J. G. VON. Adrastea. . . . Vierten Bandes, zweites Stück. Leipsic. 1802.

See pp. 234-52. 'Swift setzte den Yahoo's wenigstens seine ehrlichen Huynhms entgegen: Mandeville macht alle Staatsbürger zu Yahoo's nur in verschiednen Masken und Functionen. Er vernichtet jede Blüthe der Mensch-heit, indem er sie, Samenlos gleichsam aus Eiter und Gift entsprießen läßt,—welche teuflische Schöpfung! . . . . Wird man ein Concert nennen, wo nicht nur jede Stimme falsch spielet, sondern wo auf dies falsche Spiel jeder Stimme die Wirkung des Ganzen berechnet seyn soll? Eben so wenig kann eine Zusammensetzung von Mißformen, politisch und philosophisch, je ein System heißen. Eine fata Morgana ists, ein häßlicher Traum!' (pp. 239-40).

[1803] THE MONTHLY MIRROR Reflecting Men and Manners. 1803. [Periodical]

See xv. 291-3 for article signed 'H. J. P.', in which Mandeville is compared to Sterne. The author says (p. 292): 'But the most surprising thing of all is, that divines should have taken such universal offence at a book which supports one of the tenets of our religion, the natural corruption of human nature, unless assisted by divine grace.'

[1805] HAZLITT, WILLIAM. An Essay on the Principles of Human Action: being an Argument in Favor of the Natural Disinterestedness of the Human Mind.

See *Collected Works*, ed. Waller and Glover, vii. 467.

[NEWMAN, Jeremiah Whitaker.] The Lounger's Commonplace Book or Miscellaneous Collections. . . . Third Edition. 3 vol. 1805.
See above, i. xxvi, *n.* 4.

PEIGNOT, G. Dictionnaire Critique, Littéraire et Bibliographique [1806] des Principaux Livres Condamnés au Feu, Supprimés, ou Censurés. 2 vol. Paris. 1806.
See i. 282–4. ' Ce livre a été condamné aux flammes, comme renfermant beaucoup de principes pernicieux ' (i. 282).

TABARAUD, Mathieu Mathurin. Histoire Critique du Philosophisme Anglois, depuis son Origine jusqu'à son Introduction en France, inclusivement. 2 vol. Paris. 1806.
See ii. 229 and 248–97. ' Tout le système de Mandeville se réduit en dernière analyse aux quatre points suivans : 1°. Que l'homme n'est point naturellement sociable ; 2°. que les sociétés ne se sont formées et ne se soutiennent que par les vices et par des illusions ; 3°. que la distinction de la vertu et du vice est une affaire de pure convention... ; 4°. que les sentimens de pudeur..., de compassion, et les actions qui en résultent n'ont rien qui mérite réellement le nom de vertu, parce qu'elles sont ordinairement viciées par le motif qui les anime ' (ii. 264).

HAZLITT, William. A Reply to the Essay on Population, by the [1807] Rev. T. R. Malthus. 1807.
See *Collected Works*, ed. Waller and Glover, 1902, iv. 2.

MALTHUS, T. R. An Essay on the Principle of Population or a View of its Past and Present Effects on Human Happiness. . . . With a Biography . . . and Critical Introduction by G. T. Bettany. London, New York, and Melbourne. 1890.
' In saying this let me not be supposed to give the slightest sanction to the system of morals inculcated in the *Fable of the Bees*, a system which I consider as absolutely false, and directly contrary to the just definition of virtue. The great art of Dr. Mandeville consisted in misnomers ' (p. 553, *n.*).
This reference is in an appendix added to the fourth edition.

THE EDINBURGH REVIEW, or CRITICAL JOURNAL : for [1810] Nov. 1810 . . . Feb. 1811. Edinburgh. 1810. [Periodical]
See pp. 59–64, in a review of Joseph Fox's *A Comparative View of the Plans of Education, as Detailed in the Publications of Dr Bell and Mr Lancaster.* This review maintains both the resemblance of Dr. Bell's opinions on charity-schools to Mandeville's and their inferiority to Mandeville's. It also criticizes the latter.

[GREEN, Thomas.] Extracts from the Diary of a Lover of Literature. Ipswich. 1810.
See pp. 96–7. ' With respect to his capital and offensive paradox, that private vices are public benefits, Mandeville's whole art consists, in denominating our passions by the appellation assigned to their vicious excess ; and then proving them, under this denomination, useful to society. There is a lively force, and caustic though coarse wit, in his performance, which occasionally reminds one of Paine ' (p. 97).

HAZLITT, William. On Self-Love.   [1812]
See *Collected Works*, ed. Waller and Glover, xi. 143.

ROBINSON, HENRY CRABB. Diary, Reminiscences, and Correspondence.... Edited by Thomas Sadler. 3 vol. 1869.
' " What are you reading Mr. Robinson ? " she [Mrs. Buller] said. " The wickedest cleverest book in the English language, if you chance to know it." " I have known the ' Fable of the Bees ' more than fifty years." She was right in her guess ' (i. 392).

[1813] FORTSETZUNG ... ZU ... JÖCHERS ALLGEMEINEM GE-LEHRTEN-LEXICO. .... Angefangen von Johann Christoph Adelung und vom Buchstaben K fortgesetzt von Heinrich Wilhelm Rotermund. Leipsic and Bremen. 1784–1897.
See iv. 552–4.

[1814] [D'ISRAELI, ISAAC.] Quarrels of Authors ; or Some Memoirs for our Literary History. 3 vol. 1814.
See the footnote to iii. 65–8.

HAZLITT, WILLIAM. On Rochefoucault's Maxims. [In the *Examiner* for 23 Oct. 1814.]
See *Collected Works*, ed. Waller and Glover, ii. 254.

[1815] HAZLITT, WILLIAM. On the Tatler. [In the *Round Table* for 5 March 1815.]
See *Collected Works*, ed. Waller and Glover, i. 9.

[1818] ASCHER, S. See his preface and commentary to his German version of the *Fable—Bernhard von Mandeville's Fabel von den Bienen,* Leipsic, 1818.
' Großes dichterisches Verdienst, lebhafte Einbildungskraft, Neuheit in Bildern und Wendungen ist das wenigste was man an dem Gedichte bewundern môchte. Ja ich glaube sogar, daß Mandeville die Idee zu demselben aus einer Aeuße-rung Lucians hergenommen [a note adds—groundlessly—' Im Charon oder die Weltbeschauer.']. .... Und in dieser Rücksicht [knowledge of human nature] ... kônnte Mandeville beinahe mit einem Simonides und Archilochus wetteifern '(pp. vi–vii).

[1819] HAZLITT, WILLIAM. Lectures on the English Comic Writers. 1819.
See *Collected Works*, ed. Waller and Glover, viii. 94, *n.*, 99, and 157, *n.*

HAZLITT, WILLIAM. A Letter to William Gifford, Esq. 1819.
' This doctrine [of the complete selfishness of man] which has been sedulously and confidently maintained by the French and English metaphysicians of the two last centuries, by Hobbes, Mandeville, Rochefoucault, Helvetius, and others ... has done a great deal of mischief ...' (*Collected Works*, ed. Waller and Glover, i. 403).

[1821] HAZLITT, WILLIAM. Character of Cobbett. [In *Table-Talk ; or, Original Essays.* 1821.]
'... the picturesque satirical description of Mandeville ...' (*Collected Works*, ed. Waller and Glover, vi. 50).

[1822] HAZLITT, WILLIAM. On the Conduct of Life ; or, Advice to a Schoolboy. [First published 1836 in *Literary Remains*.]
' The best antidote I can recommend to you hereafter against the disheartening effect of such writings as those of Rochefoucault, Mandeville, and others, will

be to look at the pictures of Raphael and Correggio. You need not be altogether ashamed, my dear little boy, of belonging to a species which could produce such faces as those . . .' (*Collected Works*, ed. Waller and Glover, xii. 426).

B., R.   See the article on Mandeville ('Moral Criticisms.—No. 1') [1823] in the *Newcastle Magazine*, new series, for Feb. 1823, ii. 59–62.
'. . . the author was a man of great penetration. . . . His system, however, has been little read, and almost all writers . . . have denounced him as . . . an . . . avowed patron of immorality . . .' (ii. 59). ' Besides, there is throughout . . . a . . . disposition to satire . . . , which is at all times unbecoming the calm unruffled dignity of a philosopher' (ii. 62).

D'ISRAELI, Isaac.   A Second Series of Curiosities of Literature. 3 vol. 1823.
' It is not surprising that before " private vices were considered as public benefits ", the governors of nations instituted sumptuary laws . . .' (iii. 256).

HAZLITT, William.   Common Places. [In the *Literary Examiner*, Sept.–Dec. 1823.]
See *Collected Works*, ed. Waller and Glover, xi. 543.

ROBINSON, Henry Crabb.   Schlosser, *History of the Eighteenth Century*, trans. Davison, 1843, i. 51, *n.*, cites from a personal letter from Robinson :
' This book [the *Fable*] has anticipated the French writers in all their offensive representations of human nature, and it is remarkable that the severely religious parties have always had a sneaking kindness for Mandeville, at least, they hate the Shaftesbury school more, and for an obvious reason. If man's nature be as Shaftesbury represented it, religion is by no means necessary. Mandeville, on the contrary, shows man in his fallen state, and so points out the necessity of a Redeemer.'

HAZLITT, William.   The Spirit of the Age : or Contemporary [1825] Portraits. 1825.
See *Collected Works*, ed. Waller and Glover, iv. 269 (in ' Mr. Southey') and iv. 351 (in ' Mr. Campbell and Mr. Crabbe').

MACAULAY, T. B.   Works. . . . Edited by . . . Lady Trevelyan. 8 vol. 1866.
' If Shakespeare had written a book on the motives of human actions, it is . . . . extremely improbable that it would have contained half so much able reasoning on the subject as is to be found in the Fable of the Bees.' (v. 5, in the essay on Milton.)

DISRAELI, Benjamin.   Vivian Grey.   [1826]
See *Novels and Tales* (1900) i. 132 : ' " Do not, therefore, conclude, with Hobbes and Mandeville, that man lives in a state of civil warfare with man. . . ."'

HAZLITT, William.   The Plain Speaker. 1826.
See *Collected Works*, ed. Waller and Glover, vii. 166, *n.*, in the essay ' On Egotism'. Also, the essay ' On Novelty and Familiarity' : ' Mandeville has endeavoured to shew that if it were not for envy, malice, and all uncharitableness, mankind would perish of pure chagrin and *ennui* ; and I am not in the humour to contradict him' (*Collected Works* vii. 309).

HAZLITT, William—NORTHCOTE, James. Conversations of James Northcote, Esq., R.A. [In *New Monthly Magazine*, Nov. 1826, as 'Boswell Redivivus'.]
See *Collected Works*, ed. Waller and Glover, vi. 353 (in Conversation 4).

[1827] HAZLITT, William. On Disagreeable People. [In the *Monthly Magazine* for Aug. 1827.]
See *Collected Works*, ed. Waller and Glover, xii. 177.

HAZLITT, William. The Same Subject [Knowledge of the World] Continued. [In the *London Weekly Review* for 15 Dec. 1827.]
See *Collected Works* xii. 308.

[1828] THE EDINBURGH REVIEW, OR CRITICAL JOURNAL: for September. . . . December 1828. Edinburgh. 1828. [Periodical]
See pp. 173 and 175 (in a review of the current Oxford lectures on economics): '. . . celebrated work, the Fable of the Bees . . .—celebrated, inasmuch as there are few who have not heard of it ; yet so little read, that though seldom mentioned without some indication of contempt and abhorrence, there is no inconsiderable number of these very abhorrers . . . who unconsciously advocate his doctrines' (p. 173).

HAZLITT, William. Self-Love and Benevolence. [In the *New Monthly Magazine*, Oct. and Dec. 1828.]
See *Collected Works*, ed. Waller and Glover, xii. 96 and 98.

STEWART, Dugald. The Philosophy of the Active and Moral Powers of Man.
See *Collected Works*, ed. Hamilton, 1854-60, vi. 256 and 263-72. 'The great object of Mandeville's *Inquiry into the Origin of Moral Virtue*, is to show that all our moral sentiments are derived from *education* (vi. 264) . . . a fundamental error which is common to the system of Mandeville and that of Locke . . .' (vi. 265). 'When we read Mandeville we are ashamed of the species to which we belong . . .' (vi. 271).

[1829] HAZLITT, William—NORTHCOTE, James. Real Conversations. [In Richardson's *London Weekly Review* for 11 April 1829.]
See *Collected Works*, ed. Waller and Glover, vi. 387 (in Conversation 9): ' "[Northcote :] Did you ever read Rochefoucault ?"—[Hazlitt :] Yes. "[Northcote :] And don't you think he is right ?" [Hazlitt :] In a great measure : but I like Mandeville better. He goes more into his subject. "[Northcote :] Oh ! he is a devil. There is a description of a clergyman's hand he has given [see *Fable* i. 133], which I have always had in my eye whenever I have had to paint a fine gentleman's hand." '

[1830] MACKINTOSH, Sir James. Dissertation Second; Exhibiting a General View of the Progress of Ethical Philosophy. [In the *Encyclopædia Britannica*. . . . *Seventh Edition*. Edinburgh. 1842.]
See i. 323 : '. . . Mandeville, the buffoon and sophister of the ale-house. . . .'

[1831] HAZLITT, William. Aphorisms on Man. [In the *Monthly Magazine*, Oct. 1830–June 1831.]
'The error of Mandeville, as well as of those opposed to him, is in concluding that man is a simple and not a compound being' (*Collected Works*, ed. Waller and Glover, xii. 228).

WHATELY, Richard. Introductory Lectures on Political Economy, Being Part of a Course Delivered in Easter Term, MDCCCXXXI. 1831.

See pp. 44-52 for one of the best analyses of Mandeville. ' . . . his originality was shewn chiefly in bringing into juxtaposition, notions which, separately, had long been current, (and indeed are not yet quite obsolete,) but whose *inconsistency* had escaped detection ' (p. 45). ' His argument does not go to shew *categorically* that vice ought to be encouraged, but *hypothetically*, that, *if* the notions which were afloat were admitted, respecting the character of virtue and vice, and respecting the causes and consequences of wealth, then national virtue and national wealth must be irreconcilable . . .' (p. 46).

COLERIDGE, S. T. The Table Talk and Omniana. Oxford Uni- [1833] versity Press. 1917.

' . . . great Hudibrastic vigour . . .' (pp. 250-1).

[MILL, James.] A Fragment on Mackintosh : Being Strictures on [1835] some Passages in the Dissertation by Sir James Mackintosh, Prefixed to the Encyclopædia Britannica. 1835.

See pp. 55-63 for an excellent exposition of Mandeville in the form of an attack on Mackintosh for misrepresenting Mandeville.—Cf. Mackintosh under year 1830.

SOUTHERN LITERARY JOURNAL, and MONTHLY MAGA- [1837] ZINE. 1837. [Periodical]

See the April issue, i. 167-73. ' . . . now nearly forgotten . . .' (i. 167).

MAURICE, F. D. See the introductory matter to Maurice's edition [1844] of William Law's *Remarks on the Fable of the Bees,* Cambridge, 1844.

' . . . a *reductio ad absurdum* of many prevalent practices and dogmas . . .' (p. ix).

McCULLOCH, J. R. The Literature of Political Economy : a [1845] Classified Catalogue. 1845.

See pp. 352-3. Good.

THE GENTLEMAN'S MAGAZINE, by Sylvanus Urban, Gent. [1846] Volume xxv. New Series. MDCCCXLVI. January to June inclusive. 1846. [Periodical]

See pp. 584-5 for a comparison of Mandeville and Paley. The comparison is in a series of essays, begun in this magazine in July 1845 under the title of *Extracts from the Portfolio of a Man of the World,* the first being dated ' 1813.—Stockholm'.

WHEWELL, William. Lectures on the History of Moral Philosophy [1852] in England. 1852.

' . . . the well-known *Fable of the Bees.* . . . possesses little or no literary merit ; and is only remarkable for the notice it excited . . .' (pp. 79-80).

VORLÄNDER, Franz. Geschichte der philosophischen Moral, [1855] Rechts- und Staats-Lehre der Engländer und Franzosen. Marburg. 1855.

See pp. 425-33.

444 *References to Mandeville's Work.*

[1856] HETTNER, HERMANN. Literaturgeschichte des achtzehnten Jahrhunderts. 3 vol. Brunswick. 1856-70.

> See i. 195-203. '[Mandeville] . . . rühmt sich mehrfach, daß er hierin den Lehren des Christenthums weit näher stehe als Shaftesbury. Gewiß ist es richtig. Aber die Frage, die sich hier unwillkürlich erhebt, ist nicht die Frage, ob Mandeville in diesem Tugendbegriff mit dem Christenthum, sondern ob er mit sich selbst übereinstimmt. Diese Forderung der Tugend ist bei Mandeville so durchaus äusserlich und mit dem Kern seiner Denkweise so wenig zusammenhängend, daß es wohl erlaubt ist, sie bei ihm für eine leere Heuchelei . . . zu erklären . . .' (i. 202-3).

[1857] BUCKLE, H. T. History of Civilization in England. 3 vol. 1872. See ii. 218.

[1863] TAINE, H. A. Histoire de la Littérature Anglaise. 4 vol. Paris. 1863-4.

> 'Les professeurs d'irréligion, Toland, Tindal, Mandeville, Bolingbroke, rencontrent des adversaires plus forts qu'eux' (iii. 60).

[1865] JOWETT, BENJAMIN. Letter dated 28 May 1865.

> 'I send you some books, one very good book among them, the works of a Saint, and one very bad book, *Fable of the Bees*—one of those books which are condemned equally by the world and the Church ; by the world because it is partly true, and by the Church because it is partly false, or vice versa—one of those books which delight in turning out the seamy side of society to the light. (Don't read it if you object to the coarseness of parts.) . . . Nor do I think it a bad thing to read the book with patience and ask how much is true of ourselves' (in Abbott and Campbell, *Life and Letters of Benjamin Jowett*, ed. 1897, i. 411).

[1866] ERDMANN, J. E. Grundriss der Geschichte der Philosophie. 2 vol. Berlin. 1866.

> See ii. 124-7 sqq. for relation to history of philosophy.
> 'Dass die Moral der Britten so viel idealen und so vielen sociablen Inhalt hat, das ist es, was ihr selbst für Solche, die auf einem ganz anderen Standpunkt stehn, etwas Bestechendes gibt. Nichts desto weniger bleibt es eine Inconsequenz, dass ganz Heterogenes verbunden wird. Der Punkt, wo diese Verbindung sich löst, wird daher, sollte dies auch einen noch so widerwärtigen Anblick gewähren, einen Fortschritt in der Entwicklung des Realismus bezeichnen.
> ' 2. Einen solchen macht deswegen . . . *Mandeville* . . .' (ii. 125-6).

LANGE, F. A. Geschichte des Materialismus. Leipsic. 1887. See the index.

[1867] MARX, KARL. Das Kapital. Hamburg. 1872.

> 'Was Mandeville, ein ehrlicher Mann und heller Kopf, noch nicht begreift, ist, dass der Mechanismus des Akkumulationsprocesses selbst mit dem Kapital die Masse der "arbeitsamen Armen" vermehrt . . .' (i. 640). Cf. also i. 367, *n*. 57 for Marx's opinion that Adam Smith was greatly indebted to Mandeville.

STEPHEN, JAMES FITZJAMES. Mandeville. [In the *Saturday Review* for 20 April 1867.]

> This uncomprehending study was afterwards reprinted in Stephen's *Horae Sabbaticae*, 2nd series (1892), pp. 193-210.

BAIN, ALEXANDER. Mental and Moral Science. 1872. [1868]
See pp. 593-8 for a summary of Mandeville's position.

LECKY, W. E. H. History of European Morals from Augustus to [1869] Charlemagne. 2 vol. 1869.
See i. 6-8 and footnotes to these pages.

ELWIN, WHITWELL, AND COURTHOPE, W. J. The Works of [1871] Alexander Pope. 10 vol. 1871–1889.
See the remarks as to Pope's indebtedness to Mandeville, ii. 307-8; iii. 121 ; iv. 339 ; v. 358 ; and viii. 513. Cf. above, i. cxviii, *n.* 1.
[Of the volumes cited only vol. 2 appeared in 1871, the other four appearing later.]

MINTO, WILLIAM. A Manual of English Prose Literature. 1891. [1872] See pp. 404-5.

SPICKER, GIDEON. Die Philosophie des Grafen von Shaftesbury. Freiburg. 1872.
See pp. 71 sqq. for relation of Shaftesbury to Mandeville.

STEPHEN, LESLIE. Essays on Freethinking and Plainspeaking. 1907. [1873]
See pp. 277-316 for perhaps the most interesting of all essays on Mandeville. This essay appeared in *Every Saturday : a Journal of Choice Reading*, new series, iv. 64-71. It appeared also in *Fraser's Magazine* (ed. Froude), new series, vii. 713-27, for June 1873.

STEPHEN, LESLIE. History of English Thought in the Eighteenth [1876] Century. 2 vol. 1902.
See index for a large number of noteworthy references to Mandeville.

JODL, FRIEDRICH. Geschichte der Ethik in der neueren Philosophie. [1882] 2 vol. Stuttgart. 1882.
See i. 186-9.

MINTO, WILLIAM. Article on Mandeville in the *Encyclopædia* [1883] *Britannica*, 9th edition.
Excellent summary. Professor Minto argues, incidentally, that Mandeville meant his work to be taken humorously rather than philosophically, and that the *Grumbling Hive* is a specific satire animated by the elections of 1705. There seems small ground for this latter assumption : the allusions in the poem are of the most general nature, and Mandeville himself states (*Fable* i. 6) that ' The Satyr . . . was not made to injure and point to particular Persons '.
Another article (by John Malcolm Mitchell) has been substituted in the eleventh edition of the *Encyclopædia*.

GOLDBACH, PAUL. Bernard de Mandeville's Bienenfabel. In- [1886] augural-Dissertation. Halle. 1886.
Of little value.

ROBERTSON, JOHN M. Essays towards a Critical Method. 1889.
See pp. 201-31. Intelligent and sympathetic. Among the best analyses of Mandeville. This same essay appears also in Robertson's *Pioneer Humanists* (1907), pp. 230-70. It first appeared in *Our Corner* for 1886, vii. 92-103.

SIDGWICK, HENRY. Outlines of the History of Ethics. 1888.

'. . . though . . . a considerable share of philosophical penetration, his anti moral paradoxes have not even apparent coherence' (p. 190).

[1887] BROWNING, ROBERT. Parleyings with Certain People of Importance in their Day : to wit : Bernard de Mandeville. . . . 1887.

See pp. 31–50. Cf. above, i. vi.

[1889] PAULSEN, FRIEDRICH. System der Ethik. 2 vol. Berlin. 1900.

See i. 180 and 308, *n.* 1.

[1890] HASBACH, W. Larochefoucault und Mandeville. [In Gustav Schmoller's *Jahrbuch für Gesetzgebung, Verwaltung und Volkswirtschaft im Deutschen Reich.* Leipsic. 1890.]

See pp. 1–43. 'So steht Mandeville als derjenige da, welcher alle niedrigen Vorstellungen von der menschlichen Natur, welche im 16. und 17. Jahrhundert ausgeprägt worden waren, in seinem Werke vereinigte. Selbst von französicher Abstammung, wird er der Kanal, durch welchen der epikureisch-skeptisch-mechanische Gedanke der Franzosen endgültig in die englische Ethik und Politik hinübergeführt wird' (p. 17). '. . . kein originaler Schriftsteller im höchsten Sinne. . . . Seine Originalität besteht in der selbständigen Weiterbildung des Fremden und in der geistvollen Verknüpfung einer ethischen mit einer nationalökonomischen Theorie' (p. 40).

[1891] GLOCK, JOH. PH. Die Symbolik der Bienen und ihrer Produkte in Sage, Dichtung, Kultus, Kunst und Bräuchen der Völker. Heidelberg. 1891.

See pp. 337–57 for consideration of the *Fable* ; pp. 358–79 contain the *Grumbling Hive* in both English and German. 'Aber beide, Mandeville wie Hogarth, haben ihrem Zeitalter nur den Spiegel vorgehalten' (p. 348).

SHAW, GEORGE BERNARD. The Quintessence of Ibsenism. 1913.

'. . . purblindly courageous moralists like Mandeville and Larochefoucauld, who merely state unpleasant facts without denying the validity of current ideals, and who indeed depend on those ideals to make their statements piquant' (p. 23).

[1892] JOHNSON, LIONEL. The Art of Thomas Hardy. 1894.

See pp. 18–19. That the book was finished in 1892 is stated in its Bibliography, p. iii.

[1893] BONAR, JAMES. Philosophy and Political Economy in Some of their Historical Relations. 1893.

See index for references to good criticism.

HASBACH, W. Les Fondements Philosophiques de l'Économie Politique de Quesnay et de Smith. [In *Revue d'Économie Politique* for 1893, vii. 747–95.]

See pp. 779–82 and 785. 'Plus encore que Bayle, Mandeville relève que ce n'est pas dans la raison et dans une conduite morale, mais bien dans ce qui est irrationnel, dans l'énergie des appétits, dans ce qui moralement est laid, que se trouve la semence de toute culture.

'C'est sur ce terrain que Mandeville établit les fondements éthiques et sociaux de l'économie nationale. . . .

'Un économiste beaucoup lu du siècle passé, Vanderlint, se place dans son livre *Money answers all things* pour ainsi dire sur les épaules de Mandeville' (p. 780).

' Les bases psychologiques et morales de l'économie politique de Smith se présentent à nous comme pénétrées des théories de Shaftesbury et de Mandeville' (p. 782).

SAINTSBURY, George. In *English Prose*, ed. Craik, 1894, iii. 438–9. [1894]
'. . . a coarseness which does not consist so much in the use of offensive language as in an almost incredible vulgarity and foulness of tone. . . . his prose is frequently incorrect and never in any way polished ; but he makes up for this by many of the merits of Defoe. . . .'

TEXTE, Joseph. Jean-Jacques Rousseau et les Origines du Cosmo- [1895] politisme Littéraire. Paris. 1895.
' En même temps il [Diderot] se nourrit de . . . Mandeville, dont la *Fable des abeilles* lui fournit la plupart des idées qu'il développera plus tard dans le fameux *Supplément au voyage de Bougainville*' (p. 135).

KREIBIG, Josef C. Geschichte und Kritik des ethischen Skepti- [1896] cismus. Vienna. 1896.
See pp. 85–97.

GOSSE, Edmund. Modern English Literature a Short History. [1897] 1905.
See pp. 225–6. ' His style is without elegance, but . . . of a remarkable homeliness and picturesque vigour.'

LAVIOSA, G. La Filosofia Scientifica del Diritto in Inghilterra. Turin. 1897.
See pt. 1, pp. 656–95. '. . . Mandeville avanza una congettura affine alla dottrina *patriarchistica* di Sumner-Maine' (p. 669).

SAKMANN, Paul. Bernard de Mandeville und die Bienenfabel-Controverse Eine Episode in der Geschichte der englischen Aufklärung. Freiburg I. B., Leipsic, and Tübingen. 1897.
The most elaborate work on Mandeville to date, analysing his thought at length, and describing the controversy precipitated by his book.

SELBY-BIGGE, L. A. British Moralists Being Selections from Writers principally of the Eighteenth Century. 2 vol. Oxford. 1897.
See i. xiv–xvii. ' Regarding Mandeville as a satirist, I see no reason to suppose, as some have supposed, that his introduction of " self-sacrifice " as the touchstone of merit was meant by him as a backhanded attack upon ascetic and theological ethics. It is so essential to his theory and is introduced with such aptitude that I do not think he meant or indeed could afford to play a double game with it ' (i. xvi).

SAINTSBURY, George. A Short History of English Literature. [1898] 1900.
' . . . his style, plebeian as it is, may challenge comparison with the most famous literary vernaculars in English for racy individuality ' (p. 544).

WILDE, Norman. Mandeville's Place in English Thought. [In *Mind a Quarterly Review of Psychology and Philosophy. New Series*, for 1898, vii. 219–32.]
' What Voltaire was to the optimism of Leibniz, Mandeville was to that of Shaftesbury ' (p. 231). ' It was owing to Mandeville and the spirit which he represented that the abstract benevolence of Shaftesbury was tempered by the rational self-love of later theory ' (p. 232).

[1899] ROBERTSON, JOHN M. A Short History of Free Thought Ancient and Modern. 2 vol. New York. 1906.

'Shaftesbury had impugned the religious conception of morals ; and Mandeville had done so more profoundly, laying the foundations of scientific utilitarianism' (ii. 168).

[1900] CANEPA, ANT. La Morale Utilitaria Secondo i Sistemi di Mandeville, Elvezio e Bentham. Sanremo. 1900. [Cited from A. Pagliaini, *Catalogo Generale della Libreria Italiana,* first supplement, Milan, 1912.]

ROBERTSON, JOHN M. Introduction to his edition of Shaftesbury's *Characteristics* (1900) i. xxxviii–xlii.

' "... all our relish for beauty ... is either from advantage, or custom, or education ; " and the argument as to morals was on all fours. Mandeville made it classic' (i. xxxviii). '... a sardonic humour all his own' (i. xl).

[1902] ESPINAS, ALFRED. La Troisième Phase et la Dissolution du Mercantilisme. (Mandeville, Law, Melon, Voltaire, Berkeley.) [In *Revue Internationale de Sociologie* for March 1902, pp. 161–80.]

'Les conceptions de Melon s'inspirent de celles de Petty et de Mandeville ...' (p. 166). '... un livre dont nous sommes assuré que la plupart des hommes du xviii siècle ont pris connaissance, la *Fable des Abeilles* ...' (p. 162).

[1903] SCHATZ, ALBERT. Bernard de Mandeville. (Contribution à l'Étude des Origines du Libéralisme Économique.) [In *Vierteljahrschrift für Social- und Wirtschaftsgeschichte.* Leipsic. 1903.]

See i. 434–80. One of the most valuable articles on Mandeville. '... MANDEVILLE est le seul à avoir analysé minutieusement le concept d'intérêt personnel qui, pour D. HUME et A. SMITH, est accepté comme un tout donné' (p. 440). '... chacun poursuivant son propre bonheur contribue (à son insu) à réaliser le progrès économique. Telle est la thèse de MANDEVILLE, telle est l'idée originale qui s'exprime pour la première fois dans l'histoire de la pensée économique. Aussi bien est ce à ce titre, plus qu'à tout autre, que MANDEVILLE donne à l'école libérale l'essence même de sa philosophie' (p. 449). 'Spencer, donnant à la doctrine de MANDEVILLE sa forme contemporaine ...' (p. 471).

[1904] CANNAN, EDWIN. See his introduction to his edition of Adam Smith's *Wealth of Nations* (1904) :

'If we bear in mind Smith's criticism of Hutcheson and Mandeville in adjoining chapters of the *Moral Sentiments,* and remember further that he must almost certainly have become acquainted with the *Fable* ... when attending Hutcheson's lectures or soon afterwards, we can scarcely fail to suspect that it was Mandeville who first made him realize that " it is not from the benevolence of the butcher, the brewer or the baker that we expect our dinner, but from their regard to their own interest ". Treating the word " vice " as a mistake for self-love, Adam Smith could have repeated with cordiality Mandeville's line ... :

" Thus vice nursed ingenuity ..." ' (i. xlvi).

DANZIG, SAMUEL. Drei Genealogien der Moral. Bernard de Mandeville, Paul Rée und Friedrich Nietzsche. Pressburg. 1904. See pp. 1–27.

TICHY, G. Mandeville. [In *Česka Mysl* for 1904.] [Cited from *Enciclopedia Universal Ilustrada Europeo-Americana* xxxii. 770.]

BRUNETIÈRE, Ferdinand. Les Origines de l'Esprit Encyclo- [1905] pédique. Huit Leçons Rédigées en Mai 1905, Publiées par MM. René Doumic et Victor Giraud. [In *La Revue Hebdomadaire* for 9, 16, and 23 Nov. 1907, pp. 141–55, 281–97, 421–37.]

' On peut négliger, dans cet examen de l'influence anglaise [on French thought], celle des *Free thinkers*. . . .

' Il en est autrement de Shaftesbury et de Bernard de Mandeville.

' . . . L'Etat est conçu comme une " association pour le luxe " ; et de là vient la subordination de l'intérêt individuel à l'intérêt général, . . . et la transformation de la " question morale " en " question sociale ". Portée de cette formule. On la retrouvera dans Toussaint et Helvétius ' (pp. 425–6).

INGE, William Ralph. Studies of English Mystics St. Margaret's Lectures 1905. 1906.

' Mandeville's essay was a clever and cynical defence of licence and selfishness ' (p. 129).

BOUZINAC, J. Les Doctrines Economiques au XVIIIme Siècle Jean- [1906] François Melon Économiste. Toulouse. 1906.

See index. ' . . . son [Mandeville's] influence directe sur Melon est certaine ' (p. 154).

JOFFE, A. Zu Mandevilles Ethik und Kants " Sozialismus ". [In *Die Neue Zeit*, Stuttgart, for 7 April 1906, xxiv (2). 45–50.]

' Mandeville ist in der Ethik der typischste Repräsentant der Bourgeoisie. . . . Wir werden auch sehen, dass Kants Ethik die logische Konsequenz der englischen Moralphilosophie und von Mandevilles Lehre im besonderen bildet ' (p. 45).

SCHATZ, Albert. L'Individualisme Économique et Social. Paris. [1907] 1907.

See pp. 61–79 for relation to origins of *laissez-faire* theory.

DEDIEU, Joseph. Montesquieu et la Tradition Politique Anglaise [1909] en France. Paris. 1909.

Dedieu attempts the proof that Montesquieu was greatly influenced by Mandeville's *Fable* and *Free Thoughts*. That Montesquieu was somewhat affected by Mandeville Dedieu has shown, but he has proved it no more than possible that Montesquieu was greatly affected.

' Nous croyons que de pareils exemples dispensent de tout commentaire. Il paraît étrange que deux esprits, s'occupant d'une même question, l'envisagent sous un même angle, la développent dans une série de dissertations qui se suivent dans un ordre semblable, l'enrichissent de fines analyses identiques. Cela ne peut être que l'effet d'une influence profonde d'un esprit sur l'autre ; il nous semble, en effet, que l'évêque Warburton et l'incrédule Mandeville ont exercé, peut-être indirectement, mais, croyons-nous, en des temps différents, une maîtrise incontestable sur le génie de Montesquieu ' (pp. 260–1). ' Il nous paraît que Montesquieu lut et utilisa la *Fable* . . . vers 1724. En effet, . . . les *Réflexions sur la Monarchie Universelle*, écrites en 1724, s'inspirent largement de ce livre ' (p. 307, *n*. 1).

MORIZE, André. L'Apologie du Luxe au XVIIIe siècle et " Le Mondain " de Voltaire. Paris. 1909.

A large part of this interesting dissertation is devoted to demonstrating the indebtedness of Voltaire to the *Fable*, and to a consideration of Mandeville's influence on economics. ' Son [Mandeville's] importance est capitale, car, dans cette féconde période de préparation, il représente le moment décisif où le courant épicurien et sceptique français vient se fondre avec les conceptions économiques anglaises, — et où, à des doctrines morales venues de Montaigne, La Rochefoucauld, Saint-Évremond et Bayle, s'ajoutent les théories plus scientifiques de William Petty, Dudley North, Davenant et les autres ' (p. 69).

WACKWITZ, FRIEDRICH. Entstehungsgeschichte von ... " Robinson Crusoe ". Inaugural-Dissertation. Berlin. 1909.

' Bernard de Mandeville . . . ist schliesslich noch als reiche Fundgrube für Defoesche Gedanken zu nennen ' (p. 53). This may be true, but Wackwitz's arguments are worthless.

[1910] GRIFFIN, W. HALL—MINCHIN, HARRY CHRISTOPHER. The Life of Robert Browning. 1910.

' Browning . . . made him [Mandeville] the mouthpiece of his own views [in his *Parleyings with Certain People*] . . . . and it would seem probable that these *Vindications* [Mandeville's] were not without influence upon the evolution of his own later defences of a Blougram and a Sludge . . .' (p. 19).

SAINTSBURY, GEORGE. A History of English Prose Rhythm. 1912.

See pp. 239-40 : ' As for Mandeville, his liking for, and practice in, the actual Dialogue may make it seem rather unfair to say much of him ; but he certainly belongs to the vulgar class [of writers who use contractions].'

[1913] MORE, PAUL ELMER. The Drift of Romanticism. Shelburne Essays Eighth Series. Boston and New York. 1913.

See pp. 159-61. ' The poem [the *Grumbling Hive*] in itself was not much more than a clever *jeu d'esprit*, but the *Remarks* . . . are among the acutest psychological tracts of the age. . . . [Mandeville's] theory of the passions is a legitimate, if onesided, deduction from the naturalistic philosophy as it left the hands of Locke ; the ethical conclusions . . . have a curious similarity with the later system of Nietzsche.'

[1914] BOBERTAG, OTTO. See the preface to his German edition of the *Fable* (cf. above, ii. 400).

' Seine Art, höchst verwickelte seelische Tatbestände zu behandeln, sie zu analysieren, bis ihre verborgensten Teilglieder aufgefunden sind, und sie auf dem Wege eines allmählichen Entwicklungsprozesses synthetisch vor den Augen des Lesers entstehen zu lassen, war für die damalige Zeit etwas ganz Unerhörtes und wird es für viele heute noch sein. Im 18. Jahrhundert gab es nur einen Mann, der etwas gleich Grosses—und Grösseres—geleistet hat : David Hume . . .' (pp. xxiv-xxv).

[1916] MASSON, PIERRE MAURICE. La Religion de J. J. Rousseau. 3 vol. Paris. 1916.

' . . . à mesure que les Locke, les Mandeville, les Fréret . . . s'ingénient, à la suite de Montaigne, à dissoudre . . . les principes, en apparence, les plus solides de la morale universelle, et que les psychologues du sensualisme, en reléguant parmi les chimères désuètes le système des idées innées, semblent enlever à la loi morale son privilège transcendant, — les défenseurs de la conscience sont de plus en plus tentés de la soustraire aux enquêtes positives, et d'en faire une espèce de "faculté à part dans l'âme", comme un sens intime dont la sûreté est infaillible ' (i. 237).

MOORE, C. A. Shaftesbury and the Ethical Poets in England, 1700–1760. [In *Pub. Mod. Lang. Ass.* for 1916, xxxi. 264–325.]
See pp. 274–5, 279–80, 303–5, and 323.

PATTEN, Simon N. Mandeville in the Twentieth Century. [1918] [In *American Economic Review* for March 1918, viii. 88–98.]
Generalizations concerning the likeness of certain aspects of modern economic theory to the *Fable*, based on a very superficial knowledge of Mandeville.
This article was answered by Professors Jacob H. Hollander and E. R. A. Seligman in the *American Economic Review* for June 1918, viii. 338–9 and 339–49.

STAMMLER, Rudolf. Mandeville's Bienenfabel die letzten Gründe einer wissenschaftlich geleiteten Politik. Berlin. 1918.
This pamphlet outlines some general aspects of the *Fable* as a point of departure for Stammler's own speculation.

MEIJER, W. De Bijen als Symbol in de Letterkunde. [In *De* [1919] *Vrijmetselaar* for July 1919.]

BERNBAUM, Ernest. See the preface to his edition of Swift's [1920] *Gulliver's Travels* (1920), pp. ix–xii.

ROBERTSON, J. M. A Short History of Morals. 1920.
See especially pp. 9–12 and 268–72 for illuminating comment on and summary of Mandeville's position.

WRENN, H. B., and WISE, Thomas J. Catalogue of the Library of . . . John Henry Wrenn. 5 vol. Austin, Texas. 1920.
This catalogue ascribes to Mandeville twenty-one pieces not mentioned in my 'Writings of Bernard Mandeville' (see below under the year 1921). All these attributions are either demonstrably erroneous or highly improbable. [P.S. in final proof: I have considered this matter in my 'The Mandeville Canon: a Supplement', in *Notes and Queries* for 3 May 1924.]

KAYE, F. B. The Writings of Bernard Mandeville: a Bibliographical [1921] Survey. [In the *Journal of English and Germanic Philology* for Oct. 1921, xx. 419–67.]
This article attempted a description of all known works which are by Mandeville or have been ascribed to him, and tried to establish a canon of his writings. Some emendations are made above, i. xxxi–xxxii.

LOVEJOY, Arthur O. 'Pride' in Eighteenth Century Thought. [In *Modern Language Notes* for Jan. 1921.]
'Mandeville was one of those who helped to give currency to the premise accepted by the primitivists: science, industry, the arts, luxury and trade are all born of pride. But from this premise he drew the opposite inference; since civilization, if not a good, is at least a necessary evil, "pride", which is its moving force, is a kind of useful folly' (p. 37, *n.* 11).

KAYE, F. B. The Influence of Bernard Mandeville. [In *Studies in* [1922] *Philology* for Jan. 1922, xviii. 83–108.]
This article offers in somewhat different form the information given in the present edition, introduction, ch. 5. Where there is difference, the present edition is the more authoritative.

LOVEJOY, Arthur O.   Personal letter to me dated 3 March 1922.

' I don't feel so sure as you do that Mandeville adhered to what you call the " rigoristic point of view ".   His writing is so largely ironic that it is hard to be sure when he is serious ; but he strikes me as far too acute a writer not to have realized the logical consequences of his own most characteristic doctrine.   You yourself attribute to him [above, i. cxxxiv, *n.*] an explicitly utilitarian position. . . .
' . . . you perhaps give to M. a slightly greater place than belongs to him in the development of utilitarianism. . . . [The present edition modifies the claim made in the article—" The Influence of Bernard Mandeville "—criticized by Professor Lovejoy.]   M.'s chief significance, I think, lay not in his contribution to or influence upon the development of ethical theory, but in his place in the history of what would nowadays be called social psychology. In insisting upon the sub-rational determination of most (if not all) of our motives, and in regarding the reasons which men give for their acts as largely a " rationalizing " explanation, necessitated by self-esteem, of these subconscious motivations, he, of course, anticipated a very recent fashion in psychology.   But what is especially noteworthy about him is his recognition of the immense part played in human life, and especially in what the sociologists' lingo now calls " social control", of the " passion" which he calls " pride " or " glory". . . . he traced this spring of action and of feeling through its countless disguises and ramifications more subtly, and recognized its pervasiveness more fully, than any writer I know of before his time, or for long after.   He clearly realized that it is the existence of this class of self-conscious desires which is the specific differentia of *human* nature, and the *point d'appui* of the moral appeal, or of the control which society exercises over its members, by means of what are commonly called moral influences. Adam Smith, of course, afterwards carried out the same general idea with more detail, and in a more constructive and less satirical spirit, in his *Theory of the Moral Sentiments*, where the influence of Mandeville is not less marked, I think, than in the *Wealth of Nations*.   Nearly all of the fundamental ideas of Mr. Thorstein Veblen's *Theory of the Leisure Class*—regarded, when it appeared, as a very important and original contribution to economic theory and social psychology—may be found in Mandeville's " *Remark M.*", and elsewhere in his prose appendices to the *Fable*. . . .
' . . . M., of course, didn't see the whole truth, or the full significance of the psychological fact, of which he had caught a glimpse ; he was too eager to *épater le bourgeois* to do that.   But he nevertheless has, I think, a pretty notable place in the history of the working out of this insight into the psychology of man's moral behavior.'

MORIZE, André.   Problems and Methods of Literary History. Boston.   [1922.]

' [All the reviews] . . . were of one mind in stressing Mandeville's ideas on luxury. . . . As a result, a chapter that is really supplementary . . . appeared to the French public the most important and original part ' (p. 277).

[1923]   BREDVOLD, Louis I.   Personal letter to me dated 19 Dec. 1923.

' The evolutionary theory, in the form in which it was current before Mandeville, had in all ages tended towards revolt in ethical theory. . . . The " moral atmosphere" of the theory was on the whole the same before Mandeville as it was in his book.'

LINK, Henry C.   Review of Z. C. Dickinson's *Economic Motives* (1922).   [In *Management and Administration* for July 1923, vi. 111.]

'Psychology . . . hardly existed at that time [of Adam Smith] ; and yet Mandeville, a still earlier writer, interpreted economic facts in terms of human motives approximating those described by modern psychologists far more closely than . . . Adam Smith and his immediate followers.'

LOVEJOY, ARTHUR O. The Supposed Primitivism of Rousseau's *Discourse on Inequality.* [In *Modern Philology* for Nov. 1923.]

'... it is this Hobbesian and Mandevillian social psychology that—even more than the primitivistic tradition represented by Montaigne and Pope—prevented the evolutionistic tendency in the thought of the *Discourse* from issuing in a doctrine of universal progress ...' (xxi. 183). 'And the chief cause of the latter process ["increasing estrangement of men from one another, an intensification of ill-will and mutual fear, culminating in a monstrous epoch of universal conflict and mutual destruction "] Rousseau, following Hobbes and Mandeville, found ... in that unique passion of the self-conscious and social animal—pride, self-esteem ...' (xxi. 185).

Undated

MONTESQUIEU, BARON DE LA BRÈDE ET DE.

'J'entrerai volontiers dans les idées de celui qui a fait la fable des Abeilles, et je demanderai qu'on me montre de graves citoyens, dans aucun pays, qui y fassent autant de bien qu'en font, a de certaines nations commerçantes, leurs petits-maîtres' (*Pensées et Fragments Inédits*, Bordeaux, 1899–1901, ii. 405–6).

COLERIDGE, S. T. MS. note in Southey's copy of the *Fable* :

'Can any one read Mandeville's fable of the Bees, and not see that it is a keen satire on the inconsistencies of Christianity, and so intended ? S. T. C.'

[I have cited this remark and reference from a note on the fly-leaf of a copy of the *Fable* (ed. 1732) in the Yale Library—call no. K8. M32–C732–v. 1.]

COLERIDGE, S. T. MS. note on fly-leaf of copy of *Fable* (ed. 1724 ; bookplate of Joshua Henry Green) in possession of Major Christopher Stone :

'P. 35. It is, perhaps, a piece of simplicity to treat of Mandeville's works as other than an exquisite *bon bouche* of Satire and Irony ! But as there have been, and are, Mortals and man-shaped Mortals too, very plausible Anthropöeids, who have adopted his positions in downright *opake* earnest, it may be worth while to ask—how ? by what strange chance there happened to start up among this premier species of Ouran Outangs, yclept man, these *Wise Men* (p. 28) these Law-givers, who so cleverly took advantage of this *Peacock* Instinct of Pride and Vanity.'

PIOZZI, HESTER LYNCH. Anecdotes of ... Samuel Johnson.

'The natural depravity of mankind ... were so fixed in Mr. Johnson's opinion ... [he] used to say sometimes, half in jest half in earnest, that they were the remains of his old tutor Mandeville's instructions. As a book however, he took care always loudly to condemn the Fable of the Bees, but not without adding, "that it was the work of a thinking man"' (*Johnsonian Miscellanies*, ed. Hill, i. 268). Cf. also *Miscellanies* i. 207. [Mrs. Thrale's *Anecdotes* purports to refer to the years 1764–84.]

CORRIGENDA IN VOLUME II

INDEX TO THE COMMENTARY

ROMAN numerals refer to the pagination of the Prefatory Note and
Introduction in vol. 1. The superior figures indicate the numbers of
the notes; where a note is a continuation from the preceding page it is
distinguished by the letter *n*. Mandeville's Indexes to the Text will be found
in vol. 1, pp. 371–9, and vol. 2, pp. 359–77.